EHRLICH'S BLACKSTONE

EHRLICH'S BLACKSTONE

PART ONE: *Rights of Persons*
⚖   *Rights of Things*

J. W. EHRLICH

Capricorn Books, New York

CONTENTS

INTRODUCTION

Sir William Blackstone was born in London July 10th, 1723. In 1746 he commenced the practice of law; he was deficient in the art of elocution, had no traits of an advocate and was an unsuccessful lawyer. Blackstone was appointed professor of law when a chair was first established at Oxford in 1758. His first series of lectures was delivered there in the same year. In 1761 he was elected a Member of Parliament and soon became Solicitor General. The first volume of his *Commentaries* was published in 1765; the second in 1766; the third in 1768; and the fourth and final volume in 1769.

The great English lawyer Bracton was rivaled by no judicial writer till Blackstone arose five centuries later. By virtue both of his knowledge of law and of his literary genius, Blackstone produced the one treatise on the common law which for all time must remain a part of English literature. Here you will find that it is not the wording of the law, but the internal sense of it, that makes the law. It consists of a body and a soul; the letter of the law is the body, and the sense and reason of the law is its soul. This law is the guardian of our natural and legal rights.

Blackstone's *Commentaries*, more than any other single book, is the codification of English and American law. In accordance with the practices of lawyers in the early part of the century and preceding that, each edition of Blackstone has been overwhelmed with a larger avalanche of footnotes and commentaries on the *Commentaries*. I have taken Blackstone's original editions, excised the unnecessary and confusing passages and digressions which are not of interest to the law today, translated any necessary Latin, and deleted all footnotes.

While man expects to retain certain rights and privileges, what reason is there for the duties owed him by the government which he created and of which he believes himself to be a part? Telling someone that the law is a rule of action prescribed by a superior power, without giving the reason why such superior power came into being and whence came its authority, is leaving him to search for some mystical premise.

We speak of the right of liberty of conscience, the right of privacy, the right of self-defense, security of life and limb. How did all these things develop? What philosophy of government and what thinking of men brought these into being? Bear in mind that all but a few men were serfs when these rights began to be talked about and created, little by very little.

We are a government of laws; yet few understand the sense and reason of the law, and many fear the mass of words in which it is embodied. Nor does the citizen appreciate how these rules came into being. There is a beautiful history and philosophy to this system, and it is to be found only in the Blackstone *Commentaries*. Herein is my endeavor to give you this history and philosophy without the timeworn and obsolete phraseology. When, as here, the *Commentaries* are released from encrusting obscurities, the brilliance of Blackstone's thought and language remains undimmed by the two centuries that have passed since he assumed the chair as Oxford's first teacher of law.

The *Commentaries* continue to be the Bible of the student and of the learned reader. Large as is the proportion of the rules and usages described by Blackstone which have been modified by statute or have become obsolete, the best book in which to gain a comprehensive view of the rudiments of English and American law is still the *Commentaries*. The principles of law which they unfold remain the same.

Year after year, hundreds of superficial workers are preparing themselves to glean in the fields of legal controversy. The true workers in the law, the men who are to reap its harvests and bear away its tempting prizes, do not spare themselves the labor of acquiring an intimate acquaintance with the work of Blackstone.

The student of American law ought to be well grounded in English history, and in the development of its constitutional principles. It is idle to examine the United States Constitution without some familiarity with that from which it sprung. It is impossible to understand the full force and meaning of the maxims of personal liberty, which are so important a part of our law, without first learning how and why it was that they became incorporated into our legal system.

From a study of the *Commentaries*, the student and the scholar will derive increased love of liberty and a strengthened attachment to the laws under which we live. He will also learn to discern in the dry rule of law the principle which underlies it, and how to correctly apply that principle in new cases, as they arise, by noting how it had been earlier applied by the great minds which thus become his preceptors.

Of a work which has been so long before the public as Blackstone's *Commentaries*, it is not necessary to utter one word of approbation. For luminous method, for profound research, for purity of diction, for comprehensive brevity, and pregnancy of matter, for richness in classical allusions, and for extent and variety of knowledge of foreign jurisprudence, whether introduced for illustration, or ornament, or instruction, it is not too much to say that it stands unrivaled in ours and, perhaps, in every language.

Perhaps it is well when we think of the law that we go to that other original source, the Bible, where it is written in Deuteronomy: "But as for thee, stand thou here by me, and I will speak unto thee all the commandments, which thou shall teach them, that they may do them."

J. W. EHRLICH

San Francisco, California

PREFACE

In this volume, containing Book I and Book II of the *Commentaries*, special attention is given to the legislative, the executive and the judicial branches of government.

Here is discussed the nature of laws in general, the rights of persons, and the rights of things. The individual is most important in our civilization. It is necessary that we know his rights and responsibilities as well as the rights and duties that he has delegated to his government.

Specific attention is given to such subjects as Master and Servant, Husband and Wife, Parent and Child, Guardian and Ward, and Wills, as well as to those unseen, figurative persons called Corporations.

Not only is the right of the person important, but also the rights of things that are to be protected for his benefit. We treat here of the laws applying to property in general, inheritance, and title to real property; also how title to property is acquired by descent, by purchase, or by occupancy, all of which form an important part of this subject and about which very few lawyers have specialized knowledge.

To the student of law who is fitting himself to be a minister of justice there must be a dedication of will, of purpose, and of desire to serve his clients and the courts, as well as the community, by learning and by constant effort to fit himself for the responsible trust he is to assume as a lawyer. For without the lawyer there would be no justice. There would be no rights or wrongs. There would be no civilization. There would be anarchy, hate, intolerance and fear.

The Study, Nature, and Extent of the Law

THE NATURE OF LAWS
IN GENERAL

⚖️ MEANING OF LAW — Law, in its most general and comprehensive
sense, signifies a rule of action; and is applied indiscriminately to all
kinds of action, whether animate or inanimate, rational or irrational. Thus
we say, the laws of motion, of gravitation, of optics, or mechanics, as well
as the laws of nature and of nations.

⚖️ LAW AS ORDER OF THE UNIVERSE — Thus when the Supreme Being
formed the universe, and created matter out of nothing, He impressed
certain principles upon that matter, from which it can never depart, and
without which it would cease to be. When He put the matter into motion,
He established certain laws of motion, to which all movable bodies must
conform. To descend from the greatest operations to the smallest, when a
workman forms a clock, or other piece of mechanism, he establishes at his
own pleasure certain arbitrary laws for its direction; as that the hand
shall describe a given space in a given time; to which law as long as the
work conforms, so long it continues in perfection, and answers the end of
its formation.

If we further advance, from mere inactive matter to vegetable and
animal life, we shall find them still governed by laws; more numerous
indeed, but equally fixed and invariable. The whole progress of plants,
from the seed to the root, and from thence to the seed again;—the method
of animal nutrition, digestion, secretion and all other branches of vital
economy;—are not left to chance, or the will of the creature itself, but
are performed in a wondrous involuntary manner, and guided by unerring
rules laid down by the great Creator.

⚖️ LAW AS A ROLE OF HUMAN ACTION — This, then, is the general signification of law, a rule of action dictated by some superior being:
and, in those creatures that have neither the power to think, nor the will,
such laws must be invariably obeyed, so long as the creature itself subsists,
for its existence depends on that obedience. But laws, in their more con-

fined sense, and in which it is our present business to consider them, denote the rules, not of action in general, but of human action or conduct: that is, the precepts by which man, the noblest of all sublunary beings, a creature endowed with both reason and free will, is commanded to make use of these facilities in the general regulation of his behavior.

Man, considered as a creature, must necessarily be subject to the laws of his Creator, for he is entirely a dependent being. A being, independent of any other, has no rule to pursue, but such as he prescribes to himself; but a state of dependence will inevitably oblige the inferior to take the will of him, on whom he depends, as the rule of his conduct: not indeed in every particular, but in all those points wherein his dependence consists. This principle, therefore, has more or less intent and effect, in proportion as the superiority of the one and the dependence of the other is greater or less, absolute or limited.

☙ LAW OF NATURE — This will of his Maker is called the law of nature.

For as God, when He created matter, and endured it with a principle of mobility, established certain rules for the perpetual direction of that motion; so, when He created man, and endued him with free will to conduct himself in all parts of life, He laid down certain immutable laws of human nature, whereby that free will is in some degree regulated and restrained, and gave him also the faculty of reason to discover the purport of those laws.

Considering the Creator only as a Being of infinite power, He was able unquestionably to have prescribed whatever laws He pleased to His creature, man, however unjust or severe. But as He is also a Being of infinite wisdom, He has laid down only such laws as were founded in those relations of justice, that existed in the nature of things antecedent to any positive precept. These are the eternal, immutable laws of good and evil, to which the Creator Himself in all His dispensations conforms: and which He has enabled human reason to discover, so far as they are necessary for the conduct of human actions. Such, among others, are these principles: that we should live honestly, should hurt nobody, and should render to everyone his due; to which three general precepts Justinian has reduced the whole doctrine of law.

But if the discovery of these first principles of the law of nature depended only upon the due exertion of right reason, and could not otherwise be obtained than by a chain of metaphysical disquisitions, mankind would have wanted some inducement to have quickened their inquiries, and the greater part of the world would have rested content in mental indolence, and ignorance its inseparable companion. As, therefore, the Creator is a Being, not only of infinite power, and wisdom, but also of infinite goodness, He has been pleased so to contrive the constitution and frame of humanity, that we should want no other prompter to inquire after and pursue the rule of right, but only our own self-love, that universal principle of action. For He has so intimately connected, so inseparably interwoven the laws of eternal justice with the happiness of each individual, that the latter cannot be attained but by observing the former; and, if the former be punctually obeyed, it cannot but induce the latter. In consequence of which mutual connection of justice and human felicity, He has not perplexed the law of nature with a multitude of abstracted rules and precepts, referring merely to the fitness or unfitness of things, as some have vainly surmised; but has graciously reduced the rule of obedience to this one paternal precept, "that man should pursue his own true and substantial happiness." This is the foundation of what we call ethics, or natural law. For the several articles into which it is branched in our systems, amount to no more than demonstrating, that this or that action tends to man's real happiness, and therefore very justly concluding that the performance of it is a part of the law of nature; or, on the other hand, that this or that action is destructive of man's real happiness and therefore that the law of nature forbids it.

⚖ LAW OF NATIONS — If man were to live in a state of nature, unconnected with other individuals, there would be no occasion for any other laws, than the law of nature, and the law of God. Neither could any other law possibly exist: for a law always supposes some superior who is to make it; and in a state of nature we are all equal, without any other superior but Him who is the author of our being. But man was formed for society; and, as is demonstrated by the writers on this subject, is neither capable of living alone, nor indeed has the courage to do it.

However, as it is impossible for the whole race of mankind to be united in one great society, they must necessarily divide into many; and form separate states, commonwealths, and nations, entirely independent of each other, and yet liable to a mutual intercourse. Hence arises a third kind of law to regulate this mutual intercourse called "the law of nations"; which, as none of these states will acknowledge a superiority in the other, cannot be dictated by any; but depends entirely upon the rules of natural law, or upon mutual compacts, treaties, leagues, and agreements between these several communities: in the construction also of which compacts we have no other rule to resort to, but the law of nature; being the only one to which both communities are equally subject: and therefore the civil law very justly observes, that that rule which natural reason has dictated to all men, is called the law of nations.

☙ MUNICIPAL LAW — This much I thought it necessary to premise concerning the law of nature, and the law of nations, before I proceeded to treat more fully of the principal subject of this section, municipal or civil law; that is, the rule by which particular districts, communities, or nations are governed. I call it municipal law, in compliance with common speech; for, though strictly that expression denotes the particular customs of one single municipium or free town, yet it may with sufficient propriety be applied to any one state or nation, which is governed by the same laws and customs.

Municipal law, thus understood, is properly defined to be "a rule of civil conduct, prescribed by the supreme power in a state, commanding what is right and prohibiting what is wrong." Let us endeavor to explain its several properties, as they arise out of this definition.

☙ IT IS A "RULE" — First, it is a rule: not a transient, sudden order from a superior to or concerning a particular person; but something permanent, uniform, and universal. Therefore, a particular act of legislature to confiscate the goods of Titius, or to attaint him of high treason, does not enter into the idea of a municipal law: for the operation of this act is spent upon Titius only, and has no relation to the community in general; it is rather a sentence than a law. But an act to declare that the crime of which Titius is accused shall be deemed high treason; this has permanency, uniformity, and universality, and therefore is properly a rule. It also is called a rule, to distinguish it from advice or counsel, which we are at liberty to follow or not, as we see proper, and to judge upon the reasonableness or unreasonableness of the thing advised: whereas our obedience to the law depends not upon our approbation, but upon the Maker's will. Counsel is only matter of persuasion, law is matter of injunction; counsel acts only upon the willing, law upon the unwilling also.

It is also called a rule to distinguish it from a compact or agreement; for a compact is a promise proceeding from us, law is, "I will, or will not, do this"; that of a law is, "thou shalt, or shalt not, do it." It is true there is an obligation which a compact carries with it, equal in point of conscience to that of a law; but then the original of the obligation is different. In compacts, we ourselves determine and promise what shall be done, before we are obliged to do it; in laws, we are obliged to act without ourselves determining or promising anything at all. Upon these accounts law is defined to be "a rule."

⚖ IT IS "A RULE OF CIVIL CONDUCT" — Municipal law is also "a rule of civil conduct." This distinguishes municipal law from the natural or revealed; the former of which is the rule of moral conduct, and the latter not only the rule of moral conduct, but also the rule of faith. These regard man as a creature, and point out his duty to God, to himself, and to his neighbor, considered in the light of an individual. But municipal or civil law regards him also as a citizen, and bound to other duties towards his neighbor, than those of mere nature and religion: duties which he has engaged in by enjoying the benefits of the common union; and which amount to no more than that he do contribute on his part to the subsistence and peace of the society.

⚖ IT IS "A RULE PRESCRIBED" — It is likewise "a rule prescribed." Because a bare resolution, confined in the breast of the legislator, without manifesting itself by some external sign, can never be properly a law. It is requisite that this resolution be notified to the people who are to obey it. But the manner in which this notification is to be made, is matter of very great indifference. It may be notified by universal tradition and long practice, which supposes a previous publication, and is the case of the common law of England. It may be notified viva voce (by word of mouth), by officers appointed for that purpose, as is done with regard to proclamations, and such acts of parliament as are appointed, to be notified by writing, printing, or the like, which is the general course taken with all our acts of parliament. Yet, whatever way is made use of, it is incumbent on the promulgators to do it in the most public and perspicuous manner.

There is still a more unreasonable method than this, which is called making of laws ex post facto (after the fact), when after an action, indifferent in itself, is committed, the legislator then for the first time declares it to have been a crime, and inflicts a punishment upon the person who has committed it. Here it is impossible that the party could foresee that an action, innocent when it was done, should be afterwards converted to guilt by a subsequent law; he had therefore no cause to abstain from it; and all punishment for not abstaining must of consequence be cruel and unjust. All laws should be therefore made to commence in futuro (at a future period), and be notified before their commencement; which is implied in the term "prescribed." But when this rule is in the usual manner notified or prescribed, it is then the subject's business to be thoroughly acquainted therewith; for if ignorance of what he might know, were admitted as a legitimate excuse, the laws would be of no effect, but might always be eluded with impunity.

⚖ IT IS "A RULE PRESCRIBED BY THE SUPREME POWER IN A STATE" —

But further: municipal law is "a rule of civil conduct prescribed by the supreme power in a state." For legislature, as was before observed, is the greatest act of superiority that can be exercised by one being over another. Wherefore it is requisite to the very essence of a law, that it be made by the supreme power. Sovereignty and legislature are indeed convertible terms; one cannot subsist without the other.

This may lead us into a short inquiry concerning the nature of society and civil government; and the natural, inherent right that belongs to the sovereignty of a state, wherever that sovereignty be lodged, of making and enforcing laws.

⚖ FOUNDATIONS OF SOCIETY — The only true and natural foundations of society are the wants and the fears of individuals. Not that we can believe, with some theoretical writers, that there ever was a time when there was no such thing as society either natural or civil; but that, from the impulse of reason, and through a sense of their wants and weaknesses, individuals met together in a large plain, entered into an original contract, and chose the tallest man present to be their governor. This notion, of an actually existing unconnected state of nature, is too wild to be seriously admitted: and besides it is plainly contradictory to the revealed accounts of the primitive origin of mankind, and their preservation two thousand years afterwards; both which were effected by the means of single families. These formed the first natural society, among themselves; which, every day extending its limits, laid the first though imperfect rudiments of civil or political society: and when it grew too large to subsist with convenience in that pastoral state, wherein the patriarchs appear to have lived, it necessarily subdivided itself by various migrations into more.

Afterwards, as agriculture increased, which employs and can maintain a much greater number of hands, migrations became less frequent: and various tribes, which had formerly separated, reunited again; sometimes by compulsion and conquest, sometimes by accident, and sometimes perhaps by compact. But though society had not its formal beginning from any convention of individuals, actuated by their wants and their fears; yet it is the sense of their weakness and imperfection that keeps mankind together; that demonstrates the necessity of this union; and that therefore is the solid and natural foundation, as well as the cement of civil society. This is what we mean by the original contract of society; which, though perhaps in no instance it has ever been formally expressed at the first institution of a state, yet in nature and reason must always be understood and implied, in the very act of associating together: namely, that the whole should protect all its parts, and that every part should pay obedience to the will of the whole; or, in other words, that the community should guard the rights of each individual member, and that (in return for this protection) each individual should submit to the laws of the community; without which submission of all it was impossible that protection could be certainly extended to any.

ESTABLISHMENT OF GOVERNMENT — For when civil society is once formed, government at the same time results of course, as necessary to preserve and to keep that society in order. Unless some superior be constituted, whose commands and decisions all the members are bound to obey, they would still remain as in a state of nature, without any judge upon earth to define their several rights, and redress their several wrongs. But, as all the members which compose this society were naturally equal, it may be asked, in whose hands are the reins of government to be entrusted? To this the general answer is easy; but the application of it to particular cases has occasioned one-half of those mischiefs, which are apt to proceed from misguided political zeal.

In general, all mankind will agree that government should be reposed in such persons, in whom those qualities are most likely to be found, the perfection of which is among the attributes of Him who is emphatically styled the Supreme Being; the three grand requisites, I mean, of wisdom, of goodness, and of power: wisdom, to discern the real interest of the community; goodness, to endeavor always to pursue that real interest; and strength, or power, to carry this knowledge and intention into action. There are the natural foundations of sovereignty, and these are the requisites that ought to be found in every well-constituted frame of government.

MERITS AND DEMERITS OF DIFFERENT FORMS OF GOVERNMENT — In a democracy, where the right of making laws resides in the people at large, public virtue, or goodness of intention, is more likely to be found, than either of the other qualities of government. Popular assemblies are frequently foolish in their contrivance, and weak in their execution; but generally mean to do the thing that is right and just, and have always a degree of patriotism or public spirit. In aristocracies there is more wisdom to be found, than in the other frames of government; being composed, or intended to be composed, of the most experienced citizens; but there is less honesty than in a republic, and less strength than in a monarchy. A monarchy is indeed the most powerful of any; for by the entire conjunction of the legislative and executive powers all the sinews of government are knit together, and united in the hand of the prince; but then there is imminent danger of his employing that strength to improvident or oppressive purposes.

Thus these three species of government have, all of them, their several perfections and imperfections. Democracies are usually the best calculated to direct the end of a law; aristocracies to invent the means by which that end shall be obtained; and monarchies to carry those means into execution. The ancients, as was observed, had in general no idea of any other permanent form of government but these three: for though Cicero declares himself of opinion, "that the best constituted republic, is that which is duly compounded of these three forms, the monarchical, aristocratic, and democratic"; yet Tacitus treats this notion of a mixed government, formed out of them all, and partaking of the advantages of each, as a visionary whim, and one that, if effected, could never be lasting or secure.

⚖ THE BRITISH CONSTITUTION — But, happily for us of this island, the British constitution has long remained, and I trust will long continue, a standing exception to the truth of this observation. For, as with us the executive power of the laws is lodged in a single person, they have all the advantages of strength and dispatch, that are to be found in the most absolute monarchy: and as the legislature of the kingdom is entrusted to three distinct powers, entirely independent of each other: first, the king; secondly, the lords, spiritual and temporal, which is an aristocratical assembly of persons selected for their piety, their birth, their wisdom, their valor, or their property; and, thirdly, the house of commons, freely chosen by the people from among themselves, which makes it a kind of democracy; as this aggregate body, actuated by different springs, and attentive to different interests, composes the British parliament, and has the supreme disposal of everything; there can be no inconvenience attempted by either of the three branches, but will be withstood by one of the other two; each branch being armed with a negative power, sufficient to repel any innovation which it shall think inexpedient or dangerous.

⚖ LEGISLATIVE POWER SUPREME — Having thus cursorily considered the three usual species of government, and our own singular constitution, selected and compounded from them all, I proceed to observe, that, as the power of making laws constitutes the supreme authority, so wherever the supreme authority in any state resides, it is the right of that authority to make laws; that is, in the words of our definition, to prescribe the rule of civil action. This may be discovered from the very end and institution of civil states. For a state is a collective body, composed of a multitude of individuals, united for their safety and convenience, and intending to act together as one man. If it therefore is to act as one man, it ought to act by one uniform will. But, inasmuch as political communities are made up of many natural persons, each of whom has his particular will and inclination, these several wills cannot by any natural union be joined together, or tempered and disposed into a lasting harmony, so as to constitute and produce that one uniform will of the whole. It can therefore be no otherwise produced than by a political union; by the consent of all persons to submit their own private wills to the will of one man, or of one or more assemblies of men, to whom the supreme authority is entrusted: and this will of that one man, or assemblage of men, is in different states, according to their different constitutions, understood to be law.

Thus far as to the right of the supreme power to make laws; but further, it is its duty likewise. For since the respective members are bound to conform themselves to the will of the state, it is expedient that they receive directions from the state declaratory of that its will. But, as it is impossible, in so great a multitude, to give injunctions to every particular man, relative to each particular action, it is therefore incumbent on the state to establish general rules, for the perpetual information and direction of all persons in all points, whether of positive or negative duty. This, in order, that every man may know what to look upon as his own, what as another's; what absolute and what relative duties are required at his hands, what is to be esteemed honest, dishonest, or indifferent; what degree every man retains of his natural liberty; what he has given up as the price of the benefits of society; and after what manner each person is to moderate the use and exercise of those rights which the state assigns him, in order to promote and secure the public tranquillity.

⚖ DEFINITION OF LAW CONTINUED — From what has been advanced, the truth of the former branch of our definition, is (I trust) sufficiently evident; that "municipal law is a rule of civil conduct prescribed by the supreme power in a state." I proceed now to the latter branch of it; that it is a rule so prescribed, "Commanding what is right, and prohibiting what is wrong."

☙☙ "COMMANDING WHAT IS RIGHT, PROHIBITING WHAT IS WRONG" —
Now, in order to do this completely, it is first of all necessary that
the boundaries of right and wrong be established and ascertained by law.
And when this is once done, it will follow, of course, that it is likewise the
business of the law, considered as a rule of civil conduct, to enforce these
rights and to restrain or redress these wrongs. It remains, therefore, only
to consider in what manner the law is said to ascertain the boundaries of
right and wrong; and the methods which it takes to command the one and
prohibit the other.

For this purpose every law may be said to consist of several parts:
one, declaratory; whereby the rights to be observed, and the wrongs to be
eschewed, are clearly defined and laid down: another, directory; whereby
the subject is instructed and enjoined to observe those rights, and to abstain from the commission of those wrongs: a third, remedial; whereby a
method is pointed out to recover a man's private rights, or redress his
private wrongs: to which may be added a fourth, usually termed the
sanction, or vindicatory branch of the law; whereby it is signified what
evil or penalty shall be incurred by such as commit any public wrongs,
and transgress or neglect their duty.

☙☙ DECLARATORY PART — With regard to the first of these, the declaratory part of the municipal law, this depends not so much upon the
law of revelation or of nature, as upon the wisdom and will of the legislator. This doctrine, which before was slightly touched, deserves a more
particular explication. Those rights, then, which God and nature have
established, are therefore called natural rights, such as are life and liberty,
need not the aid of human laws to be more effectually invested in every
man than they are; neither do they receive any additional strength when
declared by the municipal laws to be inviolable. On the contrary, no
human legislature has power to abridge or destroy them, unless the owner
shall himself commit some act that amounts to a forfeiture. Neither do
divine or natural duties (such as, for instance, the worship of God, the
maintenance of children, and the like) receive any stronger sanction from
being also declared to be duties by the law of the land. The case is the
same as to crimes and misdemeanors, that are forbidden by the superior
laws, and therefore styled mala in se (crimes in themselves), such as
murder, theft, and perjury; which contract no additional turpitude from
being declared unlawful by the inferior legislature. For that legislature in
all these cases acts only, as was before observed, in subordination to the
great lawgiver, transcribing and publishing His precepts. So that, upon the

whole, the declaratory part of the municipal law has no force or operation at all, with regard to actions that are naturally and intrinsically right or wrong.

But, with regard to things in themselves indifferent, the case is entirely altered. These become either right or wrong, just or unjust, duties or misdemeanors, according as the municipal legislator sees proper, for promoting the welfare of the society, and more effectually carrying on the purposes of civil life. Thus our own common law has declared, that the goods of the wife do instantly upon marriage become the property and right of the husband; and our statute law has declared all monopolies a public offense: yet that right, and this offense, have no foundation in nature; but are merely created by the law, for the purposes of civil society. Sometimes, where the thing itself has its rise from the law of nature, the particular circumstances and mode of doing it becomes right or wrong, as the laws of the land shall direct. Thus, for instance, in civil duties; obedience to superiors is the doctrine of revealed as well as natural religion: but who those superiors shall be, and in what circumstances, or to what degrees they shall be obeyed, it is the province of human laws to determine. And so, as to injuries or crimes, it must be left to our own legislature to decide, in what cases the seizing another's cattle shall amount to "a trespass or a theft"; and where it shall be a justifiable action, as when a landlord takes them by way of distress for rent.

⚖ DIRECTORY PART — Thus much for the declaratory part of the municipal law: and the directory stands much upon the same footing; for this virtually includes the former, the declaration being usually collected from the direction. The law that says, "thou shalt not steal," implies a declaration that stealing is a crime. And we have seen that, in things naturally indifferent, the very essence of right and wrong depends upon the direction of the laws to do or to omit them.

⚖ REMEDIAL PART — The remedial part of a law is so necessary a consequence of the former two, that laws must be very vague and imperfect without it. For in vain would rights be declared, in vain directed to be observed, if there were no method of recovering and asserting those rights, when wrongfully withheld or invaded. This is what we mean properly, when we speak of the protection of the law. When, for instance, the declaratory part of the law has said, "that the field or inheritance, which belonged to Titius' father, is vested by his death in Titius"; and the directory part has "forbidden anyone to enter on another's property, without the leave of the owner": if Gaius after this will presume to take possession of the land, the remedial part of the law will then interpose its office: will make Gaius restore the possession to Titius, and also pay him damages for the invasion.

⚖ VINDICATORY PART, OR SANCTION — With regard to the sanction of laws, or the evil that may attend the breach of public duties; it is observed, that human legislators have for the most part chosen to make the sanction of their laws rather vindicatory than remuneratory, or to consist rather in punishments, than in actual particular rewards. Because, in the first place, the quiet enjoyment and protection of all our civil rights and liberties, which are the sure and general consequence of obedience to the municipal law, are in themselves the best and most valuable of all rewards. Because also, were the exercise of every virtue to be enforced by the proposal of particular rewards, it were impossible for any state to furnish stock enough for so profuse a bounty. And further, because the dread of evil is a much more forcible principle of human actions than the prospect of good. For which reasons, though a prudent bestowing of rewards is sometimes of exquisite use, yet we find that those civil laws, which enforce and enjoin our duty, do seldom, if ever, propose any priviliege or gift to such as obey the law; but do constantly come armed with a penalty denounced against transgressors, either expressly defining the nature and quantity of the punishment, or else leaving it to the discretion of the judges, and those who are entrusted with the care of putting the laws in execution.

Of all the parts of a law the most effectual is the vindicatory. For it is but lost labor to say, "do this, or avoid that," unless we also declare, "this shall be the consequence of your noncompliance." We must therefore observe, that the main strength and force of a law consists in the penalty annexed to it. Herein is to be found the principal obligation of human laws.

Legislators and their laws are said to compel and oblige; not that by any natural violence they so constrain a man, as to render it impossible for him to act otherwise than as they direct, which is the strict sense of obligation: but because, by declaring and exhibiting a penalty against offenders, they bring it to pass that no man can easily choose to transgress the law; since by reason of the impending correction, compliance is in a high degree preferable to disobedience. And even where rewards are proposed as well as punishments threatened, the obligation of the law seems chiefly to consist in the penalty: for rewards, in their nature can only persuade and allure; nothing is compulsory but punishment.

⚖   MALA IN SE AND MALA PROHIBITA — It is true, it hath been holden, and very justly, by the principal of our ethical writers, that human laws are binding upon men's consciences. But if that were the only, or most forcible obligation, the good only would regard the laws, and the bad would set them at defiance. And true as this principle is, it must still be understood with some restriction. It holds, I apprehend, as to rights; and that, when the law has determined the field to belong to Titius, it is matter of conscience no longer to withhold or to invade it. So also in regard to natural duties, and such offenses as are mala in se: here we are bound in conscience, because we are bound by superior laws, before those human laws were in being, to perform the one and abstain from the other. But in relation to those laws which enjoin only positive duties, and forbid only such things as are not male in se but mala prohibita merely, without any intermixture of moral guilt, annexing a penalty to noncompliance, here I apprehend conscience is no further concerned, than by directing a submission to the penalty, in case of our breach of those laws: for otherwise the multitude of penal laws in a state would not only be looked upon as an impolitic, but would also be a very wicked thing; if every such law were a snare for the conscience of the subject. But in these cases the alternative is offered to every man; "either abstain from this, or submit to such a penalty": and his conscience will be clear, whichever side of the alternative he thinks proper to embrace.

Thus, by the statutes for preserving the game, a penalty is denounced against every unqualified person that kills a hare, and against every person who possesses a partridge in August. And so, too, by other statutes, pecuniary penalties are inflicted for exercising trades without serving an apprenticeship thereto, for not burying the dead in woolen, for not performing the statute work on the public roads, and for innumerable other positive misdemeanors. Now these prohibitory laws do not make the transgression a moral offense, or sin: the only obligation in conscience is to submit to the penalty, if levied. It must, however, be observed, that we are here speaking of laws that are simply and purely penal, where the thing forbidden or enjoined is wholly a matter of indifference, and where the penalty inflicted is an adequate compensation for the civil inconvenience supposed to arise from the offense. But where disobedience to the law involves in it also any degree of public mischief or private injury, there it falls within our former distinction, and is also an offense against conscience.

⚖️ INTERPRETATION OF LAWS — I have now gone through the definition laid down of a municipal law; and have shown that it is "a rule—of civil conduct—prescribed—by the supreme power in state—commanding what is right, and prohibiting what is wrong": in the explication of which I have endeavored to interweave a few useful principles, concerning the nature of civil government, and the obligation of human laws. Before I conclude this section, it may not be amiss to add a few observations concerning the interpretation of laws.

⚖️ INTERPRETATION BY THE USUAL MEANING OF WORDS — The fairest and most rational method to interpret the will of the legislator is by exploring his intentions at the time when the law was made, by signs the most natural and probable. And these signs are either the words, the context, the subject matter, the effects and consequence, or the spirit and reason of the law. Let us take a short view of them all.

Words are generally to be understood in their usual and most known signification; not so much regarding the propriety of grammar, as their general and popular use. Thus the law which forbade a layman to lay hands on a priest, was adjudged to extend to him, who had hurt a priest with a weapon. Again: terms of art, or technical terms, must be taken according to the acceptation of the learned in each art, trade, and science. So in the act of settlement, where the crown of England is limited "to the Princess Sophia, and the heirs of her body, being Protestants," it becomes necessary to call in the assistance of lawyers, to ascertain the precise idea of the words "heirs of her body"; which in a legal sense comprise only certain of her lineal descendants.

Lastly, where words are clearly repugnant in two laws, the later law takes place of the elder: "later laws repeal prior ones in conflict therewith" is a maxim of universal law, as well as of our own constitutions. Accordingly it was laid down by law of the twelve tables at Rome, "let that which the people have last decreed be considered law."

⚖️ ACCORDING TO CONTEXT — If words happen to be still dubious, we may establish their meaning from the context; with which it may be of singular use to compare a word, or a sentence, whenever they are ambiguous, equivocal, or intricate. Thus the proem, or preamble, is often called in to help the construction of an act of parliament. Of the same nature and use is the comparison of a law with other laws, that are made by the same legislator, that have some affinity with the subject, or that expressly relate to the same point. Thus, when the law of England declares murder to be felony without benefit of clergy, we must resort to the same law of England to learn what the benefit of clergy is: and when the common law censures simoniacal contracts, it affords great light to the subject to consider what the canon law has adjudged to be simony.

⚖ ACCORDING TO SUBJECT MATTER — As to the subject matter, words are always to be understood as having a regard thereto; for that is always supposed to be in the eye of the legislator, and all his expressions directed to that end. Thus, when a law forbids all ecclesiastical persons to purchase provisions at Rome, it might seem to prohibit the buying of grain and other victuals: but when we consider that the statute was made to repress the usurpations of the papal see, and that the nominations to benefices by the pope were called provisions, we shall see that the restraint is intended to be laid upon such provisions only.

⚖ ACCORDING TO THE EFFECT — As to the effects and consequence, the rule is, that where words bear either none, or a very absurd signification, if literally understood, we must a little deviate from the received sense of them. Therefore the law, which enacted "that whoever drew blood in the streets should be punished with the utmost severity," was held after long debate not to extend to the surgeon, who opened the vein of a person that fell down in the street with a fit.

⚖ ACCORDING TO THE REASON OF THE LAW — But, lastly, the most universal and effectual way of discovering the true meaning of a law, when the words are dubious, is by considering the reason and spirit of it; or the cause which moved the legislator to enact it. For when this reason ceases, the law itself ought likewise to cease with it. An instance of this is given in a case put by Cicero, or whoever was the author of the rhetorical treatise inscribed to Herennius. There was a law, that those who in a storm forsook the ship should forfeit all property therein; and the ship and lading should belong entirely to those who stayed in it. In a dangerous tempest all the mariners forsook the ship, except only one sick passenger, who by reason of his disease was unable to get out and escape. By chance the ship came safe to port. The sick man kept possession, and claimed the benefit of the law. Now here all the learned agree, that the sick man is not within the reason of the law; for the reason of making it was, to give encouragement to such as should venture their lives to save the vessel; but this is a merit which he could never pretend to, who neither stayed in the ship upon that account, nor contributed anything to its preservation.

⚖ EQUITY — From this method of interpreting laws, by the reason of them, arises what we call equity; which is defined "the correction of that, wherein the law (by reason of its universality) is deficient." For since in laws all cases cannot be foreseen or expressed, it is necessary, that when the general decrees of the law come to be applied to particular cases, there should be somewhere a power vested of defining those circumstances, which (had they been foreseen) the legislator himself would have expressed. And these are the cases, which "the law does not define exactly, but leaves something to the discretion of a just and wise judge."

Equity thus depending, essentially, upon the particular circumstances of each individual case, there can be no established rules and fixed precepts of equity laid down, without destroying its very essence, and reducing it to a positive law. On the other hand, the liberty of considering all cases in an equitable light must not be indulged too far, lest thereby we destroy all law, and leave the decision of every question entirely in the breast of the judge. And law, without equity, though hard and disagreeable, is much more desirable for the public good, than equity without law: which would make every judge a legislator, and introduce most infinite confusion; as there would then be almost as many different rules of action laid down in our courts, as there are differences of capacity and sentiment in the human mind.

THE LAWS OF ENGLAND

⚖ DIVISIONS OF THE LAW OF ENGLAND — The municipal law of England, or the rule of civil conduct prescribed to the inhabitants of this kingdom, may with sufficient propriety be divided into two kinds: the unwritten or common law; and the written or statute law.

⚖ THE UNWRITTEN, OR COMMON, LAW — The unwritten law, includes not only general customs, or the common law properly so called; but also the particular customs of certain parts of the kingdom; and likewise those particular laws, that are by custom observed only in certain courts and jurisdictions.

When I call these parts of our law the unwritten or common law, I would not be understood as if all those laws were at present merely oral, or communicated from the former ages to the present solely by word of mouth.

It is true, indeed, that, in the profound ignorance of letters which formerly overspread the whole western world, all laws were entirely traditional, for this plain reason, that the nations among which they prevailed had but little idea of writing. Thus the British as well as the Gallic Druids committed all their laws as well as learning to memory; and it is said of the primitive Saxons here, as well as their brethren on the Continent, that they retained their laws solely by memory and custom. But with us at present, the monuments and evidences of our legal customs are contained in the records of the several courts of justice, in books of reports and judicial decisions, and in the treatises of learned sages of the profession, preserved and handed down to us from the times of highest antiquity.

However, I style these parts of our law, the unwritten law, because their original institution and authority are not set down in writing, as acts of parliament are, but they receive their binding power, and the force of laws, by long and immemorial usage, and by their universal reception throughout the kingdom. In like manner unwritten law is that which is expressed or sanctioned by the tacit and unwritten customs and consent of men.

🔱 ANCIENT CUSTOMS — Our ancient lawyers insist with abundance of warmth, that these customs are as old as the primitive Britons, and continued down, through the several mutations of government and inhabitants, to the present time, unchanged and unadulterated.

This may be the case as to some: but in general this assertion must be understood with many grains of allowance; and ought only to signify, as the truth seems to be, that there never was any formal exchange of one system of laws for another: Though doubtless by the intermixture of adventitious nations; the Romans, the Picts, the Saxons, the Danes, and the Normans, they must have insensibly introduced and incorporated many of their own customs with those that were before established: thereby in all probability improving the texture and wisdom of the whole by the accumulated wisdom of diverse particular countries.

🔱 ALFRED'S LAWS — Our first historians do all positively assure us that our body of laws is of this compounded nature. They tell us that in the time of Alfred, the local customs of the several provinces of the kingdom were grown so various, that he found it expedient to compile his dome-book for the general use of the whole kingdom.

This book is said to have been extant so late as the reign of King Edward IV, but is now unfortunately lost. It contained, we may probably suppose, the principal maxims of the common law, the penalties for misdemeanors, and the forms of judicial proceedings. Thus much may at least be collected from that injunction to observe it, which we find in the laws of King Edward the Elder, the son of Alfred: "to all who preside over the republic, my positive and repeated injunction is, that they conduct themselves toward all as just judges, as it is written in the dome-book, and without fear boldly and freely declare the common law."

The maxims and customs collected are of higher antiquity than memory or history can reach: nothing being more difficult than to ascertain the precise beginning of an ancient and long-established custom. Whence it is that in our law the goodness of a custom depends upon its having been used time out of mind; or, in the solemnity of our legal phrase, time whereof the memory of man runneth not to the contrary.

🔱 DIVISIONS OF THE COMMON LAW — This unwritten, or common law, is properly distinguishable into three kinds:

1. General customs; which are the universal rule of the whole

kingdom, and form the common law, in its stricter and more usual signification.

2. Particular customs: which for the most part affect only the inhabitants of particular districts.

3. Certain particular laws; which by custom are adopted and used by some particular courts of pretty general and extensive jurisdiction.

⚖ GENERAL CUSTOMS — As to general customs, of the common law; this is that law, by which proceedings and determinations in the king's ordinary courts of justice are guided and directed.

This, for the most part, settles the course in which lands descend by inheritance; the manner and form of acquiring and transferring property; the solemnities and obligations of contracts; the rules of expounding wills, deeds, and the acts of parliament; the respective remedies of civil injuries; the several species of temporal offenses, with the manner and degree of punishment; and an infinite number of minuter particulars, which diffuse themselves as extensively as the ordinary distribution of common justice requires.

Thus, for example, that there shall be four superior courts of record, the chancery, the king's bench, the common pleas, and the exchequer; that the eldest son alone is heir to his ancestor; that property may be acquired and transferred by writing; that a deed is of no validity unless sealed and delivered; that wills shall be construed more favorably, and deeds more strictly; that money lent upon bond is recoverable by action of debt; that breaking the public peace is an offense, and punishable by fine and imprisonment;—all these are doctrines that are not set down in any written statute or ordinance, but depend merely upon immemorial usage, that is, upon common law, for their support.

Some have divided the common law into two principal grounds or foundations:

1. Established customs; such as that, where there are three brothers, the eldest brother shall be heir to the second, in exclusion of the youngest and;

2. Established rules and maxims; as, "that the king can do no wrong, that no man shall be bound to accuse himself," and the like. But I take these to be one and the same thing. For the authority of these maxims rests entirely upon general reception and usage: and the only method of proving, that this or that maxim is a rule of the common law, is by showing that it hath been always the custom to observe it.

⚖️   PRECEDENTS — How are these customs or maxims to be known, and by whom is their validity to be determined? The answer is, by the judges in the several courts of justice. They are the depositaries of the law, who must decide in all cases of doubt, and who are bound by an oath to decide according to the law of the land.

Their knowledge of the law is derived from experience and study; and from being long personally accustomed to the judicial decisions of their predecessors. These judicial decisions are the principal and most authoritative evidence, that can be given, of the existence of such a custom as shall form a part of the common law. The judgment itself, and all the proceedings previous thereto, are carefully registered and preserved in public repositories set apart for that particular purpose, and to them frequent recourse is had, when any critical question arises, in the determination of which former precedents may give light or assistance.

It is an established rule to abide by former precedents, where the same points come again in litigation: as well to keep the scale of justice even and steady, and not liable to waver with every new judge's opinion; as also because the law in that case being solemnly declared and determined, what before was uncertain, and perhaps indifferent, is now become a permanent rule, which it is not in the breast of any subsequent judge to alter or vary from, according to his private sentiments; he being sworn to determine not according to his own private judgment, but according to the known laws and customs of the land; not delegated to pronounce a new law, but to maintain and expound the old one.

Yet this rule admits of exception, where the former determination is most evidently contrary to reason. But even in such cases the subsequent judges do not pretend to make a new law, but to vindicate the old one from misrepresentation. If it be found that the former decision is manifestly absurd or unjust, it is declared, not that such a sentence was bad law, but that it was not law; that is, that it is not the established custom of the realm, as has been erroneously determined.

Our lawyers tells us, that the law is the perfection of reason, that it always intends to conform thereto, and that what is not reason is not law. Not that the particular reason of every rule in the law can at this distance of time be always precisely assigned; but it is sufficient that there be nothing in the rule flatly contradictory to reason, and then the law will presume it to be well founded.

⚖️   EVIDENCE OF COMMON LAW: JUDICIAL DECISIONS — The doctrine of the law then is this: that precedents and rules must be followed, unless flatly absurd or unjust: for though their reason be not obvious at first view, yet we owe such a deference to former times as not to suppose they acted wholly without consideration. Upon the whole, however, we may take it as a general rule, "that the decisions of courts of justice are the evidence of what is common law."

⚖ REPORTS — The decisions, therefore, of courts are held in the highest regard, and are not only preserved as authentic records, but are handed out to public view in the numerous volumes of reports which furnish the lawyer's library. These reports are histories of cases, and the reasons the court gave for its judgment. The reports are extant in a regular series from the reign of King Edward II, to that of Henry VIII, and are published annually.

⚖ RULES AND REQUISITES OF PROOF RELATING TO PARTICULAR CUSTOMS — The rules relating to particular customs regard whither the proof of their existence; their legality when proved; or their usual method of allowance.

When a custom is actually proved to exist, the next inquiry is into the legality of it; for, if it is not a good custom, it ought to be no longer used. A bad custom should be abolished. This is an established maxim of the law.

To make a particular custom good, the following are necessary requisites:

⚖ THAT THEY BE IMMEMORIAL — That it has been used so long, that the memory of man runneth not to the contrary. So that, if anyone can show the beginning of it, it is no good custom. For which reason no custom can prevail against an express act of parliament; since the statute itself is a proof of a time when such a custom did not exist.

⚖ THAT THEY BE CONTINUED — It must have been continued. Any interruption would cause a temporary ceasing: The revival gives it a new beginning, which will be within time of memory, and thereupon the custom will be void. But this must be understood with regard to an interruption of the right; for an interruption of the possession only, for ten or twenty years, will not destroy the custom. As if the inhabitants of a parish have a customary right of watering their cattle at a certain pool, the custom is not destroyed, though they do not use it for ten years; it only becomes more difficult to prove: but if the right be anyhow discontinued for a day, the custom is quite at an end.

⚖ THAT THEY BE PEACEABLE — It must have been peaceable, and acquiesced in; not subject to contention and dispute. For as customs owe their original to common consent, their being immemorially disputed, either at law or otherwise is a proof that such consent was wanting.

🐝   THAT THEY BE REASONABLE — Customs must be reasonable; or rather, taken negatively, they must not be unreasonable. Upon which account a custom may be good, though the particular reason of it cannot be assigned; for it sufficeth, if no good legal reason can be assigned against it. Thus a custom in a parish, that no man shall put his beast into a common till the 3d of October, would be good; and yet it would be hard to show the reason why that day in particular is fixed upon, rather than the day before or after. But a custom, that no cattle shall be put in till the lord of the manor has first put in his, is unreasonable, and therefore bad: for peradventure the lord will never put in his; and then the tenants will lose all their profits.

🐝   THAT THEY BE CERTAIN — Customs ought to be certain. A custom, that lands shall descend to the most worthy of the owner's blood, is void; for how shall this worth be determined? But a custom to descend to the next male of the blood, exclusive of females, is certain and therefore good. A custom to pay two pence an acre in lieu of tithes, is good; but to pay sometimes two pence and sometimes three pence, as the occupier of the land pleases, is bad for its uncertainty. The maxim of the law is: That is certain which can be made certain.

🐝   THAT THEY BE COMPULSIVE — Customs, though established by consent, must be when established compulsory; and not left to the option of every man, whether he will use them or no. Therefore, a custom, that all the inhabitants shall be rated toward the maintenance of a bridge, will be good; but a custom, that every man is to contribute thereto at his own pleasure, is idle and absurd, and indeed no custom at all.

🐝   THAT THEY BE CONSISTENT — Lastly, customs must be consistent with each other: One custom cannot be set up in opposition to another. For if both are really customs, then both are of equal antiquity, and both established by mutual consent. Therefore, if one man prescribes that by custom he has a right to have windows looking into another's garden, the other cannot claim a right by custom to stop up or obstruct those windows: For these two contradictory customs cannot both be good, nor both stand together. He ought rather to deny the existence of the former custom.

🐝   METHOD OF ALLOWANCE — Next, as to the allowance of special customs. Customs, in derogation of the common law, must be construed strictly. Thus, by custom an infant of fifteen years may by one species of conveyance convey away his lands in fee simple, or forever. Yet this custom does not empower him to use any other conveyance, or even to lease them for seven years: for the custom must be strictly pursued.

⚖ SPECIAL KINDS OF LAW — The third branch of them are those peculiar laws, which by custom are adopted and used only in certain peculiar courts and jurisdictions. Viz., the civil and canon law.

It may seem a little improper at first view to rank these laws under the head of unwritten laws, seeing they are set forth by authority in their pandects, their codes, and their institutions; their councils, decrees, and decretals; and enforced by an immense number of expositions, decisions, and treatises of the learned in both branches of the law.

It is most plain, that it is not on account of their being written laws, that either the canon law, or the civil law, have any obligation within this kingdom; neither do their force and efficacy depend upon their own intrinsic authority; which is the case of our written laws, or acts of parliament. They bind not the subjects of England.

But all the strength that either the papal or imperial laws have obtained in this realm is only because they have been admitted and received by immemorial usage and custom in some particular cases, and some particular courts; and then they form a branch of the unwritten law or customary law; or else, because they are in some other cases introduced by consent of parliament, and then they owe their validity to the statute law. This is expressly declared in those remarkable words of the statute (Peter-pence, 1534), addressed to the king's royal majesty.—"This is your grace's realm, recognizing no superior under God but only your grace, hath been and is free from subjection to any man's laws, but only to such as have been devised, made, and ordained within this realm for the wealth of the same; or to such other as, by sufferance of your grace and your progenitors, the people of this your realm have taken at their free liberty, by their own consent, to be used among them; and have bound themselves by long use and custom to the observance of the same: not as to the observance of the laws of any foreign prince, potentate, or prelate; but as to the customed and ancient laws of this realm. Originally established as laws of the same, by the said sufferance, consents, and custom; and none otherwise."

⚖ THE WRITTEN LAW, OR STATUTES — Let us next proceed to the written laws of the kingdom; which are statutes, acts, or edicts, made by the king's majesty, by and with the advice and consent of the lord's spiritual and temporal and commons in parliament assembled. The oldest of these now extant, and printed in our statute-books, is the famous Magna Carta; as confirmed in parliament (1225); though doubtless there were many acts before that time, the records of which are not lost, and the determinations of them perhaps at present currently received for the maxims of the old common law.

The manner of making these statutes will be better considered hereafter, when we examine the constitution of parliaments. At present we will only take notice of the different kinds of statutes; and some of general rules with regard to their construction.

PUBLIC, SPECIAL OR PRIVATE ACTS — Statutes are either general or special, public or private. A general or public act is an universal rule, that regards the whole community; and of this the courts of law are bound to take notice judicially without the statute being particularly pleaded, or formally set forth by the party who claims an advantage under it.

Special or private acts are rather exceptions than rules, being those which only operate upon particular persons, and private concerns; such as the Romans entitled "decrees of the Senate," in contradistinction to the "acts of the Senate," which regarded the whole community: and of these (which are not promulgated with the same notoriety as the former) the judges are not bound to take notice, unless they be formally shown and pleaded.

Thus, to show the distinction, the Statute (Dilapidations 1571), to prevent spiritual persons from making leases for longer terms than twenty-one years, or three lives, is a public act; it being a rule prescribed to the whole body of spiritual persons in the nation; but an act to enable the Bishop of Chester to make a lease to A for sixty years, is an exception to this rule: it concerns only the parties and the Bishop's successors; and is therefore a private act.

CLASSES OF STATUTES: DECLARATORY — Statutes also are either declaratory of the common law, or remedial of some defects therein. Declaratory, where the old custom of the kingdom is almost fallen in disuse, or become disputable; in which case the parliament has thought proper, as a lasting testimony of the thing, and for avoiding all doubts and difficulties, to declare what the common law is and ever hath been. Thus the statute (Treasons, 1351), doth not make any new species of treasons; but only, for the benefit of the subject, declares and enumerates those several kinds of offense, which before were treason at the common law.

REMEDIAL — Remedial statutes are those which are made to supply such defects, and abridge such superfluities, in the common law, as arise either from the general imperfection of all human laws, from change of time and circumstances, from the mistakes and unadvised determinations of unlearned (or even learned) judges, or from any other cause whatsoever. This being done, either by enlarging the common law where it was too narrow and circumscribed, or by restraining it where it was too lax and luxuriant, hath occasioned another subordinate division of remedial acts of parliament into enlarging and restraining statutes.

To instance again in the case of Treason. Clipping the current coin of the kingdom was an offense not sufficiently guarded against by the common law; therefore, it was thought expedient by Statute (Clipping of Coins, 1562), to make it high treason, which it was not at the common law: so that this was an enlarging statute. At common law also spiritual corporations might lease out their estates for any term of years, till prevented by the Statute before mentioned; this was therefore a restraining statute.

⚖ CONSTRUCTION OF REMEDIAL STATUTES — There are three points to be considered in the construction of all remedial statutes; the old law, the mischief, and the remedy: that is, how the common law stood at the making of the act; what the mischief was, for which the common law did not provide; and what remedy the parliament hath provided to cure this mischief. It is the business of the judges so to construe the act, as to suppress the mischief and advance the remedy.

Let us instance again in the restraining statute (Dilapidations, 1571). By the common law, ecclesiastical corporations might let as long leases as they thought proper: the mischief was, that they let long and unreasonable leases, to the impoverishment of their successors: the remedy applied by the statute was by making void all leases by ecclesiastical bodies for longer terms than three lives or twenty-one years.

In the construction of this statute it is held, that leases, though for a longer term, if made by a bishop, are not void during the bishop's continuance in his see, or if made by a dean and chapter, they are not void during the continuance of the dean: for the act was made for the benefit and protection of the successor. The mischief is therefore sufficiently suppressed by vacating them after the determination of the interest of the grantors; but the leases, during their continuance, being not within the mischief, are not within the remedy.

⚖ CONSTRUCTION OF PENAL STATUTES — Penal statutes must be construed strictly. Thus the statute (Criminal Law, 1547), having enacted that those who are convicted of stealing horses should not have the benefit of clergy, the judges conceived that this did not extend to him that should steal but one horse, and therefore procured a new act for that purpose in the following year. To come nearer our own times, by statute (cattle-stealing, 1740), stealing sheep or other cattle, was made felony without benefit of clergy. But these general words "or other cattle," being looked upon as much too loose to create a capital offense, the act was held to extend to nothing but mere sheep. Therefore, in the next sessions, it was found necessary to make another statute (cattle-stealing, 1741); extending the former to bulls, cows, oxen, steers, bullocks, heifers, calves, and lambs by name.

CONSTRUCTION OF STATUTES AGAINST FRAUDS — Statutes against fraud are to be liberally and beneficially expounded. This may seem a contradiction to the last rule; most statutes against frauds being in their consequences penal. But this difference is here to be taken: where the statute acts upon the offender, and inflicts a penalty, as the pillory or a fine, it is then to be taken strictly: but when the statute acts upon the offense by setting aside the fraudulent transaction, here it is to be construed liberally. Upon this footing the statute (Fraudulent Conveyances, 1571), which avoids all gifts of goods, etc., made to defraud creditors and others, was held to extend by the general words to a gift made to defraud the queen of a forfeiture.

CONSTRUCTION BY CONTEXT — One part of a statute must be so construed by another that the whole may (if possible) stand: That the whole subject matter may rather operate than be annulled. As if land be vested in the king and his heirs by act of parliament, saving the right of A; and A has at that time a lease of it for three years; here A shall hold it for his term of three years, and afterwards it shall go to the king.

REPUGNANT CLAUSES — If, therefore, an act of parliament vests land in the king and his heirs, saving the right of all persons whatsoever: or vests the land of A in the king, saving the right of A: in either of these cases the saving is totally repugnant to the body of the statute, and (if good) would render the statute of no effect or operation; and therefore the saving is void, and the land vests absolutely in the king.

STATUTES SUPERSEDE THE COMMON LAW — Where the common law and a statute differ, the common law gives place to the statute; and an old statute gives place to a new one. This upon the general principle that, later laws repeal prior ones in conflict therewith. But this is to be understood only when the latter statute is couched in negative terms, or by its matter necessarily implies a negative. As if a former act says, that a juror upon such a trial shall have twenty pounds a year; and new statute afterwards enacts, that he shall have twenty marks; here the later statute, though it does not express, yet necessarily implies a negative, and virtually repeals the former. For if twenty marks be made qualification sufficient, the former statute which requires twenty pounds is at an end. But if both acts be merely affirmative, and the substance such that both may stand together, here the latter does not repeal the former, but they shall both have a concurrent efficacy.

⚖ EFFECT OF REPEAL OF A REPEALING ACT — If a statute, that repeals another, is itself repealed afterwards, the first statute is revived, without any formal words for that purpose. So when the statutes (1534 and 1543), declaring the king to be the supreme head of the church, were repealed by a statute (1554), and this latter statute was afterwards repealed (1558), there needed not any express words of revival in the latter statute, but these acts of King Henry VIII were impliedly and virtually revived.

⚖ IRREPEALABLE LEGISLATION — Acts of parliament derogatory from the power of subsequent parliaments bind not. So the statute (Treason, 1495), which directs, that no person for assisting a king de facto (in fact) shall be attainted of treason by act of parliament or otherwise, is held to be good only as to common persecutions for high treason; but will not restrain or clog any parliamentary attainder. Because the legislature, being in truth the sovereign power, is always of equal, always of absolute authority: it acknowledges no superior upon earth, which the prior legislature must have been, if its ordinances could bind a subsequent parliament.

⚖ IMPOSSIBLE AND UNREASONABLE ACTS — Lastly, acts of parliament that are impossible to be performed are of no validity: and if there arise out of them collaterally any absurd consequences, manifestly contradictory to common reason, they are, with regard to those collateral consequences, void.

I lay down the rule with these restrictions; though I know it is generally laid down more largely, that acts of parliament contrary to reason are void. But if the parliament will positively enact a thing to be done which is unreasonable, I know of no power that can control it: and the examples usually alleged in support of this sense of the rule do none of them prove, that, where the main object of a statute is unreasonable, the judges are at liberty to reject it; for that were to set the judicial power above that of the legislature, which would be subversive of all government.

But where some collateral matter arises out of the general words, and happens to be unreasonable, there the judges are in decency to conclude that this consequence was not foreseen by the parliament, and therefore they are at liberty to expound the statute by equity, and only as to this disregard it.

⚖️ COURTS OF EQUITY — What equity is, and how impossible in its very essence to be reduced to stated rules, hath been shown in the preceding section. I shall therefore only add, that there are also peculiar courts of equity established for the benefit of the subject, to detect latent frauds and concealments, which the process of the courts of law is not adapted to reach, to enforce the execution of such matters of trust and confidence, as are binding in conscience, though not cognizable in a court of law; to deliver from such dangers as are owing to misfortune or oversight; and to give a more specific relief, and more adapted to the circumstances of the case, than can always be obtained by the generality of the rules of the common law.

This is the business of our courts of equity, which, however, are only conversant in matters of property. For the freedom of our constitution will not permit, that in criminal cases a power should be lodged in any judge, to construe the law otherwise than according to the letter. This caution, while it admirably protects the public liberty, can never bear hard upon individuals. A man cannot suffer more punishment than the law assigns, but he may suffer less. The laws cannot be strained by partiality to inflict a penalty beyond what the letter will warrant; but, in cases where the letter induces any apparent hardship, the crown has the power to pardon.

THAT WHICH IS SUBJECT
TO THE LAWS OF ENGLAND

⚖️ ENGLISH COLONIES IN AMERICA — Our distant plantations in America, and elsewhere, are in some respect subject to the English laws. Plantations or colonies in distant countries are either such where the lands are claimed by right of occupancy only, by finding them desert and uncultivated, and peopling them from the mother country; or where, when already cultivated, they have been either gained by conquest or ceded to us by treaties. Both these rights are founded upon the law of nature, or at least upon that of nations.

But there is a difference between these two species of colonies, with respect to the laws by which they are bound. For it hath been held, that if an uninhabited country be discovered and planted by English subjects, all the English laws then in being, which are the birthright of every subject are immediately there in force. But this must be understood with very many and very great restrictions. Such colonists carry with them only so much of the English law as is applicable to their own situation and the condition of an infant colony; such, for instance, as the general rules of inheritance, and of protection from personal injuries.

The artificial refinements and distinctions incident to property of a great and commercial people, the laws of police and revenue (such especially as are enforced by penalties), the mode of maintenance for the established clergy, the jurisdiction of spiritual courts, and a multitude of other provisions, are neither necessary nor convenient for them and therefore are not in force. What shall be admitted and what rejected, at what times, and under what restrictions, must, in case of dispute, be decided in the first instance by their own provincial judicature, subject to the revision and control of the king in council: the whole of their constitution being also liable to be new-modeled, and reformed by the general superintending power of the legislature in the mother country.

But in conquered or ceded countries, that have already laws of their own, the king may indeed alter and change those laws; but, till he does actually change them, the ancient laws of the country remain, unless such as are against the law of God, as in the case of an infidel country. Our American plantations are principally of this latter sort, being obtained in the last century either by right of conquest and driving out the natives (with what natural justice I shall not at present inquire) or by treaties. Therefore the common law of England as such has no allowance or authority there; they being no part of the mother country, but distinct (though dependent) dominions. They are subject, however, to the control of the parliament; though not bound by any acts of parliament, unless particularly named.

THE HIGH SEA — We come now to consider the Kingdom of England in particular, the direct and immediate subject of those laws concerning which we are to treat in the ensuing commentaries.

The main or high seas are part of the realm of England, for thereon our courts of admiralty have jurisdiction; but they are not subject to the common law.

The main sea begins at the low-water mark. But between the high-water mark and the low-water mark, where the sea ebbs and flows, the common law and the admiralty have a divided authority, an alternate jurisdiction; one upon the water, when it is full sea; and the other upon the land, when it is an ebb.

DIVISIONS OF ENGLAND — The territory of England is liable to two divisions; the one ecclesiastical, the other civil.

THE ECCLESIASTICAL DIVISION: The ecclesiastical division is primarily, into two provinces, those of Canterbury and York. A province is the circuit of an archbishop's jurisdiction. Each province contains divers dioceses, or sees; whereof Canterbury includes twenty-one, and York three. Every diocese is divided into arch-deaconries, whereof there are sixty in all; each arch-deaconry into rural deaneries, which are the circuit of the archdeacon's and rural Dean's jurisdiction, of whom hereafter; and every deanery is divided into parishes.

PARISHES: A parish is that circuit of ground which is committed to the charge of one parson, or vicar, or other minister, having cure of souls therein. These districts are computed to be near ten thousand in number. How ancient the division of parishes is, may at present be difficult to ascertain; for it seems to be agreed on all hands that in the early ages of Christianity in this island, parishes were unknown, or at least signified the same that a diocese does now. There was then no appropriation of ecclesiastical dues to any particular church: But every man was at liberty to contribute his tithes to whatever priest or church he pleased, provided only that he did it to some: or, if he made no special appointment or appropriation thereof, they were paid into the hands of the bishop, whose duty it was to distribute them among the clergy, and for other pious purposes, according to his own discretion.

The kingdom was then universally divided into parishes; which division happened probably not all at once, but by degrees. For it seems pretty clear and certain, that the boundaries of parishes were originally ascertained by those of a manor or manors: since it very seldom happens that a manor extends itself over more parishes than one, though there are often many manors in one parish.

The lords, as Christianity spread itself, began to build churches upon their own demesnes or wastes, to accommodate their tenants in one or two adjoining lordships; and in order to have divine service regularly performed therein, obliged all their tenents to appropriate their tithes to the maintenance of the one officiating minister, instead of leaving them at liberty to distribute them among the clergy of the diocese in general: and this tract of land, the tithes whereof were so appropriated, formed a distinct parish.

Thus parishes were gradually formed, and parish churches endowed with the tithes that arose within the circuit assigned. But some lands, either because they were in the hands of irreligious and careless owners, or were situated in forests and desert places, or for other now unsearchable reasons, were never united to any parish, and therefore continue to this day extraparochial; and there tithes are now by immemorial custom payable to the king instead of the bishop, in trust and confidence that he will distribute them for the general good of the church.

⚖ THE CIVIL DIVISION: The civil division of the territory of England is into counties, of those counties into hundreds, of those hundreds into tithings or towns, which division, as it now stands, seems to owe its original to King Alfred: who to prevent the rapines and disorders which formerly prevailed in the realm, instituted tithings; so called, from the Saxon, because ten freeholders with their families composed one. These all dwelt together, and were sureties or free pledges to the king for the good behavior of each other; and, if any offense was committed in their district, they were bound to have the offender forthcoming. Therefore anciently no

man was suffered to abide in England above forty days, unless he were enrolled in some tithing or decennary. One of the principal inhabitants of
the tithing is annually appointed to preside over the rest, being called the
tithing man.

The Rights of
Persons

THE ABSOLUTE RIGHT
OF INDIVIDUALS

⚖ OBJECTS OF THE LAW: RIGHTS AND WRONGS — As municipal law is
a rule of civil conduct, commanding what is right, and prohibiting
what is wrong; it follows, that the primary and principal objects of the
law are rights and wrongs. I shall in the first place consider the rights that
are commanded, and secondly, the wrongs that are forbidden by the laws
of England.

Rights are, however, liable to another subdivision: being either,
first, those which concern and are annexed to the persons of men; and are
then called the rights of persons; or they are secondly, such as a man
may acquire over external objects, or things unconnected with his person,
which are styled the rights of things. Wrongs also are divisible into, first,
private wrongs, which, being in infringement merely of particular rights,
concern individuals only, and are called civil injuries; and secondly, public wrongs, which, being a breach of general and public rights, affect the
whole community, and are called crimes and misdemeanors.

⚖ DIVISION OF THESE COMMENTARIES — The objects of the laws of England falling into this fourfold division, the present commentaries will
therefore consist of the four following parts:

1. The rights of persons; with the means whereby such rights may
be either acquired or lost.

2. The rights of things; with the means also of acquiring and losing
them.

3. Private wrongs, or civil injuries; with the means of redressing
them by law.

4. Public wrongs; or crimes and misdemeanors; with the means of
prevention and punishment.

⚖ RIGHTS OF PERSONS — Now the rights of persons that are commanded
to be observed by the municipal law are of two sorts: First, such as
are due from every citizen, which are usually called civil duties; and

secondly, such as belong to him, which is the more popular acceptation of rights. Both may, indeed, be comprised in this latter division; for, as all social duties are of a relative nature, at the same time that they are due from one man, or set of men, they must also be due to another.

But I apprehend it will be more clear and easy to consider many of them as duties required from, rather than as rights belonging to particular persons. Thus, for instance, allegiance is usually, and therefore most easily, considered as the duty of the people, and protection as the duty of the magistrate; and yet they are reciprocally, the rights as well as duties of each other. Allegiance is the right of the magistrate, and protection the right of the people.

⚖ DIVISION OF PERSONS — Persons also are divided by the law into either natural persons, or artificial. Natural persons are such as the God of nature formed us; artificial are such as are created and devised by human laws for the purpose of society and government, which are called corporations or bodies politic.

⚖ DIVISION OF RIGHTS OF PERSONS — The rights of persons considered in their natural capacities are also of two sorts, absolute and relative. Absolute, which are such as appertain and belong to particular men, merely as individuals or single persons: relative, which are incident to them as members of society, and standing in various relations to each other. The first, that is, absolute rights, will be the subject of the present chapter.

⚖ ABSOLUTE RIGHTS — By the absolute rights of individuals we mean those which are so in their primary and strictest sense; such as would belong to their persons merely in a state of nature, and which every man is entitled to enjoy, whether out of society or in it. But with regard to the absolute duties, which man is bound to perform considered as a mere individual, it is not to be expected that any human municipal law should at all explain or enforce them. For the end and intent of such laws being only to regulate the behaviour of mankind, as they are members of society and stand in various relations to each other, they have consequently no business or concern with any but social or relative duties.

Let a man therefore be ever so abandoned in his principles, or vicious in his practice, provided he keeps his wickedness to himself, and does not offend against the rules of public decency, he is out of the reach of human laws. But if he makes his vices public, though they be such as seem principally to affect himself (as drunkness, or the like), they then become, by the bad example they set, of pernicious effects to society; and therefore it is then the business of human laws to correct them. Here the circumstance of publication is what alters the nature of the case. Public sobriety is a relative duty, and therefore enjoined by our laws; private sobriety is an absolute duty, which, whether it can be performed or not, human tribunals can never know; and therefore they can never enforce it by any civil sanction.

But with respect to rights, the case is different. Human laws define and enforce as well those rights which belong to a man considered as an individual, as those which belong to him considered as related to others.

PROTECTION OF ABSOLUTE RIGHTS — For the principal aim of society is to protect individuals in the enjoyment of those absolute rights, which were vested in them by the immutable laws of nature; but which could not be preserved in peace without that mutual assistance and intercourse, which is gained by the institution of friendly and social communities. Hence it follows, that the first and primary ends of human laws is to maintain and regulate these absolute rights of individuals.

Such rights as are social and relative result from, and are posterior to, the formation of states and societies; so that to maintain and regulate there is clearly a subsequent consideration. Therefore the principal view of human laws is, or ought always to be, to explain, protect, and enforce such rights as are absolute, which in themselves are few and simple; and, then, such rights as are relative, which arising from a variety of connections, will be far more numerous and more complicated. These will take up a greater space in any code of laws, and hence may appear to be more attended to, though in reality they are not, than the rights of the former kind. Let us therefore proceed to examine how far all laws ought, and how far the laws of England actually do, take notice of these absolute rights, and provide for their lasting security.

NATURAL LIBERTY — The absolute rights of man considered as a free agent, endowed with discernment to know good from evil, and with power of choosing those measures which appear to him to be most desirable, are usually summed up in one general appellation, and denominated the natural liberty of mankind. This natural liberty consists properly in a power of acting as one thinks fit, without any restraint or control, unless by the law of nature; being a right inherent in us by birth, and one of the gifts of God to man at his creation, when he endued him with the faculty of free will.

But every man, when he enters into society, gives up a part of his natural liberty, as the price of so valuable a purchase; and, in consideration of receiving the advantages of mutual commerce, obliges himself to conform to those laws, which the community has thought proper to establish. This species of legal obedience and conformity is infinitely more desirable than that wild and savage liberty which is sacrificed to obtain it.

⚖ CIVIL LIBERTY — For no man, that considers a moment, would wish to retain the absolute and uncontrolled power of doing whatever he pleases: the consequence of which is, that every other man would also have the same power; and then there would be no security to individuals in any of the enjoyments of life. Political, therefore, or civil, liberty, which is that of a member of society, is no other than natural liberty so far restrained by human laws as is necessary and expedient for the general advantage of the public.

Hence we may collect that the law, which restrains a man from doing mischief to his fellow citizens, though it diminishes the natural, increases the civil liberty of mankind; but that every wanton and causeless restraint of the will of the subject, whether practiced by a monarch, a nobility, or a popular assembly, is a degree of tyranny: nay, that even laws themselves, whether made with or without our consent, if they regulate and constrain our conduct in matters of mere indifference, without any good end in view, are regulations destructive of liberty; whereas if any public advantage can arise from observing such precepts, the control of our private inclinations, in one or two particular points, will conduce to preserve our general freedom in others of more importance; by supporting that state of society which alone can secure our independence; so that laws, when prudently framed, are by no means subversive but rather introductive of liberty; for where there is no law there is no freedom.

But then, that constitution or frame of government, that system of laws, is alone calculated to maintain civil liberty, which leaves the subject entire master of his own conduct, except in those points wherein the public good requires some direction or restraint.

⚖ CIVIL LIBERTY IN ENGLAND — The idea and practice of this political or civil liberty flourish in their highest vigor in these kingdoms, where it falls little short of perfection, and can only be lost or destroyed by the folly or demerits of its owner; the legislature, and the course the laws of England, being peculiarly adapted to the preservation of this inestimable blessing even in the meanest subject.

This spirit of liberty is so deeply implanted in our constitution, and rooted even in our very soil, that a slave or a negro, the moment he lands in

England, falls under the protection of the laws, and so far becomes a freeman; though the master's right to his service may possibly still continue.

⚖ VICISSITUDES OF ENGLISH LIBERTIES — The absolute rights of every Englishman as they are founded on nature and reason, so they are coeval with our form of government; though subject at times to fluctuate and change: their establishment being still human. At some times we have seen them depressed by overbearing and tyrannical princes; at others so luxuriant as ever to tend to anarchy, a worse state than tyranny itself, as any government is better than none at all.

But the vigor of our free constitution has always delivered the nation from these embarrassments: and, as soon as the convulsions consequent on the struggle have been over, the balance of our rights and liberties has settled to its proper level; and their fundamental articles have been from time to time asserted in parliament, as often as they were thought to be in danger.

⚖ CHARTERS OF LIBERTY — First, by the great charter of liberties, which was obtained, sword in hand, from King John, and afterwards, with some alterations confirmed in parliament by King Henry III, his son. Which charter contained very few new grants; but was for the most part declaratory of the principal grounds of the fundamental laws of England. Then, after a long interval, by the petition of right; which was a parliamentary declaration of the liberties of the people, assented to by King Charles I in the beginning of his reign. Which was closely followed by the still more ample concessions made by that unhappy prince to his parliament before the fatal rupture between them; and by the many salutary laws, particularly the habeas corpus act, passed under Charles II.

To these succeeded the Bill of Rights, or declaration delivered by the lords and commons to the Prince and Princess of Orange, 13 February, 1688; and afterwards enacted in parliament, when they became king and queen: which declaration concludes in these remarkable words: "and they do claim, demand, and insist upon all and singular the premises, as their undoubted rights and liberties. And the act of parliament itself recognizes all and singular the rights and liberties asserted and claimed in the said declaration to be the true, ancient, and indubitable rights of the people of this kingdom."

⚖ CLASSIFICATION OF PERSONAL RIGHTS — The rights thus defined by these several statutes, consist in a number of private immunities; which will appear, from what has been premised, to be indeed no other than either that remainder of natural liberty, which is not required by the laws of society to be sacrificed to public convenience; or else those civil privileges, which society hath engaged to provide, in lieu of the natural liberties so given up by individuals.

These may be reduced to three principal or primary articles; the right of personal security, the right of personal liberty, and the right of private property; because as there is no other known method of compulsion, or of abridging man's natural free will, but an infringement or diminution of one or other of these important rights, the preservation of these, inviolate, may justly be said to include the preservation of our civil immunities in their largest and most extensive sense.

PERSONAL SECURITY — The right of personal security consists of a person's legal and uninterrupted enjoyment of his life, his limbs, his body, his health, and his reputation.

LIFE — Life is the immediate gift of God, a right inherent by nature in every individual; and it begins in contemplation of law as soon as an infant is able to stir in the mother's womb. For if a woman is quick with child, and by a potion or otherwise killeth it in her womb; or if anyone beat her, whereby the child dieth in her body, and she is delivered of a dead child; this, though not murder, was by the ancient law homicide or manslaughter.

An infant in the mother's womb, is supposed in law to be born for many purposes. It is capable of having a legacy, or a surrender of a copyhold estate made to it. It may have a guardian assigned to it, and it is enabled to have an estate limited to its use, and to take afterwards by such limitation, as if it were then actually born.

LIMBS — A man's limbs (by which for the present we only understand those members which may be useful to him in fight and the loss of which alone amounts to mayhem by the common law) are also the gift of the wise Creator; to enable man to protect himself from external injuries in a state of nature. To these, therefore, he has a natural inherent right; and they cannot be wantonly destroyed or disabled without a manifest breach of civil liberty.

SELF-DEFENSE — Both the life and limbs of a man are of such high value, in the estimation of the law of England, that it pardons even homicide if committed in self-defense, or in order to preserve them. For whatever is done by a man, to save either life or member, is looked upon as done upon the highest necessity and compulsion. Therefore, if a man through fear of death or mayhem is prevailed upon to execute a deed, or do any other legal act; these, though accompanied with all other the requisite solemnities, may be afterwards avoided, if forced upon him by a well-grounded apprehension of losing his life, or even his limbs in case of his noncompliance. The same is also a sufficient excuse for the commission of many misdemeanors, as will appear in the fourth book.

⚖ DURESS — The constraint a man is under in these circumstances is called in law duress; there are two sorts; duress of imprisonment, where a man actually loses his liberty, of which we shall presently speak; and the duress by threats, where the hardship is only threatened and impending, which is that we are now discoursing of. Duress is either for fear of loss of life, or else for fear of mayhem, or loss of limb. This fear must be upon sufficient reason; it must not be the apprehension of a foolish and fearful man, but such as a courageous man may be susceptible of; it should be, for instance, such a fear as consists in an apprehension of bodily pain, or danger to life.

A fear of battery, or being beaten, though never so well grounded, is no duress; neither is the fear of having one's house burned, or one's goods taken away and destroyed; because in these cases, should the threat be performed, a man may have satisfaction by recovering equivalent damages; but no suitable atonement can be made for the loss of life or limb. He is justified who has acted in pure defense of his own life or limb.

The law not only regards life and member, and protects every man in the enjoyment of them, but also furnishes him with everything necessary for their support. For there is no man so indigent or wretched, but he may demand a supply sufficient for all the necessities of life from the more opulent part of the community, by means of the several statutes enacted for the relief of the poor.

⚖ CIVIL DEATH — These rights, of life and member, can only be determined by the death of the person; which is either a civil or natural death. The civil death commences, if any man be banished the realm by the process of the common law, or enters into religion; that is, goes into a monastery, and becomes there a monk professed; in which case he is absolutely dead in law, and his next heir shall have his estate. For, such banished man is entirely cut off from society; and such a monk, upon his profession, renounces solemnly all secular concerns; and besides, as the clergy claimed an exemption from the duties of civil life and the commands of the temporal magistrate, the genius of the English laws would not suffer those persons to enjoy the benefits of society, who secluded themselves from it, and refused to submit to its regulations.

A monk was therefore accounted dead in law, and when he entered into religion might, like other dying men, make his testament and executors; or, if he made none, the ordinary might grant administration to his next of kin, as if he were actually dead intestate. Such executors and administrators had the same power, and might bring the same actions for debts due to the religious, and were liable to the same actions for those due from him, as if he were naturally deceased.

⚖ FORFEITURE OF LIFE — This natural life being, as was before observed, the immediate donation of the great Creator, cannot legally be disposed of or destroyed by any individual, neither by the person himself nor by any other of his fellow-creatures, merely upon their own authority. Yet, it may be frequently forfeited for the breach of those laws of society, which are enforced by the sanction of capital punishments; of the nature, restrictions, expedience, and legality of which we may hereafter more conveniently inquire in the concluding book of these commentaries.

⚖ DUE PROCESS OF LAW — The statute law of England does, therefore, very seldom, and the common law does never inflict any punishment extending to life or limb, unless upon the highest necessity: and the constitution is an utter stranger to any arbitrary power of killing or maiming the subject without the express warrant of law.

No freeman shall be deprived of life but by the lawful judgment of his peers, or by the law of the land. No man shall be forejudged of life and limb, contrary to the great charter and the law of the land: and again, that no man shall be put to death without being brought to answer by due process of law.

⚖ BODILY IMMUNITY — Besides those limbs and members that may be necessary to a man, in order to defend himself or annoy his enemy, the rest of his person or body is also entitled by the same natural right, to security from the corporal insults of menaces, assaults, beating, and wounding; though such insults amount not to destruction of life or member.

⚖ PRESERVATION OF HEALTH — The preservation of a man's health from such practices as may prejudice or annoy, and

⚖ SECURITY OF REPUTATION — The security of his reputation or good name from the arts of detraction and slander, are rights to which every man is entitled, by reason and natural justice; since without these it is impossible to have the perfect enjoyment of any other advantage or right.

⚖ PERSONAL LIBERTY — Next to personal security the law of England regards, asserts, and preserves the personal liberty of individuals.

This personal liberty consists in the power of locomotion, of changing situation, or removing one's person to whatsoever place one's own inclination may direct; without imprisonment or restraint, unless by due course of law.

⚖ LAW OF THE LAND — Here again the language of the great charter is, that no freeman shall be taken or imprisoned, but by the lawful judgment of his equals, or by the law of the land. Many subsequent old statutes expressly direct, that no man shall be taken or imprisoned by suggestion or petition to the king or his council, unless it be by legal indictment, or the process of the common law. By the petition of right, it is enacted, that no freeman shall be imprisoned or detained without cause shown, to which he may make answer according to law.

⚖ HABEAS CORPUS — If any person be restrained of his liberty by order or decree of any illegal court, or by command of the king's majesty in person, or by warrant of the council board, or of any of the privy council; he shall upon demand of his consel, have a writ of habeas corpus, to bring his body before the court of king's bench or common pleas; who shall determine whether the cause of his commitment be just and thereupon do as to justice shall appertain.

By the commonly called habeas corpus act, the methods of obtaining this writ are so plainly pointed out and enforced, that so long as this statute remains unimpeached no subject of England can be long detained in prison, except in those cases in which the law requires and justifies such detainer. Lest this act should be evaded by demanding unreasonable bail, or sureties for the prisoner's appearance, it is declared by the Bill of Rights (1689), that excessive bail ought not to be required.

⚖ SUSPENSION OF WRIT OF HABEAS CORPUS — Of great importance to the public is the preservation of this personal liberty: for it once it were left in the power of any magistrate to imprison arbitrarily whomever he or his officers thought proper, there would soon be an end of all other rights and immunities. Some have thought that unjust attacks, even upon life, or property, at the arbitrary will of the magistrate, are less dangerous to the commonwealth, than such as are made upon the personal liberty of the subject.

To bereave a man of life, or by violence to confiscate his estate, without accusation or trial, would be so gross and notorious an act of despotism, as must at once convey the alarm of tyranny throughout the whole kingdom. But confinement of the person, by secretly hurrying him to jail, where his sufferings are unknown or forgotten, is a less public, a less striking, and therefore, a more dangerous engine of arbitrary government.

Yet, sometimes, when the state is in real danger, even this may be a necessary measure. But the happiness of our constitution is, that it is not left to the executive power to determine when the danger of the state is so great, as to render this measure expedient. For the parliament only, or legislative power, whenever it sees proper, can authorize the crown, by suspending the habeas corpus act for a short and limited time, to imprison suspected persons without giving any reason for so doing. This experiment ought only to be tried in cases of extreme emergency; and in these the nation parts with its liberty for a while, in order to preserve it forever.

FALSE IMPRISONMENT — The confinement of the person, in any wise, is an imprisonment. So that the keeping of a man against his will in a private house, putting him in the stocks, arresting or forcibly detaining him in the street, is an imprisonment. The law so much discourages unlawful confinement, that if a man is under duress of imprisonment, which we before explained to mean a compulsion by an illegal restraint of liberty, until he seals a bond or a like; he may allege this duress, and avoid the extorted bond.

But if a man be lawfully imprisoned, and either to procure his discharge, or on any other fair account, seals a bond or a deed, this is not by duress of imprisonment, and he is not at liberty to avoid it. To make imprisonment lawful, it must either be by process from the courts of judicature, or by warrant from some legal officer having authority to commit to prison; which warrant must be in writing, under the hand and seal of the magistrate, and express the causes of the commitment, in order to be examined into (if necessary) upon a habeas corpus. If there be no cause expressed, the jailer is not bound to detain the prisoner.

BANISHMENT — A natural and regular consequence of this personal liberty is, that every Englishman may claim a right to abide in his own country so long as he pleases; and not to be driven from it unless by the sentence of the law. The king indeed, by his royal prerogative, may issue out his writ ne exeat regnum (let him not leave the kingdom), and prohibit any of his subjects from going into foreign parts without license. This may be necessary for the public service and safeguard of the commonwealth.

But no power on earth, except the authority of parliament, can send any subject of England out of the land against his will; no, not even a criminal. For exile, or transportation is a punishment unknown to the common law; and, whenever it is now inflicted, it is either by the choice of the criminal himself to escape a capital punishment, or else by the express direction of some modern act of parliament.

To this purpose, the great charter declares, that no freeman shall be banished, unless by the judgment of his peers, or by the law of the land; and that the person, who shall dare to commit another contrary to this law, shall be disabled from bearing any office, and be incapable of receiving the king's pardon: and the party suffering shall also have his private action against the person committing, and all his aiders, advisers and abettors, and shall recover treble costs; besides his damages, which no jury shall assess at less than five hundred pounds.

The law is in this respect so benignly and liberally construed for the benefit of the subject, that, though within the realm the king may command the attendance and service of all his liegemen, yet he cannot send any man out of the realm, even upon the public service; excepting sailors and soldiers, the nature of whose employment necessarily implies an exception: for this might in reality be no more than an honorable exile.

RIGHT OF PRIVATE PROPERTY — The third absolute right, inherent in every Englishman, is that of property: which consists in the free use, enjoyment, and disposal of all his acquisitions, without any control or diminution, save only by the laws of the land.

The original of private property is probably founded in nature, as will be more fully explained in the second book of the ensuing commentaries; but certainly the modifications under which we at present find it, the method of conserving it in the present owner, and of translating it from man to man, are entirely derived from society; and are some of those civil advantages, in exchange for which every individual has resigned a part of his natural liberty. The laws of England are therefore, in point of honor and justice, extremely watchful in ascertaining and protecting this right.

Upon this principle the great charter has declared that no freeman shall be disseized or divested of his freehold, or of his liberties, or free customs, but by the judgment of his peers, or by the law of the land. By a variety of ancient statutes it is enacted, that no man's lands or goods shall be seized into the king's hands, against the great charter, and the law of the land; and that no man shall be disinherited, nor put out of his franchises or freehold, unless he be duly brought to answer, and be forejudged by course of law; and if anything be done to the contrary, it shall be redressed, and holden for none.

⚖ RIGHT OF EMINENT DOMAIN — So great, moreover, is the regard of the law for private property, that it will not authorize the least violation of it; no, not even for the general good of the whole community. If a new road, for instance, were to be made through the grounds of a private person, it might perhaps be extensively beneficial to the public; but the law permits no man, or set of men, to do this without consent of the owner of the land.

In vain may it be urged, that the good of the individual ought to yield to that of the community; for it would be dangerous to allow any private man, or even any public tribunal, to be the judge of this common good, and to decide whether it be expedient or not. Besides, the public good is in nothing more essentially interested than in the protection of every individual's private rights, as modeled by the municipal law. In this and similar cases the legislature alone can, and indeed frequently does, interpose, and compel the individual to acquiesce. But how does it interpose and compel? Not by absolutely stripping subject of his property in an arbitrary manner; but by giving him a full indemnification and equivalent for the injury thereby sustained. The public is now considered as an individual, threating with an individual for an exchange. All that the legislature does is to oblige the owner to alienate his possessions, for a reasonable price; and even this is an exertion of power, which the legislature indulges with caution, and which nothing but the legislature can perform.

⚖ TAXATION AND REPRESENTATION — Nor is this the only instance in which the law of the land has postponed even public necessity to the sacred and inviolable rights or private property. For no subject of England can be constrained to pay any aids or taxes, even for the defense of the realm or the support of government, but such as are imposed by his own consent, or that of his representatives in parliament.

⚖ BULWARKS OF PERSONAL RIGHTS — In the three preceding articles we have taken a short view of the principal absolute rights which appertain to every Englishman. But in vain would these rights be declared, ascertained, and protected by the dead letter of the laws, if the constitution had provided no other method to secure their actual enjoyment. It has therefore established certain other auxiliary subordinate rights of the subject, which serve principally as barriers to protect and maintain inviolate the three great and primary rights of personal security, personal liberty, and private property. These are,

⚖ PARLIAMENT — The constitution, powers, and privileges of parliament, of which I shall treat at large in the ensuing chapter.

⚖️ LIMITATION OF KING'S PREROGATIVE — The limitation of the king's prerogative, by bounds so certain and notorious, that it is impossible he should exceed them without the consent of the people. Of this also I shall treat in its proper place, the former of these keeps the legislative power in due health and vigor, so as to make it improbable that laws should be enacted destructive of general liberty: the latter is a guard upon the executive power by restraining it from acting either because or in contradiction to the laws that are framed and established by the other.

⚖️ DUE PROCESS OF LAW — A third subordinate right of every Englishman is that of applying to the courts of justice for redress or injuries. Since the law is in England the supreme arbiter of every man's life, liberty, and property, courts of justice must at all times be open to the subject, and the law be duly administered therein. The emphatical words of Magna Carta: "to none will we sell, to none deny, to none delay either right or justice."

⚖️ RIGHT OF PETITION — If there should happen any uncommon injury, or infringement of the rights before mentioned, which the ordinary course of law is too defective to reach, there still remains a fourth subordinate right, appertaining to every individual, namely, the right of petitioning the king, or either house of parliament, for the redress of grievances.

⚖️ RIGHT TO BEAR ARMS — The fifth and last auxiliary right of the subject is that of having arms for their defense, suitable to their condition and degree, and such as are allowed by law.

THE PARLIAMENT

⚖️ RELATIONS OF PERSONS — We are next to treat of the right and duties of persons, as they are members of society, and stand in various relations to each other. These relations are either public or private: and we will first consider those that are public.

⚖️ GOVERNMENT — The most universal public relation, by which men are connected together, is that of government; namely, as governors and governed, or, in other words, as magistrates and people. Of magistrates some also are supreme, in whom the sovereign power of the state resides; others are subordinate, deriving all their authority from the supreme magistrate, accountable to him for their conduct, and acting in an inferior secondary sphere.

⚖️ DEPARTMENTS OF GOVERNMENT — In all tyrannical governments the supreme magistracy, or the right both of making and of enforcing the laws, is vested in one and the same man, or one and the same body of men; and wherever these two powers are united together, there can be no public liberty.

The magistrate may enact tyrannical laws, and execute them in a tyrannical manner, since he is possessed in quality of dispenser of justice, with all the power which he as legislative and executive authority are in distinct hands, the former will take care not to entrust the latter with so large a power, as may tend to the subversion of its own independence, and therewith of the liberty of the subject. With us, therefore, in England this supreme power is divided into two branches; the one legislative, to wit: the parliament, consisting of king, lords, and commons; the other, executive, consisting of the king alone.

⚖️ THE MODERN PARLIAMENT: MAGNA CARTA — It is generally agreed that in the main the constitution of parliament, as it now stands, was marked out so long ago as the seventeenth year of King John (1215), in the great charter granted by that prince.

⚖ THE HOUSE OF COMMONS — The commons consist of all such men of any property in the kingdom as have not seats in the house of lords; every one of which has a voice in parliament, either personally or by his representatives.

⚖ PRINCIPLE OF REPRESENTATION — In a free state, every man, who is supposed a free agent, ought to be, in some measure his own governor; and therefore a branch at least of the legislative power should reside in the whole body of the people. This power, when the territories of the state are small and its citizens easily known, should be exercised by the people in their aggregate or collective capacity, as was wisely ordained in the petty republics of Greece, and the first rudiments of the Roman state.

⚖ SUPREME POWER OF PARLIAMENT — The power and jurisdiction of Parliament so transcendent and absolute, that it cannot be confined, either for causes or persons, within any bounds. It hath sovereign and uncontrollable authority in making, confirming, enlarging, restraining, abrogating, repealing, reviving, and expounding of laws, concerning matters of all possible denominations, ecclesiastical, or temporal, civil, military maritime, or criminal: this being the place where that absolute despotic power, which must in all governments reside somewhere, is entrusted by the constitution of these kingdoms.

All mischiefs and grievances, operations and remedies, that transcend the ordinary course of laws, are within the reach of this extraordinary tribunal. It can regulate or new-model the succession to the crown; as was done in the reign of Henry VIII and William III. It can alter the established religion of the land; as was done in a variety of instances, in the reigns of King Henry VIII and his three children. It can change and create afresh even the constitution of the kingdom and of parliaments themselves; as was done by the act of union, and the several statutes for triennial and septennial elections. It can, in short, do everything that is not naturally impossible; and therefore some have not scrupled to call its power the omnipotence of parliament. True it is, that what the parliament doth, no authority upon earth can undo. So that it is a matter most essential to the liberties of this kingdom, that such members be delegated to this important trust, as are most eminent for their probity, their fortitude, and their knowledge.

THE KING AND HIS TITLE

THE KING: THE SUPREME EXECUTIVE — The supreme executive power of these kingdoms is vested by our laws in a single person, the king or queen: for it matters not to which sex the crown descends; but the person entitled to it, whether male or female, is immediately invested with all the ensigns, rights, and prerogatives of sovereign power.

SUCCESSION TO THE THRONE — The grand fundamental maxim upon which right of succession to the throne of these kingdoms, depends, I take to be this: "that the crown is, by common law and constitutional custom, hereditary; and this is a manner peculiar to itself: but that the right of inheritance may from time to time be changed or limited by act of parliament; under which limitations the crown still continues hereditary."

THE ROYAL SUCCESSION IS HEREDITARY — First, it is in general hereditary, or descendible to the next heir, on the death or demise of the last proprietor. All regal governments must be either hereditary or elective: and, as I believe there is no instance wherein the crown of England has ever been asserted to be elective, except by the regicides at the infamous and unparalleled trial of King Charles I, it must of consequence be hereditary.

Yet while I assert an hereditary, I by no means intend a "divine right" title to the throne. Such a title may be allowed to have subsisted under the theocratic establishments of the children of Israel in Palestine; but it never yet subsisted in any other country; save only so far kingdoms like other human fabrics, are subject to the general and ordinary dispensations of providence.

THE ROYAL SUCCESSION IS FEUDAL IN CHARACTER — But, secondly, as to the particular mode of inheritance, it in general corresponds with the feudal path of descents, chalked out by the common law in the succession to landed estates; yet with one or two material exceptions. Like estates, the crown will descend lineally to the issue of the reigning monarch; as it did from King John to Richard II, through a regular pedigree of six lineal generations. As in common descents, the preference of males to females, and the right of primogeniture among the males, are strictly adhered to. Thus Edward V succeeded to the crown, in preference to Richard, his younger brother, and Elizabeth, his elder sister. Like lands or tenements, the crown, on failure of the male line, descends to the issue female.

⚖ THE ROYAL SUCCESSION IS NOT INDEFEASIBLE — The doctrine of hereditary right does by no means imply an indefeasible right to the throne. No man will, I think, assert this, that has considered our law, constitution, and history, without prejudice, and with any degree of attention. It is unquestionably in the breast of the supreme legislative authority of this kingdom, the king and both houses of parliament, to defeat this hereditary right; and, by particular entails, limitations, and provisions, to exclude the immediate heir, and vest the inheritance in anyone else. This is strictly consonant to our laws and constitution; as may be gathered from the expression so frequently used in our statute book, of "the king's majesty, his heirs, and successors." In which we may observe, that as the word, "heirs," necessarily implies and inheritance or hereditary right, generally subsisting in the royal person; so the word, "successors," distinctly taken, must imply that this inheritance may sometimes be broken through; or, that there may be a successor without being the heir, of the king.

This is so extremely reasonable, that without such a power, lodged somewhere, our polity would be very defective. For, let us barely suppose so melancholy a case, as that the heir apparent should be a lunatic, an idiot, or otherwise incapable of reigning: how miserable would be the condition of the nation, if he were also incapable of being set aside! It is therefore necessary that this power should be lodged somewhere: and yet the inheritance, and regal dignity, would be very precarious indeed, if this power were expressly and avowedly lodged in the hands of the subject only, to be exerted whenever prejudice, caprice, or discontent should happen to take the lead.

Consequently it can nowhere be so properly lodged as in the two houses of parliament, by and with the consent of the reigning king; who, it is not to be supposed, will agree to anything improperly prejudicial to the rights of his own descendants. Therefore in the king, lords, and commons, in parliament assembled, our laws have expressly lodged it.

⚖️ THE ROYAL SUCCESSION IS PERPETUAL — But, fourthly; however the crown may be limited or transferred, it still retains its descendible quality, and becomes hereditary in the wearer of it. Hence in our law the king is said never to die, in his political capacity; though, in common with other men, he is subject to mortality in his natural.

THE KING'S ROYAL FAMILY

☙ THE QUEEN — The first and most considerable branch of the king's royal family, regarded by the laws of England, is the Queen.

☙ QUEEN, REGENT, REGNANT, OR SOVEREIGN — The queen of England is either queen regent, queen consort, or queen dowager. The queen regent, regnant, or sovereign, is she who holds the crown in her own right; as the first (and perhaps the second) Queen Mary, Queen Elizabeth, and Queen Anne; and such a one has the same powers, prerogatives, rights, dignities, and duties, as if she had been a king.

☙ THE PRINCE CONSORT — The husband of a queen regnant, as Prince George of Denmark was to Queen Anne, is her subject; and may be guilty of high treason against her; but, in the instance of conjugal infidelity, he is not subjected to the same penal restrictions. For which the reason seems to be that, if a queen consort is unfaithful to the royal bed, this may debase or bastardize the heirs to the crown; but no such danger can be consequent on the infidelity of the husband to a queen regnant.

☙ THE HEIR APPARENT — The Prince of Wales, or heir apparent to the crown, and also his royal consort, and the princess royal, or eldest daughter of the king, are likewise peculiarly regarded by the laws. To compass or conspire the death of the former, or to violate the chastity of either of the latter, are as much high treason as to conspire the death of the king, or violate the chastity of the queen. This upon the same reason, as was before given: because the Prince of Wales is next in succession to the crown, and to violate his wife might taint the blood royal with bastardy; and the eldest daughter of the king is also alone inheritable to the crown, on failure of issue male, and therefore more respected by the laws than any of her younger sisters; insomuch that upon this, united with other (feudal) principles, while our military tenures were in force, the king might levy an aid for marrying his eldest daughter, and her only. The heir apparent to the crown is usually made Prince of Wales and Earl of Chester, by special creation, and investiture; but, being the king's eldest son, he is by inheritance Duke of Cornwall, without any new creation.

THE COUNCILS BELONGING
TO THE KING

🐝 VARIOUS COUNCILS OF THE KING — The third point of view, in which we are to consider the king, is with regard to his councils. For, in order to assist him in the discharge of his duties, the maintenance of his dignity, and the exertion of his prerogative, the law hath assigned him a diversity of councils to advise with. The first of these is the high court of parliament, whereof we have already treated.

🐝 PEERS OF THE REALM — Secondly, the peers of the realm are by their birth hereditary counselors of the crown, and may be called together by the king to impart their advice in all matters of importance to the realm, either in time of parliament, or, which hath been their principal use, when there is no parliament in being.

🐝 JUDGES OF THE COURTS OF JUSTICE — A third council belonging to the king, are his judges of the courts of law, for law matters. So that when the king's council is mentioned generally, it must be defined, particularized, and understood according to the subject matter; and, if the subject be of a legal nature, then by the king's council is understood his council for matters of law; namely, his judges.

🐝 PRIVY COUNCIL — But the principal council belonging to the king is his privy council, which is generally called, by way of eminence, the council. This is a noble, honorable, and revered assembly of the king and such as he wills to be of his privy council, in the king's court or palace. The king's will is the sole constituent of a privy counselor; and this also regulates their number, which of ancient times was twelve or thereabouts. King Charles II in 1679 limited it to thirty: whereof fifteen were to be the principal officers of state, and those to be counselors by virtue of their office; and the other fifteen were composed of ten lords and five commoners of the king's choosing. But since that time the number has been much augmented, and now continues indefinite.

🙦 DUTIES OF PRIVY COUNSELORS — The duty of a privy counselor appears from the oath of office, which consists of seven articles: 1. To advise the king according to the best of his cunning and discretion. 2. To advise for the king's honor and good of the public, without partiality through affection, love, need, doubt, or dread. 3. To keep the king's counsel secret. 4. To avoid corruption. 5. To help and strengthen the execution of what shall be there resolved. 6. To withstand all persons who would attempt the contrary. And, lastly, in general, 7. To observe, keep and do all that a good and true counselor ought to do to his sovereign lord.

🙦 JURISDICTION OF THE PRIVY COUNCIL — The power of the privy council is to inquire into all offenses against the government, and to commit the offenders to safe custody, in order to take their trial in some of the courts of law. But their jurisdiction herein is only to inquire, and not to punish: and the persons committed by them are entitled to their habeas corpus as much as if committed by an ordinary justice of the peace.

In plantation or admiralty causes, which arise out of the jurisdiction of this kingdom; and in matters of lunacy or idiocy, although they may eventually involve questions of extensive property, the privy council continues to have cognizance, being the court of appeal in such cases: or rather, the appeal lies to the king's majesty himself in council.

Whenever also a question arises between two provinces in America or elsewhere, as concerning the extent of their charters and the like, the king in his council exercises original jurisdiction therein, upon the principles of feudal sovereignty. Likewise, when any person claims an island or a province, in the nature of a feudal principality, by grant from the king or his ancestors, the determination of that right belongs to his majesty in council.

But from all the dominions of the crown, excepting Great Britain and Ireland, an appellate jurisdiction (in the last resort) is vested in the same tribunal; which usually exercises its judicial authority in a committee of the whole privy council, who hear the allegations and proofs, and make their report to his majesty in council, by whom the judgment is finally given.

🙦 DISSOLUTION OF THE PRIVY COUNCIL — The dissolution of the privy council depends upon the king's pleasure; and he may, whenever he thinks proper, discharge any particular member, or the whole of it, and appoint another. By the common law also it was dissolved ipso facto by the king's demise. But now, to prevent the inconveniences of having no council in being at the accession of a new prince, it is enacted by statute that the privy council shall continue for six months after the demise of the crown, unless sooner determined by the successor.

THE KING'S DUTIES

CONSTITUTIONAL DUTIES OF THE KING — I proceed next to the duties, incumbent on the king by our constitution; in consideration of which duties his dignity and prerogative are established by the laws of the land: it being a maxim in the law, that protection and subjection are reciprocal.

KING'S DUTY TO GOVERN ACCORDING TO THE LAW — The principal duty of the king is, to govern his people according to law. The king ought not to be subject to man, but to God, and to the law; for the law maketh the king. Let the king therefore render to the law, what the law has invested in him with regard to others; dominion, and power: for he is not truly king, where will and pleasure rules, and not the law. The king also hath a superior, namely God, and also the law, by which he was made a king.

The king of England must rule his people according to the decrees of the laws thereof: insomuch that he is bound by an oath at his coronation to the observance and keeping of his own laws. But, to obviate all doubts and difficulties concerning this matter, it is expressly declared by statute "That the laws of England are the birthright of the people thereof; and all the kings and queens who shall ascend the throne of this realm ought to administer the government of the same according to the said laws; and all their officers and ministers ought to serve them respectively according to the same: therefore all the laws and statutes of this realm, for securing the established religion, and the rights and liberties of the people thereof, and all other laws and statutes of the same now in force, are by his majesty, by and with the advice and consent of the lords spiritual and temporal and commons, and by authority of the same, ratified and confirmed accordingly."

THE KING'S PREROGATIVE

⚖️ CONSTITUTIONAL LIMITATIONS ON THE ROYAL PREROGATIVE — One of the principal bulwarks of civil liberty, or (in other words) of the British constitution, was the limitation of the king's prerogative by bounds so certain and notorious, that it is impossible he should ever exceed them, without the consent of the people, on the one hand; or without, on the other, a violation of that original contract, which in all states impliedly, and in ours most expressly, subsists between the prince and the subject.

⚖️ FORMER PRETENSIONS — There cannot be a stronger proof of that genuine freedom, which is the boast of this age and country, that the power of discussing and examining, with decency and respect, the limits of the king's prerogative. A topic, that in some former ages was thought too delicate and sacred to be profaned by the pen of a subject.

The glorious Queen Elizabeth herself made no scruple to direct her parliaments to abstain from discoursing of matters of state; and it was the constant language of this favorite princess and her ministers, that even that august assembly "ought not to deal, to judge, or to meddle, with her majesty's prerogative royal." Her successor, King James I, who had imbibed high notions of the divinity of regal sway, more than once laid it down in his speeches, that "as it is atheism and blasphemy in a creature to dispute what the Deity may do, so it is presumption and sedition in a subject to dispute what a king may do in the height of his power: Good Christians, he adds, will be content with God's will, revealed in his words; and good subjects will rest in the king's will, revealed in his law."

⚖️ MEANING OF PREROGATIVE — By the word "prerogative" we usually understand that special pre-eminence, which the king hath over and above all other persons, and out of the ordinary course of the common law, in right of his regal dignity. It signifies, in its etymology something that is required or demanded before, or in preference to all others. Hence, it follows, that it must be in its nature singular and eccentrical;

that it can only be applied to those rights and capacities which the king enjoys alone, in contradistinction to others, and not to those which he enjoys in common with any of his subjects: for if once any one prerogative of the crown could be held in common with the subject, it would cease to be prerogative any longer.

⚖ SOVEREIGNTY — First, the law ascribes to the king the attribute of sovereignty, or pre-eminence. The king is the viceregent and minister of God on earth: All are subject to him; and he is subject to none but to God alone. He is said to have imperial dignity; and in charters before the conquest is frequently styled king and emperor.

His realm is declared to be an empire, and his crown imperial, by many acts of parliament, which at the same time declare the king to be the supreme head of the realm in matters both civil and ecclesiastical, and of consequence inferior to no man upon earth, dependent on no man, accountable to no man. Formerly, there prevailed a ridiculous notion, propagated by the German and Italian civilians, that an emperor could do many things which a king could not and that all kings were in some degree subordinate and subject to the emperor of Germany or Rome. The meaning, therefore, of the legislature, when it uses these terms of empire and imperial, and applies them to the realm and crown of England, is only to assert that our king is equally sovereign and independent within these his dominions, as any emperor is in his empire; and owes no kind of subjection to any other potentate upon earth.

Hence it is, that no suit or action can be brought against the king, even in civil matters, because no court can have jurisdiction over him. For all jurisdiction implies superiority of power: authority to try would be vain and idle, without an authority to redress; and the sentence of a court would be contemptible, unless that court had power to command the execution of it: but who, shall command the king? It is likewise, that by law the person of the king is sacred, even though the measures pursued in his reign be completely tyrannical and arbitrary: for no jurisdiction upon earth has power to try him in a criminal way; much less to condemn him to punishment. If any foreign jurisdiction had this power, as was formerly claimed by the pope, the independence of the kingdom would be no more: and, if such a power were vested in any domestic tribunal, there would soon be an end of the constitution, by destroying the free agency of one of the constituent parts of the sovereign legislative power.

⚖ PROTECTION OF THE SUBJECT — Are then, it may be asked, the subjects of England totally destitute of remedy, in case the crown should invade their rights, either by private injuries, or public oppressions? To this we may answer, that the law has provided a remedy in both cases.

⚖ IN CASES OF PRIVATE INJURIES — First, as to private injuries: if any person has, in point of property, a just demand upon the king, he must petition him to his court of chancery, where his chancellor will administer right as a matter of grace, though not upon compulsion.

⚖ IN CASES OF PUBLIC OPPRESSION — Next, as to cases of ordinary public oppression, where the vitals of the constitution are not attacked, the law hath also assigned a remedy. For as a king cannot misuse his power, without the advice of evil counselors, and the assistance of wicked ministers, these men may be examined and punished. The constitution has therefore provided, by means of indictments, and parliamentary impeachments, that no man shall dare to assist the crown in contradiction to the laws of the land.

⚖ "THE KING CAN DO NO WRONG" — Besides the attribute of sovereignty the law also ascribes to the king, in his political capacity, absolute perfection. The king can do no wrong. Which ancient and fundamental maxim is not to be understood, as if everything transacted by the government was of course just and lawful, but means only two things. First, that whatever is exceptionable in the conduct of public affairs is not to be imputed to the king, nor is he answerable for it personally to his people: for this doctrine would totally destroy that constitutional independence of the crown, which is necessary for the balance of power, in our free and active, and therefore compounded constitution. Secondly, it means that the prerogative of the crown extends not to do any injury; it is created for the benefit of the people, and therefore cannot be exerted to their prejudice.

⚖ EXECUTIVE DEPARTMENT OF GOVERNMENT — We are next to consider those branches of the royal prerogative, which invest his kingly capacity, with a number of authorities and powers; in the exertion whereof consists the executive part of government.

This is wisely placed in a single hand by the British constitution, for the sake of unanimity, strength, and dispatch. Were it placed in many hands, it would be subject to many wills: many wills, if disunited and drawing different ways, create weakness in a government; and to unite those several wills, and reduce them to one, is a work of more time and delay than the exigencies of state will afford. The king of England is therefore not only the chief, but properly the sole, magistrate of the nation; all others acting by commission from, and in due subordination to him.

THE KING AS FOUNTAIN OF JUSTICE — The king is considered in domestic affairs as the foundation of justice and general conservator of the peace of the kingdom. By the fountain of justice the law does not mean the author or original, but only the distributor. Justice is not derived from the king, as from his free gift; but he is the steward of the public, to dispense it to whom it is due. He is not the spring, but the reservoir; from whence right and equity are conducted, by a thousand channels, to every individual.

The original power of judicature, by the fundamental principles of society, is lodged in the society at large: but as it would be impracticable to render complete justice to every individual, by the people in their collective capacity, therefore every nation has committed that power to certain select magistrates, who with more ease and expedition can hear and determine complaints; and in England this authority has immemorially been exercised by the king or his substitutes. He therefore has alone the right of erecting courts of judicature: for, though the constitution of the kingdom hath entrusted him with the whole executive power of the laws, it is impossible, as well as improper, that he should personally carry into execution this great and extensive trust; it is consequently necessary, that courts should be erected, to assist him in executing this power; and equally necessary, that, if erected, they should be erected by his authority. Hence, it is that all jurisdictions of courts are either mediately or immediately derived from the crown, their proceedings run generally in the king's name, they pass under his seal, and are executed by his officers.

CRIMINAL JURISDICTION — In criminal proceedings, or prosecutions for offenses, it would still be a higher absurdity, if the king personally sat in judgment; because in regard to these he appears in another capacity, that of prosecutor.

All offenses are either against the king's peace or his crown and dignity: and are so laid in every indictment. For though in their consequences they generally seem (except in the case of treason and a very few others) to be rather offenses against the kingdom than the king; yet, as the public, which is an invisible body, has delegated all its power and rights, with regard to the execution of the laws, to one visible magistrate, all affronts to that power, and breaches of those rights, are immediately offenses against him, to whom they are so delegated by the public. He is therefore the proper person to prosecute for all public offenses and breaches of the peace, being the person injured in the eye of the law.

⚖ PARDONING POWER — Hence, also arises another branch of the prerogative, that of pardoning offenses; for it is reasonable that he only who is injured should have the power of forgiving.

⚖ THEORY OF SEPARATE DEPARTMENTS — In this distinct and separate existence of the judicial power in a peculiar body of men, nominated indeed, but not removable at pleasure, by the crown, consists one main preservative of the public liberty; which cannot subsist long in any state, unless the administration of common justice be in some degree separated both from the legislative and also from the executive power. Were it joined with the legislative, the life, liberty, and property, of the subject would be in the hands of arbitrary judges, whose decisions would be then regulated only by their own opinions, and not by any fundamental principles of law; which, though legislators may depart from, yet judges are bound to observe. Were it joined with the executive, this union might soon be an overbalance for the legislative. Nothing, therefore, is more to be avoided, in a free constitution, than uniting the provinces of a judge and a minister of state.

MASTER AND SERVANT

⚖ THE DOMESTIC RELATIONS — The three great relations in private life
   are:

1. That of master and servant, which is founded in convenience,
whereby a man is directed to call in the assistance of others, where his own
skill and labor will not be sufficient to answer the cares incumbent upon
him.

2. That of husband and wife, which is founded in nature, but modified by civil society: the one directing man to continue and multiply his
species, the other prescribing the manner in which that natural impulse
must be confined and regulated.

3. That of parent and child, which is consequential to that of marriage, being its principal end and design: and it is by virtue of this relation that infants are protected, maintained, and educated. But, since the
parents, on whom this care is primarily incumbent, may be snatched
away by death before they have completed their duty, the law has therefore provided a fourth relation.

4. That of guardian and ward, which is a kind of artificial parentage, in order to supply the deficiency, whenever it happens, of the natural.

⚖ MASTER AND SERVANT — In discussing the relation of master and
   servant, I shall, first, consider the several sorts of servants and how
this relation is created and destroyed: secondly, the effect of this relation
with regard to the parties themselves: and, lastly, its effect with regard to
other persons.

⚖ CLASSES OF SERVANTS — I have formerly observed that pure and
   proper slavery does not, nay cannot, subsist in England; such I mean,
whereby an absolute and unlimited power is given to the master over the
life and fortune of the slave. It is repugnant to reason, and the principles
of natural law, that such a state should subsist anywhere.

The three origins of the right of slavery, assigned by justinian, are all of them built upon false foundations. First, slavery is held to arise by the law of nations from a state of captivity in war. The conqueror, say the civilians, had a right to the life of his captive; and, having spared that, has a right to deal with him as he pleases. But it is an untrue position, when taken generally, that, by the law of nature or nations, a man may kill his enemy: he has only a right to kill him, in particular cases; in cases of absolute necessity, for self-defense; and it is plain this absolute necessity did not subsist, since the victor did not actually kill him, but made him prisoner.

War is itself justifiable only on principles of self-preservation; and therefore it gives no other right over prisoners but merely to disable them from doing harm to us, by confining their persons: much less can it give a right to kill, torture, abuse, plunder, or even to enslave an enemy, when the war is over. Since, therefore, the right of making slaves by captivity, depends on a supposed right of slaughter, that foundation failing, the consequence drawn from it must fail likewise.

Secondly, it is said that slavery may begin by the civil law; when one man sells himself to another. This, if only meant of contracts to serve or work for another, is very just: but when applied to strict slavery, in the sense of the laws of old Rome or modern Barbary, is also impossible. Every sale implies a price, a quid pro quo (value for value), an equivalent can be given for life, and liberty, both of which (in absolute slavery) are held to be in the master's disposal? His property also, the very price he seems to receive, desolves to his master, the instant he becomes a slave. In this case, therefore, the buyer gives nothing, and the seller receives nothing: of what validity, than can a sale be, which destroys the very principles upon which all sales are founded?

Lastly, we are told, that besides these two ways by which slaves are acquired they may also be hereditary: They are born slaves; the children of acquired slaves are by the law of nature by a negative kind of birthright, slaves also. But this, being built on the two former rights, must fall together with them. If neither captivity, nor the sale of one's self, can by the law of nature and reason reduce the parent to slavery, much less can they reduce the offspring.

⚖ NO SLAVERY IN ENGLAND — Upon these principles the law of England abhors, and will not endure the existence of slavery within this nation. A slave or negro, the instant he lands in England, becomes a freeman; that is, the law will protect him in the enjoyment of his person, and his property.

Yet, with regard to any right which the master may have lawfully acquired to the perpetual service of John or Thomas, this will remain exactly in the same state as before: for this is no more than the same state of subjection for life, which every apprentice submits to for the space of seven years, or sometimes for a longer term. Hence, too, it follows, that the infamous and unchristian practice of withholding baptism from negro servants, lest they should thereby gain their liberty, is totally without foundation, as well as without excuse.

The law of England acts upon general and extensive principles: it gives liberty, rightly understood, that is, protection to a Jew, a Turk, or a heathen, as well as to those who profess the true religion of Christ; and it will not dissolve a civil obligation between master and servant, on account of the alteration of faith in either of the parties: but the slave is entitled to the same protection in England before, as after, baptism; and, whatever service the heathen negro owed of right to his American master, by general not by local law, the same (whatever it be) is he bound to render when brought to England and made a Christian.

MENIAL SERVANTS — The first sort of servants, therefore, acknowledged by the laws of England are menial servants; so called from being within the walls, or domestics. The contract between them and their masters arises upon the hiring. If the hiring be general without any particular time limited, the law construes it to be a hiring for a year, upon a principle of natural equity, that the servant shall serve, and the master maintain him throughout all the revolutions of the respective seasons; as well when there is work to be done as when there is not: but the contract may be made for any larger or smaller term.

All single men between twelve years old and sixty, and married ones under thirty years of age, and all single women between twelve and forty, not having any visible livelihood, are compellable by two justices to go out to service in husbandry or certain specific trades, for the promotion of honest industry; and no master can put away his servant, or servant leave his master, after being so retained, either before or at the end of his term, without a quarter's warning; unless upon reasonable cause to be allowed by a justice of the peace: but they may part by consent, or make a special bargain.

APPRENTICES — Another species of servants are called apprentices and are usually bound for a term of years, by deed indented or indentures, to serve their masters, and be maintained and instructed by them. This is usually done to persons of trade, in order to learn their art and mystery; and sometimes very large sums are given with them, as a premium for such their instruction: but it may be done to husbandmen, nay to gentlemen, and others. Children of poor persons may be apprenticed out by the overseers, with consent of two justices, till twenty-four years of age, to such persons as are thought fitting; who are also compellable to take them: and it is held, that gentlemen of fortune, and clergymen, are equally liable with others to such compulsion: for which purposes our statutes have made the indentures obligatory, even though such parish apprentice be a minor.

Apprentices to trades may be discharged on reasonable cause, either at the request of themselves or masters, at the quarter sessions, or by one justice, with appeal to the sessions, who may, by the equity of the statute, if they think it reasonable, direct restitution of a ratable share of the money given with the apprentice: and parish apprentices may be discharged in the same manner, by two justices. But if an apprentice, with whom less than ten pounds hath been given, runs away from his master, he is compellable to serve out his time of absence, or make satisfaction for the same, at any time within seven years after the expiration of his original contract.

⚖ LABORERS — A third species of servants are laborers, who are only hired by the day or the week, and do not live as part of the family; concerning whom the statutes before cited have made many very good regulations; 1. Directing that all persons who have no visible effects may be compelled to work; 2. Defining how long they must continue at work in summer and in winter; 3. Punishing such as leave or desert their work; 4. Empowering the justices at sessions, or the sheriff of the county, to settle their wages; and 5. Inflicting penalties on such as either give, or exact, more wages than are so settled.

⚖ STEWARDS, FACTORS AND BAILIFFS — There is yet a fourth species of servants, if they may be so called, being rather in a superior, a ministerial, capacity; such as stewards, factors, and bailiffs: whom however, the law considers as servants pro tempore (for a time), with regard to such of their acts, as affect their master's or employer's property.

⚖ RELATION OF SERVICE — First, by hiring and service for a year, or apprenticeship under indentures, a person gains a settlement in that parish wherein he last served forty days. In the next place persons, serving seven years as apprentices to any trade, have an exclusive right to exercise that trade in any part of England.

This law, with regard to the exclusive part of it, has by turns been looked upon as a hard law, or as a beneficial one, according to the prevailing humor of the times: which has occasioned a great variety of resolutions in the courts of law concerning it; and attempts have been frequently made for its repeal, though hitherto without success. This reason indeed only extends to such trades, in the exercise whereof skill is required: but another of their arguments goes much further; viz, that apprenticeships are useful to the commonwealth, by employing of youth, and learning them to be early industrious; but that no one would be induced to undergo a seven years' servitude, if others, though equally skillful, were allowed the same advantages without having undergone the same discipline: and in this there seems to be much reason.

However, the resolutions of the courts have in general rather confined than extended the restriction. No trades are held to be within the statute, but such as were in being at the making of it: for trading in a country village, apprenticeships are not requisite: and following the trade seven years is sufficient without any binding; for the statute only says, the person must serve as an apprentice, and does not require an actual apprenticeship to have existed.

⚖ MASTER'S RIGHT OF CORRECTION — A master may by law correct his apprentice for negligence or other misbehavior, so it be done with moderation: though, if the master or master's wife beats any other servant of full age, it is good cause of departure. But if any servant, workman, or laborer assaults his master or dame, he shall suffer one year's imprisonment, and other open corporal punishment, not extending to life or limb.

⚖ SERVANT'S WAGES — By service all servants and laborers, except apprentices, become entitled to wages: according to their agreement, if menial servants; or according to the appointment of the sheriff or sessions, if laborers or servants in husbandry: for the statutes for regulation of wages extend to such servants only, it being impossible for any magistrate to be a judge of the employment of menial servants, or of course to assess their wages.

⚖ RELATION OF SERVICE AS TO THIRD PERSONS — Let us, lastly, see how strangers may be affected by this relation of master and servant: or how a master may behave towards others on behalf of his servant; and what a servant may do on behalf of his master.

First, the master may abet and assist his servant in any action at law against a stranger: whereas, in general, it is an offense against public justice to encourage suits and animosities, by helping to bear the expenses of them, and is called in law maintenance. A master also may bring an action against any man for beating or maiming his servant: but in such case he must assign, as a special reason for so doing, his own damage by the loss of his service; and this loss must be proved upon the trial.

A master likewise may justify an assault in defense of his servant, and a servant in defense of his master: the master, because he has an interest in his servant, not to be deprived of his service; the servant, because it is part of his duty, for which he received his wages, to stand by and defend his master. Also if any person do hire or retain my servant, being in my service, for which the servant departeth from me and goeth to serve the other, I may have an action for damages against both the new master and the servant or either of them. But if the new master did not know that he is my servant, no action lies; unless he afterwards refuse to restore him upon information and demand. The reason and foundation, upon which all this doctrine is built, seem to be the property that every man has in the service of his domestics; acquired by the contract of hiring and purchased by giving them wages.

⚖ RESPONSIBILITY OF MASTER — As for those things which a servant may do on behalf of his master, they seem all to proceed upon this principle, that the master is answerable for the act of his servant, if done by his command, either expressly given, or implied: for he who does a thing by the agency of another, does it himself. Therefore, if the servant commit a trespass by the command or encouragement of his master, the master shall be guilty of it: not that the servant is excused, for he is only to obey his master in matters that are honest and lawful.

If an innkeeper's servants rob his guests, the master is bound to restitution: for as there is a confidence reposed in him, that he will take care to provide honest servants, his negligence is a kind of implied consent to the robbery; for he who does not forbid a crime while he may, sanctions it. So likewise if the drawer at a tavern sells a man bad wine, whereby his health is injured, he may bring an action against the master: for although the master did not expressly order the servant to sell it to that person in particular, yet his permitting him to draw and sell it at all is impliedly a general command.

⚖ SCOPE OF EMPLOYMENT — In the same manner, whatever a servant is permitted to do in the usual course of his business, is equivalent to a general command. If I pay money to a banker's servant, the banker is answerable for it: if I pay it to a clergyman's or a physician's servant, whose usual business it is not to receive money for his master, and he embezzles it, I must pay it over again. If a steward lets a lease of a farm, without the owner's knowledge, the owner must stand to the bargain; for this is the steward's business. A wife, a friend, a relation, that use to transact business for a man, are as to this his servants; and the principal must answer for their conduct: for the law implies, that they act under a general command; and without such a doctrine as this no mutual intercourse between man and man could subsist with any tolerable convenience.

If I usually deal with a tradesman by myself, or constantly pay him ready money, I am not answerable for what my servant takes up upon trust; for here is no implied order to the tradesman to trust my servant; but if I usually send him upon trust, or sometimes on trust and sometimes with ready money, I am answerable for all he takes up for the tradesman cannot possibly distinguish when he comes by my order, and when upon his own authority.

⚖ NEGLIGENCE OF SERVANT — If a servant, lastly, by his negligence does any damage to a stranger, the master shall answer for his neglect: if a smith's servant lames a horse while he is shoeing him, an action lies against the master, and not against the servant. But in these cases the damage must be done, while he is actually employed in the master's service; otherwise the servant shall answer for his own misbehavior. Upon this principle, by the common law, if a servant kept his master's fire negligently, so that his neighbor's house was burned down thereby, an action lay against the master; because this negligence happened in his master's immediate service: and must himself answer the damage personally.

Now the common law is in the former case, altered by statute (1707), which ordains that no action shall be maintained against any, in whose house or chamber any fire shall accidentally begin; for their own loss is sufficient punishment for their own or their servant's carelessness. But if such fire happens through negligence of any servant (whose loss is commonly very little) such servant shall forfeit 100 pounds, to be distributed among the sufferers; and, in default of payment, shall be committed to some workhouse and there kept to hard labor for eighteen months.

A master is, lastly, chargeable if any of his family layeth or casteth anything out of his house into the street or common highway, to the damage of any individual, or the common nuisance of his majesty's liege people: for the master hath the superintendence and charge of all his household. This also agrees with the civil law; which holds, that the head of the family, in this and similar cases, is held accountable for the fault of another, whether of his servant, or his child.

We may observe, that in all the cases here put, the master may be frequently a loser by the trust reposed in his servant, but never can be a gainer: he may frequently be answerable for his servant's misbehavior, but never can shelter himself from punishment by laying the blame on his agent. The reason of this is still uniform and the same; that the wrong done by the servant is looked upon in law as the wrong of the master himself; and it is a standing maxim, that no man shall be allowed to make any advantage of his own wrong.

HUSBAND AND WIFE

⚖ MARRIAGE — The second private relation of persons is that of marriage, which includes the reciprocal rights and duties of husband and wife; in the consideration of which I shall in the first place inquire, how marriages may be contracted or made; shall next point out the manner in which they may be dissolved; and shall, lastly, take a view of the legal effects and consequence of marriage.

⚖ MARRIAGE, A CIVIL CONTRACT — Our law considers marriage in no other light than as a civil contract. The holiness of the matrimonial state is left entirely to the ecclesiastical law: the temporal courts not having jurisdiction to consider unlawful marriage as a sin, but merely as a civil inconvenience. The punishment, therefore, or annulling, of incestuous or other unscriptural marriages, is the province of the spiritual courts; which act for the welfare of the soul. Taking it in this civil light, the law treats it as it does all other contracts: allowing it to be good and valid in all cases, where the parties at the time of making it were, in the first place, willing to contract; secondly, able to contract; and, lastly, actually did contract, in the proper forms and solemnities required by law.

⚖ CONSENT OF THE PARTIES — First, they must be willing to contract. Consent, no cohabitation, makes the marriage, is the maxim of the civil law in this case: and it is adopted by the common lawyers, who indeed have borrowed almost all their notions of the legitimacy of marriage from the canon and civil laws.

⚖ CAPACITY OF THE PARTIES — Secondly, they must be able to contract. In general, all persons are able to contract themselves in marriage, unless they labor under some particular disabilities and incapacities.

⚖ DISABILITIES — These disabilities are of two sorts: First, such as are canonical, and therefore sufficient by the ecclesiastical laws to avoid the marriage in the spiritual court; but these in our law only make the ·marriage voidable, and not ipso facto void, until sentence of nullity be obtained. Of this nature are pre-contract; consanguinity, or relation by blood and affinity, or relation by marriage; and some particular corporal infirmities.

These canonical disabilities are either grounded upon the express words of the divine law, or are consequences plainly deducible from thence: It therefore being sinful in the persons, who labor under them, to attempt to contract matrimony together, they are properly the object of the ecclesiastical magistrate's coercion; in order to separate the offenders, and inflict penance for the offense, for the welfare of their souls.

Such marriages not being void from the beginning, but voidable only by sentence of separation, they are esteemed valid to all civil purposes, unless such separation is actually made during the life of the parties. For, after the death of either of them, the courts of common law will not suffer the spiritual court to declare such marriages to have been void, because such declaration cannot tend to the reformation of the parties. These canonical disabilities being entirely the province of the ecclesiastical courts, our books are perfectly silent concerning them. But there are a few statutes, which serve as directories to those courts, of which it will be proper to take notice.

By statute (Marriage, 1540), it is declared, that all persons may lawfully marry, but such as are prohibited by God's law; and that all marriages contracted by lawful persons in the face of the church, and consummate with bodily knowledge, and fruit of children, shall be indissoluble. It is declared by the same statute, that nothing (God's law except) shall impeach any marriage, but within the levitical degrees; the furtherest of which is that between uncle and niece.

⚖ CIVIL DISABILITIES — The other sort of disabilities are those which are created, or at least enforced, by the municipal laws. Though some of them may be grounded on natural law, yet they are regarded by the laws of the land, not so much in the light of any moral offense, as on account of the civil inconveniences they draw after them. These civil disabilities make the contract void from the beginning and not merely voidable; not that they dissolve a contract already former, but they render the parties incapable of forming any contract at all: they do not put assunder those who are joined together, but they previously hinder the junction. If any persons under these legal incapacities come together, it is a meretricious, and not a matrimonial union.

⚖ EXISTING PRIOR MARRIAGE — The first of these legal disabilities is a prior marriage, or having another husband or wife living; in which case, besides the penalties consequent upon it as a felony, the second marriage is to all intents and purposes void; polygamy being condemned both by the law of the New Testament, and the policy of all prudent states, especially in these northern climates. Justinian, even in the climate of modern Turkey, is express, that it is not lawful to have two wives at one time.

⚖️ WANT OF AGE — The next legal disability is want of age. This is sufficient to avoid all other contracts, on account of the imbecility of judgment in the parties contracting; therefore, it ought to avoid this, the most important contract of any. Therefore, if a boy under fourteen, or a girl under twelve years of age, marries, this marriage is only inchoate and imperfect; and, when either of them comes to the age of consent aforesaid, they may disagree and declare the marriage void, without any divorce or sentence in the spiritual court. This is founded on the civil law. But the canon law pays a greater regard to the constitution than the age of the parties: for if they are fit for marriage, it is a good marriage, whatever their age may be.

In our law it is so far a marriage, that if at the age of consent they agree to continue together, they need not be married again. If the husband be of years of discretion, and the wife under twelve, when she comes to years of discretion he may disagree as well as she: for in contracts the obligation must be mutual; both must be bound, or neither: and so it is, vice versa, when the wife is of years of discretion and the husband under.

⚖️ NONCONSENT OF PARENTS — Another incapacity arises from want of consent of parents or guardians. By the common law, if the parties themselves were of the age of consent, there wanted no other concurrence to make the marriage valid: and this was agreeable to the canon law. By statute, whosoever marries any woman child under the age of sixteen years, without the consent of parents or guardians, shall be subject to fine, or five years' imprisonment; and her estate during the husband's life shall go to and be enjoyed by the next heir.

The civil law, indeed, required the consent of the parent or tutor at all ages; unless the children were emancipated, or out of the parents' power and if such consent from the father was wanting, the marriage was null, and the children illegitimate; but the consent of the mother or guardians, if unreasonably withheld, might be redressed and supplied by the judge, or the president of the province: and if the father was non compos, a similar remedy was given.

It has lately been enacted that all marriages celebrated by license where either of the parties is under twenty-one (not being a widow or widower, who are supposed emancipated), without the consent of the father, or, if he be not living, of the mother or guardians, shall be absolutely void. A like provision is made as in the civil law, where the mother or guardian is non compos, beyond sea, or unreasonably froward, to dispense with such consent at the discretion of the lord chancellor: but no provision is made, in case the father should labor under any mental or other incapacity.

Much may be said both for and against this innovation upon our ancient laws and constitution. On the one hand, it prevents the clandestine marriages of minors, which are often a terrible inconvenience to those private families wherein they happen. On the other hand, restraints upon marriages, especially among the lower class, are evidently detrimental to the public, by hindering the increase of people; and to religion and morality, by encouraging licentiousness and debauchery among the single of both sexes; and thereby destroying one end of society and government, which is to forbid a promiscuous intercourse.

⚖ MENTAL INCAPACITY — A fourth incapacity is want of reason; without a competent share of which no matrimonial contract is valid. It was formerly adjudged that the issue of an idiot was legitimate, and consequently that his marriage was valid. A strange determination, since consent is absolutely requisite to matrimony, and neither idiots nor lunatics are capable of consenting to anything. The civil law judged much more sensibly when it made such deprivations of reason a previous impediment, though not a cause of divorce if they happened after marriage.

Modern resolutions have adhered to the reason of the civil law, by determining that the marriage of a lunatic, not being in a lucid interval, was absolutely void. But as it might be difficult to prove the exact state of the party's mind at the actual celebration of the nuptials, upon this account the statute (Marriage of Lunatics, 1741), has provided, that the marriage of lunatics and persons under frenzies (if found lunatics under a commission, or committed to the care of trustees by any act of parliament) before they are declared of sound mind by the lord chancellor or the majority of such trustees, shall be totally void.

⚖ CELEBRATION OF MARRIAGE — Lastly, the parties must not only be willing and able to contract, but actually must contract themselves in due form of law, to make it a good civil marriage. Any contract made in words of the present tense, and in case of cohabitation in words of the future tense also, between persons able to contract; was before the late act deemed a valid marriage to many purposes; and the parties might be compelled in the spiritual courts to celebrate it in the face of the church. But these verbal contracts are now of no force to compel a future marriage. Neither is any marriage at present valid that is not celebrated in some parish church or public chapel, unless by dispensation from the Archbishop of Canterbury. It must also be preceded by publication of banns, or by license from the spiritual judge. Many other formalities are likewise prescribed by the act; the neglect of which, though penal, does not invalidate the marriage.

It is held to be also essential to a marriage, that it be performed by a person in orders; it being said that Pope Innocent III was the first who ordained the celebration of marriage in the church; before which it was totally a civil contract. In the times of the grand rebellion, all marriages were performed by the justices of the peace; and these marriages were declared valid, without any fresh solemnization, by statute (Confirmation of Marriages, 1660). But, as the law now stands, we may upon the whole collect, that no marriage by the temporal law is ipso facto void, that is celebrated by a person in orders, in a parish church or public chapel (or elsewhere, by special dispensation) in pursuance of banns or a license, between single persons, consenting, of sound mind, and of the age of twenty-one years; or of the age of fourteen in males and twelve in females, with consent of parents or guardians, or without it, in the case of widowhood.

⚖ DISSOLUTION OF MARRIAGE — The manner in which marriages may be dissolved is either by death, or divorce.

⚖ DIVORCE FROM THE BONDS OF MATRIMONY — There are two kinds of divorce, the one total, the other partial; the one from the bond of matrimony, the other merely from bed and board. The total divorce must be for some of the canonical causes of impediment before mentioned; and those existing before the marriage, as is always the case in consanguinity; not supervenient, or arising afterwards, as may be the case in affinity or corporal imbecility. For in cases of total divorce, the marriage is declared null, as having been absolutely unlawful from the beginning; and the parties are therefore separated for the welfare of their souls: for which reason, as was before observed, no divorce can be obtained, but during the life of the parties. The issue of such marriage as is thus entirely dissolved are bastards.

⚖ DIVORCE FROM BED AND BOARD — Divorce from bed and board is when the marriage is just and lawful ab initio, and therefore the law is tender of dissolving it; but, for some supervenient cause, it becomes improper or impossible for the parties to live together: as in the case of intolerable ill temper, or adultery, in either of the parties. For the canon law, which the common law follows in this case, deems so highly and with such mysterious reverence of the nuptial tie, that it will not allow it to be unloosed for any cause whatsoever, that arises after the union is made.

The civil law, which is partly of pagan origin, allows many causes of absolute divorce; and some of them pretty severe ones (as if a wife goes to the theater or the public games, without the knowledge and consent of the husband): but among them adultery is the principal, and with reason named the first. With us in England adultery is only a cause of separation from bed and board: for which the best reason that can be given, is, that if divorces were allowed to depend upon a matter within the power of either the parties, they would probably be extremely frequent; as was the case when divorces were allowed for canonical disabilities, on the mere confession of the parties, which is now prohibited by canons.

☙ ALIMONY — In case of divorce from bed and board the law allows alimony to the wife: which is that allowance which is made to a woman for her support out of the husband's estate; being settled at the discretion of the ecclesiastical judge, on consideration of all the circumstances of the case. This is sometimes called her estovers; for which, if he refuses payment, there is (besides the ordinary process of excommunication) a writ at common law of recovering estovers. It is generally proportioned to the rank and quality of the parties. But in case of elopement, and living with an adulterer, the law allows her no alimony.

☙ LEGAL CONSEQUENCES OF MARRIAGE — Having thus shown how marriages may be made, or dissolved, I come now to the legal consequences of such making or dissolution.

By marriage, the husband and wife are one person in law: that is, the very being or legal existence of the woman is suspended during the marriage, or at least is incorporated and consolidated into that of the husband; under whose wing, protection, and cover, she performs everything; and is therefore called in our law-French, a feme covert, and is said to be under the protection and influence of her husband, her baron, or lord; and her condition during her marriage is called her coverture.

Upon this principle, of an union of person in husband and wife, depend almost all the legal rights, duties and disabilities, that either of them acquire by the marriage. I speak not at present of the rights of property, but of such as are merely personal.

TRANSACTIONS BETWEEN HUSBAND AND WIFE — For this reason, a man cannot grant anything to his wife, or enter into covenant with her: for the grant would be to suppose her separate existence; and to covenant with her, would be only to covenant with himself; and it is also generally true, that all compacts made between husband and wife, when single, are voided by the intermarriage.

A woman, indeed, may be attorney for her husband; for that implies no separation from, but is rather a representation of, her lord. A husband may also bequeath anything to his wife by will; for that cannot take effect till the coverture is determined by his death.

LIABILITIES OF HUSBAND — The husband is bound to provide his wife with necessaries by law, as much as himself: and if she contracts debts for them, he is obliged to pay them; but, for anything besides necessaries, he is not chargeable. Also if a wife elopes, and lives with another man, the husband is not chargeable even for necessaries; at least if the person, who furnishes them, is sufficiently appraised of her elopement. If the wife be indebted before marriage, the husband is bound afterwards to pay the debt; for he has adopted her and her circumstances together.

SUITS BY AND AGAINST WIFE — If the wife be injured in her person or her property, she can bring no action for redress without her husband's concurrence, and in his name, as well as her own; neither can she be sued, without making the husband a defendant. There is, indeed, one case where the wife shall sue and be sued as feme sole, viz., where the husband has abjured the realm, or is banished: for then he is dead in law; and, the husband being thus disabled to sue for or defend the wife, it would be most unreasonable if she had no remedy, or could make no defense at all. In criminal prosecutions, it is true, the wife may be indicted and punished separately, for the union is only a civil union.

INCAPACITY AS WITNESSES — But, in trials of any sort, they are not allowed to be evidence for, or against, each other, partly because it is impossible their testimony should be indifferent; but principally because of the union of person: and therefore, if they were admitted to be witnesses for each other, they would contradict one maxim of law, "no one may be a witness in his own cause"; and if against each other, they would contradict another maxim, "no one is bound to accuse himself."

But, where the offense is directly against the person of the wife, this rule has been dispensed with: by statute (abduction, 1487), in case a woman be forcibly taken away, and married, she may be a witness against such her husband, in order to convict him of felony. For in this case she can with no propriety be reckoned his wife; because a main ingredient, her consent, was wanting to the contract: and also there is another maxim of law, that no man shall take advantage of his own wrong; which the ravisher here would do, if by forcibly marrying a woman, he could prevent her from being a witness, who is perhaps the only witness, to that very fact.

⚖ IN ECCLESIASTICAL COURTS — In the civil law the husband and wife are considered as two distinct persons; and may have separate estates, contracts, debts, and injuries: and therefore, in our ecclesiastical courts, a woman may sue and be sued without her husband.

⚖ SEPARATE ACTS OF WIFE — But, though our law in general considers man and wife as one person, yet there are some instances in which she is separately considered; as inferior to him, and acting by his compulsion. Therefore all deeds executed, and acts done, by her, during her coverture, are void; except it be a fine, or the like matter of record, in which case she must be solely and secretly examined, to learn if her act be voluntary. She cannot by will devise lands to her husband, unless under special circumstances; for at the time of making it she is supposed to be under his coercion. In some felonies, and other inferior crimes, committed by her, through constraint of her husband, the law excuses her: but this extends not to treason or murder.

⚖ HUSBAND'S RIGHT OF CORRECTION — The husband also (by the old law) might give his wife moderate correction. For as he is to answer for her misbehavior, the law thought it reasonable to entrust him with this power of restraining her, by domestic chastisement, in the same moderation that a man is allowed to correct his apprentices or children; for whom the master or parent is also liable in some cases to answer.

This power of correction was confined within reasonable bounds, and the husband was prohibited from using any violence to his wife, otherwise than lawfully and reasonably belongs to the husband for the due government and correction of his wife. The civil law gave the husband the same, or a larger, authority over his wife; allowing him, for some misdemeanors to beat his wife severely with scourges and sticks; for others, only to use moderate chastisement.

But, with us, in the politer reign of Charles II, this power of correction began to be doubted: and a wife may now have security of the peace against her husband; or, in return, a husband against his wife. Yet the lower rank of people, who were always fond of the old common law, still claim and exert their ancient privilege: and the courts of law will still permit a husband to restrain a wife of her liberty, in case of any gross misbehavior.

These are the chief legal effects of marriage during the coverture; upon which we may observe, that even the disabilities, which the wife lies under, are for the most part intended for her protection and benefit.

PARENT AND CHILD

♂♂ PARENT AND CHILD — The most universal relation in nature, is that between parent and child.

Children are of two sorts: legitimate and spurious, or bastards.

♂♂ LEGITIMATE CHILDREN — A legitimate child is he that is born in lawful wedlock or within a competent time afterwards. With us in England the rule is narrowed, for the nuptials must be precedent to the birth; of which more will be said when we come to consider the case of bastardy. At present let us inquire into: 1. The legal duties of parents to their legitimate children. 2. Their power over them. 3. The duties of such children to their parents.

♂♂ DUTIES OF PARENTS — First, the duties of parents, to legitimate children: which principally consist in three particulars; their maintenance, their protection, and their education.

The duty of parents to provide for the maintenance of their children, is a principle of natural law; an obligation laid on them not only by nature itself, but by their own proper act, in bringing them into the world; for they would be in the highest manner injurious to their issue, if they only gave their children life, that they might afterwards see them perish. By begetting them, therefore, they have entered into a voluntary obligation, to endeavor, as far as in them lies, that the life which they have bestowed shall be supported and preserved. Thus the children will have a perfect right of receiving maintenance from their parents.

The establishment of marriage in all civilized states is built on this natural obligation of the father to provide for his children; for that ascertains and makes known the person who is bound to fulfill this obligation; whereas, in promiscuous and illicit conjunctions, the father is unknown; and the mother finds a thousand obstacles in her way— shame, remorse, the constraint of her sex, and the rigor of laws;—that stifle her inclinations to perform this duty; and besides, she generally wants ability.

The municipal laws of all well-regulated states have taken care to enforce this duty: though Providence has done it more effectually than any laws, by implanting in the breast of every parent that natural or insuperable degree of affection, which not even the deformity of person or mind, not even the wickedness, ingratitude, and rebellion of children, can totally suppress or extinguish.

⚖ DUTY OF SUPPORT UNDER THE CIVIL LAW — The civil law obliges the parent to provide maintenance for his child; and, if he refuses, the judge shall take cognizance of that matter. Nay, it carries this matter so far, that it will not suffer a parent at his death totally to disinherit his child without expressly giving his reason for so doing; and there are fourteen such reasons reckoned up, which may justify such disinherison. If the parent alleged no reason, or a bad, or a false one, the child might set the will aside, as an undutiful will, a testament contrary to the natural duty of the parent.

It is remarkable under what color the children were to move for relief in such a case: by suggesting that the parent had lost the use of his reason, when he made the inofficious testament. This, was not to bring into dispute the testator's power of disinheriting his own offspring; but to examine the motives upon which he did it: and, if they were found defective in reason, then to set them aside. But perhaps this is going rather too far: every man has, or ought to have, by the laws of society, a power over his own property: and, as Grotius very well distinguishes, natural right obliges to give a necessary maintenance to children; but what is more than that they have no other right to, than as it is given to them by the favor of their parents, or the positive constitutions of the municipal law.

⚖ DUTY OF SUPPORT UNDER ENGLISH LAW — It is a principle of law, that there is an obligation on every man to provide for those descended from his loins; and the manner in which this obligation shall be performed, is thus pointed out. The father, and mother, grandfather, and grandmother of poor impotent persons shall maintain them at their own charges, if of sufficient ability, according as the quarter sessions shall direct: and if a parent runs away, and leaves his children, the church wardens and overseers of the parish shall seize his rents, goods, and chattels, and dispose of them toward their relief.

But the interpretations which the courts of law have made upon these statutes, if a mother or grandmother marries again, and was before such second marriage of sufficient ability to keep the child, the husband shall be charged to maintain it: for this being a debt of hers, when single, shall like others extend to charge the husband. But at her death, the relation being dissolved, the husband is under no further obligation.

No person is bound to provide a maintenance for his issue, unless where the children are impotent and unable to work, either through infancy, disease, or accident; and then is only obliged to find them with necessaries, the penalty on refusal being no more than twenty shillings a month. For the policy of our laws, which are ever watchful to promote industry, did not mean to compel a father to maintain his idle and lazy children in ease and indolence: but thought it unjust to oblige the parent, against his will, to provide them with superfluities, and other indulgences of fortune; imagining they might trust to the impulse of nature, if the children were deserving of such favors.

DISINHERITING OF CHILDREN — Our law has made no provision to prevent the disinheriting of children by will: leaving every man's property in his own disposal, upon a principle of liberty in this, as well as every other, action: though perhaps it had not been amiss, if the parent had been bound to leave them at the least a necessary subsistence. Indeed, among persons of any rank or fortune, a competence is generally provided for younger children, and the bulk of the estate settled upon the eldest, by the marriage articles. Heirs also, and children, are favorites of our courts of justice, and cannot be disinherited by any dubious or ambiguous words; there being required the utmost certainty of the testator's intentions to take away the right of an heir.

DUTY TO PROTECT CHILDREN — From the duty of maintenance we may easily pass to that of protection; which is also a natural duty, but rather permitted than enjoined by any municipal laws: nature, in this respect, working so strongly as to need rather a check than a spur. A parent may, by our laws, maintain and uphold his children in their lawsuits, without being guilty of the legal crime of maintaining quarrels. A parent may also justify an assault and battery in defense of the persons of his children: nay, where a man's son was beaten by another boy, and the father went near a mile to find him, and there revenged his son's quarrel by beating the other boy, of which beating he afterwards unfortunately died; it was not held to be murder, but manslaughter merely.

DUTY TO EDUCATE CHILDREN — The last duty of parents to their children is that of giving them an education suitable to their station in life: a duty pointed out by reason, and of far the greatest importance of any. For, it is not easy to imagine or allow, that a parent has conferred any considerable benefit upon his child, by bringing him into the world; if he afterwards entirely neglects his culture and education, and suffers him to grow up like a mere beast, to lead a life useless to others, and shameful to himself.

Our laws have in one instance made a wise provision for breeding up the rising generation: since the poor and laborious part of the community, when past the age of nurture, are taken out of the hands of their parents, by the statutes of apprenticing poor children; and are placed out by the public in such a manner, as may render their abilities, in their several stations, of the greatest advantage to the commonwealth. The rich, indeed, are left at their own option, whether they will breed up their children to be ornaments or disgraces to their family.

⚖ PARENTAL AUTHORITY UNDER ENGLISH LAW — The parent may lawfully correct his child, being under age, in a reasonable manner; for this is for the benefit of his education. The consent or concurrence of the parent to the marriage of his child under age, was also directed by our ancient law to be obtained: but now it is absolutely necessary; for without it the contract is void. This also is another means, which the law has put into the parent's hands, in order the better to discharge his duty; first, of protecting his children from the snares of artful and designing persons; and, next, of settling them properly in life, by preventing the ill consequences of too early and precipitate marriages.

A father has no other power over his son's estate, than as his trustee or guardian; for, though he may receive the profits during the child's minority, yet he must account for them when he comes of age. He may indeed have the benefit of his children's labor while they live with him, and are maintained by him: but this is no more than he is entitled to from his apprentices or servants. The legal power of a father (for a mother, as such, is entitled to no power, but only to reverence and respect), over the persons of his children ceases at the age of twenty-one: for they are then enfranchised by arriving at years of discretion, or that point which the law has established (as some must necessarily be established) when the empire of the father, or other guardian, gives place to the empire of reason. Yet, till that age arrives, this empire of the father continues even after his death; for he may by his will appoint a guardian to his children. He may also delegate part of his parental authority, during his life, to the tutor or schoolmaster, of his child; who is then in loco parentis (in the place of a parent), and has such a portion of the power of the parent committed to his charge, viz., that of restraint and correction, as may be necessary to answer the purposes for which he is employed.

⚖ DUTIES OF CHILDREN — The duties of children to their parents arise from a principle of natural justice and retribution. For to those, who gave us existence, we naturally owe subjection and obedience during our minority, and honor and reverence ever after: they, who protected the weakness of our infancy, are entitled to our protection in the infirmity of their age; they who by sustenance and education have enabled their offspring to prosper, ought in return to be supported by that offspring, in case they stand in need of assistance. Upon this principle, proceed all the duties of children to their parents which are enjoined by positive laws.

The law does not hold the tie of nature to be dissolved by any misbehavior of the parent; and therefore, a child is equally justifiable in defending the person, or maintaining the cause of suit, of a bad parent, as a good one; and is equally compellable, if of sufficient ability, to maintain and provide for a wicked and unnatural progenitor, as for one who has shown the greatest tenderness and parental piety.

⚖ ILLEGITIMATE CHILDREN, OR BASTARDS — We are next to consider the case of illegitimate children, or bastards, with regard to whom let us inquire: 1. Who are bastards.   2. The legal duties of the parents towards a bastard child.   3. The rights and incapacities attending such bastard children.

⚖ WHO ARE BASTARDS: LEGITIMATION — A bastard, by our English laws, is one that is not only begotten, but born out of lawful matrimony. The civil and canon laws do not allow a child to remain a bastard, if the parents afterwards intermarry: and herein they differ most materially from our law; which, though not so strict as to require that the child shall be begotten, yet makes it an indispensable condition that it shall be born, after lawful wedlock. The reason of our English law is surely much superior to that of the Roman, if we consider the principal end and design of establishing the contract of marriage. Taken in a civil light; abstractedly from any religious view, which has nothing to do with the legitimacy or illegitimacy of the children. The main end and design of marriage, therefore, being to ascertain and fix upon some certain person, to whom the care, the protection, the maintenance, and the education of the children should belong; this end is undoubtedly better answered by legitimating all issue born after wedlock, than by legitimating all issue of the same parties, even born before wedlock, so as wedlock afterwards ensues:

1. Because of the very great uncertainty there will generally be, in the proof that the issue was really begotten by the same man; whereas, by confining the proof to the birth, and not to begetting, our law has rendered it perfectly certain, what child is legitimate, and who is to take care of the child.   2. Because of the Roman law a child may be continued a bastard, or made legitimate, at the option of the father and mother, by a marriage ex post facto, thereby opening a door to many frauds and partialities, which by our law are prevented.   3. Because by those laws a man may remain a bastard till forty years of age, and then become legitimate, by the subsequent marriage of his parents; whereby the main end of marriage, the protection of infants, is totally frustrated. 4. Because this rule of the Roman law admits of no limitations as to the time or number of bastards so to be legitimated; but a dozen of them may, twenty years after their birth, by the subsequent marriage of their parents be admitted to all the privileges of legitimate children.

This is plainly a great discouragement to the matrimonial state; to which one main inducement is usually not only the desire of having children, but also the desire of procreating lawful heirs. Whereas our constitutions guard against this indecency, and at the same time give sufficient allowance to the frailties of human nature. For if a child be begotten while the parents are single, and they will endeavor to make an early reparation for the offense, by marrying within a few months after, our law is so indulgent as not to bastardize the child, if it be born, though not begotten, in lawful wedlock, for this is an incident that can happen but once; since all future children will be begotten, as well as born, within the rules of honor and civil society. Upon reasons like these we may suppose the peers to have acted at the parliament of Merton, when they refused to enact that children born before marriage should be esteemed legitimate.

☙ CHILDREN OF DUBIOUS PARENTAGE — From what has been said it appears, that all children born before matrimony are bastards by our law; and so it is of all children born so long after the death of the husband, that, by the usual course of gestation, they could not be begotten by him. But, this being a matter of some uncertainty, the law is not exact as to a few days. This gives occasion to a proceeding at common law, where a widow is suspected to feign herself with child, in order to produce a supposititious heir to the estate: an attempt which the rigor of the Gothic constitutions esteemed equivalent to the most atrocious theft, and therefore punished with death. In this case with us the heir presumptive may have a writ for inspecting whether a woman be pregnant, to examine whether she be with child or not; and, if she be, to keep her under proper restraint, till delivered; which is entirely conformable to the practice of the civil law: but, if the widow be upon due examination found not pregnant, the presumptive heir shall be admitted to the inheritance, though liable to lose it again, on the birth of a child within forty weeks from the death of the husband.

But if a man dies, and his widow soon after marries again, and a child is born within such a time, as that by the course of nature it might have been the child of either husband; in this case he is said to be more than ordinarily legitimate; for he may, when he arrives to years of discretion, choose which of the fathers he pleases. To prevent this, among other inconveniences, the civil law ordained that no widow should marry within the year of mourning.

⚖ BASTARDS BORN DURING WEDLOCK — As bastards may be born before the coverture or marriage state is begun, or after it is determined, so also children born during wedlock may in some circumstances be bastards. As if the husband be out of the kingdom of England (or, as the law somewhat loosely phrases it, beyond the four seas), for above nine months, so that no access to this wife can be presumed, her issue during that period shall be bastards. But generally, during the coverture access of the husband shall be presumed, unless the contrary can be shown; which is such a negative as can only be proved by showing him to be elsewhere: for the general rule is that the presumption is in favor of legitimacy.

In a divorce from bed and board, if the wife breeds children, they are bastards; for the law will presume the husband and wife conformable to the sentence of separation, unless access be proved: but in a voluntary separation of agreement, the law will suppose access, unless the negative be shown. So, also, if there is an apparent impossibility of procreation on the part of the husband, as if he be only eight years old, or the like, there the issue of the wife shall be bastard. Likewise, in case of divorce in the spiritual court from the bond of matrimony, all the issue born during the coverture are bastards, because such divorce is always upon some cause, that rendered the marriage unlawful and null from the beginning.

ᛒᛒ   SUPPORT OF BASTARDS — Let us next see the duty of parents to their bastard children, by our law; which is principally that of maintenance. For, though bastards are not looked upon as children of any civil purposes, yet the ties of nature, of which maintenance is one, are not so easily dissolved: and they hold indeed as to many other intentions; as particularly, that a man shall not marry his bastard sister or daughter. The civil law, therefore, when it denied maintenance to bastards begotten under certain atrocious circumstances, was neither consonant to nature, nor reason.

The method in which the English law provides maintenance for them is as follows: when a woman is delivered, or declares herself with child, of a bastard, and will be oath before a justice of peace charge any person having got her with child, the justice shall cause such person to be apprehended, and commit him till he gives security, either to maintain the child, or appear at the next quarter sessions to dispute and try the fact. But if the woman dies, or is married before delivery, or miscarries, or proves not to have been with child, the person shall be discharged: otherwise the sessions, or two justices out of sessions, upon original application to them, may take order for the keeping of the bastard, by charging the mother or the reputed father with the payment of money or other sustentation for that purpose.

If such putative father, or lewd mother, run away from the parish, the overseers by directions of two justices may seize their rents, goods and chattels, in order to bring up the said bastard child. Yet such is the humanity of our laws, that no woman can be compulsively questioned concerning the father of her child, till one month after her delivery: which indulgence is, however, very frequently a hardship upon parishes, by giving the parents opportunity to escape.

ᛒᛒ   RIGHTS AND INCAPACITIES OF BASTARDS — The rights are very few, being only such as he can acquire; for he can inherit nothing, being looked upon as the son of nobody. Yet he may gain a surname by reputation, though he has none by inheritance. All other children have their primary settlement in their father's parish; but a bastard in the parish where born, for he hath no father. However, in case of fraud, as if a woman be sent either by order of justices, or comes to beg as a vagrant, to a parish which she does not belong, and drops her bastard there; the bastard shall, in the first case, be settled in the parish from whence she was illegally removed; or, in the latter case, in the mother's own parish, if the mother be apprehended for her vagrancy. Bastards also, born in any licensed hospital for pregnant women, are settled in the parishes to which the mothers belong. The incapacity of a bastard consists principally in this, that he cannot be heir to anyone, neither can he have heirs, but of his own body; for he is a kin to nobody, and has no ancestor from whom any inheritable blood can be derived.

A bastard was also, in strictness, incapable of holy orders; and, though that were dispensed with, yet he was utterly disqualified from holding any dignity in the church: but this doctrine seems now obsolete; and in all other respects, there is no distinction between a bastard and another man. Really any other distinction, but that of not inheriting, which civil policy renders necessary, could, with regard to the innocent offspring of his parents' crimes, be odious, unjust and cruel to the last degree, and yet the civil law, so boasted of for its equitable decisions, made bastards in some cases incapable even of a gift from their parents. A bastard may, lastly, be made legitimate, and capable of inheriting, by the transcendent power of an act of parliament, and not otherwise.

GUARDIAN AND WARD

⚖️ GUARDIAN AND WARD — The only general private relation, now remaining to be discussed, is that of guardian and ward; which bears a very near resemblance to the last, and is plainly derived out of it: the guardian being only a temporary parent; that is, for so long time as the ward is an infant, or under age.

⚖️ GUARDIANS — The guardian with us performs the office both of the tutor and curator of the Roman laws; the former of which had the charge of the maintenance and education of the minor, the latter the care of his fortune; or, according to the language of the court of chancery, the tutor was the committee of the person, the curator the committee of the estate. But this office was frequently united in the civil law, as it is always in our law with regard to minors, though as to lunatics and idiots it is commonly kept distinct.

⚖️ KINDS OF GUARDIANS — Of the several species of guardians, the first are guardians by nature: viz., the father and (in some cases) the mother of the child. For if an estate be left to an infant, the father is by common law the guardian, and must account to his child for the profits. With regard to daughters, it seems by the statute (Abduction, 1558), that the father might by deed or will assign a guardian to any woman child under the age of sixteen; and, if none be so assigned, the mother shall in this case be guardian.

There are also guardians for nurture; which are, of course, the father or mother, till the infant attains the age of fourteen years; in default of father or mother, the ordinary usually assigns some discreet person to take care of the infant's personal estate, and to provide for his maintenance and education.

Next are guardians in socage (an appelation which will be fully explained in the second book of these commentaries), who are also called guardians by the common law. These take place only when the minor is entitled to some estate in lands, and then by the common law the guardianship devolves upon his next of kin, to whom the inheritance cannot possibly descend; as, where the estate descended from his father, in this case his uncle by the mother's side cannot possibly inherit this estate, and therefore shall be the guardian.

The law judges it improper to trust the person of an infant in his hands, who may by possibility become heir to him; that there may be no temptation, nor even suspicion of temptation, for him to abuse his trust. These guardians in socage, like those for nurture, continue only till the minor is fourteen years of age; for then, in both cases, he is presumed to have discretion, so far as to choose his own guardian. This he may do, unless one be appointed by the father, by virtue of the statute (Military Tenures, 1660), which, considering the imbecility of judgment in children of the age of fourteen, and the abolition of guardianship in chivalry (which lasted till the age of twenty-one, and of which we shall speak hereafter) enacts, that any father, under age or of full age, may by deed or will dispose of the custody of his child, either born or unborn, to any person, except a popish recusant, either in possession or reversion, till such child attains the age of one and twenty years. These are called guardians by statute, or testamentary guardians.

⚖ RECIPROCAL RIGHTS AND DUTIES — The power and reciprocal duty of a guardian and ward are the same as that of a father and child; and therefore I shall not repeat them: but shall only add, that the guardian, when the ward comes of age, is bound to give him an account of all that has been transacted on his behalf, and must answer for all losses by his willful default or negligence. In order, therefore, to prevent disagreeable contests with young gentlemen, it has become a practice for many guardians, of large estates especially, to indemnify themselves by applying to the court of chancery, acting under its direction, and accounting annually before the officers of that court.

The lord chancellor is, by right derived from the crown, the general and supreme guardian of all infants, as well as idiots and lunatics; that is, of all such persons as have not discretion enough to manage their own concerns. In case, therefore, any guardian abuses his trust, the court will check and punish him; nay, sometimes will proceed to the removal of him, and appoint another in his stead.

⚖ WARDS — Let us next consider the ward or person within age, for whose assistance and support these guardians are constituted by law. The ages of male and female are different for different purposes. A male at twelve years old may take the oath of allegiance; at fourteen is at years of discretion, and therefore may consent or disagree to marriage, may choose his guardian, and if his discretion be actually proved, may make his testament of his personal estate; at seventeen may be an executor; and at twenty-one is at his own disposal, and may alien his lands, goods and chattels.

A female at seven years of age may be betrothed or given in marriage; at nine is entitled to dower, at twelve is at years of maturity, and therefore may consent or disagree to marriage, and, if proved to have sufficient discretion, may bequeath her personal estate; at fourteen is at years of legal discretion, and may choose a guardian; at seventeen may be executrix; and at twenty-one may dispose of herself and her lands. So that full age in male or female is twenty-one years, which age is completed on the day preceding the anniversary of a person's birth; who till that time is an infant, and so styled in law.

PRIVILEGES AND DISABILITIES OF INFANTS — Infants have various privileges, and various disabilities: but their very disabilities are privileges; in order to secure them from hurting themselves by their own inprovident acts. An infant cannot be sued but under the protection, and joining the name, of his guardian; for he is to defend him against all attacks as well by law as otherwise. He may sue either by his guardian, or his next friend who is not his guardian. This next friend may be any person who will undertake the infant's cause; and it frequently happens that an infant, by his next friend, institutes a suit in equity against a fraudulent guardian.

In criminal cases, an infant of the age of fourteen years may be capitally punished for any capital offense: but under the age of seven he cannot. The period between seven and fourteen is subject to uncertainty: for the infant shall, generally speaking be judged prima facie innocent; yet if he was capable of deceit; and could discern between good and evil at the time of the offense committed, he may be convicted and undergo judgment and execution of death, though he hath not attained to years of puberty or discretion. In such cases the maxim of law is, that malice, or the intention to do a wrongful act, makes up for the want of mature years.

With regard to estates and civil property, an infant hath many privileges, which will be better understood when we come to treat more particularly to those matters; but this may be said in general, that an infant shall lose nothing by nonclaim, or neglect of demanding his right;

nor shall any other laches or negligence be imputed to an infant, except in some very particular cases.

⚖ CONTRACTS AND CONVEYANCES OF INFANTS — It is generally true, that an infant can neither alien his lands nor do any legal act, nor make a deed, nor, indeed, any manner of contract, that will bind him. But still to all these rules there are some exceptions: part of which were just now mentioned in reckoning up the different capacities which they assume at different ages; and there are others, a few of which it may not be improper to recite, as a general specimen of the whole. First, it is true that infants cannot alien their estates, but infant trustees or mortgagees, are enabled to convey, under the direction of the court of chancery or exchequer, or other courts of equity, the estates they hold in trust or mortgage, to such person as the court shall appoint. Also it is generally true, that an infant can do no legal act.

An infant may also purchase lands, but his purchase is incomplete: for, when he comes to age, he may either agree or disagree to it, as he thinks prudent or proper, without alleging any reason; and so may his heirs after him, if he dies without having completed his agreement. It is, further, generally true, that an infant, under twenty-one can make no deed but what is afterwards voidable: yet in some cases he may bind himself apprentice by deed indented or indentures, for seven years; and he may by deed or will appoint a guardian to his children, if he has any.

Lastly, it is generally true, that an infant can make no other contract that will bind him: yet he may bind himself to pay for his necessary meat, drink, apparel, physic, and such other necessaries; and likewise for his good teaching and instruction, whereby he may profit himself afterwards.

CORPORATIONS

⚖ CORPORATIONS: ARTIFICIAL PERSONS — We have hitherto considered
persons in their natural capacities, and have treated of their rights
and duties. But, as all personal rights die with the person, and, as the
necessary forms of investing a series of individuals, one after another,
with the same identical rights, would be very inconvenient, if not impracticable; it has been found necessary when it is for the advantage of
the public to have any particular rights kept on foot and continued, to
constitute artificial persons, who may maintain a perpetual succession,
and enjoy a kind of legal immortality.

These artificial persons are called bodies politic, or corporations
of which there is a great variety subsisting, for the advancement of
religion, of learning, and of commerce; in order to preserve entire and
forever those rights and immunities, which, if they were granted only
to those individuals of which the body corporate is composed, would
upon their death be utterly lost and extinct.

To show the advantages of these incorporations, let us consider
the case of a college in either of our universities, founded for study and
prayer, for the encouragement and support of religion and learning. If
this was a mere voluntary assembly, the individuals which compose it
might indeed read, pray, study, and perform scholastic exercises together, so long as they could agree to do so: but they could neither frame,
nor receive any laws or rules for their conduct; none at least, which
would have any binding force, for want of a coercive power to create
a sufficient obligation. Neither could they be capable of retaining any
privileges or immunities: for, if such privileges be attacked, which of all
this unconnected assembly has the right, or ability to defend them?
When they are dispersed by death or otherwise, how shall they
transfer these advantages to another set of students, equally unconnected
as themselves?

So, also, with regard to holding estates or other property, if land be granted for the purposes of religion or learning to twenty individuals not incorporated, there is no legal way of continuing the property to any other persons for the same purposes, but by endless conveyances from one to the other, as often as the hands are changed. But when they are consolidated and united into a corporation, they and their successors are then considered as one person in law: as one person, they have one will, which is collected from the sense of the majority of the individuals: this one will may establish rules and orders for the regulation of the whole, which are a sort of municipal laws of this little republic; or rules and statutes may be prescribed to it at its creation, which are then in the place of natural laws: the privileges and immunities, the estates and possessions, of the corporation, when once invested in them, will be forever vested, without any new conveyance to new successions; for all the individual members that have existed from the foundation to the present time, or that shall ever hereafter exist, are but one person in law, a person that never dies; in like manner as the River Thames is still the same river, though the parts which compose it are changing every instant.

CORPORATIONS AGGREGATE: CORPORATIONS SOLE — The first division of corporations is into aggregate and sole. Corporations aggregate consist of many persons united together into one society, and are kept up by a perpetual succession of members, so as to continue forever: of which kind are the mayor and commonalty of a city, the head and fellows of a college, the dean and chapter of a cathedral church. Corporations sole consist of one person only and his successors, in some particular station, who are incorporated by law, in order to give them such legal capacities and advantages, particularly that of perpetuity, which in their natural persons they could not have had. In this sense the king is a sole corporation: so is a bishop: so is every parson and vicar.

The necessity, or at least use, of this institution will be very apparent, if we consider the case of a parson of a church. At the original endowment of parish churches, the freehold of the church, the churchyard, the parsonage house, the glebe, and the tithes of the parish, were vested in the parson by the bounty of the donor, as a temporal recompense to him for his spiritual care of the inhabitants, and with intent that the same emoluments should ever afterwards continue as a recompense for the same care. But how was this to be effected? The freehold was vested in the parson; and, if we suppose it vested in his natural capacity, on his death it might descend to his heir, and would liable to his debts and encumbrances: or, at best, the heir might be compellable, at some trouble and expense, to convey these rights to the succeeding incumbent. The law, therefore, has wisely ordained that the parson, as parson, shall never die, any more than the king; by making him and his successors a corporation. By which means all the original rights of the parsonage are preserved entire to the successor: for the present incumbent, and his predecessor who lived seven centuries ago, are in law one and the same person; and what was given to the one was given to the other also.

⚖ ECCLESIASTICAL CORPORATIONS — Another division of corporations, either sole or aggregate, is into ecclesiastical and lay. Ecclesiastical corporations are where the members that compose it are entirely spiritual persons; such as bishops; certain deans, archdeacons, parsons, and vicars; which are sole corporations: deans and chapters at present, and formerly prior and convent, abbot and monks, and the like, bodies aggregate. These are erected for the furtherance of religion, and perpetuating the rights of the church.

⚖ LAY CORPORATIONS: (1) CIVIL CORPORATIONS, (2) ELEEMOSYNARY CORPORATIONS — Lay corporations are of two sorts: civil and eleemosynary. The civil are such as are erected for a variety of temporal purposes. The king, for instance, is made a corporation to prevent in general the possibility of vacancy of the throne, and to preserve the possession of the crown entire; for, immediately upon the demise of one king, his successor, is, as we have formerly seen, in full possession of the regal rights and dignity.

Other lay corporations are erected for the good government of a town or particular district, as a mayor and commonalty, or the like: some for the advancement and regulation of manufacturers and commerce; as the trading companies of London, and other towns: and some for the better carrying on of divers special purposes; as churchwardens, for conservation of the goods of the parish; the college of physicians and company of surgeons of London, for the improvement of the medical science; the general corporate bodies of the universities of Oxford and Cambridge: for it is clear they are not spiritual or ecclesiastical corporations, being composed of more laymen than clergy: neither are they eleemosynary foundations, though stipends are annexed to particular magistrates and professors, any more than other corporations where the acting officers have standing salaries; for these are rewards for work and labor, not charitable donations only, since every stipend is preceded by service and duty: they seem therefore, to be merely civil corporations.

The eleemosynary sort are such as are constituted for the perpetual distribution of the free alms, or bounty, of the founder of them to such persons as he has directed. Of this kind are all hospitals for the maintenance of the poor, sick and impotent; and all colleges, both in our universities and out of them: which colleges, are founded for two purposes; 1. For the promotion of piety and learning by proper regulations and ordinances. 2. For imparting assistance to the members of those bodies, in order to enable them to prosecute their devotion and studies with greater ease and assiduity. All these eleemosynary corporations are, strictly speaking, lay and not ecclesiastical, even though composed of ecclesiastical persons, and although they in some things partake of the nature, privileges, and restrictions of ecclesiastical bodies.

Having thus marshaled the several species of corporations, let us next proceed to consider, 1. How corporations, in general, may be created. 2. What are their powers, capacities, and incapacities. 3. How corporations are visited. 4. How they may be dissolved.

CREATION OF CORPORATIONS — Corporations, by the civil law, seem to have been created by the mere act, and voluntary association of their members; provided such convention was not contrary to law. It does not appear that the prince's consent was necessary, but merely that the original founders of these voluntary and friendly societies (for they were little more than such) should not establish any meetings in opposition to the laws of the state.

CORPORATIONS BY COMMON LAW, CORPORATIONS BY PRESCRIPTION — The king's consent is absolutely necessary to the erection of any corporation, either impliedly or expressly given. The king's implied consent is to be found in corporations which exist by force of the common law, to which our former kings were supposed to have given their concurrence. Of this sort are the king himself, all bishops, parsons, vicars, churchwardens, and some others; who by common law have ever been held (as far as our books can show us) to have been corporations.

Another method of implication whereby the king's consent is presumed, is as to all corporations by prescription, such as the city of London, and many others, which have existed as corporations, time whereof the memory of man runneth not to the contrary; and therefore are looked upon in law to be well created. For though the members thereof can show no legal charter of incorporation, yet in cases of such high antiquity the law presumes there once was one; and that by the variety of accidents, which a length of time may produce, the charter is lost or destroyed.

CONSENT OF KING, HOW GIVEN: BY PARLIAMENT — The methods, by which the king's consent is expressly given, are either by act of parliament or charter. By act of parliament, of which the royal assent is a necessary ingredient, corporations may undoubtedly be created; but it is observable, that most of those statutes, which are usually cited as having created corporations, do either confirm such as have been before created by the king; as in the case of the college of physicians, erected by charter (1518), which charter was afterwards confirmed in parliament; or, they permit the king to erect a corporation in futuro with such and such powers; as is the case of the bank of England. So that the immediate creative act is usually performed by the king alone, in virtue of his royal prerogative.

BY CHARTER — All the other methods, therefore, whereby corporations exist, by common law, by prescription, and by act of parliament, are for the most part reducible to this of the king's letters patent, or charter of incorporation.

POWER OF PARLIAMENT TO CREATE CORPORATIONS — The parliament, we observe, by its absolute and transcendent authority, may perform this, or any other act whatsoever: and actually did perform it to a great extent, by statute (Workhouses, 1597), which incorporated all hospitals and houses of correction founded by charitable persons, without further trouble: and the same has been done in other cases of charitable foundations. But otherwise it has not formerly been usual thus to intrench upon the prerogative of the crown, and the king may prevent it when he pleases.

CREATION OF CORPORATIONS BY PATENT — The king (it is said) may grant to a subject the power of erecting corporations, though the contrary was formerly held: that is, he may permit the subject to name the persons and powers of the corporation at his pleasure; but it is really the king that erects, and the subject is but the instrument; for though none but the king can make a corporation, yet he who does a thing by the agency of another, does it himself.

CORPORATE NAME — When a corporation is erected, a name must be given to it; and by that name alone it must sue, and be sued, and do all legal acts; though a very minute variation therein is not material.

Such name is the very being of its constitution; and, though it is the will of the king that erects the corporation, yet the name is the knot of its combination, without which it could not perform its corporate functions.

POWERS OF A CORPORATION — After a corporation is so formed and named; it acquires many powers, rights, capacities, and incapacities, which we are next to consider. Some of these are necessarily and inseparably incident to every corporation; which incidents, as soon as a corporation is duly erected, are tacitly annexed of course, as

1. To have perpetual succession. This is the very end of its incorporation: for there cannot be a succession forever without an incorporation; and therefore all aggregate corporations have a power necessarily implied of electing members in the room of such as go off.

2. To sue or be sued, implead or be impleaded, grant or receive, by its corporation name, and do all other acts as natural persons may.

3. To purchase lands, and hold them, for the benefit of themselves and their successors: which two are consequential to the former.

4. To have a common seal. For a corporation, being an invisible body, cannot manifest its intentions by any personal act or oral discourse; it therefore acts and speaks only by its common seal. For, though the particular members may express their private consents to any act, by words, or signing their names, yet this does not bind the corporation; it is the fixing of the seal, and that only, which unites the several assents of the individuals, who compose the community, and makes one joint assent of the whole.

5. To make by-laws or private statutes for the better government of the corporation; which are binding upon themselves, unless contrary to the laws of the land, and then they are void. This is also included by law in the very act of incorporation: for, as natural reason is given to the natural body for the governing it, so by-laws or statutes are a sort of political reason to govern the body politic. But no trading company is allowed to make by-laws, which may affect the king's prerogative, or the common profit of the people, under penalty of 40 pounds, unless they be approved by the chancellor, treasurer, and chief justices, or the judges of assize in their circuits: and, even though they be so approved, still if contrary to law they are void.

These five powers are inseparably incident to every corporation, at least to every corporation aggregate: for two of them, though they may be practiced, yet are very unnecessary to a corporation sole; viz., to have a corporate seal to testify his sole assent, and to make statutes for the regulations of his own conduct.

⚖️   PRIVILEGES AND DISABILITIES — There are also certain privileges and disabilities that attend an aggregate corporation, and are not applicable to such as are sole; the reason for them ceasing, and of course the law. It must always appear by attorney: for it cannot appear in person. It can neither maintain nor be made defendant to, an action of battery or such like personal injuries; for a corporation can neither beat, nor be beaten, in its body politic. A corporation cannot commit treason, or felony, or other crime, in its corporate capacity: though its members may, in their distinct individual capacities.

Neither is it capable of suffering a traitor's or felon's punishment, for it is not liable to corporal penalties, not to attainder, forfeiture, or corruption of blood. It cannot be executor or administrator, or perform any personal duties; for it cannot take an oath for the due execution of the office. It cannot be seised of lands to the use of another; for such kind of confidence is foreign to the end of its institution. Neither can it be committed to prison; for its existence being ideal, no man can apprehend or arrest it.

It cannot be outlawed; for outlawry always supposes a precedent right of arresting, which has been defeated by the parties absconding, and that also a corporation cannot do: for which reasons the proceedings to compel a corporation to appear to any suit by attorney are always by distress on their lands and goods. Neither can a corporation be excommunicated; for it has no soul.

There are also other incidents and powers, which belong to some sort of corporations and not to others. An aggregate corporation may take goods and chattels for the benefit of themselves and their successors, but a sole corporation cannot; for such movable property is liable to be lost or embezzled, and would raise a multitude of disputes between the successor and executor; which the law is careful to avoid.

In ecclesiastical and eleemosynary foundations, the king or the founder may give them rules, laws, statutes, and ordinances, which they are bound to observe: but corporations merely lay, constituted for civil purposes, are subject to no particular statutes; but to the common law, and to their own by-laws, not contrary to the laws of the realm.

Aggregate corporations also, that have by their constitution a head, as a dean, warden, master, or the like, cannot do any acts during the vacancy of the headship, except only appointing another: neither are they then capable of receiving a grant; for such corporation is incomplete without a head. But there may be a corporation aggregate constituted without a head: as the governors of the Charter-house, London, who have no president or superior, but are all of equal authority.

⚖ CORPORATIONS ACT BY MAJORITY — In aggregate corporations also, the act of the major part is esteemed the act of the whole. By the civil law this major part must have consisted of two-thirds of the whole; also no act could be performed: which, perhaps, may be one reason why they required three at least to make a corporation. But, with us, any majority is sufficient to determine the act of the whole body. Whereas, notwithstanding the law stood thus, some founders of corporations had made statutes in derogation of the common law, making very frequently the unanimous assent of the society to be necessary to any corporate act; it was therefore enacted by statute (Corporation, 1541), that all private statutes shall be utterly void, whereby any grant or election, made by the head, with the concurrence of the major part of the body, is liable to be obstructed by any one or more, being the minority: but this statute extends not to any negative or necessary voice, given by the founder to the head of any such society.

⚖ POWER TO PURCHASE LANDS — We before observed that it was incident to every corporation, to have a capacity to purchase lands for themselves and successors: and this is regularly true at the common law. But they are excepted out of the statute of wills: so that no devise of lands to a corporation by will is good: except for charitable uses, by statute (Charitable Gifts, 1601): Which exception is again greatly narrowed by the statute (Charitable Uses, 1736). Also, by a great variety of statutes, their privilege even of purchasing from any living grantor is much abridged; so that now a corporation, either ecclesiastical or lay, must have a license from the king to purchase, before they can exert that capacity which is vested in them by the common law: nor is even this in all cases sufficient. These statutes are generally called the statutes of mortmain; all purchases made by corporate bodies being said to be purchases in a dead-hand: for the reason that these purchases being usually made by ecclesiastical bodies, the members of which (being professed) were reckoned dead persons in law, land therefore, holden by them, might with great propriety be said to be held in a dead-hand.

⚖ DUTIES OF CORPORATIONS — The general duties of all bodies politic, considered in their corporate capacity, may, like those of natural persons, be reduced to this single one; that of acting up to the end or design, whatever it be, for which they were created by their founder.

⚖ VISITATION OF CORPORATIONS — I proceed, therefore, next to inquire, how these corporations may be visited. For corporations being composed of individuals, subject to human frailties, are liable as well as private persons, to deviate from the end of their institution. For that reason the law has provided proper persons to visit, inquire into, and correct all irregularities that arise in such corporations, either sole or aggregate, and whether ecclesiastical, civil, or eleemosynary.

With regard to all ecclesiastical corporations, the ordinary is their visitor, so constituted by the canon law, and from whence derived to us. The pope formerly, and now the king, as supreme ordinary, is the visitor of the archbishop or metropolitan; the metropolitan has the charge and coercion of all his suffragan bishops; and the bishops in their several dioceses are in ecclesiastical matters the visitors of all deans and chapters, of all persons and vicars, and of all other spiritual corporations.

⚖ CIVIL CORPORATIONS — I know it is generally said, that civil corporations are subject to no visitation, but merely to the common law of the land; and this shall be presently explained. But first, as I have laid it down as a rule that the founder, his heirs, or assigns, are the visitors of all lay corporations, let us inquire what is meant by the founder.

The founder of all corporations in the strictest and original sense is the king alone, for he only can incorporate a society; and in civil incorporations, such as mayor and commonalty, etc., where there are no possession or endowments given to the body, there is no other founder but the king: but in eleemosynary foundations, such as colleges and hospitals, where there is an endowment of lands, the law distinguishes, and makes two species of foundation; the one, the incorporation, in which sense the king is the general founder of all colleges and hospitals; the other the dotation of it, in which sense the first gift of the revenues is the foundation, and he who gives them is in law the founder: it is this last sense that we generally call a man the founder of a college or hospital. But here the king has his prerogative: for if the king and a private man join in endowing an eleemosynary foundation, the king alone shall be the founder of it. In general, the king being the sole founder of all civil corporations, and the endower the perficient founder of all eleemosynary ones, the right of visitation of the former results, according to the laid down, to the king; and of the latter to the patron or endower.

The king being thus constituted by law visitor of all civil corporations, the law has also appointed the place, wherein he shall exercise this jurisdiction: which is the court of king's bench; where and where only, all misbehaviors of this kind of corporations are inquired into and redressed, and all their controversies decided. This is what I understand to be the meaning of our lawyers, when they say that these civil corporations are liable to no visitation; that is, that the law having by immemorial usage appointed them to be visited and inspected by the king their founder, in his majesty's court of king's bench, according to the rules of the common law, they ought not to be visited elsewhere, or by any other authority.

This is so strictly true, that though the king by his letters patent had subjected the college of physicians to the visitation of four very respectable persons, the lord chancellor, the two chief justices, and the chief baron; though the college had accepted this charter with all possible marks of acquiescence; and had acted under it for near a century; yet in 1753, the authority of this provision coming in dispute, on an appeal preferred to these supposed visitors, they directed the legality of their own appointment to be argued: and as this college was merely a civil and not an eleemosynary foundation, they at least determined, upon several days solemn debate, that they had no jurisdiction as visitors; and remitted the appellant (if aggrieved) to his regular remedy in his majesty's court of king's bench.

⚖ ELEEMOSYNARY CORPORATIONS — As to eleemosynary corporations, by the dotation the founder and his heirs are of common right the legal visitors, to see that such property is rightly employed, as might otherwise have descended to the visitor himself: but, if the founder has appointed and assigned any other person to be visitor, then his assignee so appointed is invested with all the founder's power, in exclusion of his heir. Eleemosynary corporations are chiefly hospitals, or colleges in the universities.

⚖ COLLEGES — Colleges in the universities (whatever the common law may now, or might formerly, judge) were certainly considered by the popish clergy, under whose direction they were as ecclesiastical, or at least as clerical corporations; and therefore the right of visitation was claimed by the ordinary of the diocese. But, whatever might be formerly the opinion of the clergy, it is now held as established common law that colleges are lay corporations, though sometimes totally composed of ecclesiastical persons; and that the right of visitation does not arise from any principles of the canon law, but of necessity was created by the common law.

⚖ DISSOLUTION OF CORPORATIONS — We come now, in the last place, to consider how corporations may be dissolved. Any particular member may be disfranchised, or lose his place in the corporation, by acting contrary to the laws of the society, or the laws of the land: or he may resign it by his own voluntary act. But the body politic may also itself be dissolved in several ways; which dissolution is the civil death of the corporation: and in this case their lands and tenements shall revert to the person, or his heirs, who granted them to the corporation; for the law doth annex a condition to every such grant, that if the corporation be dissolved, the grantor shall have the lands again, because the cause of the grant faileth. The grant is, indeed, only during the life of the corporation, which may endure forever: but, when that life is determined by the dissolution of the body politic, the grantor takes it back by reversion, as in the case of every other grant for life.

The debts of a corporation, either to or from it, are totally extinguished by its dissolution; so that the members thereof cannot recover, or be charged with them, in their natural capacities: Agreeable to that maxim of the civil law—"whatever be due to a corporation is not due to each member singly; nor is each singly answerable for the debts due from the corporation."

METHODS OF DISSOLUTION — A corporation may be dissolved:

1. By act of parliament, which is boundless in its operations.

2. By the natural death of all its members, in cases of an aggregate corporation.

3. By surrender of its franchises into the hands of the king, which is a kind of suicide.

4. By forfeiture of its charter, through negligence or abuse of its franchises; in which case the law judges that the body politic has broken the condition upon which it was incorporated, and thereupon the incorporation is void.

The regular course is to bring an information in nature of a writ of quo warranto (by what warrant or authority), to inquire by what warrant the members now exercise their corporate power, having forfeited it by such and such proceedings. Because by the common law corporations were dissolved, in case the mayor or head officer was not duly elected on the day appointed in the charter or established by prescription, it is now provided, that for the future no corporation shall be dissolved upon that account; and ample directions are given for appointing a new officer, in case there be no election, or a void one, made upon the charter or prescriptive day.

The Rights of
Things

PROPERTY IN GENERAL

☙☙ RIGHT OF PROPERTY — The former book of these commentaries having treated at large of the rights and duties as are annexed to the persons of men, the objects of our inquiry in this second book will be those rights which a man may acquire in and to such external things as are unconnected with his person. These are what the writers on natural law style the rights of dominion, or property concerning in nature and original of which I shall first premise a few observations, before I proceed to distribute and consider its several objects.

☙☙ ORIGIN OF PROPERTY — There is nothing which so generally strikes the imagination, and engages the affections of mankind, as the right of property; or that sole and despotic dominion which one man claims and exercises over the external things of the world, in total exclusion of the right of any other individual in the universe.

Yet there are very few that will give themselves the trouble to consider the original and foundation of this right. Pleased as we are with the possession, we seem afraid to look back to the means by which it was acquired, as if fearful of some defect in our title; or at best we rest satisfied with the decision of the laws in our favor, without examining the reason or authority upon which these laws have been built.

We think it enough that our title is derived by the grant of the former proprietor, by descent from our ancestors, or by the last will and testament of the dying owners; not caring to reflect that (accurately and strictly speaking) there is no foundation in nature or in natural law shy a set of words upon parchment should convey the dominion of land; why the son should have a right to exclude his fellow-creatures from a determinate spot of ground, because his father had done so before him; or why the occupier of a particular field of a jewel, when lying on his death-bed and no longer able to maintain possession, should be entitled to tell the rest of the world which of them should enjoy it after him.

These inquiries, it must be owned, would be useless and even troublesome in common life. It is well if the mass of mankind will obey the laws when made, without scrutinizing too nicely into the reasons of making them. But, when law is to be considered not only as a matter of practice, but also as a rational science, it cannot be improper or useless to examine more deeply the rudiments and grounds of these positive constitutions of society.

In the beginning of the world, we are informed by holy writ, the all-bountiful Creator gave to man "dominion over all the earth; and over the fish of the sea, and over the fowl of the air, and over every living thing that moveth upon the earth." This is the only true and solid foundation of man's dominion over external things, whatever airy metaphysical notions may have been started by fanciful writers upon this subject.

The earth, therefore, and all things therein, are the general property of all mankind, exclusive of other beings, from the immediate gift of the Creator. And, while the earth continued bare of inhabitants, it is reasonable to suppose, that all was in common among them, and that everyone took from the public stock to his own use such things as his immediate necessities required.

OWNERSHIP IN COMMON — These general notions of property were then sufficient to answer all the purposes of human life; and might perhaps still have answered them had it been possible for mankind to have remained in a state of primeval simplicity: as may be collected from the manners of many American nations when first discovered by the Europeans; and from the ancient method of living among the first Europeans themselves, if we may credit either the memorials of them preserved in the golden age of the poets or the uniform accounts given by historians of those times, wherein all things were common and undivided, as if there were but one patrimony for them all. Not that this communion of goods seems ever to have been applicable, even in the earliest ages, to aught but the substance of the thing; nor could it be extended to the use of it.

By the law of nature and reason, he who first began to use it acquired therein a kind of transient property, that lasted so long as he was using it and no longer; or, to speak with greater precision, the right of possession continued for the same time only that the act of possession lasted. Thus the ground was in common, and no part of it was the permanent property of any man in particular; yet whoever was in the occupation of any determinate spot of it, for rest, for shade, or the like, acquired for the time a sort of ownership, from which it would have been unjust, and contrary to the law of nature, to have driven him by force; but the instant that he quitted the use or occupation of it, another might seize it without injustice.

Thus also a vine or other tree might be said to be in common, as all men were equally entitled to its produce; and yet any private individual might gain the sole property of the fruit, which he had gathered for his own repast. A doctrine well illustrated by Cicero, who compares the world to a great theater, which is common to the public, and yet the place which any man has taken is for the time his own.

INDIVIDUAL OWNERSHIP — But when mankind increased in number, craft and ambition, it became necessary to entertain conceptions of more permanent dominion; and to appropriate to individuals not the immediate use only, but the very substance of the thing to be used. Otherwise, innumerable tumults must have arisen, and the good order of the world been continually broken and disturbed, while a variety of persons striving who should get the first occupation of the same thing, or disputing which of them had actually gained it. As human life also grew more and more refined, abundance of conveniences were devised to render it more easy, commodious, and agreeable; as, habitations for shelter and safety, and raiment for warmth and decency. But no man would be at the trouble to provide either, so long as he had only an usufructuary property in them, which was to cease the instant that he quitted possession; if, as soon as he walked out of his tent, or pulled off his garment, the next stranger who came by would have a right to inhabit the one, and to wear the other.

In the case of habitations in particular, it was natural to observe, that even the brute creation, to whom everything else was in common, maintained a kind of permanent property in their dwellings, especially for the protection of their young; that the birds of the air had nests, and the beasts of the field had caverns, the invasion of which they esteemed a very flagrant injustice, and would sacrifice their lives to preserve them. Hence a property was soon established in every man's house and homestall; which seems to have been originally mere temporary huts or movable cabins, suited to the design of Providence for more speedily peopling the earth, and suited to the wandering life of their owners, before any extensive property in the soil or ground was established.

There can be no doubt but that movables of every kind become sooner appropriated than the permanent substantial soil: partly because they were more susceptible of a long occupancy, which might be continued for months together without any sensible interruption, and at length by usage ripen into an established right; but principally because few of them could be fit for use, till improved and ameliorated by the bodily labor of the occupant: which bodily labor, bestowed upon any subject which before lay in common to all men, is universally allowed to give the fairest and most reasonable title to an exclusive property therein.

⚖   OWNERSHIP OF ANIMALS AND WELLS — The article of food was a more immediate call, and therefore a more early consideration. Such as were not contented with the spontaneous product of the earth sought for a more solid refreshment in the flesh of beasts, which they obtained by hunting. But the frequent disappointments, incident to that method of provision, induced them to gather together such animals as were of a more tame and sequacious nature; and to establish a permanent property in their flocks and herds, in order to sustain themselves in a less precarious manner, partly by the milk of their dams and partly by the flesh of the young.

The support of these their cattle made the article of water also a very important point. And therefore the book of Genesis (the most venerable monument of antiquity, considered merely with a view to history) will furnish us with frequent instances of violent contentions concerning wells; the exclusive property of which appears to have been established in the first digger or occupant, even in such places where the ground and herbage remained yet in common. Thus we find Abraham, who was but a sojourner, asserting his right to a well in the country of Abimelech, and exacting an oath for his security, "because he had digged that well." And Isaac, about ninety years afterwards, reclaimed this his father's property; and, after much contention with the Philistines, was suffered to enjoy it in peace.

⚖   OWNERSHIP OF LAND — All this while the soil and pasture of the earth remained still in common as before, and open to every occupant: except, perhaps, in the neighborhood of towns, where the necessity of a sole and exclusive property in lands (for the sake of agriculture) was earlier felt, and therefore more readily complied with. Otherwise when the multitude of men and cattle had consumed every convenience on one spot of ground, it was deemed a natural right to seize upon and occupy such other lands as would more easily supply their necessities

We have a striking example of the same kind in the history of Abraham and his nephew Lot. When their joint substance became so great that pasture and other conveniences grew scarce, the natural consequence was that a strife arose between their servants; so that it was no longer practicable to dwell together. This contention Abraham thus endeavored to compose: "Let there be no strife, I pray thee, between thee and me. Is not the whole land before thee? Separate thyself, I pray thee, from me. If thou wilt take the left hand then I will go to the right; or if thou depart to the right hand, then I will go to the left." This plainly implies an acknowledged right, in either, to occupy whatever ground he pleased, that was not preoccupied by other tribes. "And Lot lifted up his eyes, and beheld all the plain of Jordan, that it was well watered everywhere, even as the garden of the lord. Then Lot chose him all the plain of Jordan, and journeyed east; and Abraham dwelt in the land of Canaan."

Upon the same principle was founded the right of migration, or sending colonies to find out new habitation, when the mother country was overcharged with inhabitants.

As the world by degrees grew more populous, it daily became more difficult to find out new spots to inhabit, without encroaching upon former occupants; and, by constantly occupying the same individual spot, the fruits of the earth were consumed, and its spontaneous produce destroyed, without any provision for a future supply or succession. It therefore became necessary to pursue some regular method of providing a constant subsistence; and this necessity produced, or at least promoted and encouraged, the art of agriculture. The art of agriculture, by a regular connection and consequence, introduced and established the idea of a more permanent property in the soil than had hitherto been received and adopted.

It was clear that the earth would not produce her fruits in sufficient quantities, without the assistance of tillage: but who would be at the pains of tilling it, if another might watch an opportunity to seize upon and enjoy the product of his industry, art and labor? Had not, therefore, a separate property in lands, as well as movables, been vested in some individuals, the world must have continued a forest, and men have been mere animals of prey; which, according to some philosophers, is the genuine state of nature. Necessity begat property; and in order to insure that property, recourse was had to civil society, which brought along with it a long train of inseparable concomitants; states, government, laws, punishments, and the public exercise of religious duties. Thus connected together, it was found that a part only of society was sufficient to provide, by their manual labor, for the necessary subsistence of all; and leisure was given to others to cultivate the human mind, to invent useful arts, and to lay the foundations of science.

⚖ OCCUPANCY, ORIGINAL TITLE TO PROPERTY — The only question remaining is, how this property became actually vested: or what it is that gave a man an exclusive right to retain in a permanent manner that specific land, which before belonged generally to everybody, but particularly to nobody. And, as we before observed that occupancy gave the right to the temporary use of the soil, as it is agreed upon all hands that occupancy gave also the original right to the permanent property in the substance of the earth itself; which excludes everyone else but the owner from the use of it.

Property, both in lands and movables, being thus originally acquired by the first taker, which taking amounts to a declaration that he intends to appropriate the thing to his own use, it remains in him, but the principles of universal law, till such time as he does some other act which shows an intention to abandon it; for then it becomes, naturally speaking, of public right once more, and is liable to be again appropriated by the next occupant.

So if one is possessed of a jewel, and casts it into the sea or a public highway, this is such an express dereliction, that a property will be vested in the first fortunate finder that will seize it to his own use. But if he hides it privately in the earth or other secret place, and it is discovered, the finder acquires no property therein; for the owner hath not by this act declared any intention to abandon it, but rather the contrary; and if he loses or drops it by accident, it cannot be collected from thence that he designed to quit the possession; and therefore in such a case the property still remains in the loser, who may claim it again of the finder.

⚖ TRANSFER OF OWNERSHIP — But this method, of one man's abandoning his property, and another seizing the vacant possession, however well founded in theory, could not long subsist in fact. It was calculated merely for the rudiments of civil society, and necessarily ceased among the complicated interests and artificial refinements of polite and established governments. In these it was found, that what became inconvenient or useless to one man, was highly convenient and useful to another; who was ready to give in exchange for it some equivalent, that was equally desirable to the former proprietor.

This mutual convenience introduced commercial traffic, and the reciprocal transfer of property by sale, grant, or conveyance: which may be considered either as a continuance of the original possession which the first occupant had; or as an abandoning of the thing by the present owner, and an immediate successive occupancy of the same by the new proprietor. The voluntary dereliction of the owner, and delivering the possession to another individual, amount to a transfer of the property; the proprietor declaring his intention no longer to occupy the thing himself, but that his own right of occupancy shall be vested in the new acquirer.

⚖ SUCCESSION TO PROPERTY ON DEATH — The most universal and effectual way of abandoning property is by the death of the occupant: when both the actual possession and intention of keeping possession ceasing, the property which is founded upon such possession and intention ought also to cease of course. For, naturally speaking, the instant a man ceases to be, he ceases to have any dominion: else, if he had a right to dispose of his acquisitions one moment beyond his life, he would also have a right to direct their disposal for a million of ages after him; which would be highly absurd and inconvenient. All property must therefore cease upon death, considering men as absolute individuals, and unconnected with civil society: for then, by the principles before established, the next immediate occupant would acquire a right in all that the deceased possessed.

But as, under civilized governments which are calculated for the peace of mankind, such a constitution would be productive of endless disturbances, the universal law of almost every nation has either given the dying person a power of continuing his property by disposing of his possession by will; or, in case he neglects to dispose of it, or is not permitted to make any disposition at all, the municipal law of the country then steps in, and declares who shall be the successor, representative, or heirs of the deceased; that is, who alone shall have a right to enter upon this vacant possession, in order to avoid that confusion, which its becoming again common would occasion.

Further, in case no testament be permitted by the law, or none be made, and no heir can be found so qualified as the law requires, still, to prevent the robust title of occupancy from again taking place, the doctrine of escheats is adopted in almost every country whereby the sovereign of the state, and those who claim under his authority, are the ultimate heirs, and succeed to those inheritances, to which no other title can be formed.

☙☙ INTERSTATE SUCCESSION — The right of inheritance, or descent to the children and relations of the deceased, seems to have been allowed much earlier than the right of devising by testament. It is certainly wise and effectual, but clearly a political, establishment; since the permanent right of property, vested in the ancestor himself, was no natural, but merely a civil, right. It is true, that the transmission of one's possessions to posterity has an evident tendency to make a man a good citizen and a useful member of society; it sets the passions on the side of duty, and prompts a man to deserve well of the public, when he is sure that the reward of his services will not die with himself, but be transmitted to those with whom he is connected by the dearest and most tender affections.

Yet, reasonable as this foundation of the right of inheritance may seem it is probable that its immediate original arose not from speculations altogether so delicate and refined, and if not from fortuitous circumstances, at least, from a plainer and more simple principle. A man's children or nearest relations are usually about him on his death-bed, and are the earliest witnesses of his decease. They become, there-fore, generally the next immediate occupants, till at length in process of time this frequent usage ripened into general law. Also in the earliest ages, on failure of children, a man's servants born under his roof were allowed to be his heirs; being immediately on the spot when he died. For we find the old patriarch Abraham expressly declaring that "since God had given him no seed," his steward Eliezer, one born in his house, was his heir.

☙☙ TESTAMENTARY SUCCESSION — While the property continued only for life, testaments were useless and unknown; and, when it became in-heritable, the inheritance was long indefeasible, and the children or heirs at law were incapable of exclusion by will. Till at length it was found that so strict a rule of inheritance made heirs disobedient and headstrong, defrauded creditors on their just debts, and prevented many provident fathers from dividing or charging their estates as the exigency of their families required. This introduced pretty generally the right of disposing of one's property, or a part of it, by testament; that is, by written or oral instructions properly witnessed and authenticated, according to the pleasure of the deceased; which we therefore emphatically style his will.

In personal estates the father may succeed to his children; in landed property he never can be their immediate heir, by any the re-motest possibility: in general, only the eldest son, in some places the youngest, in others all the sons together, have a right to succeed to the inheritance: in real estate males are preferred to females, and the eldest male will usually exclude the rest; in the division of personal estates, the females of equal degree are admitted together with the males, and no right of primogeniture is allowed.

The positive law of England, directs it to vest in such person as the last proprietor shall by will, attended with certain requisites, appoint; and, in defect of such appointment, to go to some particular person, who from the result of certain local constitutions, appears to be the heir at law. Hence it follows, that, where the appointment is regularly made, there cannot be a shadow of right in anyone but the person appointed.

THINGS IN COMMON — But, after all, there are some few things, which notwithstanding the general introduction and continuance of property, must still unavoidably remain in common; being such wherein nothing but an usufructuary property is capable of being had: and therefore they still belong to the first occupant, during the time he holds possession of them, and no longer. Such (among others) are the elements of light, air, and water; which a man may occupy by means of his windows, his gardens, his mills, and other conveniences. Such, also, are the generality of those animals which are said to be wild by nature, or of a wild and untamable disposition which any man may seize upon and keep for his own use or pleasure. All these things, so long as they remain in possession, every man has a right to enjoy without disturbance; but if once they escape from his custody, or he voluntarily abandons the use of them, they return to the common stock, and any man else has an equal right to seize and enjoy them afterwards.

OWNERLESS THINGS — Again there are other things, in which a permanent property may subsist, not only as to the temporary use, but also the solid substance; and which yet would be frequently found without a proprietor, had not the wisdom of the law provided a remedy to obviate this inconvenience. Such are forests and other waste grounds, which were omitted to be appropriated in the general distribution of lands. Such also are wrecks, estrays, and that species of wild animals, which the arbitrary constitutions of positive law have distinguished from the rest by the well-known appellation of game.

With regard to these and some others, as disturbances and quarrels would frequently arise among individuals contending about the acquisition of this species of property by first occupancy, the law has therefore wisely cut up the root of dissension, by vesting the things themselves in the sovereign of the state; or else in his representatives appointed and authorized by him, being usually the lords of manors.

CORPOREAL HEREDITAMENTS

The objects of dominion or property are things, as contradistinguished from persons; and things are distributed into two kinds; things real, and things personal. Things real are such as are permanent, fixed and immovable, which cannot be carried out of their place; as lands and tenements; things personal are goods, money, and all other movables; which may attend the owner's person wherever he thinks proper to go.

In treating of things real, let us consider, first, their several sorts or kinds; secondly, the tenures by which they may be holden; thirdly, the estates which may be had in them; and fourthly, the title to them, and the manner of acquiring and losing it.

First, with regard to their several sorts or kinds, things real are usually said to consist in lands, tenements, or hereditaments.

⚖ LAND — Land comprehends all things of a permanent, substantial nature; being a word of a very extensive signification, as will presently appear more at large.

⚖ TENEMENTS — Tenement is a word of greater extent, and though in its vulgar acceptation is only applied to houses and other buildings, yet in its original, and legal sense it signifies everything that may be holden, provided it be of a permanent nature; whether it be of a substantial and sensible or of an unsubstantial kind. Thus frank-tenement, or freehold, is applicable not only to lands and other solid objects, but also to offices, rents, commons, and the like: and, as lands and houses are tenements, so is an advowson a tenement; and a franchise, an office, a right of common, a peerage, or other property of the like unsubstantial kind, are, all of them, legally speaking, tenements.

⚖ HEREDITAMENTS — But an hereditament is by much the largest and most comprehensive expression: for it includes not only lands and tenements, but whatsoever may be inherited, be it corporeal, or incorporeal, real, personal or mixed. Thus an heirloom, or implement of furniture which by custom descends to the heir together with an house, is neither land, nor tenement, but a mere movable; yet, being inheritable is comprised under the general word "hereditament": and so a condition, the benefit of which may descend to a man from his ancestor, is also an hereditament.

Hereditaments, then are of two kinds: corporeal and incorporeal. Corporeal consist of such as affect the senses; such as may be seen and handled by the body: incorporeal are not the object of sensation, can neither be seen nor handled, are creatures of the mind, and exist only in contemplation.

Corporeal hereditaments consist wholly of substantial and permanent objects; all which may be comprehended under the general denomination of land only. For land comprehendeth in its legal signification any ground, soil, or earth whatsoever; as arable meadows, pastures, woods, moors, waters, marshes and heath. It legally includeth also all castles, houses, and other buildings: for they consist of two things; land, which is the foundation, and structure thereupon: so that, if I convey the land or ground, the structure or building passeth therewith.

It is observable that water is here mentioned as a species of land, which may seem a kind of solecism; but such is the language of the law: and therefore I cannot bring an action to recover possession of a pool or other piece of water, by the name of water only; either by calculating its capacity, as, for so many cubical yards; or, by superficial measure, for twenty acres of water; or by general description, as for a pond, a watercourse, or a rivulet; but I must bring my action for the land that lies at the bottom, and must call it twenty acres of land covered with water. For water is a movable, wandering thing, and must of necessity continue common by the law of nature; so that I can only have a temporary, transient, property therein; wherefore, if a body of water runs out of my pond into another man's, I have no right to reclaim it. But the land which that water covers is permanent, fixed, and immovable: and therefore in this I may have a certain, substantial property; of which the law will take notice.

Land hath also, in its legal signification, an indefinite extent, upwards as well as downwards. He who owns the ground possesses also to the sky, is the maxim of the law, upwards; therefore no man may erect any building, or the like to overhang another's land; and, downwards, whatever is in a direct line between the surface of any land and the center of the earth, belongs to the owner of the surface; as is every day's experience in mining countries. So that the word "land" includes not only the face of the earth, but everything under it, or over it. Therefore, if a man grants all his lands, he grants thereby all his mines of metal and other fossils, his woods, his waters, and his houses, as well as his fields and meadows. The particular names of the things are equally sufficient to pass them, except in the instance of water; by a grant of which, nothing passes but a right of fishing; but the capital distinction in this; that by the name of a castle, messuage, toft, croft, or the like, nothing else will pass, except what falls with the ulmost propriety under the term made use of, but by the name of land, which is the most general name, everything terrestrial will pass.

INCORPOREAL HEREDITAMENTS

CHARACTER OF AN INCORPOREAL HEREDITAMENT — An incorporeal hereditament is a right issuing out of a thing corporate (whether real or personal) or concerning, or annexed to, or exercisable within, the same, it is not the thing corporate itself, which may consist in lands, houses, jewels, or the like; but something collateral thereto, as a rent issuing out of those lands or houses, or an office relating to those jewels. As the logicians speak, corporeal hereditaments are the substance, which may be always seen, always handled: incorporeal hereditaments are but a sort of accidents, which inhere in and are supported by that substance; and may belong or not belong to it, without any visible alteration therein. Their existence is merely in idea and abstracted contemplation; though their effects and profits may be frequently objects of our bodily senses. Indeed, if we would fix a clear notion of an incorporeal hereditament, we must be careful not to confound together the profits produced, and the thing, or hereditament, which produces them.

An annuity, for instance, is an incorporeal hereditament: for though the money, which is the fruit or product of this annuity, is doubtless of a corporeal nature, yet the annuity itself, which produces that money, is a thing invisible, has only a mental existence, and cannot be delivered over from hand to hand. So tithes, if we consider the produce of them, as the tenth sheaf or tenth lamb, seem to be completely corporeal; yet they are indeed incorporeal hereditaments: for they, being merely a contingent right, collateral to or issuing out of lands, can never be the object of sense: they are neither capable of being shown to the eye, nor of being delivered into bodily possession.

KINDS OF INCORPOREAL HEREDITAMENTS — Incorporeal hereditaments are principally of ten sorts; advowsons, tithes, commons, ways, offices, dignities, franchises, corodies or pensions, annuities, and rents.

⚖ ADVOWSONS — Advowson is the right of presentation to a church, or ecclesiastical benefice. Advowson signifies the taking into protection; and therefore is synonymous with patronage; and he who has the right of advowson is called the patron of the church. For, when lords of manors first built churches on their own demesnes, and appointed the tithes of those manors to be paid to the officiating ministers, the lord, who thus built a church, and endowed it with land, had of common right a power annexed of nominating such minister as he pleased (provided he were canonically qualified) to officiate in that church, of which he was the founder, endower, maintainer, or, in one word, the patron.

This instance of an advowson will completely illustrate the nature of an incorporeal hereditament. It is not itself the bodily possession of the church and its appendages; but it is a right to give some other man a title to such bodily possession.

The advowson is the object of neither the sight nor the touch; and yet it perpetually exists in the mind's eye, and in contemplation of law. It cannot be delivered from man to man by any visible bodily transfer, nor can corporal possession be had of it. If the patron takes corporal possession of the church, the churchyard, the land or the like, he introduces on another man's property; for to these the parson has an exclusive right.

The patronage can therefore be only conveyed by operation of law, by verbal grant, either oral or written, which is a kind of invisible, mental transfer: and being so vested, it lies dormant and unnoticed, till occasion calls it forth: when it produces a visible, corporeal fruit, by entitling some clerk, whom the patron shall please to nominate, to enter and receive bodily possession of the lands and tenements of the church.

⚖ TITHES — A second species of incorporeal hereditaments is that of tithes; which are defined to be the tenth part of the increase, yearly arising and renewing from the profits of lands, the stock upon lands, and the personal industry of the inhabitants: the first species being such as of corn, grass, hops, and wood; the second mixed, as of wool, milk, pigs, etc., consisting of natural products, but nurtured and preserved in part by the care of man; and of these the tenth must be paid in gross; the third personal, as of manual occupations, trades, fisheries, and the like; and of these only the tenth part of the clear gains and profits is due.

⚖ ORIGIN OF TITHES — As to their original, I will not put the title of the clergy to tithes upon any divine right; though such a right certainly commenced, and I believe as certainly ceased, with the Jewish theocracy. Besides the positive precepts of the New Testament, natural reason will tell us, that an order of men, who are separated from the world, and excluded from other lucrative professions, for the sake of the rest of mankind, have a right to be furnished with the necessaries, conveniences, and moderate enjoyments of life, at their expense, for whose benefit they forego the usual means of providing them. Accordingly all municipal laws have provided a liberal and decent maintenance for their national priests or clergy: ours in particular have established this of tithes, probably in imitation of the Jewish law.

⚖ TITHES, TO WHOM DUE — We are next to consider the persons to whom they are due. Upon their first introduction though every man was obliged to pay tithes in general, yet he might give them to what priests he pleased; or he might pay them into the hands of the bishop, who distributed among his diocesan clergy the revenues of the church, which were then in common. But, when dioceses were divided into parishes, the tithes of each parish were allotted to its own particular minister; first by common consent, or the appointments of lords of manors, and afterwards by the written law of the land.

⚖ EXEMPTION FROM TITHES — We observed that tithes are due to the parson of common right, unless by special exemption: let us therefore see, thirdly, who may be exempted from the payment of tithes, and how lands, and their occupiers, may be exempted or discharged from the payment of tithes, either in part or totally first, by a real composition; or, secondly, by a custom or prescription.

⚖ BY A REAL COMPOSITION — First, a real composition is when an agreement is made between the owner of the lands, and the parson or vicar, with the consent of the ordinary and the patron, that such lands shall for the future be discharged from payment of tithes, by reason of some land or other real recompense given to the parson, in lieu and satisfaction thereof.

⚖ BY DISCHARGE BY CUSTOM OR PRESCRIPTION — Secondly, a discharge by custom or prescription, is where time out of mind such persons or such lands have been, either partially or totally, discharged from the payment of tithes. This immemorial usage is binding upon all parties; as it is in its nature an evidence of universal consent and acquiescence, and with reason supposes a real composition to have been formerly made.

⚖ COMMONS — Common, or right of common, appears from its very definition to be an incorporeal hereditament: being a profit which a man hath in the land of another; as to feed his beasts, to catch fish, to dig turf, to cut wood, or the like. And hence common is chiefly of four sorts; common of pasture, of piscary, of turbary, and of the estovers.

⚖ COMMON OF PASTURE — Common of pasture is a right of feeding one's beasts on another's land; for in those waste grounds, which are usually called commons, the property of the soil is generally in the lord of the manor; as in common fields it is in the particular tenants. This kind of common is either appendant, appurtenant, because of vicinage, or in gross.

⚖ COMMON APPENDANT — Common appendant is a right, belonging to the owners or occupiers of arable land, to put commonable beasts upon the lord's waste, and upon the lands of other persons within the same manor. Commonable beasts are either beasts of the plow, or such as manure the ground. This is a matter of most universal right. It was originally permitted, not only for the encouragement of agriculture, but for the necessity of the thing. For, when lords of manors granted out parcels of land to tenants, for services either done or to be done, these tenants could not plow or manure the land without beasts; these beasts could not be sustained without pasture; and pasture could not be had but in the lord's wastes, and on the uninclosed fallow grounds of themselves and the other tenants. The law therefore annexed this right of common, as inseparable incident, to the grant of the lands; and this was the original of common appendant.

⚖ COMMON APPURTENANT — Common appurtenant ariseth from no connection of tenure, nor from any absolute necessity, but may be annexed to lands in other lordships, or extend to other beasts, besides such as are generally commonable: as hogs, goats, or the like, which neither plow nor manure the ground.

This not arising from any natural propriety or necessity, like common appendant, it is therefore not of general right; but can only be claimed by immemorial usage and prescription, which the law esteems sufficient proof of a special grant or agreement for this purpose.

⚖ COMMON BECAUSE OF VICINAGE — Common because of vicinage, or neighborhood, is where the inhabitants of two townships, which lie contiguous to each other, have usually intercommoned with one another; and the beasts of the one straying mutually into the other's fields, without any molestation from either. This is indeed only a permissive right, intended to excuse what in strictness is a trespass in both, and to prevent a multiplicity of suits. Either township may inclose and bar out the other, though they have intercommoned time out of mind. Neither hath any person of one town a right to put his beasts originally into the other's common: but if they escape, and stray thither of themselves, the law winks at the trespass.

⚖ COMMON IN GROSS — Common in gross, or at large, is such as is neither appendant nor appurtenant to land, but is annexed to a man's person; being granted to him and his heirs by deed: or it may be claimed by prescriptive right, as by a parson of a church, or the like corporation sole. This is a separate inheritance, entirely distinct from any landed property, and may be vested in one who has not a foot of ground in the manor.

⚖ RESTRICTIONS ON COMMONS OF PASTURE — All these species, of pasturable common, may be and usually are limited as to number and time; but there are also commons without stint, and which last all the year. By the statute of Merton, however, and other subsequent statutes, the lord of a manor may inclose so much of the waste as he pleases, for tillage or wood ground, provided he leaves common sufficient for such as are entitled thereto.

⚖ COMMON OF PISCARY — Common of piscary is a liberty of fishing in another man's water.

⚖ COMMON OF TURBARY — Common of turbary is a liberty of digging turf upon another's ground. There is also a common of digging for coals, minerals, stones, and the like. All these bear a resemblance to common of pasture in many respects; though in one point they go much further: common of pasture being only a right of feeding on the herbage and vesture of the soil, which renews annually; but common of turbary, and the rest, are a right of carrying away the very soil itself.

⚖ COMMON OF ESTOVERS — Common of estovers is a liberty of taking necessary wood, for the use or furniture of a house or farm, from off another's estate.

⚖ WAYS — A fourth species of incorporeal hereditaments is that of ways; or the right of going over another man's ground. I speak not here of the king's highways, which lead from town to town; nor yet of common ways, leading from a village into the fields; but of private ways, in which a particular man may have an interest and a right, though another be owner of the soil.

This may be grounded on a special permission; as when the owner of the land grants to another a liberty of passing over his grounds, to go to church, to market, or the like: in which case the gift or grant is particular; and confined to the grantee alone; it dies with the person; and, if the grantee leaves the country, he cannot assign over his right to any other; nor can he justify taking another person in his company.

A way may be also by prescription; as if all the owners and occupiers of such a farm have immemorially used to cross another's ground: for this immemorial usage supposes an original grant, whereby a right of way thus appurtenant to land may clearly be created.

A right of way may also arise by act and operation of law: for, if a man grants me a piece of ground in the middle of his field, he at the same time tacitly and impliedly gives me a way to come at it; and I may cross his land for that purpose without trespass. For when the law doth give anything to one, it giveth impliedly whatsoever is necessary for enjoying the same.

⚖️ OFFICES — Offices, which are a right to exercise a public or private employment, and to take the fees and emoluments thereunto belonging, are also incorporeal hereditaments: whether public, as those of magistrates; or private, as of bailiffs, receivers, and the like. For a man may have an estate in them, either to him and his heirs, or for life, or for a term of years, or during pleasure only: save only that offices of public trust cannot be granted for a term of years, especially if they concern the administration of justice, for then they might perhaps vest in executors or administrators.

Neither can any judicial office be granted in reversion; because though the grantee may be able to perform it at the time of the grant, yet before the office falls he may become unable and insufficient: but ministerial offices may be so granted: for those may be executed by deputy. Also, by statute (Sale of Offices, 1552), no public office shall be sold, under pain of disability to dispose of or hold it. For the law presumes that he who buys an office will be bribery, extortion, or other unlawful means, make his purchase good, to the manifest detriment of the public.

⚖️ DIGNITIES — Dignities bear a near relation to offices. Of the nature of these we treated at large in the former book: it will therefore be here sufficient to mention them as a species of incorporeal hereditaments, wherein a man may have a property or estate.

⚖️ FRANCHISES — Franchises are a seventh species. Franchise and liberty are used as synonymous terms: and their definition is, a royal privilege, or branch of the king's prerogative, subsisting in the hands of a subject. Being therefore derived from the crown, they must arise from the king's grant; or, in some cases, may be held by prescription, which, as has been frequently said, presupposes a grant. The kinds of them are various, and almost infinite: I will here briefly touch upon some of the principal; premising only, that they may be vested in either natural persons or bodies politic; in one man, or in many: but the same identical franchise that has before been granted to one cannot be bestowed on another, for that would prejudice the former grant.

It is a franchise for a number of persons to be incorporated, and subsist as a body politic; with a power to maintain perpetual succession and do other corporate acts: and each individual member of such corporation is also said to have a franchise or freedom.

Other franchises are, to have a fair or market; with the right of taking toll, either there or at any other public places, as to bridges, wharfs, or the like; which tolls must have a reasonable cause of commencement (as in consideration of repairs, or the like), else the franchise is illegal and void: or, lastly, to have a forest, chase, park, warren, or fishery, endowed with privileges of royalty; which species of franchise may require a more minute discussion.

FRANCHISE OF FOREST — As to a forest: this, in the hands of a subject, is properly the same thing with a chase; being subject to the common law, and not to the forest laws. But a chase differs from a park, in that it is not inclosed, and also in that a man may have a chase in another man's ground as well as in his own; being indeed the liberty of keeping beasts of chase or royal game therein, protected even from the owner of the land with a power of hunting them thereon.

A park is an inclosed chase, extending only over a man's own grounds. The word park indeed properly signifies an inclosure; but yet it is not every field or common, which a gentleman pleases to surround with a wall or paling, and to stock with a herd of deer, that is thereby constituted a legal park: for the king's grant, or at least immemorial prescription, is necessary to make it so.

It is unlawful at common law for any person to kill any beasts of park or chase, except such as possess these franchises of forest, chase, or park.

FRANCHISE OF FREEWARREN — Freewarren is a similar franchise, erected for preservation or custody (which the word signifies) of beasts and fowls of warren; which, being of a wild nature, everyone had a natural right to kill as he could; but upon the introduction of the forest laws, at the Norman Conquest, as will be shown hereafter, these animals being looked upon as royal game and the sole property of our savage monarchs, this franchise of freewarren was invented to protect them; by giving the grantee a sole and exclusive power of killing such game so far as his warren extended, on condition of his preventing other persons.

A man, therefore, that has the franchise of warren, is in reality no more than a royal gamekeeper; but no man, not even a lord of a manor, could by common law justify sporting on another's soil, or even on his own, unless he had the liberty of freewarren. This franchise is almost fallen into disregard, since the new statutes for preserving the game.

There are many instances of keen sportsmen in ancient times, who have sold their estates, and reserved the freewarren, or right of killing game, to themselves; by which means it comes to pass that a man and his heirs have sometimes freewarren over another's ground.

FRANCHISE OF FREE FISHERY — A free fishery, or exclusive right of fishing in a public river, is also a royal franchise: and is considered as such in all countries where the feudal polity has prevailed: though the making such grants, and by that means appropriating what seems to be unnatural to restrain, the use of running water, was prohibited for the future by King John's great charter; and the rivers that were fenced in his time were directed to be laid open, as well as the forests to be disafforested.

This differs from a several fishery; because he that has a several fishery must also be the owner of the soil, which in a free fishery is not requisite. It differs also from a common of piscary before mentioned, in that the free fishery is an exclusive right, the common of piscary is not so: and therefore, in a free fishery, a man has a property in the fish before they are caught; in a common of piscary not till afterwards.

CORODIES — Corodies are a right of substance, or to receive certain allotments of victual and provision for one's maintenance. In lieu of which (especially when due from ecclesiastical persons), a pension or sum of money is sometimes substituted. And these may be reckoned another species of incorporeal hereditaments; though not chargeable on, or issuing from, any corporeal inheritance, but only charged on the person of the owner in respect of such his inheritance.

ANNUITIES — Annuities, which are much of the same nature; only that these arise from temporal, as the former from spiritual persons. An annuity is a thing very distinct from a rent-charge, with which it is frequently confounded: a rent-charge being a burden imposed upon and issuing out of lands, whereas an annuity is a yearly sum chargeable only upon the person of the grantor. Therefore, if a man by deed grant to another the sum of 2ol per annum, without expressing out of what lands it shall issue, no land at all shall be charged with it; but it is a mere personal annuity: which is of so little account in the law, that if granted to an eleemosynary corporation, it is not within the statutes of mortmain: and yet a man may have a real estate in it, though his security is merely personal.

RENTS — Rents are the last species of incorporeal hereditaments. The word, "Rent" or "Render," signifies a compensation or return, it being in the nature of an acknowledgment given for the possession of some corporeal inheritance. It is defined to be a certain profit issuing yearly out of lands and tenements corporeal. It must be a profit; yet there is no occasion for it to be, as it usually is, a sum of money: for spurs, capons, horses, corn, and other matters may be rendered, and frequently are rendered by way of rent. It may also consist in services or manual operations; as, to plow so many acres of ground, to attend the king or the lord to the wars, and the like; which services in the eyes of the law are profits.

This profit must also be certain; or that which may be reduced to a certainty by either party. It must also issue yearly though there is no occasion for it to issue every successive year; but it may be reserved every second, third or fourth year: yet, as it is to be produced out of the profits and lands and tenements, as a recompense for being permitted to hold or enjoy them, it ought to be reserved yearly, because those profits do annually arise and are annually renewed. It must issue out of the thing granted, and not be part of the land or thing itself; wherein it differs from an exception in the grant, which is always of part of the thing granted.

It must, lastly, issue out of lands and tenements corporeal; that is, from some inheritance whereunto the owner or grantee of the rent may have recourse to distrain. Therefore, a rent cannot be reserved out of an advowson, a common, an office, a franchise, or the like, but a grant of such annuity or sum may operate as a personal contract, and oblige the grantor to pay the money reserved, or subject him to an action of debt: though it doth not affect the inheritance, and is no legal rent in contemplation of law.

KIND OF RENTS — There are at common law three manner of rents, rent-service, rent-charge and rent-seck.

Rent-service is so called because it hath some corporal service incident to it, as at the least fealty, or the feudal oath of fidelity. For, if a tenant holds his land by fealty, and ten shillings rent; or by the service of plowing the lord's land, and five shillings rent; these pecuniary rents, being connected with personal services, are therefore called rent-service. And for these, in case they be behind, or arrear, at the day appointed, the lord may distrain of common right, without reserving any special power of distress; provided he hath in himself the reversion or future estate of the lands and tenements, after the lease or particular estate of the lessee or grantee is expired.

A rent-charge is were the owner of the rent hath no future interest, or reversion expectant in the land; as where a man by deed maketh over to others his whole estate in fee simple, with a certain rent payable thereout, and adds to the deed a covenant or clause of distress, that if the rent be arrear, or behind, it shall be lawful to distrain for the same. In this case the land is liable to the distress, not of common right, but by virtue of the clause in the deed, and therefore it is called a rent-charge, because in this manner the land is charged with a distress for the payment of it.

Rent-seck, or barren rent, is in effect nothing more than a rent reserved by deed, but without any clause of distress.

⚖ OTHER VARIETIES OF RENTS — There are other species of rents, which are reducible to these three. Rents of assize are the certain established rents of the freeholders and ancient copyholders of a manor, which cannot be departed from or varied. Those of the freeholders are frequently called chief rents, and both sorts are indifferently denominated quit-rents, because thereby the tenant goes quit and free of all other services. When these payments were reserved in silver or white money, they were anciently called white-rents, or blanch-farms, in contradistinction to rents reserved in work, grain, or baser money, which were called black-mail.

Rack rent is only a rent of the full value of the tenement or near it. A fee-farm rent is a rent-charge issuing out of an estate in fee; of at least one-fourth of the value of the lands, at the time of its reservation: for a grant of lands, reserving so considerable a rent, is indeed only letting lands to farm in fee simple instead of the usual methods for life or years.

⚖ GENERAL RULES AS TO RENTS — These are the general divisions of rent; but the difference between them (in respect to the remedy for recovering them) is now totally abolished; and all persons may have the like remedy by distress for rent-seck, rents of assize, and chief-rents, as in case of rents reserved upon lease.

Rent is regularly due and payable upon the land from whence it issues, if no particular place is mentioned in the reservation: but, in case of the king, the payment must be either to his officers at the exchequer or to his receiver in the country. And, strictly, the rent is demandable and payable before the time of sunset of the day whereon it is reserved; though perhaps not absolutely due till midnight.

With regard to the original of rents, something will be said in the next chapter: and, as to distresses and other remedies for their recovery, the doctrine relating thereto, and the several proceedings thereon, these belong properly to the third part of our Commentaries, which will treat of civil injuries, and the means whereby they are redressed.

THE FEUDAL SYSTEM

🗜 HISTORY OF THE FEUDAL SYSTEM — It is impossible to understand, with any degree of accuracy, either the civil constitution of this kingdom, or the laws which regulate its landed property, without some general acquaintance with the nature and doctrine of feuds, or the feudal law: A system so universally received throughout Europe, upwards of twelve centuries ago, yet surely no industrious student will imagine his time misemployed, when he is led to consider that the obsolete doctrines of our laws are frequently the foundation, upon which what remains is erected; and that it is impracticable to comprehend many rules of the modern law, in a scholarlike scientifical manner, without having recourse to the ancient.

🗜 ORIGIN OF FEUDS — The constitution of feuds had its original from the military policy of the northern or Celtic nations, the Goths, the Huns, the Franks, the Vandals, and the Lombards, who all migrating from the storehouse of nations who poured themselves in vast quantities into all the regions of Europe, at the declension of the Roman empire.

It was brought by them from their own countries, and continued in their respective colonies as the most likely means to secure their new acquisitions: and to that end, large districts or parcels of land were allotted by the conquering general to the superior officers of the army, and by them dealt out again in smaller parcels or allotments to the inferior officers and most deserving soldiers. These allotments were called feuds, fiefs, or fees; which last appellation in the northern languages signifies a conditional stipend or reward. Rewards of stipends they evidently were; and the condition annexed to them was, that the possessor should do service faithfully, both at home and in the wars, to him by whom they were given; for which purpose he took the oath of fealty: and in case of the breach of this condition and oath, by not performing the stipulated service, or by deserting the lord in battle, the lands were again to revert to him who granted them.

⚖ THE FEUDAL RELATION — Allotments, thus acquired, naturally engaged such as accepted them to defend them: and as they all sprang from the same right of conquest, no part could subsist independent of the whole; wherefore all givers as well as receivers were mutually bound to defend each other's possession. But, as they could not effectually be done in a tumultuous irregular way, government, and to that purpose subordination, was necessary.

Every receiver of lands, or feudatory, was therefore bound, when called upon by his benefactor, or immediate lord of his feud or fee, to do all in his power to defend him. Such benefactor or lord was likewise subordinate to and under the command of his immediate benefactor or superior; and so upwards to the prince or general himself. And the several lords were also reciprocally bound, in their respective gradations, to protect the possessions they had given.

Thus the feudal connection was established, a proper military subjection was naturally introduced, and an army of feudatories were always ready enlisted, and mutually prepared to muster, not only in defense of each man's own property, but also in defense of the whole, and of every part of this their newly acquired country: the prudence of which constitution was soon sufficiently visible in the strength and spirit, with which they maintained their conquests.

⚖ FEUDAL TENURE SUPPLANTS ALLODIAL OWNERSHIP — Scarce had these northern conquerors established themselves in their new dominions, when the wisdom of their constitutions, as well as their personal valor, alarmed all the princes of Europe; that is, of those countries which had formerly been Roman provinces, but had revolted, or were deserted by their old masters, in the general wreck of the empire. Wherefore most, if not all, of them thought it necessary to enter into the same or a similar plan of policy. For whereas, before, the possessions of their subjects were wholly independent, and hold of no superior at all, now they parceled out their royal territories, or persuaded their subjects to surrender up and retake their own landed property, under the like feudal obligations of military fealty. And thus, in the compass of a very few years, the feudal constitution, or the doctrine of tenure, extended itself over all the western world.

⚖ THE FEUDAL SYSTEM IN ENGLAND — But this feudal polity, which was thus by degrees established over all the Continent of Europe, seems not to have been received in this part of our island, at least not universally and as a part of the national constitution, till the reign of William the Norman.

⚖ THE NORMAN CONQUEST — This introduction, however, of the feudal tenures into England, by King William, does not seem to have been effected immediately after the Conquest, nor by the mere arbitrary will and power of the Conqueror; but to have been gradually established by the Norman barons, and others, in such forfeited lands as they received from the gift of the Conqueror, and afterwards universally consented to by the great council of the nation long after his title was established.

Indeed, from the prodigious slaughter of the English nobility at the battle of Hastings, and the fruitless insurrections of those who survived, such numerous forfeitures had accrued, that he was able to reward his Norman followers with very large and extensive possessions, which gave a handle to the monkish historians, and such as have implicitly followed them, to represent him as having by right of the sword seized on all the lands of England, and dealt them out again to his own favorites. A supposition, grounded upon a mistaken sense of the word conquest; which in its feudal acceptation, signifies no more than acquisition: and this had led many hasty writers into a strange historical mistake, and one which upon the slightest examination will be found to be most untrue. However, certain it is, that the Normans now began to gain very large possessions in England; and their regard for the feudal law, under which they had long lived, together with the king's recommendation of this policy to the English, as the best way to put themselves on a military footing, and thereby to prevent any future attempts from the Continent, were probably the reasons that prevailed to effect its establishment here by law.

Though the time of this great revolution in our landed property cannot be ascertained with exactness, yet there are some circumstances that may lead us to a probable conjecture concerning it. For we learn from the Saxon chronicle, that in the nineteenth year of King William's reign an invasion was apprehended from Denmark; and the military constitution of the Saxons being then laid aside, and no other introduced in its stead, the kingdom was wholly defenseless: which occasioned the king to bring over a large army of Normans and Bretons, who were quartered upon every landholder, and greatly oppressed the people. This apparent weakness, together with the grievances occasioned by a foreign force, might cooperate with the king's remonstrances, and the better incline the nobility to listen to his proposals for putting them in a posture of defense.

⚖ DOMESDAY BOOK — As soon as the danger was over, the king held a great council to inquire into the state of the nation; the immediate consequence of which was the compiling of the great survey called Domesday Book, which was finished in the next year: and in the latter end of that very year the king was attended by all his nobility at Sarum; where all the principal landholders submitted their lands to the yoke of military tenure, became the king's vassals, and did homage and fealty to his person.

This may possibly have been the era of formally introducing the feudal tenures by law; and perhaps the very law, thus made at the council of Sarum, is that which is still extant, and couched in these remarkable words: "We decree that all freemen bind themselves by homage and fealty, that within and without the whole kingdom of England, they will be faithful to King William, their lord, and everywhere preserve his lands and honors with all fidelity, and defend him against all foreign and domestic enemies."

The terms of this law are plainly feudal: for, first, it requires the oath of fealty, which made in the sense of the feudists every man that took it a tenant or vallas: and, secondly, the tenants obliged themselves to defend their lord's territories and titles against all enemies foreign and domestic. But what clearly evinces the legal establishment of this system, is another law of the same collection, which exacts the performance of the military feudal services, as ordained by the general council: "that all earls, barons, soldiers, servants, and freemen of our whole kingdom aforesaid, keep and hold themselves always well furnished with arms and horses, as is suitable and proper; and be always ready and well prepared for fulfilling and performing their entire service to us when need shall be; according to what they are by law bound to do for us by reason of their fees and tenements, and as we have ordained by the common council of our whole kingdom aforesaid."

The new polity, therefore, would seem not to have been imposed by the conqueror, but nationally and freely adopted by the general assembly of the whole realm, in the same manner as other nations of Europe had before adopted it, upon the same principle of self-security.

⚖ FEUDAL TENURES IN ENGLAND — In consequence of this change, it became a fundamental maxim and necessary principle (though in reality a mere fiction) of our English tenures, "that the king is the universal lord and original proprietor of all the lands in his kingdom; and that no man doth or can possess any part of it, but what has mediately or imme-

diately been derived as a gift from him, to be held upon feudal services."
For, this being the real case in pure, original, proper feuds, other nations
who adopted this system were obliged to act upon the same supposition,
as a substruction and foundation of their new polity, though the fact was
indeed far otherwise. And indeed by thus consenting to the introduction
of feudal tenures, our English ancestors probably meant no more than to
put the kingdom in a state of defense by establishing a military system;
and to oblige themselves (in respect of their lands) to maintain the king's
title and territories, with equal vigor and fealty, as if they had received
their lands from his bounty upon these express conditions, as pure, proper
beneficiary feudatories.

⚖ MODIFICATIONS IN THE FEUDAL SYSTEM — Our ancestors, therefore,
who were by no means beneficiaries, but had barely consented to this
fiction of tenure from the crown, as the basis of a military discipline, with
reason looked upon these deductions as grievous impositions, and arbitrary conclusions from principles that, as to them, had no foundation in
truth. However, this king, and his son, William Rufus, kept up with a
high hand all the rigors of the feudal doctrines: but their successor, Henry
I, found it expedient, when he set up his pretensions to the crown, to
promise a restitution of the laws of King Edward the Confessor, or ancient Saxon system; and accordingly, in the first year of his reign, granted
a charter, whereby he gave up the greater grievances, but still reserved the
fiction of feudal tenure, for the same military purposes which engaged
his father to introduce it. But this charter was gradually broken through,
and the former grievances were revived and aggravated, by himself and
succeeding princes; till in the reign of King John they became so intolerable, that they occasioned his barons, or principal feudatories, to rise up in
arms against him: which at length produced the famous great charter
(Magna Carta) at Runnymede, which, with some alterations, was confirmed by his son, Henry III.

Though its immunities (especially as altered on its last edition by
his son) are very greatly short of those granted by Henry I, it was justly
esteemed at the time a vast acquisition to English liberty. Indeed, by
the further alteration of tenures that has since happened, many of these
immunities may now appear, to a common observer, of much less consequence than they really were when granted; but this, properly considered,
will show, not that the acquisitions under John were small, but that those
under Charles were greater. From hence also arises another inference;
that the liberties of Englishmen are not (as some arbitrary writers would

represent them) here infringements of the king's prerogative, extorted from our princes by taking advantage of their weakness; but a restoration of that ancient constitution, of which our ancestors had been defrauded by the art and finesse of the Norman lawyers, rather than deprived by the force of the Norman arms.

LORD AND VASSAL — The grand and fundamental maxim of all feudal tenure is this; that all the lands were originally granted out by the sovereign, and are therefore holden, either mediately or immediately, of the crown. The grantor was called the proprietor, or lord; being he who retained the dominion or ultimate property of the feud or fee: and the grantee, who had only the use and possession, according to the terms of the grant, was styled the feudatory or vassal, which was only another name for the tenant or holder of the lands; though, on account of the prejudices we have justly conceived against the doctrines that were afterwards grafted on this system, we now use the word vassal opprobriously, as synonymous to slave or bondman.

The manner of the grant was by words of gratuitous and pure donation (I have given and granted); which are still the operative words in our modern infeudations or deeds of feoffment. This was perfected by the ceremony of corporal investiture, or open and notorious delivery of possession in the presence of the other vassals, which perpetuated among them the era of the new acquisition, at the time when the art of writing was very little known: and therefore the evidence of property was reposed in the memory of the neighborhood; who in case of a disputed title, were afterwards called upon to decide the difference, not only according to external proofs, adduced by the parties litigant, but also by the internal testimony of their own private knowledge.

OATH OF FEALTY: HOMAGE — Besides an oath of fealty, or profession of faith to the lord, which was the parent of our oath of allegiance, the vassal or tenant upon investiture did usually homage to his lord; openly and humbly kneeling, being ungirt, uncovered and holding up his hands both together between those of the lord, who sat before him: and there professing that "he did become his man, from that day forth, of life and limb and earthly honor": and then he received a kiss from his lord. Which ceremony was denominated manhood, by the feudists, from the stated form of words, "I become your man."

FEUDAL SERVICE — When the tenant had thus professed himself to be the man of his superior or lord, the next consideration was concerning the service, which, as such, he was bound to render, in recompense for the land he held. This was twofold: to follow or do suit to, the lord in his courts in time of peace; and in his armies or warlike retinue, when necessity called him to the field.

The lord was, in early times, the legislator and judge over all his feudatories: and therefore the vassals of the inferior lords were bound by their fealty to attend their domestic courts-baron (which were instituted in every manor or barony, for doing speedy and effectual justice to all the tenants) in order as well to answer such complaints as might be alleged against themselves, as to form a jury or homage for the trial of their fellow-tenants: and upon this account, in all the feudal institutions both here and on the Continent, they are distinguished by the appellation of the peers of the court.

In like manner the barons themselves, or lords of inferior districts, were denominated peers of the king's court, and were bound to attend him upon summons, to hear causes of greater consequence in the king's presence and under the direction of his grand justiciary: till in many countries the power of that officer was broken and distributed into other courts of judicature, the peers of the king's court still reserving to themselves (in almost every feudal government) the right of appeal from those subordinate courts in the last resort.

The military branch of service consisted in attending the lord to the wars, if called upon, with such a retinue, and for such a number of days, as were stipulated at the first donation, in proportion to the quantity of the land.

⚖️ DURATION OF FEUDS — At the first introduction of feuds, as they were gratuitous, so also they were precarious and held at the will of the lord, who was then the sole judge whether his vassal performed his services faithfully. Then they became certain for one or more years. But still feuds were not yet hereditary; though frequently granted, by the favor of the lord, to the children of the former possessor; till in process of time it became unusual, and was therefore thought hard to reject the heir, if he were capable to perform the services: and therefore infants, women and professed monks, who were incapable of bearing arms, were also incapable of succeeding to a genuine feud. But the heir, when admitted to the feud which his ancestor possessed, used generally to pay a fine or acknowledgment to the lord, in horses, arms, money, and the like, for such renewal of the feud: which was called a relief, because it re-established the inheritance, or in the words of the feudal writers, "it raised up the uncertain and fallen inheritance."

✠ FEUDS BECOME HEREDITARY — In process of time feuds came by degrees to be universally extended, beyond the life of the first vassal, to his sons, or perhaps to such one of them, as the lord should name; and in this case the form of the donation was strictly observed: for if a feud was given to a man and his sons, all his sons succeeded him in equal portions; and as they died off, their shares reverted to the lord, and did not descend to their children, or even to their surviving brothers, as not being specified in the donation. But when such a feud was given to a man and his heirs, in general terms, then a more extended rule of succession took place; and when a feudatory died, his male descendants forever were admitted to the succession.

When any such descendant, who thus had succeeded, died, his male descendants were also admitted in the first place; and, in defect of them, such of his male collateral kindred as were of the blood or lineage of the first feudatory, but no others. This was an unalterable maxim in feudal succession, that "none was capable of inheriting a feud, but such as was of the blood of, that is, lineally descended from, the first feudatory." And the descent, being thus confined to males, originally extended to all the males alike; all the sons, without any distinction of primogeniture, succeeding to equal portions of the father's feud. This being found upon many accounts inconvenient (particularly, by dividing the services, and thereby weakening the strength of the feudal union), and honorary feuds (or titles of nobility) being now introduced, which were not of a divisible nature, but could only be inherited by the eldest son; in imitation of these military feuds (or those we are now describing) began also in most countries to descend according to the same rule of primogeniture, to the eldest son, in exclusion of all the rest.

✠ FEUDS INALIENABLE — Other qualities of feuds were, that the feudatory could not alien or dispose of his feud; neither could he exchange, nor yet mortgage, nor even devise it by will, without the consent of the lord. For, the reason of conferring the feud being the personal abilities of the feudatory to serve in war, it was not fit he should be at liberty to transfer this gift, either from himself, or from his posterity who were presumed to inherit his valor, to others who might prove less able.

As the feudal obligation was looked upon as reciprocal, the feudatory being entitled to the lord's protection, in return for his own fealty and service; therefore the lord could no more transfer his seigniory or protection without consent of his vassal, then the vassal could his feud without consent of his lords; it being equally unreasonable, that the lord should extend his protection to a person to whom he had exceptions, and that the vassal should owe subjection to a superior not of his own choosing.

⚖️ SUBINFEUDATION — These were the principal, and very simple, qualities of the genuine or original feuds: which were all of a military nature, and in the hands of military persons: though the feudatories, being under frequent incapacities of cultivating and manuring their own lands, soon found it necessary to commit part of them to inferior tenants; obliging them to such returns in service, corn, cattle, or money, as might enable the chief feudatories to attend their military duties without distraction: which returns were the original of rents. By these means the feudal polity was greatly extended; these inferior feudatories being under similar obligations of fealty, to do suit of court, to answer the stipulated renders or rent-service, and to promote the welfare of their immediate superiors or lords.

⚖️ PROPER AND IMPROPER FEUDS — But this at the same time demolished the ancient simplicity of feuds; and an inroad being once made upon their constitution, it subjected them, in a course of time, to great varieties and innovations.

Feuds began to be bought and sold, and deviations were made from the old fundamental rules of tenure and succession; which were held no longer sacred, when the feuds themselves no longer continued to be purely military. These tenures began now to be divided into proper and improper feuds; under the former of which divisions were comprehended such, and such only, of which we have before spoken; and under that of improper or derivative feuds were comprised all such as do not fall within the other description: such, for instance, as were originally bartered and sold to the feudatory for a price; such as were held upon base or less honorable services, or upon a rent, in lieu of military service; such as were in themselves alienable, without mutual license; and such as might descend indifferently either to males or females. But, where a difference was not expressed in the creation, such new-created feuds did in all other respects follow the nature of an original, genuine, and proper feud.

THE ANCIENT
ENGLISH TENURES

🐝 ENGLISH TENURES, FEUDAL — In this chapter we shall take a short
view of the ancient tenures of our English estates, or the manner in
which lands, tenements and hereditaments might have been holden; as the
same stood in force, till the middle of the last century.

🐝 NATURE OF FEUDAL TENURE — Almost all the real property of this
kingdom is by the policy of our laws supposed to be granted by, dependent upon and holden of some superior lord.

The thing holden is therefore styled a tenement, the possessors
thereof tenants, and the manner of their possession a tenure. Thus all the
land in the kingdom is supposed to be holden, mediately or immediately,
of the king; who is styled the lord paramount, or above all. Such tenants
as held under the king immediately, when they granted out portions of
their lands to inferior persons, became also lords with respect to those
inferior persons, as they were still tenants with respect to the kind; and
thus partaking of a middle nature, were called mesne, or middle, lords.
So that if the king granted a manor to A, and he granted a portion of the
land to B, now B was said to hold of A, and A of the king; or in other
words, B held his lands immediately of A, but mediately of the king. The
king, therefore, was styled lord paramount; A was both tenant and lord,
or was a mesne lord; and B was called the lowest tenant; being he who
was supposed to make profit of the land. In this manner are all the lands
of the kingdom holden, which are in the hands of subjects.

🐝 TENANTS IN CAPITE — All tenures being thus derived, or supposed to
be derived, from the king, those that held immediately under him, in
right of his crown and dignity, were called his tenants in chief; which
was the most honorable species of tenure, but at the same time subjected
the tenants to greater and more burdensome services, than inferior tenures
did.

☙☙ KINDS OF FEUDAL SERVICES — There seem to have subsisted among our ancestors four principal species of lay tenures, to which all others may be reduced: the grand criteria of which were the natures of the several services or renders, that were due to the lords from their tenants. The services, in respect of their quality, were either free or base services; in respect of their quantity and the time of exacting them, were either certain or uncertain.

Free services were such as were not unbecoming the character of a soldier, or a freeman to perform; as to serve under his lord in the wars, to pay a sum of money, and the like. Base services were such as were fit only for peasants, or persons of a servile rank; as to plow the lord's land, to make his hedges, to carry out his dung, or other mean employments.

The certain services, whether free or base, were such as were stinted in quantity, and could not be exceeded on any pretense; as, to pay a stated annual rent, or to plow such a field for three days. The uncertain depended upon unknown contingencies: as, to do military service in person, or pay an assessment in lieu of it, when called upon, or to do whatever the lord should command; which is a base or villein service.

☙☙ SPECIES OF FEUDAL TENURES — From the various combinations of these services have arisen the four kinds of lay tenure which subsisted in England, till the middle of the last century; and three of which subsist to this day.

Tenements are of two kinds, frank-tenement, and villeinage. Of frank-tenements, some are held freely in consideration of homage and knight service; others in free socage with the service of fealty only. And again, of villeinages some are pure, and others privileged. He that holds in pure villeinage shall do whatsoever is commanded him, and always be bound to an uncertain service. The other kind of villeinage is called villein socage; and these villein socamen do villein services, but such as are certain and determined. Of which the sense seems to be as follows:

First, where the service was free, but uncertain, as military service with homage, that tenure was called the tenure in chivalry, or by knight service. Secondly, where the service was not only free, but also certain, as by fealty only, by rent and fealty, etc., that tenure was called free socage. These were the only free holdings or tenements; the others were servile: as, thirdly, where the service was base in its nature, and uncertain as to time and quantity, the tenure was absolute or pure villeinage. Lastly, where the service was base in its nature, but reduced to a certainty, this was still villeinage, but distinguished from the other by the name of privileged villeinage, or it might be still called socage (from the certainty of its services) but degraded by their baseness into the inferior title of villein socage.

⚖ KNIGHT SERVICE — The first, most universal, and esteemed and most honorable species of tenure, was that by knight service. This differed in very few points, as we shall presently see, from a pure and proper feud, being entirely military, and the genuine effect of the feudal establishment in England. To make a tenure by knight service, a determinate quantity of land was necessary, which was called a knight's fee; and a certain number of these knight's fees were requisite to make up a barony.

He who held this proportion of land (or a whole fee) by knight service, was bound to attend his lord to the wars for forty days in every year, if called upon: which attendance was his return, his rent or service, for the land he claimed to hold. If he held only half a knight's fee, he was only bound to attend twenty days, and so in proportion.

⚖ INCIDENTS OF KNIGHT SERVICE — This tenure of knight service had all the marks of a strict and regular feud: it was granted by words of pure donation (I have given and granted): was transferred by investiture or delivering corporal possession of the land, usually called livery of seisin; and was perfected by homage and fealty. It also drew after it these seven fruits and consequences, as inseparably incident to the tenure in chivalry; viz., aids, relief, primer seisin, wardship, marriage, fines for alienation, and escheat.

⚖ AIDS — Aids were originally mere benevolences granted by the tenant to his lord, in times of difficulty and distress; but in process of time they grew to be considered as a matter of right, and not of discretion. These aids were principally three: first, to ransom the lord's person, if taken prisoner; a necessary consequence of the feudal attachment and fidelity: insomuch that the neglect of doing it, whenever it was in the vassal's power, was by the strict rigor of the feudal law, an absolute forfeiture of his estate.

Secondly, to make the lord's eldest son a knight; a matter that was formerly attended with great ceremony, pomp, and expense. This aid could not be demanded till the heir was fifteen years old, or capable of bearing arms: the intention of it being to breed up the eldest son and heir apparent of the seigniory, to deeds of arms and chivalry, for the better defense of the nation.

Thirdly, to marry the lord's eldest daughter, by giving her a suitable portion: for daughter's portions were in those days extremely slender; few lords being able to save much out of their income for this purpose; nor could they acquire money by other means, being wholly conversant in matters of arms: nor by the nature of their tenure, could they charge their lands with this, or any other encumbrances.

From bearing their proportion to these aids no rank or profession was exempted.

But besides these ancient feudal aids, the tyranny of lords by degrees exacted more and more; as, aids to pay the lord's debts and aids to enable him to pay aids or reliefs to his superior lord; from which last, indeed, the king's tenants (in chief, i.e., of the king) were, from the nature of their tenure, excused, as they held immediately of the king who had no superior.

To prevent this abuse, King John's magna carta ordained, that no aids be taken by the king without consent of parliament, nor in any wise by inferior lords, save only the three ancient ones above mentioned. But this provision was omitted in Henry III's charter, and the same oppressions were continued till (1297), when the statute called "a confirmation of the charters" was enacted; which in this respect revived King John's charter, by ordaining that none but the ancient aids should be taken. Though the species of aids was thus restrained, yet the quantity of each aid remained arbitrary and uncertain. King John's charter indeed ordered that all aids taken by the king of his tenants should be settled by parliament. But they were never completely ascertained and adjusted till the statute (knighthood, 1275), which fixed the aids of inferior lords at twenty shillings, or the supposed twentieth part of every knight's fee, for making the eldest son a knight, or marrying the eldest daughter; and the same was done with regard to the king's tenants (King's Son and Daughter, 1351). The other aid, for ransom of the lord's person, being not in its nature capable of any certainty, was therefore never ascertained.

☟ RELIEFS — Relief, was before mentioned as incident to every feudal tenure, by way of fine or composition with the lord for taking up the estate, which was lapsed or fallen in by the death of the last tenant. But, though reliefs had their original while feuds were only life estates, yet they continued after feuds became hereditary; and were therefore looked upon, very justly, as one of the greatest grievances of tenure: especially when, at the first they were merely arbitrary and at the will of the lord; so that, if he pleased to demand an exorbitant relief, it was in effect to disinherit the heir. The English illbrooked this consequence of their new adopted policy; and therefore William the Conqueror by his laws ascertained the relief, by directing that a certain quantity of arms, and habiliments of war should be paid by the earls, barons, and vavasors respectively; and, if the latter had no arms, they should pay 100s.

⚖ PRIMER SEISIN — Primer Seisin was a feudal burden, only incident to the king's tenants and not to those who held of incident to the king's tenants and not to those who held of inferior or mesne lords. It was a right which the king had, when any of his tenants died seised of a knight's fee, to receive of the heir (provided he were of full age) one whole year's profits of the lands, if they were in immediate possession; and half a year's profits, if the lands were in reversion expectant on an estate for life.

This seems to be little more than an additional relief: but grounded upon this feudal reason that; by the ancient law of feuds, immediately upon a death of a vassal the superior was entitled to enter and take seisin or possession of the land, by way of protection against intruders, till the heir appeared to claim it and receive investiture: and for the time the lord so held it, he was entitled to take the profits; and unless the heir claimed within a year and day, it was by the strict law a forfeiture.

This practice, however, seems not to have long obtained in England, if ever, with regard to tenure under inferior lords; but, as to the king's tenures primer seisin was expressly declared, under Henry III and Edward II, to belong to the king by prerogative, in contradistinction to other lords. The king was entitled to enter and receive the whole profits of the land, till livery was sued; which suit being commonly within a year and day next after the death of the tenant, therefore the king used to take at an average the first-fruits, that is to say, one year's profits of the land.

⚖ WARDSHIP — These payments were only due if the heir was of full age; but if he was under the age of twenty-one, being a male, or fourteen, being a female, the lord was entitled to the wardship of the heir, and was called the guardian in chivalry.

This wardship consisted in having the custody of the body and lands of such heir, without any account of the profits, till the age of twenty-one in males, and sixteen in females. For the law supposed the heir male unable to perform knight service till twenty-one; but as for the female, she was supposed capable at fourteen to marry, and then her husband might perform the service. The lord, therefore, had no wardship, if at the death of the ancestor the heir male was of the full age of twenty-one, or the heir female of fourteen: yet, if she was then under fourteen, and the lord once had her in ward, he might keep her so till sixteen, by virtue of statute (Ward, 1275), the two additional years being given by the legislature for no other reason but merely to benefit the lord.

This wardship, so far as it related to land, though it was not nor could be part of the law of feuds, so long as they were arbitrary, temporary, or for life only; yet, when they became hereditary, and did consequently often descend upon infants, who by reason of their age could neither perform nor stipulate for the services of the feud, does not seem upon feudal principles to have been unreasonable. For the wardship of the land, or custody of the feud, was retained by the lord, that he might out of the profits thereof provide a fit person to supply the infant's services, til he should be of age to perform them himself.

If we consider the feud in its original import, as a stipend, fee, or reward for actual service, it could not be thought hard that the lord should withhold the stipend, so long as the service was suspended. Though undoubtedly to our English ancestors, where such a stipendiary donation was a mere supposition or figment, it carried abundance of hardship; and accordingly it was relieved by the charter of Henry I, which took this custody from the lord, and ordained that the custody, both of the land and the children should belong to the widow or next of kin. But this noble immunity did not continue many years.

The wardship of the body was a consequence of the wardship of the land; for he who enjoyed the infant's estate was the properest person to educate and maintain him in his infancy: and also, in a political view, the lord was most concerned to give his tenant a suitable education, in order to qualify him the better to perform those services which in his maturity he was bound to render.

⚖️ DELIVERY FROM WARDSHIP — When the male heir arrived to the age of twenty-one, or the heir female to that of sixteen, they might sue out their livery that is the delivery of their lands out of their guardian's hands. For this they were obliged to pay a fine, namely, half a year's profits of the land; though this seems expressly contrary to magna carta. However, in consideration of their lands having been so long in ward, they were excused all reliefs, and the king's tenants also all primer seisins.

In order to ascertain the profits that arose to the crown by these fruits of tenure, and to grant the heir his livery, the itinerant justices had it formerly in charge to make inquisition concerning them by a jury of the county, commonly called an inquisition after death; which was instituted to inquire (at the death of any man of fortune) the value of his estate, the tenure by which it was holden, and who and of what age his heir was; thereby to ascertain the relief and value of the primer seisin, or the wardship and livery accruing to the king thereupon. A manner of proceeding that came in process of time to be greatly abused, and at length an intolerable grievance; it being one of the principal accusations against Empson and Dudley, the wicked engines of Henry VII, that by color of false inquisitions they compelled many persons to sue out livery from the crown, who by no means were tenants thereunto. And, afterwards, a court of wards and liveries was erected, for conducting the same inquiries in a more solemn and legal manner.

KNIGHTHOOD — When the heir thus came of full age, provided he held a knight's fee, he was to receive the order of knighthood, and was compellable to take it upon him, or else pay a fine to the king. For in those herdical times, no person was qualified for deeds of arms and chivalry who had not received this order, which was conferred with much preparation and solemnity.

This prerogative, of compelling the vassals to be knighted, or to pay a fine, was expressly recognized in parliament, by statute (Knighthood, 1307); was exerted as an expedient for raising money by many of our best princes, particularly by Edward VI and Queen Elizabeth; but yet was the occasion of heavy murmurs when exerted by Charles I: among whose many misfortunes it was, that neither himself nor his people seemed able to distinguish between the arbitrary stretch, and the legal exertion, of prerogative.

However, among the other concessions made by that unhappy prince, he agreed to divest himself of this undoubted flower of the crown, and it was accordingly abolished by statute (Order of Knighthood, 1640).

MARRIAGE — Before they came of age, there was still another piece of authority, which the guardian was at liberty to exercise over his infant wards; I mean the right of marriage, which in its feudal sense signified the power which the lord or guardian in chivalry had of disposing of his infant ward in matrimony. While the infant was in ward, the guardian had the power of tendering him or her a suitable match, without disparagement, or inequality: which if the infant refused, they forfeited the value of the marriage to their guardian; that is, so much as a jury would assess, or anyone would bona fide give to the guardian for such an alliance: and, if the infants married themselves without the guardian's consent, they forfeited double the value. This seems to have been one of the greatest hardships of our ancient tenures.

There are indeed substantial reasons why the lord should have the restraint and control of the ward's marriage, especially of his female ward; because of their tender years, and the danger of such female ward's intermarrying with the lord's enemy. But no tolerable pretense could be assigned why the lord should have the sale or value of the marriage. Nor, indeed, is this claim of strictly feudal original; the most probable account of it seeming to be this: that by the custom of Normandy the lord's consent was necessary to the marriage of his female wards; which was introduced into England, together with the rest of the Norman doctrine of feuds: and it is likely that the lords usually took money for their consent, since in the often-cited charter of Henry I, he engages for the future to take nothing for his consent; which also he promises in general to give provided such female ward were not married to his enemy.

But this, among other beneficial parts of that charter, being disregarded, and guardians still continuing to dispose of their wards in a very arbitrary unequal manner, it was provided by King John's great charter, that heirs should be married without disparagement, the next of kin having previous notice of the contract. These provisions in behalf of the relations were omitted in the charter of Henry III; wherein the clause stands merely thus, "heirs should be married without disparagement": meaning certainly heirs female, as there are no traces before this to be found of the lord's claiming the marriage of heirs male. The king and his great lords thenceforward took a handle from the ambiguity of this expression to claim them both (whether they be male or female), and also, as nothing but disparagement was restrained by magna carta, they thought themselves at liberty to make all other advantages that they could. Afterwards this right, of selling the ward in marriage or else receiving the price or value of it, was expressly declared by the statute of Merton; which is the first direct mention of it that I have met with, in our own or any other law.

⚖ FINES — Another attendant or consequence of tenure, by knight service was that of fines due to the lord for every alienation, whenever the tenant had occasion to make over his land to another. This depended on the nature of the feudal connection; it not being reasonable nor allowed, as we have before seen, that a feudatory should transfer his lord's gift to another, and substitute a new tenant to do the service in his own stead, without the consent of the lord: and, as the feudal obligation was considered as reciprocal, the lord also could not alienate his seigniory, without the consent of his tenant, which consent of his was called an attornment.

This restraint upon the lords soon wore away; that upon the tenants continued longer. For, when everything came in process of time to be bought and sold, the lords would not grant a license to their tenant, to alien, without a fine being paid; apprehending that, if it was reasonable for the heir to pay a fine or relief on the renovation of his paternal estate, it was much more reasonable that a stranger should make the same acknowledgment on his admission to a newly purchased feud.

With us these fines seem only to have been exacted from the king's tenants who were never able to alien without a license: but, as to common persons, they were at liberty, by magna carta, and the statute of quia emptores (if not earlier), to alien the whole of their estate, to be holden of the same lord, as they themselves held it of before.

The king's tenants, not being included under the general words of these statutes, could not alien without a license: for if they did, it was in ancient strictness an absolute forfeiture of the land; though some have imagined otherwise. But this severity was mitigated by statute (Sale of Land, 1326), which ordained, that in such case the lands would not be forfeited, but a reasonable fine be paid to the king. Upon which statute it was settled, that one-third of the yearly value should be paid for a license of alienation; but, if the tenant presumed to alien without a license, a full year's value should be paid.

ESCHEAT — The last consequence of tenure in chivalry was escheat; which is the determination of the tenure, or dissolution of the mutual bond between the lord and tenant, from the extinction of the blood of the latter by either natural or civil means: if he died without heirs of his blood, or if his blood was corrupted and stained by commission of treason or felony; whereby every inheritable quality was entirely blotted out and abolished.

In such cases the land escheated, or fell back, to the lord of the fee; that is, the tenure was determined by breach of the original condition, expressed or implied in the feudal donation. In the one case, there were no heirs subsisting of the blood of the first feudatory or purchases, to which heirs alone the grant of the feud extended: in the other, the tenant, by perpetrating an atrocious crime, showed that he was no longer to be trusted as a vassal, having forgotten his duty as a subject; and therefore forfeited his feud, which he held under the implied condition that he should not be a traitor or a felon. The consequence of which in both cases was, that the gift, being determined, resulted back to the lord who gave it.

☙ OTHER SPECIES OF KNIGHT SERVICE — These were the principal qualities, fruits, and consequences of the tenure by knight service: a
tenure, by which the greatest part of the lands in this kingdom were
holden, and that principally of the kind in capite, till the middle of the
last century; and which was created for defense of the realm by the
king's own principal subjects, which was judged to be much better than to
trust to hirelings or foreigners. The description here given is that of knight
service proper; which was to attend the king in his wars.

There were also some other species of knight service; so called,
though improperly, because the service or render was of a free and honorable nature, and equally uncertain as to the time of rendering as that of
knight service proper, and because they were attended with similar fruits
and consequences. Such was the tenure by grand serjeanty, whereby the
tenant was bound, instead of serving the king generally in his wars, to do
some special honorary service to the king in person; as to carry his banner, his sword, or the like; or to be his butler, champion, or other officer,
at his coronation. It was in most other respects like knight service; only
he was not bound to pay aid; and, when tenant by knight service paid
five pounds for a relief on every knight's fee, tenant by grand serjeanty
paid one year's value of his land, were it much or little.

☙ ESCUAGE OR SCUTAGE — These services, both of chivalry and grand
serjeanty, were all personal, and uncertain as to their quantity or
duration. But, the personal attendance in knight service growing troublesome and inconvenient in many respects, the tenants found means of com-
pounding for it; by first sending others in their stead, and in process of
time making a pecuniary satisfaction to the lords in lieu of it. This pecuniary satisfaction at last come to be levied by assessments, at so much for
every knight's fee; and therefore this kind of tenure was called scutage;
being then a well-known denomination for money; and in like manner it
was called, in our Norman French, escuage; being indeed a pecuniary, instead of a military, service.

The first time this appears to have been taken was in 1158, but it
soon came to be so universal, that personal attendance fell quite into
disuse. Hence we find in our ancient histories, that, from this period, when
our kings went to war, they levied scutages on their tenants, to defray
their expenses, and to hire troops: and these assessments, in the time of
Henry II, seem to have been made arbitrarily and at the king's pleasure.
Which prerogative being greatly abused by his successors, it became matter of national clamor; and King John was obliged to consent, by his

magna carta, that no scutage should be imposed without consent of parliament.

This clause was omitted in his son Henry III's charter; where we only find, that scutages or escuage should be taken in a reasonable and moderate manner. Yet afterwards by statute (Taxation, 1297), and many subsequent statutes it was enacted, that the king should take no aids or tasks but by the common assent of the realm. Hence it is held in our old books, that escuage, or scutage could not be levied but by consent of parliament; such scutages being indeed the groundwork of all succeeding subsidies, and the land tax of later times.

Since, therefore, escuage differed from knight service in nothing, but as a compensation differs from actual service, knight service is frequently confounded with it. And thus must be understood, that tenant by homage, fealty, and escuage, was tenant by knight service: that is, that this tenure was respected as a tenure in chivalry. As the actual service was uncertain, and depended upon emergencies, so it was necessary that this pecuniary compensation would be equally uncertain, and depend on the assessments of the legislature suited to those emergencies. Had the escuage been a settled invariable sum, payable at certain times, it had been neither more nor less than a mere pecuniary rent: and the tenure instead of knight service would have been of another kind, called socage, of which we shall speak in the next chapter.

CORRUPTION OF KNIGHT SERVICE — For the present I have only to observe, that by the degenerating of knight service, or personal military duty, into escuage, or pecuniary assessments, all the advantages (either promised or real) of the feudal constitution were destroyed, and nothing but the hardships remained. Instead of forming a national militia composed of barons, knights, and gentlemen, bound by their interest, their honor, and their oaths, to defend their king and country, the whole of this system of tenures now tended to nothing else, but a wretched means of raising money to pay an army of occasional mercenaries.

In the meantime the families of all our nobility and gentry groaned under the intolerable burdens, which were introduced and laid upon them by the subtlety and finesse of the Norman lawyers. Besides the scutages to which they were liable in defect of personal attendance, which, however, were assessed by themselves in parliament, they might be called upon by the king or lord paramount for aids, whenever his eldest son was to be knighted or his eldest daughter married; not to forget the ransom of his own person.

The heir, on the death of his ancestor, if of full age, was plundered of the first emoluments arising from his inheritance, by way of relief and primer seisin; and, if under age, of the whole of his estate during infancy. And then, when he came to his own, after he was out of wardship, his woods decayed, houses fallen down, stock wasted and gone, lands let forth and plowed to be barren, to make amends he was yet to pay half a year's profits as a fine for suing out his livery; and also the price or value of his marriage, if he refuses such wife as his lord and guardian had bartered for, and imposed upon him; or twice that value, if he married another woman. Add to this the untimely and expensive honor of knighthood, to make his poverty more completely splendid. And when by these deductions his fortune was so shattered and ruined, that perhaps he was obliged to sell his patrimony, he had not even that poor privilege allowed him, without paying an exorbitant fine for a license of alienation.

♒︎   ABOLITION OF MILITARY TENURES — A slavery so complicated, and so extensive as this, called aloud for a remedy in a nation that boasted of its freedom. Palliatives were from time to time applied by successive acts of parliament, which assuaged some temporary grievances. Till at length the humanity of King James I consented for a proper equivalent to abolish them all; though the plan then proceeded not to effect; in like manner as he had formed a scheme, and began to put it in execution, for removing the feudal grievance of heritable jurisdictions in Scotland, which has since been pursued and effected by statute (Heritable Jurisdictions, 1746).

King James' plan for exchanging our military tenures seems to have been nearly the same as that which has been since pursued; only with this difference, that, by way of compensation for the loss which the crown and other lords would sustain, an annual fee-farm rent should be settled and inseparably annexed to the crown, and assured to the inferior lords, payable out of every knight's fee within their respective seigniories. An expedient, seemingly much better than the hereditary excise, which was afterwards made the principal equivalent for these concessions.

At length the military tenures, with all their heavy appendages, were destroyed at one blow by statute (Military Tenures, 1660), which enacts, "that the court of wards and liveries, and all wardships, liveries, primer seisins, values and forfeitures of marriages, by reason of any tenure of the king or others, be totally taken away. And that all fines for alienations, tenures by homage, knights service, and escuage, and also aids for marrying the daughter or knighting the son, and all tenures of the king in capite, be likewise taken away. And that all sorts of tenures, held by the king or others, be turned into free and common socage; save only tenures in frankalmoigne, copyholds, and the honorary services (without the slavish part) of grand serjeanty." A statute, which was a greater acquisition to the civil property of this kingdom than even magna carta itself: since that only pruned the luxuriances that had grown out of the military tenures, and thereby preserved them in vigor; but the statute of King Charles extirpated the whole, and demolished both root and branches.

THE MODERN
ENGLISH TENURES

Although, by the means that were mentioned in the preceding chapter, the oppressive or military part of the feudal constitution was happily done away, yet we are not to imagine that the constitution itself was utterly laid aside, and a new one introduced in its room: since by the statute (12 Charles II 1660) the tenures of socage and frankalmoigne, the honorary services of grand serjeanty, and the tenure by copy of court roll were reserved; nay, all tenures in general, except frankalmoigne, grand serjeanty, and copyhold, were reduced to one general species of tenure, then well known and subsisting, called free and common socage. This, being sprung from the same feudal original as the rest, demonstrates the necessity of fully contemplating that ancient system; since it is that alone to which we can recur to explain any seeming or real difficulties, that may arise in our present mode of tenure.

The military tenure, or that by knight service, consisted of what were reputed the most free and honorable services, but which in their nature were unavoidably uncertain in respect to the time of their performance.

The second species of tenure, or socage, consisted also of free and honorable services; but such as were liquidated and reduced to an absolute certainty. And this tenure not only subsists to this day, but has in a manner absorbed and swallowed up almost every other species of tenure. And to this we are next to proceed.

⚜ MEANING AND CHARACTER OF SOCAGE — Socage, in its most general and extensive signification, seems to denote a tenure by any certain and determinate service. And in this sense it is by our ancient writers constantly put in opposition to chivalry, or knight service, where the render was precarious and uncertain. Thus if a man holds by a rent in money, without any escuage or serjeanty that tenure may be called socage: but if you add thereto any royal service, or escuage to any, the smallest amount, that shall be called military tenure. So, too the general name of socage arises from grants to which military service, or grand serjeanty, is not incident.

The service must therefore be certain, in order to denominate it socage; as to hold by fealty and 20s. rent; or, by homage, fealty, and 20s. rent; or, by homage and fealty without rent; or, by fealty and certain corporal service, as plowing the lord's land for three days; or by fealty only without any other service: for all these are tenures in socage.

☙ FREE AND COMMON SOCAGE — But socage, as was hinted in the last chapter, is of two sorts: free socage, where the services are not only certain, but honorable: the villein socage, where the services, though certain, are of a baser nature. Such as hold by the former tenure are called tenants in free socage.

Of this tenure we are first to speak; and this, both in the nature of its service, and the fruits and consequences, appertaining thereto, was always by much the most free and independent species of any.

The word derives from the Saxon appellation, soc, which signifies liberty or privilege, and, being joined to a usual termination, is called socage, signifying a free or privileged tenure. It was the certainty that denominated it a socage tenure; and nothing sure could be a greater liberty or privilege than to have the service ascertained, and not left to the arbitrary calls of the lord, as in the tenures of chivalry.

Taking this, then, to be the meaning of the word, it seems probable that the socage tenures were the relics of Saxon liberty; retained by such persons as had neither forfeited them to the king, nor been obliged to exchange their tenure for the more honorable, as it was called, but at the same time more burdensome, tenure of knight service.

☙ KINDS OF FREE AND COMMON SOCAGE — As, therefore, the grant criterion and distinguishing mark of these species of tenure are the having its renders or services ascertained, it will include under it all other methods of holding free lands by certain and invariable rents and duties: and, in particular, petit serjeanty, tenure in burgage, and gavelkind.

☙ PETIT SERJEANTY — By the statute (1660), grand serjeanty is not itself totally abolished, but only the slavish appendages belonging to it; for the honorary services (such as carrying the king's sword or banner, officiating as his butler, carver, etc., at the coronation) are still reserved. Nor petit serjeanty bears a great resemblance to grand serjeanty; for as the one is a personal service, so the other is a rent or render, both tending to some purpose relative to the king's person.

Petit serjeanty, consists in holding lands of the king by the service of rendering to him annually some small implement of war, as a bow, a sword, a lance, an arrow or the like. This is but socage in effect; for it is no personal service, but a certain rent: and, we may add, it is clearly no predial service, or service of the plow, but in all respects free and common socage; only being held of the king, it is by way of eminence dignified with the title of petit serjeanty. And magna carta respects it in this light, when it enacts, that no wardship of the lands or body shall be claimed by the king in virtue of a tenure by petit serjeanty.

⚖ BURGAGE TENURE — Tenure in burgage is socage: and it is where the king or other person is lord of an ancient borough, in which the tenements are held by a rent certain. It is indeed only a kind of town socage; as common socage, by which other lands are holden, is usually of a rural nature. A borough, as we have formerly seen, is usually distinguished from other towns by the right of sending members to parliament; and, where the right of election is by burgage tenure, that alone is a proof of the antiquity of the borough. Tenure in burgage, therefore, is where houses, or lands which were formerly the site of houses, in an ancient borough, are held of some lord in common socage, by a certain established rent. These seem to have withstood the shock of the Norman encroachments principally on account of their insignificancy, which made it not worth while to compel them to an alteration of tenure; as a hundred of them put together would scarce have amounted to a knight's fee. Besides, the owners of them, being chiefly artificers and persons engaged in trade, could not with any tolerable propriety be put on such a military establishment, as the tenure in chivalry was. There also we have again an instance, where a tenure is confessedly in socage, and yet could not possibly ever have been held by plow service; since the tenants must have been citizens or burghers, the situation frequently a walled town, the tenement a single house; so that none of the owners was probably master of a plow, or was able to use one, if he had it.

⚖ BOROUGH-ENGLISH — The free socage, therefore, in which these tenements are held, seems to be plainly a remnant of Saxon liberty; which may also account for the great variety of customs, affecting many of these tenements so held in ancient burgage: the principal and most remarkable of which is that called borough-English, so named in contradistinction, as it were, to the Norman customs, and which is that the youngest son, and not the eldest, succeeds to the burgage tenement on the death of his father.

For the younger son, by reason of his tender age, is not so capable as the rest of his brethren to help himself.

Other authors have indeed given a much stranger reason for this custom, as if the lord of the fee had anciently a right to break the seventh commandment with his tenant's wife on her wedding-night; and that therefore the tenement descended not to the eldest, but the youngest son; who was more certainly the offspring of the tenant. But I cannot learn that even this custom prevailed in England, though it certainly did in Scotland till abolished by Malcolm III.

Perhaps a more rational account than either may be stretched from the practice of the Tartars; among whom this custom of descent to the youngest son also prevails. That nation is composed totally of shepherds and herdsmen; and the elder sons, as soon as they are capable of pastoral life, migrate from their father with a certain allotment of cattle, and go to seek a new habitation. The youngest son, therefore, who continues latest with the father, is naturally the heir of his house, the rest being already provided for.

⚖ GAVELKIND — The nature of the tenure in gavelkind affords us a still stronger argument. It is universally known what struggles the Kentishmen made to preserve their ancient liberties, and with how much success those struggles were attended. As it is principally here that we meet with the custom of gavelkind (though it was and is to be found in some other parts of the kingdom), we may fairly conclude that this was a part of those liberties. The distinguishing properties of this tenure are various. Some of the principal are these:

1. The tenant is of age sufficient to alien his estate by feoffment at the age of fifteen.

2. The estate does not escheat in case of an attainder and execution for felony; their maxim being, "the father to the bow, the son to the plow."

3. In most places he had a power of devising land by will, before the statute for that purpose was made.

4. The lands descend, not to the eldest, youngest, or any one son only, but to all the sons together; which was indeed anciently the most usual course of descent all over England, though in particular places particular customs prevailed.

These, among other properties, distinguished this tenure in a most remarkable manner: and yet it is said to be only a species of a socage tenure, modified by the custom of the country; the lands being holden by suit of court and fealty, which is a service in its nature certain.

By a charter of King John, Hubert, Archbishop of Canterbury, was authorized to exchange the gavelkind tenures holden of the see of Canterbury into tenures by knight's service; and by statute (1539), for disgaveling the lands of divers lords and gentlemen in the county of Kent, they are directed to be descendible for the future like other lands which were never holden by service of socage.

The immunities which the tenants in gavelkind enjoyed were such, as we cannot conceive should be conferred upon mere plowmen and peasants: from all which I think it sufficiently clear, that tenures in free socage are in general of a nobler original than is assigned by the bulk of our common lawyers.

☙ FREE SOCAGE OF FEUDAL CHARACTER — Having thus distributed and distinguished the several species of tenure in free socage, I proceed next to show that this also partakes very strongly of the feudal nature. Which may probably arise from its ancient Saxon original; since feuds were not unknown among the Saxons, though they did not form a part of their military policy, nor were drawn out into such arbitrary consequences as among the Normans. It seems therefore, reasonable to imagine, that socage tenure existed in much the same state before the Conquest as after: that in Kent it was preserved with a high hand, as our histories inform us it was; and that the rest of the socage tenures dispersed through England escaped the general fate of other property, partly out of favor and affection to their particular owners, and partly from their own insignificancy.

☙ TOKENS OF FEUDAL CHARACTER OF FREE SOCAGE — However this may be, the tokens of their feudal original will evidently appear from a short comparison of the incidents and consequences of socage tenure with those of tenure in chivalry; remarking their agreement or difference as we go along.

☙ HELD OF A SUPERIOR LORD — In the first place, then, both were held of superior lords; of the king as lord paramount, and sometimes of a subject or mesne lord between the king and the tenant.

☙ SERVICES — Both were subject to the feudal return, render, rent, or service of some sort or other, which arose from a supposition of an original grant from the lord to the tenant. In the military tenure, or more proper feud, this was from its nature uncertain; in socage, which was a feud of the improper kind, it was certain, fixed, and determinate (though perhaps nothing more than bare fealty), and so continues to this day.

⚖ FEALTY — Both were, from their constitution, universally subject (over and above all other renders) to the oath of fealty, or mutual bond of obligation between the lord and tenant. This oath every lord, of whom tenements are holden at this day, may and ought to call upon his tenants to take in his court-baron; if it be only for the reason that if it be neglected, it will by long continuance of time grow out of memory (as doubtless it frequently has) whether the land be holden of the lord or not; and so he may lose his seigniory, and the profit which may accrue to him by escheats and other contingencies.

⚖ AIDS — The tenure in socage was subject, of common right, to aids for knighting the son and marrying the eldest daughter: which were fixed by the statute at 20s. for every 20l. per annum so held; as in knight service. These aids, as in tenure by chivalry, were originally mere benevolences, though afterwards claimed as matter of right; but were all abolished by statute (1660).

⚖ RELIEFS — Relief is due upon socage tenure, as well as upon tenure in chivalry: but the manner of taking it is very different. The relief on a knight's fee was 5l. or one-quarter of the supposed value of the land; but a socage relief is one year's rent or render, payable by the tenant to the lord, be the same either great or small.

The statute (Confirmation of Great Charter, 1300), declares, that a free sokeman shall give no relief, but shall double his rent after the death of his ancestor, according to that which he hath used to pay his lord, and shall not be grieved above measure.

Reliefs in knight service were only payable, if the heir at the death of his ancestor was of full age: but in socage they were due, even though the heir was under age, because the lord has no wardship over him. The statute of Charles II reserves the reliefs incident to socage tenure; and therefore, wherever lands in fee simple are holden by a rent, relief is still due of common right upon the death of a tenant.

⚖ PRIMER SEISIN — Primer Seisin was incident to the king's socage tenants, as well as those by knight service. But this tenancy as well as primer seisins, are also, among the other feudal burdens, entirely abolished by the statute.

⚖ WARDSHIP — Wardship is also incident to tenure in socage; but of a nature very different from that incident to knight service. For if the inheritance descend to an infant under fourteen, the wardship of him does not, nor never did, belong to the lord of the fee; because in this tenure no military or other personal service being required, there was no occasion for the lord to take the profits, in order to provide a proper substitute for his infant tenant: but his nearest relation (to whom the inheritance cannot descend) shall be his guardian in socage, and have the custody of his land and body till he arrives at the age of fourteen.

The guardian must be such a one, at whom the inheritance by no possibility can descend. At fourteen this wardship in socage ceases; and the heir may oust the guardian, and call him to account for the rents and profits: for at this age the law supposes him capable of choosing a guardian for himself. It was in this particular, of wardship, as also in that of marriage, and in the certainty of the render or service, that the socage tenures had so much the advantage of the military ones. But as the wardship ceased at fourteen, there was this disadvantage attending it: that your heirs, being left at so tender an age to choose their own guardians till twenty-one, they might make an improvident choice. Therefore, when almost all the lands in the kingdom were turned into socage tenures, the statute (Military Tenures, 1660), enacted, that it should be in the power of any father by will to appoint a guardian, till his child should attain the age of twenty-one. If no such guardian was appointed, the court of chancery will frequently interpose, and name a guardian, to prevent an infant from improvidently exposing himself to ruin.

⚖ MARRIAGE — Marriage, or the value of the marriage, was not in socage tenure any perquisite or advantage to the guardian, but rather the reverse. If the guardian married his ward under the age of fourteen, he was bound to account to the ward for the value of the marriage, even though he took nothing for it, unless he married him to advantage. The law, in favor of infants, is always jealous of guardians, and therefore in this case it made them account, not only for what they did, but also for what they might receive on the infant's behalf; lest by some collusion the guardian should have received the value, and not brought it to account; but, the statute having destroyed all values of marriages, this doctrine of course hath ceased with them. At fourteen years of age the ward might have disposed of himself in marriage, without any consent of his guardian, till the late act for preventing clandestine marriages.

These doctrines of wardship and marriage in socage tenure were so diametrically opposite to those in knight service, and so entirely agree with those parts of King Edward's laws, that were restored by Henry I, as might alone convince us that socage was of a higher original than the Norman Conquest.

☙ FINES — Fines for alienation were, I apprehend, due for lands holden of the king by socage tenure, as well as in case of tenure by knight service: for the statutes that relate to this point, speak generally of all tenants without making any distinction: though now all fines for alienation are demolished by the statute of Charles II.

☙ ESCHEAT — Escheats are equally incident to tenure in socage, as they were to tenure by knight service; except only in gavelkind lands, which are (as is before mentioned) subject to no escheats for felony, though they are to escheats for want of heirs.

Thus much for the two grand species of tenure, under which almost all of the free lands of the kingdom were holden till the restoration in 1660, when the former was abolished and sunk into the latter: so that lands of both sorts are now holden by the one universal tenure of free and common socage.

☙ VILLEINAGE TENURE — The other grand division of tenure, is that of villeinage, as contradistinguished from frank tenure. And this is subdivided into two classes, pure and privileged, villeinage: from whence have arisen two other species of our modern tenures.

☙ PURE VILLEINAGE: COPYHOLD — From the tenure of pure villeinage have sprung our present copyhold tenures, or tenure by copy of court roll at the will of the lord: in order to obtain a clear idea of which it will be previously necessary to take a short view of the original and nature of manors.

☙ MANORS — Manors are in substance as ancient as the Saxon constitution, though perhaps differing a little, in some immaterial circumstances, from those that exist at this day: just as we observed of feuds, that they were partly known to our ancestors, even before the Norman Conquest.

A manor (from remaining), because the usual residence of the owner, seems to have been a district of ground, held by lords or great personages; who kept in their own hands so much land as was necessary for the use of their families, which were called demesne lands; being occupied by the lord and his servants. The other, or tenemental, lands they distributed among their tenants: which from the different modes of tenure were called and distinguished by two different names.

First, book-land, or charter-land, which was held by deed under certain rents and free services, and in effect differed nothing from free socage lands: and from hence have arisen most of the freehold tenants who hold of particular manors, and owe suit and service to the same. The other species was called folkland, which was held by no assurance in writing, but distributed among the common folk or people at the pleasure of the lord, and resumed at his discretion; being indeed land held in villeinage, which we shall presently describe more at large.

The residue of the manor, being uncultivated, was termed the lord's waste, and served for public roads, and for common of pasture to the lord and his tenants.

Manors were formerly called baronies, as they still are lordships: and each lord or baron was empowered to hold a domestic court, called the court-baron, for redressing misdemeanors and nuisances within the manor, and for settling disputes of property among the tenants. This court is an inseparable ingredient of every manor; and if the number of suitors should so fail as not to leave sufficient to make a jury or homage, that is, two tenants at the least, the manor itself is lost.

⚖ SUBINFEUDATION — In the early times of our legal constitution, the king's greater barons, who had a large extent of territory held under the crown, granted out frequently smaller manors to inferior persons to be held of themselves; which do, therefore, now continue to be held under a superior lord, who is called in such cases the lord paramount over all these manors: and his seigniory is frequently termed an honor, not a manor, if it hath belonged to an ancient feudal baron, or hath been at any time in the hands of the crown.

In imitation whereof, these inferior lords began to carve out and grant to others still more minute estates, to be held as of themselves; and were so proceeding downwards without limit; till the superior lords observed, that by this method of subinfeudation they lost all their feudal profits, of wardships, marriages, and escheats, which fell into the hands of these mesne or middle lords, who were the immediate superiors of him who occupied the land: and also that the mesne lords themselves were so impoverished thereby, that they were disabled from performing their services to their own superiors.

This occasioned, first, that provision in the thirty-second chapter of magna carta (1225), (which is not to be found in the first charter granted by that prince, nor in the great charter of King John) that no man should either give or sell his land, without reserving sufficient to answer the demands of his lord; and, afterwards the statute (1290), which directs, that, upon all sales or feoffments of land, the feoffee shall hold the same, not of his immediate feoffor, but of the chief lord of the fee, of whom such feoffer himself held it.

⚜ FOLKLAND — Now with regard to the folkland, or estates held in villeinage, this was a species of tenure neither strictly feudal, Norman, or Saxon; but mixed and compounded of them all.

Under the Saxon government there were a sort of people in a condition of downright servitude, used and employed in the most servile works, and belonging, both they, their children, and effects, to the lord of the soil, like the rest of the cattle or stock upon it. These seem to have been those who held what was called the folkland, from which they were removable at the lord's pleasure.

On the arrival of the Normans here, it seems not improbable that they, who were strangers to any other than a feudal state, might give some sparks of enfranchisement to such wretched persons as fell to their share, by admitting them, as well as others, to the oath of fealty; which conferred a right of protection, and raised the tenant to a kind of estate superior to down-right slavery, but inferior to every other condition. This they called villeinage, and the tenants villeins, either from the word, or else, from a village; because they lived chiefly in villages, and were employed in rustic works of the most sordid kind.

⚜ VILLEINS — These villeins, belonging principally to lords of manors, were either villeins, annexed to the manor or land: or else they were at large, that is, annexed to the person of the lord, and transferable by deed from one owner to another. They could not leave their lord without his permission; but, if they ran away, or were purloined from his, might be claimed and recovered by action like beasts or other chattels.

They held, indeed, small portions of land by way of sustaining themselves and families; but it was at the mere will of the lord, who might dispossess them whenever he pleased; and it was upon villein services, that is, to carry out dung, to hedge and ditch the lords' demesnes, and any other the meanest offices: and their services were not only base, but uncertain both as to their time and quantity.

A villein could acquire no property either in lands or goods: but if he purchased either, the lord might enter upon them, oust the villein, and seize them to his own use, unless he contrived to dispose of them again before the lord has seized them; for the lord had then lost his opportunity.

In many places, also, a fine was payable to the lord, if the villein presumed to marry his daughter to anyone without leave from the lord: and, by the common law, the lord might also bring an action against the husband for damages in thus purloining his property. For the children of villeins were also in the same state of bondage with their parents.

In case of a marriage between a freeman and a villein, the issue followed the condition of the father, being free if he was free, and villein if he was villein; contrary to the maxim of the civil law, that the offspring follows the condition of its mother. But no bastard could be born a villein, because by another maxim of our law he is the son of nobody; and as he can gain nothing by inheritance, it were hard that he should lose his natural freedom by it.

The law, however, protected the persons of villeins, as the king's subjects, against atrocious injuries of the lord: for he might not kill or maim his villein; though he might beat him with impunity, since the villein had no action or remedy at the law against his lord, but in case of the murder of his ancestor, or the maim of his own person. [Women] indeed had also an appeal of rape, in case the lord violated them by force.

⚖ ENFRANCHISEMENT OF VILLEINS — Villeins might be enfranchised by manumission, which is either express or implied: express, as where a man granted to the villein a deed of manumission: implied, as where a man bound himself in a bond to his villein for a sum of money, granted him an annuity by deed, or gave him an estate in fee, for life or years; for this was dealing with his villein on the footing of a freeman, it was in some of the instances giving him an action against his lord, and in others, vesting an ownership in him entirely inconsistent with his former state of bondage.

So, also, if the lord brought an action against his villein, this enfranchised him; for, as the lord might have a short remedy against his villein, by seizing his goods (which was more than equivalent to any damages he could recover) the law, which is always ready to catch at anything in favor of liberty, presumed that by bringing this action he meant to set his villein on the same footing with himself, and therefore held it an implied manumission. But, in case the lord indicted him for felony, it was otherwise; for the lord could not inflict a capital punishment on his villein, without calling in the assistance of the law.

⚖ EMERGENCE OF COPYHOLD TENURE — Villeins, by this and many other means, in process of time gained considerable ground on their lords; and in particular strengthened the tenure of their estates to that degree, that they came to have in them an interest in many places full as good, in others better than their lords. For the good nature and benevolence of many lords of manors having, time out of mind, permitted their villeins and their children to enjoy their possessions without interruption, in a regular course of descent, the common law, of which custom is the life, now gave them title to prescribe against their lords; and, on performance of the same services, to hold their lands in spite of any determination of the lord's will.

For, though in general they are still said to hold their estates at the will of the lord, yet it is such a will as is agreeable to the custom of the manor; which customs are preserved and evidenced by the rolls of the several courts-baron in which they are entered, or kept on foot by the constant immemorial usage of the several manors in which the lands lie. As such tenants had nothing to show for their estates, but these customs and admissions in pursuance of them, entered on those rolls, or the copies of such entries witnessed by the steward, they now began to be called tenants by copy of court roll, and their tenure itself a copyhold.

⚜ DISAPPEARANCE OF VILLEINS — Thus copyhold tenures, although very meanly descended, yet come of an ancient house; for, from what has been premised, it appears that copyholders are in truth no other but villeins, who, by a long series of immemorial encroachments on the lord, have at last established a customary right to those estates, which before were held absolutely at the lord's will. Which affords a very substantial reason for the great variety of customs that prevail in different manors, with regard both to the descent of the estates and the privileges belonging to the tenants. These encroachments grew to be so universal, that when tenure in villeinage was virtually abolished (though copyholds were reserved), by the statute of Charles II, there was hardly a pure villein left in the nation.

⚜ INCIDENTS OF COPYHOLD — As a further consequence of what has been premised, we may collect these two main principles which are held to be the supporters of the copyhold tenure, and without which it cannot exist; 1. That the lands be parcel of, and situate within that manor, under which it is held. 2. That they have been demised, or demisable, by copy of court roll immemorially. For immemorial custom is the life of all tenures by copy; so that no new copyhold can, strictly speaking, be granted at this day.

In some manors, where the custom hath been to permit the heir to succeed the ancestor in his tenure, the estates are styled copyholds of inheritance; in others, where the lords have been more vigilant to maintain their rights, they remain copyholds for life only; for the custom of the manor has in both cases so far superseded the will of the lord, that, provided the services be performed or stipulated for by fealty, he cannot, in the first instance, refuse to admit the heir of his tenant upon his death; nor in the second, can he remove his present tenant so long as he lives, though he holds nominally by the precarious tenure of his lord's will.

The fruits and appendages of a copyhold tenure, that it hath in common with free tenures, are fealty, services (as well in rents as otherwise), reliefs, and escheats. The two latter belong only to copyholds of inheritance; the former to those for life also. But besides these, copyholds have also heriots, wardship, and fines. Heriots are a render of the best beast or other good (as the custom may be) to the lord on the death of the tenant. This is plainly a relic of villein tenure; there being originally less hardship in it, when all the goods and chattels belonged to the lord, and he might have seized them even in the villein's lifetime. These are incident to both species of copyhold; but wardship and fines to those of inheritance only.

Wardship, in copyhold estates, partakes both of that in chivalry and that in socage. Like that in chivalry, the lord is the legal guardian; who usually assigns some relation of the infant tenant to act in his stead: and he, like guardian in socage, is accountable to his ward for the profits.

Of fines, some are in the nature of primer seisins, due on the death of each tenant, others are mere fines for alienation of the lands; in some manors only one of these sorts can be demanded, in some both, and in others neither. They are sometimes arbitrary and at the will of the lord, sometimes fixed by custom; but, even when arbitrary, the courts of law, in favor of the liberty of copyholders have tied them down to be reasonable in their extent; otherwise they might amount to a disherison of the estate. No fine, therefore, is allowed to be taken upon descents and alienations (unless in particular circumstances) of more than two years improved value of the estate.

From this instance we may judge of the favorable disposition of the law of England (which is a law of liberty) hath always shown to this species of tenants; by removing, as far as possible, every real badge of slavery from them, however some nominal ones may continue. It suffered custom very early to get the better of the express terms upon which they held their lands; by declaring that the will of the lord was to be interpreted by the custom of the manor; and where no custom has been suffered to grow up to the prejudice of the lord, as in the case of arbitrary fines, the law itself interposes in an equitable method, and will not suffer the lord to extend his power so far as to disinherit the tenant.

⚖ PRIVILEGED VILLEINAGE, OR VILLEINAGE SOCAGE — There is yet a fourth species of tenure under the name sometimes of privileged villeinage, and sometimes of villein socage. This is such as has been held of the kings of England from the Conquest downwards; that the tenants herein perform villein services, but certain and fixed; that they cannot alien or transfer their tenements by grant or feoffment, any more than pure villeins can; but must surrender them to the lord or his steward, to be again granted out and held in villeinage.

⚖ ANCIENT DEMESNE — Ancient demesne consists of those lands or manors, which, though now perhaps granted out to private subjects, were actually in the hands of the crown in the time of Edward the Confessor, or William the Conqueror; and so appear to have been by the great survey in the exchequer called Domesday-book. The tenants of these lands, under the crown, were not all of the same order or degree. Some of them continued for a long time pure and absolute villeins, dependent on the will of the lord: and those who have succeeded them in their tenures now differ from common copyholders in only a few points.

Others were in great measure enfranchised by the royal favor: being only bound in respect of their lands to perform some of the better sort of villein services, but those determinate and certain; as, to plow the king's land for so many days, to supply his court with such a quantity of provisions, and the like; all of which are now changed into pecuniary rents: and in consideration hereof they had many immunities and privileges granted to them; as, to try the right of their property in a peculiar court of their own, called a court of ancient demesne, by a peculiar process denominated a writ of right close: not to pay toll or taxes; not to contribute to the expenses of knights of the shire; not to be put on juries, and the like.

⚖ SERVICES OF THE TENANTS — These tenants, therefore, though their tenure be absolutely copyhold, yet have an interest equivalent to a freehold: for, though their services were of a base and villeinous original, yet the tenants were esteemed in all other respects to be highly privileged villeins; and especially for that their services were fixed and determinate, and that they could not be compelled (like pure villeins) to relinquish these tenements at the lord's will, or to hold them against their own and therefore they are called free.

⚖️   CHARACTER OF THE TENURE — Lands holden by this tenure are therefore a species of copyhold, and as such preserved and exempted from
the operation of the statute of Charles II. Yet they differ from common
copyholds, principally in the privileges before mentioned, as also they differ
from freeholders by one especial mark and tincture of villeinage., viz.,
that they cannot be conveyed from man to man by the general common-
law conveyances of feoffment, and the rest; but must pass by surrender
to the lord or his steward, in the manner of common copyholds: yet with
this difference, that, in the surrender of these lands in ancient demesne, it
is not used to say "to hold at the will of the lord" in their copies, but only
"to hold according to the custom of the manor."

Thus have we taken a compendious view of the principal and fundamental points of the doctrine of tenures, both ancient and modern, in
which we cannot but remark the mutual connection and dependence that
all of them have upon each other. And upon the whole it appears that,
whatever changes and alterations these tenures have in process of time
undergone, from the Saxon era to 1660, all lay tenures are now in effect reduced to two species; free tenure in common socage, and base tenure by
copy of court roll.

I mentioned lay tenures only; because there is still behind one
other species of tenure, reserved by the statute of Charles II, which is of a
spiritual nature, and called the tenure in frankalmoigne.

⚖️   TENURE IN FRANKALMOIGNE — Tenure in frankalmoigne, or free
alms, is that, whereby a religious corporation, aggregate or sole,
holdeth lands of the donor to them and their successors forever. The service which they were bound to render for these lands was not certainly defined: but only in general to pray for the souls of the donor and his heirs,
dead or alive; and therefore they did no fealty (which is incident to all
other services but this) because this divine service was of a higher and
more exalted nature.

This is the tenure, by which almost all the ancient monasteries and
religious houses held their lands; and by which the parochial clergy, and
very many ecclesiastical and eleemosynary foundations, hold them at this
day; the nature of the service being upon the Reformation altered, and
made conformable to the purer doctrines of the church of England.

It was an old Saxon tenure; and continued under the Norman revolution, through the great respect that was shown to religion and religious
men in ancient times. Which is also the reason that tenants in frankalmoigne were discharged of all other services, except the threefold neces-

sity of repairing the highways, building castles, and repelling invasions. Even at present, this is a tenure of a nature very distinct from all others; being not in the least feudal, but merely spiritual.

If the service be neglected, the law gives no remedy by distress or otherwise to the lord of whom the lands are holden; but merely a complaint to the ordinary or visitor to correct it. Wherein it materially differs from what was called tenure by divine service: in which the tenants were obliged to do some special divine services in certain; as to sing so many masses, to distribute such a sum in alms, and the like; which, being expressly defined and prescribed, could with no kind of propriety be called free alms; especially as for this, if unperformed, the lord might distrain, without any complaint to the visitor.

All such donations are indeed now out of use: for, since the statute (1290), none but the king can give lands to beholden by this tenure. I only mention them, because frankalmoigne is excepted by name in the statute of Charles II, and therefore subsists in many instances at this day.

FREEHOLD ESTATES
OF INHERITANCE

⚖ ESTATES — The next objects of our disquisitions are the nature and properties of estates. An estate in lands, tenements and hereditaments, signifies such interest as the tenant hath therein; so that if a man grants all his estate to A and his heirs, everything that he can possibly grant shall pass thereby. It is called in Latin, Status; it signifying the condition, or circumstance, in which the owner stands, with regard to his property.

To ascertain this with proper precision and accuracy, estates may be considered in a three-fold view: First, with regard to the quantity of interest which the tenant has in the tenement; secondly, with regard to the time at which that quantity of interest is to be enjoyed; and, thirdly, with regard to the number and connections of his tenants.

First, with regard to the quantity of interest which the tenant has in the tenement, this is measured by its duration and extent. Thus, either his right of possession is to subsist for an uncertain period, during his own life, or the life of another man; to determine at his own decease, or to remain to his descendants after him: or it is circumscribed within a certain number of years, months, or days: or, lastly, it is infinite and unlimited, being vested in him and his representatives forever. This occasions the primary division of estates, into such as are freehold, and such as are less than freehold.

⚖ ESTATES OF FREEHOLD — An estate of freehold is the possession of the soil by a freeman. The possession of the land is called in the law of England, the franktenement or freehold. Such estate, therefore, and no other, as requires actual possession of the land, is, legally speaking, freehold: which actual possession can, by the course of the common law, be only given by the ceremony called livery of seisin, which is the same as the feudal investiture.

From these principles we may extract this description of a freehold;

that it is such an estate in lands as is conveyed by livery of seisin; or, in tenements of an incorporeal nature, by what is equivalent thereto. Where a freehold shall pass, it behooveth to have livery of seisin. As, therefore, estates of inheritance and estates for life could not by common law be conveyed without livery of seisin, these are properly estates of freehold; and, as no other estates were conveyed with the same solemnity, therefore no others are properly freehold estates.

ESTATES OF INHERITANCE — Estates of freehold, then are divisible into estates of inheritance, and estates not of inheritance. The former are again divided into inheritances absolute or fee simple; and inheritances limited, one species of which we usually call fee-tail.

FEE-SIMPLE ESTATES — Tenant in fee simple (or, as he is frequently styled, tenant in fee) is he that hath lands, tenements, or hereditaments, to hold to him and his heirs forever; generally, and simply; without mentioning what heirs, but referring that to his own pleasure, or to the disposition of the law.

The true meaning of the word "fee" is the same with that of feud or fief. This is property in its highest degree; and the owner thereof hath the absolute and direct ownership, and therefore is said to be seised thereof absolutely in his own demesne. But feodum or fee, is that which is held of some superior, on condition of rendering him service; in which superior the ultimate property of the land resides.

Sir Henry Spelman defines a feud or fee to be the right which the vassal or tenant hath in lands, to use the same, and take the profits thereof to him and his heirs, rendering to the lord his due services; the mere allodial propriety of the soil always remaining in the lord. This allodial property no subject in England has; it being a received, and now undeniable, principle in the law, that all the lands in England are holden mediately or immediately of the kind but all subjects' lands are in the nature of feodum or fee; whether derived to them by descent from their ancestors, or purchased for a valuable consideration: for they cannot come to any man by either of those ways, unless accompanied with those feudal clogs, which were laid upon the first feudatory when it was originally granted.

Hence it is that, in the most solemn acts of law, we express the strongest and highest estate that any subject can have, by these words; "he is seised thereof in his demesne, as of fee." It is a man's demesne, or property, since it belongs to him and his heirs forever: yet this property, or demesne, is strictly not absolute or allodial, but qualified or feudal: it is his demesne, as of fee; that is, it is not purely and simply his own, since it is held of a superior lord, in whom the ultimate property resides.

This is the primary sense and acceptation of the word "fee." But the doctrine, "that all lands are holden," having been for so many ages a fixed and undeniable axiom, our English lawyers do very rarely (of late years especially) use the word "fee" in this its primary original sense, in contradistinction to allodium or absolute property, with which they have no concern; but generally use it to express the continuance or quantity of estate.

A fee, therefore, in general, signifies an estate of inheritance; being the highest and most extensive interest that a man can have in a feud: and, when the term is used simply, without any other adjunct, or has the adjunct of simple annexed to it (as a fee, or a fee simple) it is used in contradistinction to a fee conditional at the common law, or a fee-tail by the statute; importing an absolute inheritance, clear of any condition, limitation, or restrictions to particular heirs, but descendible to the heirs general, whether male or female, lineal or collateral.

Taking, therefore, fee for the future, unless where otherwise explained, in this its secondary sense, as a state of inheritance, it is applicable to, and may be had in, any kind of hereditaments either corporeal or incorporeal. But there is this distinction between the two species of hereditaments; that, of a corporeal inheritance a man shall be said to be seised in his demesne, as of fee; of an incorporeal one he shall only be said to be seised as of fee, and not in his demesne. For, as incorporeal hereditaments are in their nature collateral to, and issue out of, lands and houses, their owner hath no property, or demesne, in the thing itself, but that only something derived out of it; resembling the servitudes, or services, of the civil law. The property is frequently in one man, while the appendage or service is in another.

⚖ DIFFERENT INTERESTS IN THE SAME LAND — The fee simple or inheritance of lands and tenements is generally vested and resides in some person or other; though divers inferior estates may be carved out of it. As if one grants a lease for twenty-one years, or for one or two lives, the fee simple remains vested in him and his heirs; and after the determination of those years or lives, the land reverts to the grantor or his heirs, who shall hold it again in fee simple.

Yet sometimes the fee may be in abeyance, that is in expectation, remembrance, and contemplation in law; there being no person in being in whom it can vest and abide: though the law considers it as always potentially existing, and ready to vest whenever a proper owner appears.

Thus, in a grant to John for life, and afterwards to the heirs of Richard, the inheritance is plainly neither granted to John nor Richard, nor can it vest in the heirs of Richard till his death, for no one is heir of a living person: it remains, therefore, in waiting, or abeyance, during the life of Richard.

⚖ THE WORD "HEIRS" NECESSARY IN FEOFFMENTS — The word "heirs" is necessary in the grant or donation in order to make a fee, or inheritance. If land be given to a man forever, or to him and his assigns forever, this vests in him but an estate for life. This very great nicety about the insertion of the word "heirs" in all feoffments and grants, in order to vest a fee, is plainly a relic of the feudal strictness: by which we may remember it was required that the form of the donation should be punctually pursued; or donations should be construed strictly, lest anyone be presumed to have given more than is expressed in the donation. Therefore, as the personal abilities of the donee were originally supposed to be the only inducements to the gift, the donee's estate in the land extended only to his own person, and subsisted no longer than his life; unless the donor by an express provision in the grant, gave it a longer continuance, and extended it also to his heirs. This rule is now softened by many exceptions.

⚖ WHEN WORD "HEIRS" NOT NECESSARY — 1. It does not extend to devises by will; in which as they were introduced at the time when the feudal rigor was apace wearing out, a more liberal construction is allowed: and therefore by a devise to a man forever, or to one and his assigns forever, or to one in fee simple, the devisee hath an estate of inheritance; for the intention of the devisor is sufficiently plain from the words of perpetuity annexed, though he hath omitted the legal words of inheritance. But if the devise be to a man and his assigns, without annexing words of perpetuity, there the devisee shall take only an estate for life; for it does not appear that the devisor intended any more.

2. Neither does this rule extend to fines or recoveries, considered as a species of conveyance; for thereby an estate in fee passes by act and operation of law without the word "heirs": as it does also for particular reasons, by certain other methods of conveyance, which have relation to a former grant or estate, wherein the word "heirs" was expressed.

3. In creations of nobility by writ, the peer so created hath an inheritance in his title, without expressing the word "heirs"; for they are

implied in the creation, unless it be otherwise specially provided: but in creations by patent, which are of strict right, the word "heirs" must be inserted, otherwise there is no inheritance.

4. In grants of lands to sole corporations and their successors, the word "successors" supplies the place of "heirs"; for as heirs take from the ancestor, so doth the successor from the predecessor. Nay, in a grant to a bishop, or other sole spiritual corporation, the word "frankalmoigne" supplies the place of "successors" (as the word "successors" supplies the place of "heirs") by force of the term; and in all these cases a fee simple vests in such sole corporation. But in a grant of lands to a corporation aggregate, the word "successors" is not necessary, though usually inserted: for, albeit such simple grant be strictly only an estate for life, yet, as that corporation never dies, such estate for life is perpetual, or equivalent to a fee simple, and therefore the law allows it to be one.

Lastly, in the case of the king, a fee simple will vest in him, without the word "heirs" or "successors" in the grant; partly from prerogative royal and partly from a reason similar to the last, because the king in judgment of law, never dies. But the general rule is, that the word "heirs" is necessary to create an estate of inheritance.

LIMITED FEES — We are next to consider limited fees, or such estates of inheritance as are clogged and confined with conditions, or qualifications, of any sort. These we may divide into two sorts: 1. Qualified, or base fees: and 2. Fees conditional, so called at the common law; and afterwards fees-tail, in consequence of the statute de donis (of gifts).

BASE OR QUALIFIED FEES — A base, or qualified, fee is such a one as has a qualification subjoined thereto, and which must be determined whenever the qualification annexed to it is at an end. As, in the case of a grant to A and his heirs, tenants of the manor of Dale; in this instance, whenever the heirs of A cease to be tenants of that manor, the grant is entirely defeated. So, when Henry VI granted to John Talbot, lord of the manor of Kingston-Lisle in Berks, that he and his heirs, lords of the said manor, should be peers of the realm, by the title of Barons of Lisle; here John Talbot had a base or qualified fee in that dignity; and the instant he or his heirs quitted the seigniory of this manor, the dignity was at an end. This estate is a fee, because by possibility it may endure forever in a man and his heirs; yet as that duration depends upon the concurrence of collateral circumstances, which qualify and debase the purity of the donation, it is therefore a qualified or base fee.

☙☙ CONDITIONAL FEES: ESTATES-TAIL — A conditional fee at the common law was a fee restrained to some particular heirs, exclusive of others; a strict and limited donation; as to certain heirs, others being excluded from the succession: as to the heirs of a man's body, by which only his lineal descendants we.e admitted in exclusion of collateral heirs; or, to the heirs male of his body, in exclusion both of collaterals and lineal females also. It was called a conditional fee, by reason of the condition expressed or implied in the donation of it, that if the donee died without such particular heirs, the land should revert to the donor.

This was a condition annexed by law to all grants whatsoever, that on failure of the heirs specified in the grant, the grant should be at an end, and the land return to its ancient proprietor. Such conditional fees were strictly agreeable to the nature of feuds, when they first ceased to be mere estates for life, and were not yet arrived to be absolute estates in fee simple.

☙☙ THE OLD LAW OF CONDITIONAL FEES — With regard to the condition annexed to these fees by the common law, our ancestors held that such a gift (to a man and the heirs of his body) was a gift upon condition that it should revert to the donor, if the donee had no heirs of his body; but if he had, it should then remain to the donee. They therefore called it a fee simple, on condition that he had issue.

Now, we must observe that when any condition is performed, it is thenceforth entirely gone; and the thing to which it was before annexed, becomes absolute and wholly unconditional. So that, as soon as the grantee had any issue born, his estate was supposed to become absolute by the performance of the condition; at least, for these three purposes: 1. To enable the tenant to alien the land, and thereby to bar not only his own issue, but also the donor of his interest in the reversion. 2. To subject him to forfeit it for treason: which he could not do, till issue born, longer than for his own life; lest thereby the inheritance of the issue, and reversion of the donor, might have been defeated. 3. To empower him to charge the land with rents, commons, and certain other encumbrances, so as to bind his issue.

This was thought the more reasonable because, by the birth of issue, the possibility of the donor's reversion was rendered more distant and precarious; and his interest seems to have been the only one which the law, as it then stood, was solicitous to protect; without much regard to the right of succession intended to be vested in the issue. However, if the tenant did not in fact alien the land, the course of descent was not altered by this performance of the condition; for if the issue had afterwards died, and then the tenant, or original grantee, had died, without making any alienation; the land, by the terms of the donation, could descend to none but the heirs of his body, and, therefore, in default of them, must have reverted to the donor.

For which reason, in order to subject the lands to the ordinary course of descent, the donees of these conditional fee simples took care to alien as soon as they had performed the condition by having issue; and afterwards repurchased the lands, which gave them a fee-simple absolute, that would descend to the heirs general, according to the course of the common law. Thus stood the old law with regard to conditional fees; which things, though they seem ancient, are yet necessary to be known; as well for the declaring how the common law stood in such cases, as for the sake of annuities, and such like inheritances, as are not within the statutes of entail, and therefore remain as at the common law.

☙☙   THE STATUTE DE DONIS — The inconveniences, which attended these limited and fettered inheritances, were probably what induced the judges to give way to this subtle finesse of construction (for such it undoubtedly was), in order to shorten the duration of these conditional estates. But, on the other hand, the nobility, who were willing to perpetuate their possessions in their own families, to put a stop to this practice, procured the statute (commonly called the statute de donis of conditional gifts) to be made; which paid a greater regard to the private will and intentions of the donor, than to the propriety of such intentions, or any public considerations whatsoever. This statute revived in some sort the ancient feudal restraints which were originally laid on alienations, by enacting, that from thenceforth the will of the donor be observed; and that the tenements so given (to a man and the heirs of his body) should at all events go to the issue, if there were any; or, if none, should revert to the donor.

☙☙   FEE-TAIL AND REVERSION — Upon the construction of this act of parliament, the judges determined that the donee had no longer a conditional fee simple, which became absolute and at his own disposal, the instant any issue was born; but they divided the estate into two parts, leaving in the donee a new kind of particular estate, which they denominated a fee-tail; and vesting in the donor the ultimate fee simple of the land, expectant on the failure of issue; which expectant estate is what we now call a reversion.

⚖ WHAT MAY BE ENTAILED — Having thus shown the original of estates-tail, I now proceed to consider, what things may, or may not, be entailed under the statute de donis. Tenements is the only word used in the statute: and this comprehends all corporeal hereditaments whatsoever; and also all incorporeal hereditaments which savor of the realty, that is, which issue out of corporeal ones, or which concur, or are annexed to, or may be exercised within the same; as rents, estovers, commons, and the like. Also offices and dignities, which concern lands, or have relation to fixed and certain places may be entailed.

Mere personal chattels, which savor not at all of the realty, cannot be entailed. Neither can an office, which merely relates to such personal chattels; nor an annuity, which charges only the person, and not the lands, of the grantor.

In these last, if granted to a man and the heirs of his body, the grantee hath still a fee conditional at common law, as before the statute: and by his alienation may bar the heir or reversioner.

An estate to a man and his heirs for anothers life cannot be entailed; for this is strictly no estate of inheritance (as will appear hereafter), and therefore not within the statute de donis. Neither can a copyhold estate be entailed by virtue of the statute; for that would tend to encroach upon and restrain the will of the lord: but, by the special custom of the manor, a copyhold may be limited to the heirs of the body; for here the custom ascertains and interprets the lord's will.

⚖ SPECIES OF ESTATES-TAIL — Next, as to the several species of estates-tail, and how they are respectively created. Estates-tail are either general, or special.

⚖ TAIL-GENERAL — Tail-general is where lands and tenements are given to one, and the heirs of his body begotten; which is called tail-general, because, how often soever such donee in tail be married, his issue in general by all and every such marriage is, in successive order, capable of inheriting the estate-tail, by the form of the gift.

⚖ TAIL-SPECIAL — Tenant in tail-special is where the gift is restrained to certain heirs of the donee's body, and does not go to all of them in general. This may happen several ways. I shall instance in only one; as where lands and tenements are given to a man and the heirs of his body, on Mary his now wife to be begotten: here no issue can inherit, but such special issue as is engendered between them two; not such as the husband may have by another wife: and therefore it is called special tail. Here we may observe, that the words of inheritance (to him and his heirs) give him an estate in fee; but they being heirs to be by him begotten, this makes it a fee-tail; and the person being also limited, on whom such heirs shall be begotten (viz., Mary his present wife), this makes it a fee-tail special.

TAIL MALE AND TAIL FEMALE — Estates, in general and special tail, are further diversified by the distinction of sexes in such entails; for both of them may either be in tail male or tail female. As if lands be given to a man, and his heirs male of his body begotten, this is an estate in tail male general; but if to a man and his heirs female of his body on his present wife begotten, this is an estate in tail female special. In case of an entail male, the heirs female shall never inherit, nor any derived from them; on the other hand, the heirs male, in case of a gift in tail female.

Thus, if the donee in tail male hath a daughter, who dies leaving a son, such grandson in this case cannot inherit the estate-tail; for he cannot deduce his descent wholly by heirs male. As the heir male must convey his descent wholly by males, so must the heir female wholly by females. Therefore if a man hath two estates-tail, the one in tail male, the other in tail female; and he hath issue a daughter, which daughter hath issue a son; this grandson can succeed to neither of the estates: for he cannot convey his descent wholly either in the male or female line.

WORDS NECESSARY TO MAKE AN ENTAIL — As the word "Heirs" is necessary to create a fee, so in further imitation of the strictness of the feudal donation, the word body, or some other words of procreation, are necessary to make it a fee-tail, and ascertain to what heirs in particular the fee is limited. If, therefore, either the words of inheritance or words of procreation be omitted, albeit the others are inserted in the grant, this will not make an estate-tail.

As, if the grant be to a man and his issue of his body, to a man and his seed, to a man and his children, or offspring; all these are only estates for life, there wanting the words of inheritance, his heirs. So, on the other hand, a gift to a man, and his heirs male, or female, is an estate in fee simple, and not in fee-tail; for there are no words to ascertain the body out of which they shall issue.

FRANK-MARRIAGE — There is still another species of entailed estates, now indeed grown out of use, yet still capable of subsisting in law; which are estates in frank-marriage. These are defined to be, where tenements are given by one man to another, together with a wife, who is the daughter or cousin of the donor, to hold in frank-marriage. By such gift, though nothing but the word "frank-marriage" is expressed, the donees shall have the tenements to them, and the heirs of their two bodies begotten; that is, they are tenants in special tail. For this one word, frank-marriage, does not only create an inheritance, like the word frankalmoigne, but likewise limits that inheritance; supplying not only words of descent, but of procreation also. Such donees in frank-marriage are liable to no service but fealty; for a rent reserved thereon is void, until the fourth degree of consanguinity be past between the issues of the donor and donee.

✠ INCIDENTS OF TENANCY IN TAIL — The incidents to a tenancy in tail, under the statute are chiefly these:

1. That a tenant in tail may commit waste on the estate-tail, by selling timber, pulling down houses, or the like, without being impeached, or called to account, for the same.

2. That the wife of the tenant in tail shall have her dower, or thirds, of the estate-tail.

3. That the husband of a female tenant in tail may be tenant by the curtesy of the estate-tail.

4. That an estate may be barred, or destroyed by a fine, by a common recovery, or by lineal warranty descending with assets to the heir.

✠ EVILS OF ESTATES-TAIL — Thus much for the nature of estates-tail: the establishment of which family law occasioned infinite difficulties and disputes. Children grew disobedient when they knew that they could not be set aside: farmers were ousted of their leases made by tenants in tail; for, if such leases had been valid, then under color of long leases the issue might have been virtually disinherited: creditors were defrauded of their debts; for, if tenant in tail could have charged his estate with their payment, he might also have defeated his issue, by mortgaging it for as much as it was worth: innumerable latent entails were produced to deprive purchasers of the lands they have fairly bought: of suits in consequence of which our ancient books are full: and treasons were encouraged; as estates-tail were not liable to forfeiture, longer than for the tenant's life. So that they were justly branded, as the source of new contentions, and mischiefs unknown to the common law; and almost universally considered as the common grievance of the realm. But as the nobility were always fond of this statute (De Donis), because it preserved their family estates from forfeiture, there was little hope of procuring a repeal by the legislature; and therefore, by the connivance of an active and politic prince, a method was devised to evade it.

✠ COMMON RECOVERIES — About two hundred years intervened between the making of the statute De Donis (1285), and the application of common recoveries to this intent, in (1472): which were then openly declared by the judges to be a sufficient bar of an estate-tail. For though the courts had, so long before as (1326-1377), very frequently hinted their opinion that a bar might be effected upon these principles, yet it never was carried into execution; till Edward IV observing (in the disputes between the houses of York and Lancaster) how little effect attainders for treason had on families, whose estates were protected by the sanctuary of entails, gave his countenance to this proceeding, wherein, in consequence of the principles then laid down, it was in effect determined, that a common recovery suffered by tenant in tail should be an effectual destruction thereof.

What common recoveries are, both in their nature and consequences, and why they are allowed to be a bar to the estate-tail, must be reserved to a subsequent inquiry. At present I shall only say, that they are fictitious proceedings, introduced by a kind of pious fraud, to elude the statute de donis, which was found so intolerably mischievous, and which yet one branch of the legislature would not then consent to repeal: and, that these recoveries, however clandestinely begun, are now become by long use and acquiescence a most common assurance of lands; and are looked upon as the legal mode of conveyance, by which tenant in tail may dispose of his lands and tenements: so that no court will suffer them to be shaken or reflected on, and even acts of parliament have by a sidewind countenanced and established them.

☙☙ STATUTE OF TREASON (1534) — This expedient having greatly abridged estates-tail with regard to their duration, others were soon invented to strip them of other privileges. The next that was attacked was their freedom from forfeitures for treason. For, notwithstanding the large advances made by recoveries, in the compass of about threescore years, towards unfettering these inheritances, and thereby subjecting the lands to forfeiture, the rapacious prince then reigning, finding them frequently resettled in a similar manner to suit the convenience of families, had address enough to procure a statute, whereby all estates of inheritance (under which general words estates-tail were covertly included) are declared to be forfeited to the king upon any conviction of high treason.

☙☙ STATUTE OF LEASES (1540) AND FINES (1540) — The next attack which they suffered in order of time was by statute (Leaseholds, 1540), whereby certain leases made by tenants in tail, which do not tend to the prejudice of the issue, were allowed to be good in law, and to bind the issue in tail. But they received a more violent blow, in the same session of parliament, by the construction put upon the statute of fines, by the statute (Fines, 1540), which declares a fine duly levied by tenant in tail to be a complete bar to him and his heirs, and all other persons, claiming under such entail. This was evidently agreeable to the intention of Henry VII, whose policy it was (before common recoveries had obtained their full strength and authority) to lay the road as open as possible to the alienation of landed property, in order to weaken the overgrown power of his nobles. But as they, from the opposite reasons, were not easily brought to consent to such a provision, it was therefore couched, in his act, under covert and obscure expressions.

The judges, though willing to construe that statute as favorably as possible for the defeating of entailed estates, yet hesitated at giving fines so extensive a power by mere implication, when the statute de donis had expressly declared, that they should not be a bar to estates-tail. But the statute of Henry VIII, when the doctrine of alienation was better received, and the will of the prince more implicitly obeyed than before, avowed and established that intention.

⚖ EXCEPTIONS IN FAVOR OF THE CROWN — Yet, in order to preserve the property of the crown from any danger of infringement, all estates-tail created by the crown, and of which the crown has the reversion, are excepted out of this statute. The same was done with regard to common recoveries, by the statute (Fines and Recoveries, 1542), which enacts that no feigned recovery had against tenants in tail where the estate was created by the crown, and the remainder or reversion continues still in the crown, shall be of any force and effect. Which is allowing, indirectly and collaterally, their full force and effect with respect to ordinary estates-tail, where the royal prerogative is not concerned.

Lastly, by a statute of the succeeding year, all estates-tail are rendered liable to be charged for payment of debts due to the kind by record or special contract; as since, by the bankrupt laws, they are also subjected to be sold for the debts contracted by a bankrupt. By the construction put on the statute (Charitable Uses, 1601), an appointment by tenant in tail of the lands entailed, to a charitable use, is good without fine or recovery.

⚖ RESULTING CONDITION OF ESTATES-TAIL — Estates-tail, being thus by degrees unfettered, are now reduced again to almost the same state, even before issue born, as conditional fees were in at common law, after the condition was performed, by the birth of issue. For, first, the tenant in tail is now enabled to alien his lands and tenements by fine, by recovery, or by certain other means; and thereby to defeat the interest as well as his own issue, though unborn, as also of the reversioner, except in the case of the crown: secondly, he is now liable to forfeit them for high treason: and, lastly, he may charge them with reasonable leases, and also with such of his debts as are due to the crown on specialties, or have been contracted with his fellow-subjects in a course of extensive commerce.

FREEHOLDS, NOT
OF INHERITANCE

⚘ TWO KINDS OF ESTATES FOR LIFE — We are next to discourse of such estates of freehold as are not of inheritance, but for life only. And of these estates for life, some are conventional, or expressly created by the acts of the parties; others merely legal, or created by construction and operation of law.

⚘ CONVENTIONAL ESTATES FOR LIFE — Estates for life, expressly created by deed or grant (which alone are properly conventional), and where a lease is made of lands or tenements to a man, to hold for the term of his own life, or for that of any other person, or for more lives than one: in any of which cases he is styled tenant for life; only, when he holds the estate by the life of another, he is usually called tenant for the life of another.

These estates for life are, like inheritances, of a feudal nature; and were, for some time, the highest estate that any man could have in a feud, which was not in its original hereditary. They are given or conferred by the same feudal rights and solemnities, the same investiture or livery of seisin, as fees themselves are; and they are held by fealty, if demanded, and such conventional rents and services as the lord or lessor, and his tenant or lessee, have agreed on.

⚘ ESTATES FOR LIFE CREATED BY GENERAL GRANT — Estates for life may be created, not only by the express words before mentioned, but also by a general grant, without defining or limiting any specific estate. As, if one grants to A the manor of Dale, this makes him tenant for life. For though, as there are no words of inheritance, or heirs, mentioned in the grant, it cannot be construed to be a fee, it shall, however, be construed to be as large an estate as the words of the donation will bear, and therefore an estate for life. Also such a grant at large, or a grant for term of life generally, shall be construed to be an estate for the life of the grantee; in case the grantor hath authority to make such a grant: for an estate for a man's own life is more beneficial and of a higher nature than for any other life;

and the rule of law is, that all grants are to be taken most strongly against the grantor, unless in the case of the kind.

   ⚖   CONDITIONAL LIFE ESTATES — Such estates for life will, generally speaking, endure as long as the life for which they are granted: but there are some estates for life, which may determine upon future contingencies, before the life, for which they are created, expires. As, if an estate be granted to a woman during her widowhood, or to a man until he be promoted to a benefice; in these, and similar cases, whenever the contingency happens, when the widow marries, or when the grantee obtains a benefice, the respective estates are absolutely determined and gone.

     Yet, while they subsist, they are reckoned estates for life; because, the time for which they will endure being uncertain, they may by possibility last for life, if the contingencies upon which they are to determine do not sooner happen. Moreover, in case an estate be granted to a man for his life, generally, it may also determine by his civil death: as if he enters into a monastery, whereby he is dead in law: for which reason in conveyances the grant is usually made "for the term of a man's natural life"; which can only determine by his natural death.

   ⚖   INCIDENTS OF ESTATES FOR LIFE — The incidents to an estate for life are principally the following; which are applicable not only to that species of tenants for life, which are expressly created by deed; but also to those, which are created by act and operation of law.

   ⚖   ESTOVERS OR BOTES — Every tenant for life, unless restrained by covenant or agreement, may of common right take upon the land demised to him reasonable estovers or botes. For he hath a right to the full enjoyment and use of the land, and all its profits, during his estate therein. But he is not permitted to cut down timber or do other waste upon the premises: for the destruction of such things, as are not the temporary profits of the tenement, is not necessary for the tenant's complete enjoyment of his estate; but tends to the permanent and lasting loss of the person entitled to the inheritance.

   ⚖   EMBLEMENTS — Tenant for life, or his representatives, shall not be prejudiced by any sudden determination of his estate, because such a determination is contingent and uncertain. Therefore, if a tenant for his own life sows the lands, and dies before the harvest, his executors shall have the emblements, or profits of the crop: for the estate was determined by the act of God; and it is a maxim in the law, that the act of God injures no man. The representatives, therefore, of the tenant for life shall have the emblements, to compensate for the labor and expense of tilling, manuring, and sowing the lands; and also for the encouragement of husbandry, which being a public benefit, tending to the increase and plenty of provisions, ought to have the utmost security and privilege that the law can give it. Wherefore by the feudal law, if a tenant for life died between the beginning of September and the end of February, the lord, who was entitled to the reversion, was also entitled to the profits of the whole year: but, if he died between the beginning of March and the end of August, the heirs of the tenant received the whole.

So it is also, if a man be tenant for the life of another, and he on whose life the land is held, dies after the corn sown, the tenant (for the life of another) shall have the emblements. The same is also the rule, if a life estate be determined by the act of law. Therefore, if a lease be made to husband and wife during coverture (which gives them a determinable estate for life), and the husband sows the land, and afterwards they are divorced (from the bond of matrimony), the husband shall have the emblements in this case; for the sentence of divorce is the act of law.

But if an estate for life be determined by the tenants own act (as, by forfeiture for waste committed: or, if a tenant during widowhood thinks proper to marry), in these, and similar cases, the tenants, having thus determined the estate by their own acts, shall not be entitled to take the emblements.

The doctrine of emblements extends not only to corn sown, but to roots planted, or other annual artificial profit, but it is otherwise of fruit-trees, grass, and the like; which are not planted annually at the expense and labor of the tenant, but are either a permanent, or natural, profit of the earth. For even when a man plants a tree, he cannot be presumed to plant it in contemplation of any present profit; but merely with a prospect of its being useful to future successions of tenants.

The advantages also of emblements are particularly extended to the parochial clergy by statute (First-fruits, 1536). For all persons, who are presented to any ecclesiastical benefice, or to any civil office, are considered as tenants for their own lives, unless the contrary be expressed in the form of donation.

⚖ RIGHTS OF SUBTENANTS — A third incident to estates for life relates to the under-tenants or lessees. They have the same, nay greater indulgences than their lessors, the original tenants for life. The same; for the law of estovers and emblements, with regard to the tenant for life, is also law with regard to his under-tenant, who represents him and stands in his place: and greater; for in those cases where tenant for life shall not have the emblements, because the estate determines by his own act, the exception shall not reach his lessee who is a third person. As in the case of a woman who holds during widowhood; her taking husband is her own act, and therefore deprives her of the emblements: but if she leases her estate to an under-tenant, who sows the land, and she then marries, this her act shall not deprive the tenant of his emblements, who is a stranger and could not prevent her.

The lessees of tenants for life had also at the common law another most unreasonable advantage; for, at the death of their lessors the tenants for life, these undertenants might if they pleased quit the premises, and pay no rent to anybody for the occupation of the land since the last quarter day, or other day assigned for payment of rent. To remedy which it is now enacted, that the executors or administrators of tenant for life, on whose death any lease determined, shall recover of the lessee a ratable proportion of rent, from the last day of payment to the death of such lessor.

⚖️ LEGAL ESTATES FOR LIFE: ESTATE IN TAIL AFTER POSSIBILITY OF ISSUE EXTINCT — The next estate for life is of the legal kind, as contradistinguished from conventional; viz., that of tenant in tail after possibility of issue extinct.

This happens, where one is tenant in special tail, and a person, from whose body the issue was to spring, dies without issue; or, having left issue, that issue becomes extinct: in either of these cases the surviving tenant in special tail becomes tenant in tail after possibility of issue extinct. As, where one has an estate to him and his heirs on the body of his present wife to be begotten, and the wife dies without issue: in this case the man has an estate-tail, which cannot possibly descend to anyone; therefore the law makes use of this long periphrasis, as absolutely necessary to give an adequate idea of his estate. For if it had called him barely tenant in fee-tail special, that would not have distinguished him from others; and besides he had no longer an estate of inheritance, or fee, for he can have no heirs, capable of taking by the form of the gift.

Had it called him tenant in tail without issue, this had only related to the present fact, and would not have excluded the possibility of future issue. Had he been styled tenant in tail without possibility of issue, this would exclude time past as well as present, and he might under this description never have had any possibility of issue. No definition, therefore, could so exactly mark him out, as this of tenant in tail after possibility of issue extinct, which (with a precision peculiar to our own law) not only takes in the possibility of issue in tail which he once had, but also states that this possibility is now extinguished and gone.

This estate must be created by the act of God, that is, by the death of that person out of whose body the issue was to spring; for no limitation, conveyance, or other human act can make it. For, if land be given to a man and his wife, and the heirs of their two bodies begotten, and they are divorced, they shall neither of them have this estate, but be barely tenants for life, notwithstanding the inheritance once vested in them. A possibility of issue is always supposed to exist, in law, unless extinguished by the death of the parties; even though the donees be each of them an hundred years old.

This estate is of an amphibious nature, partaking partly of an estate-tail, and partly of an estate for life. The tenant is, in truth, only tenant for life, but with many of the privileges of a tenant in tail, as, not to be punishable for waste, etc.: or, he is tenant in tail, with many of the restrictions of a tenant for life; as, to forfeit his estate if he aliens it in fee simple: whereas such alienation by tenant in tail, though voidable by the issue, is no forfeiture of the estate to the reversioner: who is not concerned in interest, till all possibility of issue be extinct. But, in general, the law looks upon this estate as equivalent to an estate for life only; and, as such, will permit this tenant to exchange his estate with a tenant for life; which exchange can only be made, as we shall be hereafter, of estates that are equal in their nature.

⚖️ TENANCY BY THE CURTESY — Tenant by the curtesy of England is where a man marries a woman seised of lands and tenements in fee simple or fee-tail; that is, of an estate of inheritance; and has by her issue, born alive, which was capable of inheriting her estate. In this case, he shall on the death of his wife, hold the lands for his life, as tenant by the curtesy of England.

This estate is used within the realm of England only; and it is said to have been introduced by King Henry I; but it appears also to have been the established law of Scotland, wherein it was called curialitas: so that probably our word "curtesy" was understood to signify rather an attendance upon the lord's court or curtis (that is, being his vassal or tenant), than to denote any peculiar favor belonging to this island. Therefore it is laid down that by having issue, the husband shall be entitled to do homage to the lord, for the wife's lands, alone: whereas, before issue had, they must have both done it together.

Yet it is not generally apprehended to have been a consequence of feudal tenure, though I think some substantial feudal reasons may be given for its introduction. For, if a woman seised of lands have issue by her husband, and dies, the husband is the natural guardian of the child, and as such is in reason entitled to the profits of the lands in order to maintain it; and, therefore, the heir apparent of a tenant by the curtesy could not be in ward to the lord of the fee, during the life of such tenant. As soon, therefore, as any child was born, the father began to have a permanent interest in the lands; he became one of the peers of the court, and was called tenant by the curtesy initiate; and this estate being once vested in him by the birth of the child, was not liable to be determined by the subsequent death or coming of age of the infant.

⚖ REQUISITES TO MAKE A TENANCY BY THE CURTESY — There are four requisites necessary to make a tenancy by the curtesy; marriage, siesin of the wife, issue, and death of the wife: 1. The marriage must be canonical and legal.

2. The seisin of the wife must be an actual seisin, or possession of the lands; not a bare right to possess, which is a seisin in law, but an actual possession, which is a seisin in deed. Therefore a man shall not be tenant by the curtesy of a remainder or reversion.

But of some incorporeal hereditaments a man may be tenant by the curtesy, though there have been no actual seisin of the wife: as in case of an advowson, where the church has not become void in the lifetime of the wife; which a man may hold by the curtesy, because it is impossible to have had actual seisin of it. If the wife be an idiot, the husband shall not be tenant by the curtesy of her lands; for the king by prerogative is entitled to them, the instant she herself has any title: and since she could never be rightfully seised of the lands, and the husband's title depends entirely upon her seisin, the husband can have no title as tenant by the curtesy.

3. The issue must be born alive. Some have a notion that it must be heard to cry; but that is a mistake. Crying, indeed, is the strongest evidence of its being born alive, but it is not the only evidence. The issue also must be born during the life of the mother; for, if the mother dies in labor, and the Caesarean operation is performed, the husband in this case shall not be tenant by the curtesy: because, at the instant of the mother's death, he was clearly not entitled, as having had no issue born, but the land descended to the child, while he was yet in his mother's womb; and the estate being once so vested, shall not afterwards be taken from him.

In gavelkind lands, a husband may be tenant by the curtesy without having any issue. But in general there must be issue born; and such issue must also be capable of inheriting the mother's estate. Therefore, if a woman be a tenant in tail male, and hath only a daughter born, the husband is not thereby entitled to be tenant by the curtesy; because such issue female can never inherit the estate in tail male. This seems to be the true reason why the husband cannot be tenant by the curtesy of any lands of which the wife was not actually seised: because, in order to entitle himself to such estate, he must have begotten issue that may be heir to the wife; but no one by the standing rule of law can be heir to the ancestor of any land whereof the ancestor was not actually seised; and therefore as the husband hath never begotten any issue that can be heir to those lands, he shall not be tenant of them by the curtesy.

The time when the issue was born is immaterial, provided it were during the coverture: for, whether it were born before or after the wife's seisin of the lands, whether it be living or dead at the time of the seisin, or at the time of the wife's decease, the husband shall be tenant by the curtesy. The husband by the birth of the child becomes tenant by the curtesy initiate, and may do many acts to charge the lands: but his estate is not consummate till the death of the wife; which is the fourth and last requisite to make a complete tenant by the curtesy.

⚖ TENANCY IN DOWER — Tenant in dower is where the husband of a woman is seised of an estate of inheritance, and dies; in this case, the wife shall have the third part of all the lands and tenements whereof he was seised during the coverture, to hold to herself for the term of her natural life.

Dower is the marriage portion, which the wife brought to her husband; to which the civil law, in its original state, had nothing that bore a resemblance. Dower out of lands seems to have been unknown in the early part of our Saxon constitution; for, in the laws of King Edmond, the wife is directed to be supported wholly out of the personal estate. Afterwards, as may be seen in gavelkind tenure, the widow became entitled to a conditional estate in one-half of the lands; with a proviso that she remained chaste and unmarried; as is usual also in copyhold dowers, or free-bench.

The reason, which our law gives for adopting it, is a very plain and sensible one; for the sustenance of the wife, and the nurture and education of the younger children.

⚖ WHO MAY BE ENDOWED — In treating of this estate, let us first consider who may be endowed; secondly, of what she may be endowed; thirdly, the manner how she shall not be endowed; for where there is no marriage, there is no dower due. But a divorce from bed and board only doth not destroy the dower; no, not even for adultery itself by the common law. Yet now by statute if a woman elopes from her husband, and lives with an adulterer, she shall lose her dower, unless her husband be voluntarily reconciled to her.

It was formerly held, that the wife of an idiot might be endowed, though the husband of an idiot could not be tenant by the curtesy: but as it seems to be at present agreed, upon principles of sound sense and reason, that an idiot cannot marry, being incapable of consenting to any contract, this doctrine cannot now take place.

By the ancient law the wife of a person attainted of treason or felony could not be endowed; to the intent that if the love of a man's own life cannot restrain him from such atrocious acts, the love of his wife and children may: though it's presumed the wife was privy to her husband's crime. However, the statute (Criminal Law, 1547), abated the rigor of the common law in this particular, and allowed the wife her dower. But a subsequent statute revived this severity against the widows of traitors, who are now barred of their dower (except in the case of certain modern treasons relating to the coin), but not the widows of felons.

An alien, also, cannot be endowed, unless she be queen consort; for no alien is capable of holding lands. The wife must be above nine years old at her husband's death, otherwise she shall not be endowed.

OF WHAT ENDOWED — We are next to inquire, of what a wife may be endowed. She is now by law entitled to be endowed of all lands and tenements, of which her husband was seised in fee simple or fee-tail at any time during the coverture; and of which any issue, which she might have had, might by possibility have been heir, therefore, if a man, seised in fee simple, hath a son by his first wife, and after marries a second wife, she shall be endowed of his lands; for her issue might by possibility have been heir, on the death of the son by the former wife. But, if there be a donee in special tail, who holds lands to him and the heirs of his body begotten on Jane his wife; though Jane may be endowed of these lands, yet if Jane dies, and he marries a second wife, that second wife shall never be endowed of the lands entailed; for no issue, that she could have, could by any possibility inherit them.

A seisin in law of the husband will be as effectual as a seisin in deed, in order to render the wife dowable; for it is not in the wife's power to bring the husband's title to an actual seisin, as it is in the husband's power to do with regard to the wife's lands: which is one reason why he shall not be tenant by the curtesy, of such lands whereof the wife, or he himself in her right, was actually seised in deed. The seisin of the husband, for a transitory instant only, when the same act which gives him the estate conveys it also out of him again (as where by a fine land is granted to a man, and he immediately renders it back by the same fine), such a seisin will not entitle the wife to dower; for the land was merely passing through his hands, and never rested in the husband. But, if the land abides in him for a single moment, it seems that the wife shall be endowed thereof. In short, a widow may be endowed of all her husband's lands, tenements, and hereditaments, corporeal or incorporeal, under the restrictions, before mentioned; unless there be some special reason to the contrary.

Thus, a woman shall not be endowed of a castle, built for defense of the realm: nor of a common without stint; for, as the heir would then have one portion of this common, and the widow another, and both without stint, the common would be doubly stocked. Copyhold estates are also not liable to dower, being only estates at the lord's will; unless by the special custom of the manor, in which case it is usually called the widow's free-bench. But, where dower is allowable, it matters not, though the husband alien the lands during the coverture; for he aliens them liable to dower.

☙ HOW DOWER ATTACHES — Next, as to the manner in which a woman is to be endowed. There are now subsisting four species of dower.

1. Dower by the common law; or that which is before described.

2. Dower by particular custom; as that the wife should have half the husband's lands, or in some places the whole, and in some only a quarter.

3. Dower at the church door: which is where tenant in fee simple of full age, openly at the church door, where all marriages were formerly celebrated, after affiance made and troth plighted between them, doth endow his wife with the whole, or such quantity as he shall please, of his lands; at the same time specifying and ascertaining the same: on which the wife, after her husband's death, may enter without further ceremony.

4. Dower by assent of the father; which is only a species of dower made when the husband's father is alive, and the son by his consent, expressly given, endows his wife with parcel of his father's lands. In either of these cases, they must to prevent frauds be made in the face of the

church, and at the church door; for those made on a death-bed, in a chamber or elsewhere, where the nuptials have been private, are not valid.

⚖️ HISTORY OF DOWER — It is curious to observe the several revolutions which the doctrine of dower has undergone, since its introduction into England. It seems first to have been of the nature of the dower in gavelkind, before mentioned; viz., a modiety of the husband's lands, but forfeitable by incontinency or second marriage. By the famous charter of Henry I this condition, of widowhood and chastity, was only required in case the husband left any issue: and afterwards we hear no more of it.

Under Henry the Second, the dower at the church door was the most usual species of dower; and here as well as in Normandy, it was binding upon the wife, if by her consented to at the time of marriage. Neither, in those days of feudal rigor, was the husband allowed to endow her with more than the third part of the lands whereof he was seised, though he might endow her with less; lest by such liberal endowments the lord should be defrauded of his wardships and other feudal profits.

If no specific donation was made at the church porch, then she was endowed by the common law of the third part which was called her reasonable dower of such lands and tenements, as the husband was seised of at the time of the espousals, and no other; unless he specially engaged before the priest to endow her of his future acquisitions: and, if the husband had no lands, an endowment in goods, chattels, or money, at the time of espousals, was a bar of any dower in lands which he afterwards acquired.

In King John's magna carta, and the first charter of Henry III, no mention is made of any alteration of the common law, in respect of the lands subject to dower; but in those of 1217, and 1224, it is particularly provided, that a widow shall be entitled for her dower to the third part of all such lands as the husband had held in his lifetime: yet, in case of a specific endowment of less, the widow had still no power to waive it after her husband's death. This continued to be law, during the reigns of Henry III and Edward I. In Henry IV's time it was denied to be law, that a woman can be endowed of her husband's good and chattels: and, under Edward IV, expressly is it said that a woman may be endowed with more than a third part; and shall have her election, after her husband's death, to accept such dower, or refuse it, and betake herself to her dower at common law. Which state of uncertainty was probably the reason, that these specific dowers at the church door and by assent of the father have since fallen into total disuse.

ASSIGNMENT OF DOWER — I proceed to consider the method of endowment, or assigning dower, by the common law, which is now the only usual species.

By the old law, grounded on the feudal exactions, a woman could not be endowed without a fine paid to the lord; neither could she marry again without his license; lest she should contract herself, and so convey part of the feud to the lord's enemy. This license, the lords took care to be well paid for; and, as it seems, would sometimes force the dowager to a second marriage, in order to gain the fine.

To remedy these oppressions, it was provided, first by the charter of Henry I, and afterwards by magna carta, that the widow shall pay nothing for her marriage, nor shall be distrained to marry afresh, if she chooses to live without a husband; but shall not, however, marry against the consent of the lord: and further, that nothing shall be taken for assignment of the widow's dower, but that she shall remain in her husband's capital mansion-house for forty days after his death, during which time her dower shall be assigned. These forty days are called the widow's quarantine; a term made use of in law to signify the number of forty days, whether applied to this occasion or any other.

The particular lands to be held in dower, must be assigned by the heir of the husband or his guardian; not only for the sake of notoriety, but also to entitle the lord of the fee to demand his services of the heir, in respect of the lands so holden. For the heir by this entry becomes tenant thereof to the lord, and the widow is immediate tenant to the heir, by a kind of subinfeudation, or under tenancy, completed by this investiture or assignment; which tenure may still be created, notwithstanding the statute (1290), because the heir parts not with the fee simple, but only with an estate for life.

If the heir or his guardian do not assign her dower within the term of quarantine, or do assign it unfairly, she has her remedy at law, and the sheriff is appointed to assign it. Or if the heir (being under age) or his guardian assign, more than she ought to have, it may be afterwards remedied by writ of admeasurement of dower. If the thing of which she is endowed be divisible, her dower must be set out by metes and bounds; but, if it be indivisible, she must be endowed specially; as, of the third presentation to a church, the third toll-dish of a mill, the third part of the profits of an office, the third sheaf of tithe, and the like.

Upon preconcerted marriages, and in estates of considerable consequence, tenancy in dower happens very seldom: for, the claim of the wife to her dower at the common law diffusing itself so extensively, it became a great clog to alienations, and was otherwise inconvenient to families. Wherefore, since the alteration of the ancient law respecting dower, which hath occasioned the entire disuse of that species of dower, jointures have been introduced in their stead, as a bar to the claim at common law. Which leads me to inquire, lastly.

⚖️ BARRING DOWER — A widow may be barred of her dower not only by elopement, divorce, being an alien, the treason of her husband, and other disabilities before mentioned, but also by detaining the title deeds, or evidences of the estate from the heir; until she restores them: and, by statute if a dowager aliens the land assigned her for dower, she forfeits it ipso facto, and the heir may recover it by action. A woman also may be barred of her dower, by levying a fine or suffering a recovery of the lands, during her coverture. But the most usual method of barring dowers is by jointures, as regulated by statute (Statute of Uses, 1535).

⚖️ JOINTURES — A jointure, which, strictly speaking, signifies a joint estate, limited to both husband and wife, but in common acceptation extends also to a sole estate, limited to the wife only, is thus defined "a competent livelihood of freehold for the wife, of lands and tenements; to take effect, in profit or possession, presently after the death of the husband; for the life of the wife at least." This description is framed from the purview of the statute (1535), before mentioned; commonly called the statute of uses, of which we shall speak fully hereafter. At present I have only to observe, that before the making of that statute, the greatest part of the land of England was conveyed to uses; the property or possession of the soil being vested in one man, and the use, or profits thereof, in another; whose directions, with regard to the disposition thereof, the former was in conscience obliged to follow, and might be compelled by a court of equity to observe. Now, though a husband had the use of lands in absolute fee simple, yet the wife was not entitled to any dower therein; he not being seised thereof: wherefore it became usual, on marriage, to settle by express deed some special estate to the use of the husband and his wife, for their lives, in joint tenancy or jointure; which settlement would be a provision for the wife in case she survived her husband.

At length the statute of uses ordained, that such as had the use of lands, should, to all intents and purposes, be reputed and taken to be absolutely seised and possessed of the soil itself. In consequence of which legal seisin, all wives would have become dowable of such lands as were held to the use of their husbands, and also entitled at the same time to any special lands that might be settled in jointure: had not the same statute provide, that upon making such an estate in jointure to the wife before marriage, she shall be forever precluded from her dower.

⚖ REQUISITES OF A JOINTURE — But then these four requisites must be punctually observed:

1. The jointure must take effect immediately on the death of the husband.

2. It must be for her own life at least, and not for the life of another, or for any term of years, or other smaller estate.

3. It must be made to herself, and no other in trust for her.

4. It must be made, and so in the deed particularly expressed to be, in satisfaction of her whole dower, and not of any particular part of it.

If the jointure be made to her after marriage, she had her election after her husband's death, as in dower, and may either accept it, or refuse it and betake herself to her dower at common law; for she was not capable of consenting to it during coverture. If, by any fraud or accident, a jointure made before marriage proves to be on a bad title, and the jointress is evicted, or turned out of possession, she shall then have her dower to that amount at the common law.

⚖ RELATIVE ADVANTAGES OF DOWER AND JOINTURE — There are some advantages attending tenants in dower that do not extend to jointresses; and so vice versa, jointresses are in some respects more privileged than tenants in dower. Tenant in dower by the old common law is subject to no tolls or taxes; and hers is almost the only estate on which, when derived from the king's debtor, the king cannot distrain for his debt; if contracted during the coverture. But, on the other hand, a widow may enter at once, without any formal process, on her jointure land; as she also might have done on dower which a jointure in many points resembles; and the resemblance was still greater, while that species of dower continued in its primitive state; whereas no small trouble, and a very tedious method of proceeding, is necessary to compel a legal assignment of dower. What is more, though dower be forfeited by the treason of the husband, yet lands settled in jointure remain unimpeached to the widow.

ESTATES LESS THAN FREEHOLD

☙ KINDS OF ESTATES LESS THAN FREEHOLD — Of estates, that are less than freehold, there are three sorts:

1. Estates for years.
2. Estates at will.
3. Estates by sufferance.

☙ ESTATES FOR YEARS — An estate for years is a contract for the possession of lands or tenements, for some determinate period: it takes place where a man letteth them to another for the term of a certain number of years, agreed upon between the lessor and the lessee, and the lessee enters thereon. If the lease be but for half a year, or a quarter, or any less time, this lessee is respected as a tenant for years and is styled so in some legal proceedings; a year being the shortest term which the law in this case takes notice of. This may, not improperly, lead us into a short explanation of the division and calculation of time by the English law.

☙ COMPUTATION OF TIME — The space of a year is a determinate and well-known period, consisting commonly of 365 days: for, though in leap-years it consists properly of 366, yet by statute (1236) the increasing day in the leap-year, together with the preceding day, shall be accounted for one day only.

That of a month is more ambiguous: there being, in common use, two ways of calculating months; either as lunar, consisting of twenty-eight days, the supposed revolution of the moon, thirteen of which make a year: or, as calendar months of unequal lengths, according to the Julian division in our common almanacs, commencing at the calends of each month, whereof in a year there are only twelve.

A month in law is a lunar month, or twenty-eight days, unless otherwise expressed; not only because it is always one uniform period, but because it falls naturally into a quarterly division by weeks. There-fore, a lease for "twelve months" is only for forty-eight weeks; but if it be for "a twelve month" in the singular number, it is good for the whole year. Herein the law recedes from its usual calculation, because the ambiguity between the two methods of computation ceases; it being generally understood that by the space of time called thus, in the singular number, a twelvemonth, is meant the whole year consisting of one solar revolution.

In the space of a day all the twenty-four hours are usually reckoned, the law generally rejecting all fractions of a day, in order to avoid disputes. Therefore, if I am bound to pay money on any certain day, I discharge the obligation if I pay it before 12 o'clock at night; after which the following day commences. But to return to estates for years.

⚖ ESTATES FOR YEARS ORIGINALLY PRECARIOUS — These estates were originally granted to mere farmers or husbandmen, who every year rendered some equivalent in money, provisions, or other rent to the lessors or landlords; but, in order to encourage them to manure and cultivate the ground, they had a permanent interest granted them, not determinable at the will of the lord. Their possession was esteemed of so little consequence, that they were rather considered as the bailiffs or servants of the lord, who were to receive and account for the profits at a settled price, than as having any property of their own. They were not allowed to have a freehold estate: but their interest (such as it was) vested after their deaths in their executors, who were to make up the accounts of their testator with the lord, and his other creditors, and were entitled to the stock upon the farm. The lessee's estate might also, by the ancient law, be at any time defeated, by a common recovery suffered by the tenant of the freehold; which annihilated all leases for years then subsisting, unless afterwards renewed by the recoverer, whose title was supposed superior to his by whom those leases were granted.

⚖ DURATION OF ESTATES FOR YEARS — While estates for years were thus precarious, it is no wonder that they were usually very short, like our modern leases upon rack-rent; and indeed we are told that by the ancient law no leases for more than forty years were allowable, because any longer possession might tend to defeat the inheritance. Yet this law, if ever it existed, was soon antiquated; for we may observe, in Madox's collection of ancient instruments, some leases for years of a pretty early date, which considerably exceed that period, and long terms, for three hundred years or a thousand were certainly in use in the time of Edward III, and probably of Edward I.

But certainly, when by the statute (1529), the termor (that is, he who is entitled to the term of years) was protected against these fictitious recoveries, and his interest rendered secure and permanent, long terms began to be more frequent than before; and were afterwards extensively introduced, being found extremely convenient for family settlements and mortgages: continuing subject, however, to the same rules of succession, and with the same inferiority to freeholds, as when they were little better than tenancies at the will of the landlord.

⚖ DEFINITION OF ESTATE FOR YEARS — Every estate which must expire at a period certain and prefixed, by whatever words created, is an estate for years. Therefore this estate is frequently called a term, because its duration or continuance is bounded, limited, and determined: for every such estate must have a certain beginning, and certain end.

That is certain which can be made certain: therefore, if a man make a lease to another, for so many years as J.S. shall name, it is a good lease for years; for though it is at present uncertain, yet when J.S. hath named the years, it is then reduced to a certainty. If no day of commencement is named in the creation of this estate, it begins from the making, or delivery of the lease. A lease for so many years as J.S. shall live, is void from the beginning; for it is neither certain, nor can ever be reduced to a certainty, during the continuance of the lease.

The same doctrine holds, if a person make a lease of his glebe for so many years as he shall continue parson of Dale; for this is still more uncertain. But a lease for twenty or more years, if J.S. shall so long live, or if he should so long continue parson, is good; for there is a certain period fixed, beyond which it cannot last; though it may determine sooner, on the death of J.S. or his ceasing to be parson there.

⚖ BEGINNING OF THE TERM — We have before remarked, and endeavored to assign the reason of, the inferiority in which the law places an estate for years, when compared with an estate for life, or an inheritance: observing, that an estate for life, even if it be for the life of another, is a freehold; but that an estate for a thousand years is only a chattel, and reckoned part of the personal estate. Hence it follows, that a lease for years may be made to commence at a future time, though a lease for life cannot. As, if I grant lands to Titius to hold from Michaelmas next for twenty years, this is good; but to hold from

Michaelmas next for the term of his natural life, is void. For no estate of freehold can commence at a future time; because it cannot be created at common law without livery of seisin, or corporal possession of the land: and corporal possession cannot be given of an estate now, which is not to commence now, but hereafter.

Because no livery of seisin is necessary to a lease for years, such lessee is not said to be seised, or to have true legal seisin of the lands. Nor, indeed, does the bare lease vest any estate in the lessee; but only gives him a right of entry on the tenement, which right is called his interest in the term, but when he has actually so entered, and thereby accepted the grant, the estate is then and not before vested in him, and he is possessed, not properly of the land, but of the term of years; the possession or seisin of the land remaining still in him who hath the freehold.

Thus the word "term" does not merely signify the time specified in the lease, but the estate also and interest, that passes by that lease; and therefore the term may expire, during the continuance of the time; as by surrender, forfeiture, and the like. For which reason, if I grant a lease to A for the term of three years, and after the expiration of said term to B for six years, and A surrenders or forfeits his lease at the end of one year, B's interest shall immediately take effect: but if the remainder had been to B from and after the expiration of the said time, in this case B's interest will not commence till the time is fully elapsed, whatever may become of A's term.

♉♉ INCIDENTS OF AN ESTATE FOR YEARS — Tenant for term of years hath incident to, and inseparable from his estate, unless by special agreement, the same estovers, which we formerly observed that tenant for life was entitled to: that is to say, house-bote, fire-bote, plow-bote, and hay-bote; terms which have already been explained.

♉♉ EMBLEMENTS — With regard to emblements, or profits of land sowed by tenant for years, there is this difference between him, and tenant for life: that where the term of tenant for years depends upon a certainty, as if he holds from midsummer for ten years, and in the last year he sows a crop of corn, and it is not ripe and cut before midsummer, the end of his term, the landlord shall have it; for the tenant knew the expiration of his term, and therefore it was his own folly to sow what he never could reap the profits of.

But where the lease for years depends upon an uncertainty; as, upon the death of the lessor, being himself only tenant for life, or being a husband seised in right of his wife; or if the term of years be determinable upon a life or lives; in all these cases, the estate for years not being certainly to expire at a time foreknown, but merely by the act of God, the tenant, or his executors, shall have the emblements in the same manner that a tenant for life or his executors shall be entitled thereto. Not so, if it determine by the act of the party himself; as if tenant for years does anything that amounts to a forfeiture: in which case the emblements shall go to the lessor, and not to the lessee, who hath determined his estate by his own default.

⚖ ESTATES AT WILL — The second species of estates not freehold are estates at will. An estate at will is where lands and tenements are let by one man to another, to have and to hold at the will of the lessor; and the tenant by force of this lease obtains possession. Such tenant hath no certain indefeasible estate, nothing that can be assigned by him to any other; because the lessor may determine his will, and put him out whenever he pleases.

But every estate at will is at the will of both parties, landlord and tenant; so that either of them may determine his will, and quit his connections with the other at his own pleasure. Yet this must be understood with some restriction. For, if the tenant at will sows his land, and the landlord, before the corn is ripe, or before it is reaped, put him out, yet the tenant shall have the emblements, and free ingress, egress, and regress, to cut and carry away the profits. This for the same reason, upon which all the cases of emblements turn; viz., the point of uncertainty: since the tenant could not possibly know when his landlord would determine his will, and therefore could make no provision against it; and having sown the land, which is for the good of the public, upon a reasonable presumption, the law will not suffer him to be a loser by it. But it is otherwise, and upon reason equally good, where the tenant himself determines the will; for in this case the landlord shall have the profits of the land.

⚖ TERMINATION OF ESTATE AT WILL — What act does, or does not, amount to a determination of the will on either side, had formerly been matter of great debate in our courts. It is now, I think, settled, that (besides the express determination of the lessor's will, by declaring that the lessee shall hold no longer; which must either be made upon the land, or notice must be given to the lessee), the exertion of any act of ownership by the lessor, as entering upon the premises and cutting timber, taking a distress for rents and impounding it thereon, or making a feoffment, or lease for years of the land to commence immediately; any act of desertion by the lessee, as assigning his estate to another, or commiting waste, which is an act inconsistent with such a tenure; or the death or outlawry, of either lessor or lessee; but an end to or determines the estate at will.

☙☙ RIGHTS AFTER TERMINATION OF ESTATE AT WILL — The law is, however, careful that no sudden determination of the will by one party shall tend to the manifest and unforeseen prejudice of the other. This appears in the case of emblements before mentioned; and, by the parity of reason, the lessee after the determination of the lessor's will, shall have reasonable ingress and egress to fetch away his goods and utensils.

If rent be payable quarterly or half-yearly, and the lessee determines the will, the rent shall be paid to the end of the current quarter or half-year. Upon the same principle, courts of law have of late years learned as much as possible against construing demises, where no certain term is mentioned, to be tenancies at will; but have rather held them to be tenancies from year to year so long as both parties please, especially where an annual rent is reserved: in which case they will not suffer either party to determine the tenancy even at the end of the year, without reasonable notice to the other.

☙☙ COPYHOLDS — There is one species of estates at will that deserves a more particular regard than any other; and that is, an estate held by copy of court roll; or, as we usually call it, a copyhold estate. This, as was before observed, was in its original and foundation nothing better than a mere estate at will. But the kindness and indulgence of successive lords of manors having permitted these estates to be enjoyed by the tenants and their heirs, according to particular customs established in their respective districts; therefore, though they still are held at the will of the lord, and so are in general expressed in the court rolls to be, yet that will is qualified, restrained, and limited, to be exerted according to the custom of the manor.

This custom, being suffered to grow up by the lord, is looked upon as the evidence and interpreter of his will: his will is no longer arbitrary and precarious; but fixed and ascertained by the custom to be the same, and no other, that has time out of mind been exercised and declared by his ancestors. A copyhold tenant is therefore now fully as properly a tenant by the custom having arisen from a series of uniform wills.

☙☙ FORMS OF COPYHOLD — A copyholder may, in many manors, be tenant in fee simple, in fee-tail, for life, by the curtesy, in dower, for years, at sufferance, or on condition; subject, however, to be deprived of these estates upon the concurrence of those circumstances which the will of the lord, promulged by immemorial custom, has declared to be a forfeiture or absolute determination of those interests; as in some manors the want of issue male, in others the cutting down of timber, the nonpayment of a fine, and the like. Yet none of these interests amount to freehold; for the freehold of the whole manor abides always in the lord only, who hath granted out the use and occupation, but not the corporal seisin or true possession of certain parts and parcels thereof, to these his customary tenants at will.

⚖️ EVOLUTION OF COPYHOLD — The reason of originally granting out this complicated kind of interest, so that the same man shall, with regard to the same land, be at one and the same time tenant in fee simple and also tenant at the lord's will, seems to have arisen from the nature of villeinage tenure; in which a grant of any estate of freehold, or even for years absolutely, was an immediate enfranchisement of the villein.

The lords, therefore, though they were willing to enlarge the interest of their villeins, by granting them estates which might endure for their lives, or sometimes be descendible to their issue, yet did not care to manumit them entirely; and for that reason it seems to have been contrived, that a power of resumption at the will of the lord should be annexed to these grants, whereby the tenants were still kept in a state of villeinage, and no freehold at all was conveyed to them in their respective lands: and of course, as the freehold of all lands must necessarily rest and abide somewhere, the law supposed it to continue and remain in the lord.

Afterwards, when these villeins became modern copyholders, and had acquired by custom a sure and indefeasible estate in their lands, on performing their usual services, but yet continued to be styled in their admissions tenants at the will of the lord—the law still supposed it an absurdity to allow, that such as were thus nominally tenants at will could have any freehold interest: and therefore continued and still continues to determine, that the freehold of lands so holden abides in the lord of the manor, and not in the tenant; for though he really holds to him and his heirs forever, yet he is also said to hold to another's will.

But with regard to certain other copyholders, of free or privileged tenure, which are derived from the ancient tenants in villein socage, and are not said to hold at the will of the lord, but only according to the custom of the manor, there is no such absurdity in allowing them to be capable of enjoying a freehold interest: and therefore the law doth not suppose the freehold of such lands to rest in the lord of whom they are holden, but in the tenants themselves; who are sometimes called customary freeholders, being allowed to have a freehold interest though not a freehold tenure.

However, in common cases, copyhold estates are still ranked (for the reasons above mentioned) among tenancies at will; though custom, which is the life of the common law, has established a permanent property in the copyholders, who were formerly nothing better than bondmen, equal to that of the lord himself in the tenements holden of the manor; nay, sometimes even superior; for we may now look upon a copyholder of inheritance, with a fine certain, to be little inferior to an absolute freeholder in point of interest, and in other respects, particularly in the clearness and security of his title, to be frequently in a better situation.

⚖ ESTATES AT SUFFERANCE — An estate at sufferance is where one comes into possession of land by lawful title, but keeps it afterwards without any title at all. As if a man takes a lease for a year, and, after the year is expired, continues to hold the premises without any fresh leave from the owner of the estate. Or, if a man maketh a lease at will, and dies, the estate at will is thereby determined: but if the tenant continueth possession, he is tenant at sufferance.

But, no man can be tenant at sufferance against the king, to whom no laches, or neglect, in not entering and ousting the tenant, is ever imputed by law: but his tenant, so holding over, is considered as an absolute intruder.

In the case of a subject, this estate may be destroyed whenever the true owner shall make an actual entry on the lands and oust the tenant; for, before entry, he cannot maintain an action of trespass against the tenant by sufferance, as he might against a stranger: and the reason is, because the tenant being once in by a lawful title, the law (which presumes no wrong in any man) will suppose him to continue upon a title equally lawful, unless the owner of the land by some public and avowed act, such as entry is, will declare his continuance to be tortious, or, in common language, wrongful.

Thus stands the law, with regard to tenants by sufferance; and landlords are obliged in these cases to make formal entries upon their lands, and recover possession by the legal process of ejectment: and at the utmost, by the common law, the tenant was bound to account for the profits of the land so by him detained. Now, by statute (Landlord and Tenant, 1730), in case any tenant for life or years, or other person claiming under or by collusion with such tenant, shall willfully hold over after the determination of the term, and demand made and notice in writing given, by him to whom the remainder or reversion of the premises shall belong, for delivering the possession thereof; such person, so holding over or keeping the other out of possession, shall pay for the time he detains the lands, at the rate of double their yearly value.

By statute (Distress for Rent, 1737), in case any tenant, having power to determine his lease, shall give notice of his intention to quit the premises, and shall not deliver up the possession at the time contained in such notice, he shall thenceforth pay double the rent, for such time as he continues in possession. These statutes have almost put an end to the practice of tenancy by sufferance, unless with the tacit consent of the owner of the tenement.

ESTATES UPON CONDITION

⚖ DEFINITION AND CLASSIFICATION OF ESTATES UPON CONDITION —
There is also an estate upon condition; being such whose existence depends upon the happening or not happening of some uncertain event, whereby the estate may be either originally created, or enlarged, or finally defeated. And these conditional estates I have chosen to reserve till last, because they are indeed more properly qualifications of other estates than a distinct species of themselves; seeing that any quantity of interest, a fee, a freehold, or a term of years, may depend upon these provisional restrictions.

Estates, then, upon condition, are of two sorts: 1. Estates upon condition implied: 2. Estates upon condition expressed, under which last may be included: 3. Estates held in vadio, gage, or pledge: 4. Estates by statute merchant or statute staple: 5. Estates held by elegit.

⚖ ESTATES UPON CONDITION, IMPLIED — Estates upon condition implied in law are where a grant of an estate has a condition annexed to it inseparably from its essence and constitution, although no condition be expressed in words. As if a grant be made to a man of an office, generally, without adding other words; the law tacitly annexes hereto a secret condition that the grantee shall duly execute his office, on breach of which condition it is lawful for the grantor, or his heirs, to oust him, and grant it to another person.

⚖ GROUNDS OF FORFEITURE — An office, either public or private, may be forfeited by misuser or nonuser, both of which are breaches of this implied condition. 1. By misuser, or abuse; as if a judge takes a bribe, or a park-keeper kills deer without authority. 2. By nonuser, or neglect; which in public offices that concern the administration of justice, or the commonwealth, is of itself a direct and immediate cause of forfeiture: but nonuser of a private office is no cause of forfeiture, unless some special damage is proved to be occasioned thereby. In the one case delay must necessarily be occasioned in the affairs of the public, which require a constant attention; but, private offices not requiring so regular and unremitted a service, the temporary neglect of them is not necessarily productive of mischief; upon which account some special loss must be proved, in order to vacate these.

Franchises, also, being regal privileges in the hands of a subject, are held to be granted on the same condition of making a proper use of them; and therefore they may be lost and forfeited, like offices, either by abuse or by neglect.

Upon the same principle proceed all the forfeitures which are given by law of life estates and others; for any acts done by the tenant himself, that are incompatible with the estate which he holds. As if tenants for life or years enfeoff a stranger in fee simple: this is, by the common law, a forfeiture of their several estates; being a breach of the condition which the law annexes thereto, viz., that they shall not attempt to create a greater estate than they themselves are entitled to. So if any tenants for years, for life, or in fee, commit a felony; the king or other lord of the fee is entitled to have their tenements, because their estate is determined by the breach of the condition, "that they shall not commit felony," which the law tacitly annexes to every feudal donation.

ESTATES UPON CONDITION, EXPRESSED — An estate on condition expressed in the grant itself is where an estate is granted, either in fee simple or otherwise, with an express qualification annexed, whereby the estate granted shall either commence, be enlarged, or be defeated, upon performance or breach of such qualification or condition. These conditions are therefore either precedent or subsequent.

CONDITIONS PRECEDENT — Precedent are such as must happen or be performed before the estate can vest or be enlarged: subsequent are such, by the failure or nonperformance of which an estate already vested may be defeated. Thus, if an estate for life be limited to A upon his marriage with B, the marriage is a precedent condition, and till that happens no estate is vested in A. Or, if a man grant to his lessee for years, that upon payment of a hundred marks within the term he shall have the fee, this also is a condition precedent, and the fee simple passeth not till the hundred marks be paid.

CONDITIONS SUBSEQUENT — But if a man grant an estate in fee simple, reserving to himself and his heirs a certain rent, and that, if such rent be not paid at the times limited, it shall be lawful for him and his heirs to reenter, and avoid the estate: in this case the grantee and his heirs have an estate upon condition subsequent, which is defeasible if the condition be not strictly performed.

Thus an estate to a man and his heirs, tenants of the manor of Dale, is an estate on condition that he and his heirs continue tenants of that manor. So, if a personal annuity be granted at this day to a man and the heirs of his body; as theirs is no tenement within the statute of Westminster the Second, it remains, as at common law, a fee simple on condition that the grantee has heirs of his body.

Upon the same principle depend all the determinable estates of freehold, which we mentioned: these are estates as during widowhood, etc.; upon condition that the grantees do not marry, and the like. On the breach of any of these subsequent conditions, by the failure of these contingencies; by the grantee's not continuing tenant of the manor Dale, by not having heirs of his body, or by not continuing sole; the estates which were respectively vested in each grantee are wholly determined and void.

☸ DISTINCTION BETWEEN CONDITIONS AND LIMITATIONS — A distinction is, however, made between a condition in deed and a limitation, which Littleton denominates also a condition in law. For when an estate is so expressly confined and limited by the words of its creation that it cannot endure for any longer time than till the contingency happens upon which the estate is to fail, this is denominated a limitation: as when land•is granted to a man, so long as he is parson of Dale, or while he continues unmarried, or until out of the rents and profits he shall have made 500£. and the like.

In such case the estate determines as soon as the contingency happens (when he ceases to be parson, marries a wife, or has received the 500£.), and the next subsequent estate, which depends upon such determination, becomes immediately vested, without any act to be done by him who is next in expectancy. But when an estate is, strictly speaking, upon condition in deed (as if granted expressly upon condition to be void upon the payment of 40£. by the grantor, or so that the grantee continues unmarried, or provided he goes to York, etc.), the law permits it to endure beyond the time when such contingency happens, unless the grantor or his heirs or assigns take advantage of the breach of the conditon, and make either an entry or a claim in order to avoid the estate.

Though strict words of condition be used in the creation of the estate, yet if on breach of the condition the estate be limited over to a third person, and does not immediately revert to the grantor or his representatives (as if an estate be granted by A to B, on condition that within two years B intermarry with C, and on failure thereof then to D and his heirs), this the law construes to be a limitation and not a condition: because, if it were a conditon, then, upon the breach thereof, only A or his representatives could avoid the estate by entry, and so D's remainder might be defeated by their neglecting to enter; but, when it is a limitation, the estate of B determines, and that of D commences, the instant that the failure happens. So, also, if a man by his will devises land to his heir at law, on condition that he pays a sum of money, and for nonpayment devises it over, this shall be considered as a limitation, otherwise no advantage could be taken of the nonpayment, for none but the heir himself could have entered for a breach of condition.

In all these instances, of limitations or conditions subsequent, it is to be observed, that so long as the condition, either express or implied, either in deed or in law, remains unbroken, the grantee may have an estate of freehold, provided the estate upon which such condition is annexed be in itself of a freehold nature; as if the original grant express either an estate of inheritance, or for life, or no estate at all, which is constructively an estate for life.

The breach of these conditions being contingent and uncertain, this uncertainty preserves the freehold; because the estate is capable to last forever, or at least for the life of the tenant, supposing the condition to remain unbroken. But where the estate is at the utmost a chattel interest, which must determine at a certain time, and may determine sooner (as a grant for ninety-nine years, provided A, B, and C, or the survivor of them, shall so long live), this still continues a mere chattel, and is not, by its uncertainty, ranked among estates of freehold.

⚖ IMPOSSIBLE AND ILLEGAL CONDITIONS — Express conditions, if they be impossible at the time of their creation, or afterwards become impossible by the act of God or the act of the feoffor himself, of if they be contrary to law, or repugnant to the nature of the estate, are void. In any of which cases, if they be conditions subsequent, that is, to be performed, after the estate shall become absolute in the tenant.

As, if a feoffment be made to a man in fee simple, on condition that unless he goes to Rome in twenty-four hours; or unless he marries with Jane S. by such a day (within which time the woman dies, or the feoffor marries her himself); or unless he kills another; or in case he aliens in fee; then in any of such cases the estate shall be vacated and determine: here the condition is void, and the estate made absolute in the feoffee. For he hath by the grant the estate vested in him, which shall not be defeated afterwards by a condition either impossible, illegal, or repugnant. But if the condition be precedent, or to be performed before the estate vests, as a grant to a man that, if he kills another or goes to Rome in a day, he shall have an estate in fee; here, the void condition being precedent, the estate which depends thereon is also void, and the grantee shall take nothing by the grant: for he hath no estate until the condition be performed.

⚖ ESTATES IN GAGE OR PLEDGE — There are some estates defeasible upon condition subsequent, that require a more peculiar notice. Such are, Estates held in pledge; which are of two kinds, living pledge; and dead pledge; or mortgage.

⚖ LIVING PLEDGE — A living pledge, is when a man borrows a sum (suppose 200£.) of another; and grants him an estate, as, of 20£. per annum, to hold till the rents and profits shall repay the sum so borrowed. This is an estate conditioned to be void, as soon as such sum is raised. In this case the land or pledge is said to be living: it subsists, and suvives the debt; and, immediately on the discharge of that, results back to the borrower.

⚖ MORTGAGE — But a dead pledge, or mortgage (which is much more common than the other), is where a man borrows of another a specific sum (for example, 200£.) and grants him an estate in fee, on condition that if he, the mortgagor, shall repay the mortgagee the said sum of 200£. on a certain day mentioned in the deed, that the mortgagee shall reconvey the estate to the mortgagor: in this case the land, which so put in pledge, is by law, in case of nonpayment at the time limited, forever dead and gone, from the mortgagor; and the mortgagee's estate in the lands is then no longer conditional, but absolute. But, so long as it continues conditional, that is, between the time of lending the money and time allotted for payment, the mortgagee is called tenant in mortgage.

⚖ MORTGAGEE'S RIGHT OF POSSESSION — As soon as the estate is created, the mortgagee may immediately enter on the lands; but is liable to be dispossessed, upon performance of the condition by payment of the mortgage at the day limited. Therefore the usual way is to agree that the mortgagor shall hold the land till the day assigned for payment; when, in case of failure, whereby the estate becomes absolute, the mortgagee may enter upon it and take possession, without any possibility at law of being afterwards evicted by the mortgagor, to whom the land is now forever dead.

⚖ EQUITY OF REDEMPTION — But here again the courts of equity interpose; and, though a mortgage be thus forfeited, and the estate absolutely vested in the mortgagee at the common law, yet they will consider the real value of the tenements compared with the sum borrowed. If the estate be of greater value than the sum lent thereon, they will allow the mortgagor at any reasonable time to recall or redeem his estate; paying to the mortgagee his principal, interest, and expenses: for otherwise, in strictness of law, an estate worth 1,000£. might be forfeited for nonpayment of 100£. or a less sum.

This reasonable advantage, allowed to mortgagors, is called the equity of redemption; and thus enables a mortgagor to call on the mortgagee, who has possession of his estate, to deliver it back and account for the rents and profits received, on payment of his whole debt and interest. On the other hand, the mortgagee may either compel the sale of the estate, in order to get the whole of his money immediately; or else call upon the mortgagor to redeem his estate presently, or, in default thereof, to be forever foreclosed from redeeming the same; that is, to lose his equity of redemption without possibility of recall.

In some cases of fraudulent mortgages, the fraudulent mortgagor forfeits all equity of redemption whatsoever. It is not, however, usual for mortgagees to take possession of the mortgaged estate, unless where the security is precarious, or small; or where the mortgagor neglects even the payment of interest: when the mortgagee is frequently obliged to being an ejectment, and take the land into his own hands, in the nature of a pledge. But, by statute (Mortgage, 1733), after payment or tender by the mortgagor of principal, interest, and costs, the mortgagee can maintain no ejectment; but may be compelled to reassign his securities.

In Glanvill's time, when the universal method of conveyance was by livery of seisin or corporal tradition of the lands, no gage or pledge of lands was good unless possession was also delivered to the creditor; "if delivery of the pledge itself do not follow, the king's court is not accustomed to take cognizance of private agreements of this kind": for which the reason given is, to prevent subsequent and fraudulent pledges of the same land: since in such a case the same thing might be pledged to many creditors as well before as afterwards." The frauds which have arisen, since the exchange of these public and notorious conveyances for more private and secret bargains, have well evinced the wisdom of our ancient law.

☙ ESTATES BY STATUTE MERCHANT AND STATUTE STAPLE — A fourth species of estates, defeasible on condition subsequent, are those held by statute merchant, and statute staple; which are very nearly related to the living pledge before mentioned, or estate held till the profits thereof shall discharge a debt liquidated or ascertained.

Both the statute merchant and statute staple are securities for money; the one entered into pursuant to statute (1285), and thence called a statute merchant; the other pursuant to statute (1353), before the mayor of the staple, that is to say, the grand mart for the principal commodities or manufactures of the kingdom, formerly held by act of parliament in certain trading towns, and thence this security is called a statute staple.

They are both, I say, securities for debts, originally permitted only among traders, for the benefit of commerce; whereby the lands of the debtor are conveyed to the creditor, till out of the rents and profits of them his debt may be satisfied: and, during such time as the creditor so holds the lands, he is tenant by statute merchant or statute staple.

There is also a similar security, the recognizance in the nature of a statute staple, which extends the benefit of this mercantile transaction to all the king's subjects in general, by virtue of statute (Recognizances for Debt, 1531).

⚖ ESTATE BY ELEGIT — Another similar conditional estate, created by operation of law, for security and satisfaction of debts, is called an estate by elegit. What an elegit is, and why so called, will be explained in the third part of these commentaries. At present I need only mention, that it is the name of a writ, founded on the statute of Westm. 2. by which, after a plaintiff has obtained judgment for his debt of law, the sheriff gives him possession of one-half of the defendant's lands and tenements, to be held, occupied, and enjoyed, until his debt and damages are fully paid: and, during the time he so holds them, he is called tenant by elegit.

It is easy to observe that this is also a mere conditional estate, defeasible as soon as the debt is levied. But it is remarkable, that the feudal restraints of alienating lands, and charging them with the debts of the owner, were softened much earlier and much more effectually for the benefit of trade and commerce, than for any other consideration.

⚖ CHATTELS REAL — I shall conclude what I had to remark of these estates, by statute merchant, statute staple, and elegit, with the observation of Sir Edward Coke, "These tenants have uncertain interests in lands and tenements, and yet they have but chattels and no freeholds" (which makes them an exception to the general rule), "because though they may hold an estate of inheritance, or for life (as a freehold), until their debt be paid; yet it shall go to their executors: and though, to recover their estates, they shall have the same remedy (by assize) as a tenant of the freehold shall have, yet it is but the similitude of a freehold.

This indeed only proves them to be chattel interest, because they go to the executors, which is inconsistent with the nature of a freehold: but it does not assign the reason why these estates, in contradistinction to other uncertain interests, shall vest in the executors of the tenant and not the heir; which is probably owing to this: that, being a security and remedy provided for personal debts due to the deceased, to which debts the executor is entitled, the law has, therefore, thus directed their succession; as judging it reasonable, from a principle of natural equity, that the security and remedy should be vested in them, to whom the debts if recovered would belong.

Upon the same principle, if lands be devised to a man's executor, until out of their profits the debts due from the testator be discharged, this interest in the lands shall be a chattel interest, and on the death of such executor shall go to his executors: because they, being liable to pay the original testator's debts, so far as his assets will extend, are in reason entitled to possess that fund, out of which he has directed them to be paid.

ESTATES IN POSSESSION, REMAINDER, AND REVERSION

⚘ ESTATES IN RESPECT TO THE TIME OF ENJOYMENT — Hitherto we have considered estates solely with regard to their duration, or the quantity of interest which the owners have therein. We are now to consider them in another view; with regard to the time of their enjoyment, when the actual pernancy of the profits (that is, the taking, perception, or receipt, of the rents and other advantages arising therefrom) begins.

Estates, therefore, with respect to this consideration, may either be in possession, or in expectancy: and of expectancies there are two sorts; one created by act of law, and called a reversion. The doctrine of estates in expectancy contains some of the nicest and most abstruse learning in the English law. These will therefore require a minute discussion, and demand some degree of attention.

⚘ ESTATES IN REMAINDER — An estate in remainder may be defined to be an estate limited to take effect and be enjoyed after another estate is determined. As if a man seised in fee simple granteth lands to A for twenty years, and, after the determination of the said term, then to B and his heirs forever: here A is tenant for years, remainder to be in fee. In the first place, an estate for years is created or carved out of the fee, and given to A; and the residue or remainder of it is given to B. But both these interests are in fact only one estate; the present term of years and the remainder afterwards, when added together, being equal only to one estate in fee. They are indeed different parts, but they constitute only one whole: they are carved out of one and the same inheritance: they are both created, and may both subsist, together; the one in possession, the other in expectancy.

So if land be granted to A for twenty years, and after the determination of B's estate for life, it be limited to C and his heirs forever: this makes A tenant for years, with remainder to B for life, remainder over to C in fee. Here the estate of inheritance undergoes a division into three portions: there is first A's estate for years carved out of it; and after that B's estate for life; and then the whole that remains is limited to C and his heirs. Here also the first estate, and both the remainders, for life and in fee, are one estate only; being nothing but parts or portions of one entire inheritance: and if there were a hundred remainders, it would still be the same thing; upon a principle grounded in mathematical truth, that all the parts are equal, and no more than equal, to the whole.

⚖️ NO REMAINDER ON A FEE SIMPLE — No remainder can be limited after the grant of an estate in fee simple: because a fee simple is the highest and largest estate, that a subject is capable of enjoying; and he that is tenant in fee hath in him the whole of the estate: a remainder, therefore, which is only a portion, or residuary part, of the estate, cannot be reserved after the whole is disposed of. A particular estate, with all the remainders expectant thereon, is only one fee simple; as 40£. is a part of 100£. and 60£. is the remainder of it: wherefore, after a fee simple once vested, there can no more be a remainder limited thereon, than after the whole 100£. is appropriated there can be any residue subsisting.

⚖️ THE PARTICULAR ESTATE — And, first, there must necessarily be some particular estate, precedent to the estate in remainder. As, an estate for years to A, remainder to B for life; or, an estate for life to A, remainder to B in tail. This precedent estate is called the particular estate, as being only a small part, or particular, of the inheritance; the residue or remainder of which is granted over to another.

The necessity of creating this preceding particular estate, in order to make a good remainder, arises from this plain reason; that remainder is a relative expression, and implies that some part of the thing is previously disposed of: for, where the whole is conveyed at once, there cannot possibly exist a remainder; but the interest granted, whatever it be, will be an estate in possession.

⚖️ ESTATES IN FUTURO — An estate created to commence at a distant period of time without any intervening estate, is therefore properly no remainder: it is the whole of the gift, and not a residuary part. Such future estates can only be made of chattel interests, which were considered in the light of mere contracts by the ancient law, to be executed either now or hereafter, as the contracting parties should agree: but an estate of freehold must be created to commence immediately.

It is an ancient rule of the common law that no estate of freehold can be created to commence in futuro; but it ought to take effect presently either in possession or remainder; because at common law no freehold in lands could pass without livery of seisin: which must operate either immediately, or not at all. It would therefore be contradictory, if an estate, which is not to commence till hereafter, could be granted by a conveyance which imports an immediate possession. Therefore, though a lease to A for seven years, to commence from next Michaelmas, is good; yet a conveyance to B of lands, to hold to him and his heirs forever from the end of three years next ensuing, is void.

So that when it is intended to grant an estate of freehold, whereof the enjoyment shall be deferred till a future time, it is necessary to create a previous particular estate, which may subsist till that period of time is completed; and for the grantor to deliver immediate possession of the land to the tenant of this particular estate, which is construed to be giving possession to him in remainder, since his estate and that of the particular tenant are one and the same estate in law. As, where one leases to A for three years, with remainder to B in fee, and makes livery of seisin to A; hereby the livery the freehold is immediately created, and vested in B during the continuance of A's term of years. The whole estate passes at once from the grantor to the grantees, and the remainderman is seised of his remainder at the same time that the termor is possessed of his term. The enjoyment of it must indeed be deferred till hereafter; but it is to all intents and purposes an estate commencing immediately, though to be occupied and enjoyed in futuro (at a future time).

ESTATES AT WILL — As no remainder can be created, without such a precedent particular estate, therefore the particular estate is said to support the remainder. But a lease at will is not held to be such a particular estate, as will support a remainder over. For an estate at will is of a nature so slender and precarious, that it is not looked upon as a portion of the inheritance; and a portion must first be taken out of it, in order to constitute a remainder.

Besides, if it be a freehold remainder, livery of seisin must be given at the time of its creation; and the entry of the grantor, to do this, determines the estate at will in the very instant in which it is made: or if it be a chattel interest, though perhaps it might operate as a future contract, if the tenant for years be a party to the deed of creation, yet it is void by way of remainder: for it is a separate independent contract, distinct from the precedent estate at will; and every remainder must be part of one and the same estate, out of which the preceding particular estate is taken.

It is generally true, that if the particular estate is void in its creation, or by any means is defeated afterwards, the remainder supported thereby shall be defeated also: as where the particular estate is an estate for the life of a person not in existence; or an estate for life upon condition, on breach of which condition the grantor enters and avoids the estate; in either of these cases the remainder over is void.

⚖ REMAINDER AND PARTICULAR ESTATE COMMENCE AT SAME TIME — A second rule to be observed is this; that the remainder must commence or pass out of the grantor at the time of the creation of the particular estate. As, where there is an estate to A for life, with remainder to B in fee: here B's remainder in fee passes from the grantor at the same time that seisin is delivered to A of his life estate in possession. It is this which induces the necessity at common law of livery of seisin being made on the particular estate, whenever a freehold remainder is created.

For, if it be limited even on an estate for years, it is necessary that the lessee for years should have livery of seisin, in order to convey the freehold, and yet cannot be given to him in remainder without infringing the possession of the lessee for years, therefore the law allows such livery made to the tenant of the particular estate, to relate and inure to him in remainder, as both are but one estate in law.

⚖ VESTING OF REMAINDER — A third rule respecting remainders is this: that the remainder must vest in the grantee during the continuance of the particular estate from the instant that it determines. As, if A be tenant for life, remainder to B in tail; here B's remainder is vested in him, at the creation of the particular estate to A for life: or, if A and B be tenants for their joint lives, remainder to the survivor in fee; here though during their joint lives the remainder is vested in neither, yet on the death of either of them, the remainder vests instantly in the survivor: wherefore both these are good remainders.

But, if an estate be limited to A for life, remainder to the eldest son of B in tail, and A dies before B hath any son; here the remainder will be void, for it did not vest in anyone during the continuance, nor at the determination, of the particular estate: and, even supposing that B should afterwards have a son, he shall not take by this remainder; for as it did not vest at or before the end of the particular estate, it never can vest at all, but is gone forever.

And this depends upon the principle before laid down, that the precedent particular estate, and the remainder are one estate in law; they must therefore subsist and be in existence at one and the same instant of time, either during the continuance of the first estate or at the very instant when that determines, so that no other estate can possibly come between them. For there can be no intervening estate between the particular estate, and the remainder supported thereby: the thing supported must fall to the ground, if once its support be severed from it.

☙ DIVISION OF REMAINDERS — It is upon these rules, but principally the last, that the doctrine of contingent remainders depends. For remainders are either vested or contingent.

☙ VESTED REMAINDERS — Vested remainders (or remainders executed, whereby a present interest passes to the party, though to be enjoyed in future) are where the estate is invariably fixed, to remain to a determinate person, after the particular estate is spent. As if A be tenant for twenty years, remainder to B in fee; here B's is a vested remainder, which nothing can defeat, or set aside.

☙ CONTINGENT REMAINDERS — Contingent or executory remainders (whereby no present interest passes) are where the estate in remainder is limited to take effect, either to a dubious and uncertain person, or upon a dubious and uncertain event; so that the particular estate may chance to be determined, and the remainder never take effect.

☙ LIMITED TO UNCERTAIN PERSON — First, they may be limited to a dubious and uncertain person. As if A be tenant for life, with remainder to B's eldest son (then unborn) in tail; this is a contingent remainder, for it is uncertain whether B will have a son or no: but the instant that a son is born, the remainder is no longer contingent, but vested. Though, if A had died before the contingency happened, that is, before B's son was born, the remainder would have absolutely gone; for the particular estate was determined before the remainder could vest. Nay, by the strict rule of law, if A were tenant for life, remainder to his own eldest son in tail, and A died without issue born, but leaving his wife enciente or big with child, and after his death a posthumous son was born, this son could not take the land, by virtue of this remainder; for the particular estate determined before there was any person in existence, in whom the remainder could vest.

To remedy this hardship, it is enacted by statute (Posthumous Children, 1698), that posthumous children shall be capable of taking in remainder, in the same manner as if they had been born in their father's lifetime: that is, the remainder is allowed to vest in them, while yet in their mother's womb.

☙ COMMON POSSIBILITY — This species of contingent remainders, to a person not in being, must, however, be limited to someone, that may by common possibility, or a near possibility, be in existence at or before the particular estate determines. As if an estate be made to A for life, remainder to the heirs of B: now, if A dies before B, the remainder is at an end; for during B's life he has no heir (no one is heir of a living person): but if B dies first, the remainder then immediately vests in his heir, who will be entitled to the land on the death of A. This is a good contingent remainder, for the possibility of B's dying before A is (a near possibility), and therefore allowed in law. But a remainder to the right heirs of B (if there be no such person as B in existence is void. For here there must two contingencies happen; first, that such a person as B shall be born; and secondly, that he shall also die during the continuance of the particular estate; which make it a most improbable possibility.

A remainder to a man's eldest son, who hath none (we have seen), is good; for by common possibility he may have one; but if it be limited in particular to his son John, or Richard, it is bad, if he have no son of that name: for it is too remote a possibility that he should not only have a son, but a son of a particular name.

A limitation of a remainder to a bastard before it is born, is not good: for though the law allows the possibility of having bastards, it presumes it to be a very remote and improbable contingency. Thus may a remainder be contingent, on account of the uncertainty of the person who is to take it.

⚖ LIMITED ON UNCERTAIN EVENT — A remainder may also be contingent, where the person to whom it is limited is fixed and certain, but the event upon which it is to take effect is vague and uncertain. As, where land is given to A for life, and in case B survives him, then with remainder to B in fee; here, B is a certain person, but the remainder to him is a contingent remainder, depending upon a dubious event, the uncertainty of his surviving A. During the joint lives of A and B it is contingent; and if B dies first, it never can vest in his heirs, but is forever gone; and if A dies first, the remainder to B becomes vested.

⚖ FREEHOLDS LIMITED ONLY ON FREEHOLDS — Contingent remainders of either kind, if they amount to a freehold, cannot be limited on an estate for years, or any other particular estate, less than a freehold. Thus if land be granted to A for ten years, with remainder in fee to the right heirs of B, this remainder is void: but if granted to A for life, with a like remainder, it is good. For, unless the freehold passes out of the grantor at the time when the remainder is created, such freehold remainder is void: it cannot pass out of him, without vesting somewhere; and in the case of a contingent remainder it must vest in the particular tenant, else it can vest nowhere: unless, therefore, the estate of such particular tenant be of a freehold nature, the freehold cannot vest in him, and consequently the remainder is void.

⚖ CONTINGENT REMAINDERS, HOW DEFEATED — Contingent remainders may be defeated, by destroying or determining the particular estate upon which they depend, before the contingency happens whereby they become vested. Therefore, when there is tenant for life, with divers remainders in contingency, he may, not only by his death, but by alienation, surrender, or other methods, destroy and determine his own life estate, before any of those remainders vest; the consequence of which is that he utterly defeats them all. As, if there be tenant for life, with remainder to this eldest son unborn in tail, and the tenant for life, before any son is born, surrenders his life estate, he by that means defeats the remainder in tail to his son: for his son not being in existence, when the particular estate determined, the remainder could not then vest; and, as it could not vest then, by the rules before laid down, it never can vest at all.

⚖ HOW PRESERVED FROM DEFEAT — In these cases, therefore, it is necessary to have trustees appointed to preserve the contingent remainders; in whom there is vested an estate in remainder for the life of the tenant for life, to commence when his determines. If, therefore, his estate for life determines otherwise than by his death, their estate, for the residue of his natural life, will then take effect, and become a particular estate in possession, sufficient to support the remainders depending in contingency.

⚖ EXECUTORY DEVISES — Thus the student will observe how much nicety is required in creating and securing a remainder; and I trust he will in some measure see the general reason, upon which this nicety is founded. It were endless to attempt to enter upon the particular subtleties and refinements, into which this doctrine, by the variety of cases which have occurred in the course of many centuries, has been spun out and subdivided: neither are they consonant to the design of these elementary disquisitions.

I must not, however, omit, that in devises by last will and testament (which, being often drawn up when the party is without counsel are always more favored in construction than formal deeds, which are presumed to be made with great caution, forethought, and advice). In these devises, I say, remainders may be created in some measure contrary to the rules before laid down: though our lawyers will not allow such dispositions to be strictly remainders; but call them by another name, that of executory devises, or devises hereafter to be executed.

⚖ DIFFERENCES BETWEEN REMAINDERS AND EXECUTORY DEVISES — An executory devise of lands is such a disposition of them by will, that thereby no estate vests at the death of the devisor, but only on some future contingency. It differs from a remainder in three very material points: 1. That it needs not any particular estate to support it. 2. That by it a fee simple or other less estate may be limited after a fee simple. 3. That by this means a remainder may be limited of a chattel interest after a particular estate for life created in the same.

⚖ PARTICULAR ESTATE NOT NECESSARY IN EXECUTORY DEVISE — The first case happens when a man devises a future estate to arise upon a contingency; and, till that contingency happens, does not dispose of the fee simple, but leaves it to descend to his heir at law. As if one devises land to a feme sole and her heirs, upon her day of marriage: here is in effect a contingent remainder without any particular estate to support it; a freehold commencing in futuro (at a future period). This limitation though it would be void in a deed, yet is good in a will, by way of executory devise. For, since by a devise a freehold may pass without corporal tradition or livery of seisin (as it must do, if it passes at all), therefore it may commence in future; because the principal reason why it cannot commence in futuro in other cases is the necessity of actual seisin, which always operates immediately. Since it may thus commence in futuro, there is no need of a particular estate to support it; the only use of which is to make the remainder, by its unity with the particular estate, a present interest. And hence, also, it follows, that such an executory devise, not being a present interest, cannot be barred by a recovery, suffered before it commences.

⚖ FEE, OR LESS ESTATE, LIMITED ON EXECUTORY DEVISE — By executory devise a fee, or other less estate, may be limited after a fee. This happens where a devisor devises his whole estate in fee, but limits a remainder thereon to commence on a future contingency. As if a man devises land to A and his heirs; but, if he dies before the age of twenty-one, then to B and his heirs: the remainder, though void in a deed, is good by way of executory devise.

⚖ RULE AGAINST PERPETUITIES — But, in both these species of executory devises, the contingencies ought to be such as may happen within a reasonable time; as within one or more life or lives in being, or within a moderate term of years; for courts of justice will not indulge even wills, so as to create a perpetuity, which the law abhors: because by perpetuities (or the settlement of an interest, which shall go in the succession prescribed, without any power of alienation) estates are made incapable of answering those ends, of social commerce, and providing for the sudden contingencies of private life, for which property was at first established.

The utmost length that has been hitherto allowed for the contingency of an executory devise of either kind to happen in, is that of a life or lives in being, and one and twenty years afterwards. As when lands are devised to such unborn son of a feme covert, as shall first attain the age of twenty-one, and his heirs; the utmost length of time that can happen before the estate can vest, is the life of the mother and the subsequent infancy of her son: and this hath been decreed to be a good executory devise.

REMAINDER LIMITED ON A CHATTEL INTEREST — By executory devise a term of years may be given to one man for his life, and afterwards limited over in remainder to another, which could not be done by deed: for by law the first grant of it, to a man for life, was a total disposition of the whole term; a life estate being esteemed of a higher and larger nature than any term of years. At first, the courts were tender, even in the case of a will, of restraining the devisee for life from aliening the term; but only held, that in case he died without exerting that act of ownership, the remainder over should then take place: for the restraint of the power of alienation, especially in very long terms, was introducing a species of perpetuity.

But, soon afterwards, it was held, that the devisee for life hath no power of aliening the term, so as to bar the remainderman: yet in order to prevent the danger of perpetuities, it was settled, that though such remainders may be limited to as many persons successively as the devisor thinks proper, yet they must all be in existence during the life of the first devisee; for then all the candles are lighted and are consuming together, and the ultimate remainder is in reality only to that remainderman who happens to survive the rest: or, that such remainder may be limited to take effect upon such contingency only as must happen (if at all) during the life of the first devisee.

Thus much for such estates in expectancy, as are created by the express words of the parties themselves; the most intricate title in the law. There is yet another species, which is created by the act and operation of the law itself, and this is called a reversion.

ESTATES IN REVERSION — An estate in reversion is the residue of an estate left in the grantor, to commence in possession after the determination of some particular estate granted out by him. A reversion is the returning of land to the grantor or his heirs after the grant is over. As, if there be a gift in tail, the reversion of the fee is, without any special reservation, vested in the donor by act of law: and so also the reversion, after an estate for life, years, or at will, continues in the lessor. For the fee simple of all lands must abide somewhere; and if he, who was before possessed of the whole, carves out of it any smaller estate, and grants it away, whatever is not so granted remains in him.

A reversion is never, therefore, created by deed or writing, but arises from construction of the law; a remainder can never be limited, unless by either deed or devise. But both are equally transferable, when actually vested, being both present estates, though taking effect in futuro.

⚖ INCIDENTS OF REVERSIONS — The doctrine of reversions is plainly derived from the feudal constitution. For, when a feud was granted to a man for life, or to him and his issue male, rendering either rent, or other services; then, on his death or the failure of issue male, the feud was determined and resulted back to the lord or proprietor, to be again disposed of at his pleasure. Hence the usual incidents to reversions are said to be fealty and rent. When no rent is reserved on the particular estate, fealty, however, results of course, as an incident quite inseparable and may be demanded as a badge of tenure, or acknowledgment of superiority; being frequently the only evidence that the lands are holden to all.

Where rent is reserved, it is also, incident, though not inseparably so, to the reversion. The rent may be granted away, reserving the reversion, the rent will pass with it, an incident thereunto; though by the grant of the rent generally, the reversion will not pass. The incident passes by the grant of the principal, but not conversely: for the maxim of law is "The accessory does not precede but follows its principal."

⚖ DISTINCTIONS BETWEEN REMAINDERS AND REVERSIONS — These incidental rights of the reversion, and the respective modes of descent, in which remainders very frequently differ from reversions, have occasioned the law to be careful in distinguishing the one from the other, however inaccurately the parties themselves may describe them.

If one, seised of a paternal estate in fee, makes a lease for life, with remainder to himself and his heirs, this is properly a mere reversion, to which rent and fealty shall be incident; and which shall only descend to the heirs of his father's blood, and not to his heirs general, as a remainder limited to him by a third person would have done: for it is the old estate, which was originally in him, and never yet was out of him. Likewise, if a man grants a lease for life to A, reserving rent, with reversion to B and his heirs, B hath a remainder descendible to his heirs general, and not a re' version to which the rent is incident; but the grantor shall be entitled to the rent, during the continuance of A's estate.

STATUTE OF FRAUDULENT CONCEALMENT OF DEATHS — In order to assist such persons as have any estate in remainder, reversion, or expectancy, after the death of others, against fraudulent concealments of their deaths, it is enacted by statute (1707), that all persons on whose lives any lands or tenements are holden, shall (upon application to the court of chancery and order made thereupon) once in every year, if required, be produced to the court, or its commissioners; or upon neglect or refusal, they shall be taken to be actually dead, and the person entitled to such expectant estate may enter upon and hold the lands and tenements, till the party shall appear to be living.

DOCTRINE OF MERGER — Before we conclude the doctrine of remainders and reversions, it may be proper to observe, that whenever a greater estate and less coincide and meet in one and the same person, without any intermediate estate, the less is immediately annihilated; or, in the law phrase, is said to be merged, that is, sunk or drowned, in the greater.

Thus, if there be tenant for years, and the reversion in fee simple descends to or is purchased by him, the term of years is merged in the inheritance, and shall never exist any more. But they must come to one and the same person in one and the same right; else, if the freehold be in his own right, and he has a term in right of another there is no merger. Therefore, if tenant for years dies, and makes him who hath the reversion in fee his executor, whereby the term of years vests also in him, the term shall not in the right of the testator, and subject to his debts and legacies. So, also, if he who hath the reversion in fee marries the tenant for years, there is no merger; for he hath the inheritance in his own right, the lease in the right of his wife.

An estate-tail is an exception to this rule: for a man may have in his own right both an estate-tail and a reversion in fee; and the estate-tail, though a less estate, shall not merge in the fee. For estates-tail are protected and preserved from merger by the operation and construction, though not be the express words of statute which operation and construction have probably arisen upon this consideration; that, in the common cases of merger of estates for life or years by uniting with the inheritance, the particular tenant hath the sole interest in them, and hath full power at any time to defeat, destroy, or surrender them to him that hath the reversion; therefore, when such an estate unites with the reversion in fee, the law considers it in the light of a virtual surrender of the inferior estate.

But, in an estate-tail, the case is otherwise: the tenant for a long time had no power at all over it, so as to bar or to destroy it; and now can only do it by certain special modes, by a fine, a recovery, and the like: it would therefore have been strangely improvident, to have permitted the tenant in tail by purchasing the reversion in fee, to merge his particular estate, and defeat the inheritance of his issue: and hence it has become a maxim, that a tenancy in tail, which cannot be surrendered, cannot also be merged in the fee.

ESTATES IN SEVERALTY, JOINT TENANCY, COPARCENARY, AND COMMON

⚖️ ESTATES IN RESPECT TO THE NUMBER OF THEIR TENANTS — We come now to treat of estates, with respect to the number and connections of their owners, the tenants who occupy and hold them. Considered in this view, estates of any quantity or length of duration, and whether they be in actual possession or expectancy, may be held in four different ways; in severalty, in joint tenancy, in coparcenary, and in common.

⚖️ ESTATES IN SEVERALTY — He that holds lands and tenements in severalty, or is sole tenant thereof, is he that holds them in his own right only, without any other person being joined or connected with him in point of interest, during his estate therein. This is the most common and usual way of holding an estate.

⚖️ ESTATES IN JOINT TENANCY — An estate in joint tenancy is where lands or tenements are granted to two or more persons, to hold in fee simple, fee-tail, for life, for years, or at will. In consequence of such grants an estate is called an estate in joint tenancy, and sometimes an estate in jointure, which word as well as the other signifies a union or conjunction of interest; though in common speech the term "jointure" is now usually confined to that joint estate, which by virtue of statute (Statute of Uses, 1535), is frequently vested in the husband and wife before marriage, as a full satisfaction and bar of the woman's dower.

We will first inquire, how these estates may be created; next, their properties and respective incidents; and lastly, how they may be severed or destroyed.

⚖️ CREATION OF JOINT ESTATE — The creation of an estate in joint tenancy depends on the wording of the deed or devise, by which the tenants claim title; for this estate can only arise by purchase or grant, that is, by the act of the parties, and never by the mere act of law.

If an estate be given to a plurality of persons, without adding any restrictive, exclusive, or explanatory words, as if an estate be granted to A and B and their heirs, this makes them immediately joint tenants in fee of the lands. For the law interprets the grant so as to make all parts of it take effect, which can only be done by creating an equal estate in them both. As, therefore, the grantor has thus united their names, the law gives them a thorough union in all other respects.

⚖️ PROPERTIES OF JOINT ESTATE — The properties of a joint estate are derived from its unity, which is fourfold; the unity of interest, the unity of title, the unity of time, and the unity of possession: or, in other words, joint tenants have one and the same interest, accruing by one and the same conveyance, commencing at one and the same time, and held by one and the same undivided possession.

⚖️ UNITY OF INTEREST — First, they must have one and the same interest. One joint tenant cannot be entitled to one period of duration or quantity of interest in lands, and the other to a different; one cannot be tenant for life, and the other for years: one cannot be tenant in fee, and the other in tail. If land be limited to A and B for their lives, this makes them joint tenants of the freehold; if to A and B and their heirs, it makes them joint tenants of the inheritance. If land be granted to A and B for their lives, and to the heirs of A; here A and B are joint tenants of the freehold during their respective lives, and A has the remainder of the fee in severalty: or, if land be given to A and B, and the heirs of the body of A; here both have a joint estate for life, and A hath a several remainder in tail.

⚖️ UNITY OF TITLE — Secondly, joint tenants must also have a unity of title: their estate must be created by one and the same act, whether legal or illegal; as by one and the same grant, or by one and the same disseisin. Joint tenancy cannot arise by descent or act of law; but merely by purchase, or acquisition by the act of the party: and, unless that act be one and the same, the two tenants would have different titles; and if they had different titles, one might prove good, and the other bad, which would absolutely destroy the jointure.

⚖️ UNITY OF TIME — Thirdly, there must also be a unity of time: their estates must be vested at one and the same period, as well as by one and the same title. As in case of a present estate made to A and B; or a remainder in fee to A and B after a particular estate; in either case B and A are joint tenants of this present estate, or this vested remainder. But if, after a lease for life, the remainder be limited to the heirs of A and B; and during the continuance of the particular estate A dies, which vests the remainder of one moiety in his heirs; and then B dies, whereby the other moiety becomes vested in the heir of B: now A's heir and B's heir are not joint tenants of this remainder, but tenants in common; for one moiety vested at one time, and the other moiety vested at another.

Yet, where a feoffment was made to the use of a man, and such wife as he should afterwards marry, for term of their lives, and he afterwards married; in this case it seems to have been hold that the husband and wife had a joint estate, though vested at different times: because the use of the wife's estate was in abeyance and dormant till the intermarriage; and, being then awakened, had relation back, and took effect from the original time of creation.

⚖️ UNITY OF POSSESSION — Lastly, in joint tenancy, there must be a unity of possession. Joint tenants are said to be seised by the half and by all; that is, they each of them have the entire possession, as well of every parcel as of the whole. They have not, one of them a seisin of one-half, and the other of the other half; neither can one be exclusively seised of one acre, and his companion of another; but each as an undivided part of the whole.

⚖️ OTHER INCIDENTS OF JOINT ESTATES — Upon these principles, of a thorough and intimate union of interest and possession, depend many other consequences and incidents to the joint tenant's estate. If two joint tenants let a verbal lease of their land, reserving rent to be paid to one of them, it shall inure to both, in respect of the joint reversion. If their lessee surrenders his lease to one of them, it shall also inure to both, because of the privity, or relation to their estate.

On the same reason, livery of seisin, made to one joint tenant, shall inure to both of them; and the entry, or re-entry, fo one joint tenant is as effectual in law as if it were the act of both. In all actions also relating to their joint estate, one joint tenant cannot sue or be sued without joining the other.

Upon the same ground it is held, that one joint tenant cannot have an action against another for trespass, in respect of his land; for each has an equal right to enter on any part of it. But one joint tenant is not capable by himself to do any act, which may tend to defeat or injure the estate of the other; as to let leases, or to grant copyholds: and, if any waste be done, which tends to the destruction of the inheritance, one joint tenant may have an action of waste against the other, by statute.

Though at common law no action of account lay for one joint tenant against another, unless he had constituted him his bailiff or receiver, yet now by the statute (Joint Tenants, 1705), joint tenants may have actions of account against each other, for receiving more than their due share of the profits of the tenements held in joint tenancy.

⚖   DOCTRINE OF SURVIVORSHIP — From the same principle also arises the remaining grant incident of joint estates: viz., the doctrine of survivorship: by which when two or more persons are seised of a joint estate, of inheritance, for their own lives, or for the life of another, or are jointly possessed of any chattel interest, the entire tenancy upon the decease of any of them remains to the survivors, and at length to the last survivor; and he shall be entitled to the whole estate, whatever it be, whether an inheritance or common freehold only, or even a less estate.

This is the natural and regular consequence of the union and entirety of their interest. The interest of two joint tenants is not only equal or similar, but also is one and the same. But, while it continues, each of two joint tenants has a concurrent interest in the whole: and therefore, on the death of his companion, the sole interest in the whole remains to the survivor. For the interest, which the survivor originally had, is clearly not devested by the death of his companion: and no other person can now claim to have a joint estate with him, for no one can now have an interest in the whole, accruing by the same title, and taking effect at the same time as his own: neither can anyone claim a separate interest in any part of the tenements; for that would be to deprive the survivor of the right which he has in all, and every part. As, therefore, the survivor's original interest in the whole still remains; and as no one can now be admitted, either jointly or severally, to any share with him therein; it follows that his own interest must now be entire and several, and that he shall alone be entitled to the whole estate (whatever it be) that was created by the original grant.

This right upon the death of one joint tenant, accumulates and increases to the survivors; which I apprehend to be one reason why neither the king, nor any corporation, can be a joint tenant with a private person. For here is no mutuality; the private person has not even the remotest chance of being seised of the entirety, by benefit of survivorship; for the king and the corporation can never die.

⚖   JOINT TENANCY, HOW SEVERED AND DESTROYED — We are, lastly, to inquire, how an estate in joint tenancy may be severed and destroyed. This may be done by destroying any of its constituent unities.

⚖   DESTRUCTION OF UNITY OF TIME — 1. That of time, which respects only the original commencement of the joint estate, cannot indeed (being now past), be effected by any subsequent transactions.

But 2. The joint tenants' estate may be destroyed, without an alienation, by merely disuniting their possession. For joint tenants being seised by half and by all, everything that tends to narrow that interest, so that they shall not be seised throughout the whole, and throughout every part, is a severance or destruction of the jointure. Therefore, if two joint tenants agree to part their lands and hold them in sevaralty, they are no longer joint tenants; for they have now no joint interest in the whole, but only a several interest respectively in the several parts. For that reason, also, the right of survivorship is by such separation destroyed.

By common law all the joint tenants might agree to make partition of the lands, but one of them could not compel the other so to do: for, this being an estate originally created by the act and agreement of the parties, the law would not permit any one or more of them to destroy the united possession without a similar universal consent. But now by statutes (Partition, 1539) and (Partition, 1540), joint tenants, either of inheritances or other less estates, are compellable by writ or partition to divide their lands.

ALIENATION — 3. The jointure may be destroyed by destroying the unity of title. As if one joint tenant aliens and conveys his estate to a third person: here the joint tenancy is severed, and turned into tenancy in common; for the grantee and the remaining joint tenant hold by different titles (one derived from the original, the other from the subsequent, grantor), though, till partition made, the unity of possession continues.

But a devise of one's share by will is no severance of the jointure: for no testament takes effect till after the death of the testator, and by such death the right of the survivor (which accrued at the original creation of the estate, and has therefore a priority to the other) is already vested.

MERGER — 4. It may also be destroyed, by destroying the unity of interest. Therefore, if there be two joint tenants for life, and the inheritance is purchased by our descends upon either, it is a severance of the jointure: though, if an estate is originally limited to two for life, and after to the heirs of one of them, the freehold shall remain in jointure, without merging in the inheritance: because being created by one and the same conveyance, they are not separate estates (which is requisite in order to a merger), but branches of one entire estate.

In like manner, if a joint tenant in fee makes a lease for life of his share, this defeats the jointure: for it destroys the unity both of title and of interest. Whenever or by whatever means the jointure ceases or is severed, the right of survivorship the same instant ceases with it. Yet, if one of three joint tenants aliens his share, the two remaining tenants still hold their parts by joint tenancy and survivorship: and, if one of three joint tenants releases his share to one of his companions, though the joint tenancy is destroyed with regard to that part, yet the two remaining parts are still held in jointure; for they still preserve their original constituent unities.

But, when, by any act or event, different interests are created in the several parts of the estate, or they are held by different titles, or if merely the possession is separated; so that the tenants have no longer these four indispensable properties, a sameness of interest, and undivided possession, a title vesting at one and the same time, and by one and the same act or grant; the jointure is instantly dissolved.

⚖️ UTILITY OF SEVERANCE OF JOINT ESTATES — In general it is advantageous for the joint tenants to dissolve the jointure; since thereby the right of survivorship is taken away, and each may transmit his own part to his own heirs. Sometimes, however, it is disadvantageous to dissolve the joint estate: as if there be joint tenants for life, and they make partition, this dissolves the jointure; and, though before they each of them had an estate in the whole for their own lives and the life of their companion, now they have an estate only for their own lives merely; and, on the death of either, the reversioner shall enter. Therefore, if there be two joint tenants for life, and one grants away his part for the life of his companion, it is a forfeiture; for in the first place, by the severance of the jointure he has given himself in his own [part] only an estate for his own life; and then he grants the same land for the life of another: which grant, by a tenant for his own life merely, is a forfeiture of his estate; for it is creating an estate which may by possibility last longer than that which he is legally entitled to.

⚖️ ESTATES IN COPARCENARY — An estate held in coparcenary is where lands of inheritance descend from the ancestor to two or more persons. It arises either by common law, or particular custom. By common law: as where a person seised in fee simple or in fee-tail dies, and his next heirs are two or more females, his daughters, sisters, aunts, cousins, or their representatives; in this case they shall all inherit, as will be more fully shown, when we treat of descents hereafter: and these coheirs are then called coparceners; or, for brevity, parceners only. Parceners by particular custom are where lands descend, as in gavelkind, to all the males in equal degree, as sons, brothers, uncles, etc. in either of these cases, all the parceners put together make but one heir, and have but one estate among them.

☙☙ PROPERTIES OF PARCENERS — The properties of parceners are in some respects like those of joint tenants; they having the same unities of interest, title and possession. They may sue and be sued jointly for matters relating to their own lands: and the entry of one of them shall in some cases inure as the entry of them all. They cannot have an action or trespass against each other: but herein they differ from joint tenants, that they are also excluded from maintaining an action of waste; for coparceners could at all times put a stop to any waste by writ of partition, but till the statute of Henry the Eight, joint tenants had no such power.

Parceners also differ materially from joint tenants in four other points: 1. They always claim by descent, whereas joint tenants always claim by purchase. Therefore, if two sisters purchase lands, to hold to them and their heirs, they are not parceners, but joint tenants: and hence it likewise follows, that no lands can be held in coparcenary, but estates of inheritance, which are of a descendible nature; whereas not only estates in fee and in tail, but for life or years, may be held in joint tenancy.

2. There is no unity of time necessary to an estate in coparcenary. For if a man hath two daughters to whom his estate descends in coparcenary, and one dies before the other, the surviving daughter and the heir of the other, or, when both are dead, their two heirs, are still parceners; the estates vesting in each of them at different times, though it be the same quantity of interest, and held by the same title.

3. Parceners, though they have an unity, have not and entirety, of interest. They are properly entitled each to the whole, and of course there is no survivorship between them: for each part descends severally to their respective heirs, though the unity of possession continues. And as long as the lands continue in a course of descent and united in possession, so long are the tenants therein, whether male or female, called parceners.

But if the possession be once severed by partition, they are no longer parceners, but tenants in severalty; or if one parcener aliens her share, though no partition be made, then are the lands no longer held in coparcenary, but in common.

☙☙ PARTITION — Parceners are so called because they may be constrained to make partition. [There are] many methods of making it; four of which are by consent, and one by compulsion. The first is, where they agree to divide the lands into equal parts in severalty, and that each shall have such a determinate part.

The second, when they agree to choose some friend to make partition for them, and then the sisters shall choose each of them her part according to seniority of age; or otherwise, as shall be agreed. The privilege of seniority is in this case persona; for if the eldest sister be dead, her issue shall not choose first, but the next sister. But, if an advowson descend in coparcenary, and the sisters cannot agree in the presentation, the eldest and her issue, nay her husband, or her assigns, shall present alone, before the younger.

A third method of partition is, where the eldest divides, and then she shall choose last; for the rule of law is, "she who makes the division has the last choice."

The fourth method is where the sisters agree to cast lots for their shares. And these are the methods by consent. That by compulsion is, where one or more sue out a writ of partition against the others; whereupon the sheriff shall go to the lands, and make partition thereof by the verdict of a jury there impaneled, and assign to each of the parceners her part in severalty.

But there are some things which are in their nature impartible. The mansion-house, common of estovers, common of piscary uncertain, or any other common without stint, shall not be divided; but the elder sister, if she pleases, shall have them, and make the others a reasonable satisfaction in other parts of the inheritance: or, if that cannot be, then they shall have the profits of the thing by turns, in the same manner as they take the advowson.

⚖️   HOTCHPOT — There is yet another consideration attending the estate in coparcenary; that if one of the daughters has had an estate given with her in frank-marriage by her ancestor (which we may remember was a species of estates-tail, freely given by a relation for advancement of his kinswoman in marriage), in this case, if lands descend from the same ancestor to her and her sisters in fee simple, she or her heirs shall have no share of them, unless they will agree to divide the lands so given in frank-marriage in equal proportion with the rest of the lands descending. It is denominated bringing these lands into hotchpot: which term I shall explain in the very words of Littleton: "It seemeth that this word hotchpot, is in English a pudding; for in a pudding is not commonly put one thing alone, but one thing with other things together."

By this housewifely metaphor our ancestors meant to inform us, that the lands, both those given in frank-marriage and those descending in fee simple, should be mixed and blended together, and then divided in equal portions among all the daughters. But this was left to the choice of the donee in frank-marriage; and if she did not choose to put her lands in hotchpot, she was presumed to be sufficiently provided for, and the rest of the inheritance was divided among her other sisters.

The law of hotchpot took place then only, when the other lands descended in tail, the donee in frank-marriage was entitled to her share, without bringing her lands so given into hotchpot. And the reason is, because lands descending in fee simple are distributed by the policy of law, for the maintenance of all the daughters; and, if one has a sufficient provision out of the same inheritance, equal to the rest, it is not reasonable that she should have more: but lands, descending in tail, are not distributed by the operation of law, but by the designation of the giver (by the form of the gift); it matters not, therefore, how unequal this distribution may be.

Also no lands, but such as are given in frank-marriage, shall be brought into hotchpot; for no others are looked upon in law as given for the advancement of woman, or by way of marriage portion. And therefore, as gifts in frank-marriage are fallen into disuse, I should hardly have mentioned the law of hotchpot, had not this method of division been revived and copied by the statute for distribution of personal estates, which we shall hereafter consider at large.

DISSOLUTION OF ESTATE IN COPARCENARY — The estate in coparcenary may be dissolved, either by partition, which disunites the possession; by alienation of one parcener, which disunites the title, and may disunite the interest; or by the whole at last descending to and vesting in one single person, which brings it to an estate in severalty.

TENANCY IN COMMON — Tenants in common are such as hold by several and distinct titles, but by unity of possession; because none knoweth his own severalty, and therefore they all occupy promiscuously. This tenancy, therefore, happens, where there is a unity of possession merely, but perhaps an entire disunion of interest, of title, and of time. For, if there be two tenants in common of lands, one may hold his part in fee simple, the other in tail, or for life; so that there is no necessary unity of interest: one may hold by descent, the other by purchase; or the one by purchase from A, the other by purchase from B; so that there is no unity of title: one's estate may have been vested fifty years, the other's but yesterday; so there is no unity of time. The only unity there is, is that of possession.

CREATION OF TENANCIES IN COMMON — Tenancy in common may be created, either by the destruction of the two other estates, in joint tenancy and coparcenary, or by special limitation in a deed. By the destruction of the two other estates, I mean such destruction as does not sever the unity of possession, but only the unity of title or interest; as, if one of the two joint tenants in fee aliens his estate for the life of the alienee and the other joint tenant are tenants in common: for they now have several titles, the other joint tenant by the original grant, the alienee by the new alienation; and they also have several interests, the former joint tenant in fee simple, the alienee for his own life only.

So, if one joint tenant give his part to A in tail, and the other gives his to B in tail, the donees are tenants in common, as holding by different titles, and conveyances. If one or two parceners aliens, the alienee and the remaining parcener are tenants in common; because they hold by different titles, the parcener by descent, the alienee by purchase.

So likewise, if there be a grant to two men, or two women, and the heirs of their bodies, here the grantees shall be joint tenants of the life estate, but they shall have several inheritances; because they cannot possibly have one heir to their two bodies, as might have been the case had the limitation been to a man and woman, and the heirs of their bodies begotten: and in this, and the like cases, their issues shall be tenants in common; because they must claim by different titles, one as heir of A, and the other as heir of B; and those too not titles by purchase but descent. In short, whenever an estate in joint tenancy or coparcenary is dissolved, so that there be no partition made, but the unity of possession continues, it is turned into a tenancy in common.

⚖ JOINT TENANCIES PREFERRED TO TENANCIES IN COMMON — A tenancy in common may also be created by express limitation in a deed: but here care must be taken not to insert words which imply a joint estate; and then if lands be given to two or more, and it be not joint tenancy, it must be a tenancy in common. But the law is apt in its constructions to favor joint tenancy rather than tenancy in common; because the divisible services issuing from land (as rent, etc.) are not divided, nor the entire services (as fealty) multiplied, by joint tenancy, as they must necessarily be upon a tenancy in common. If one grants to another half his land, the grantor and grantee are tenants in common: because, as has been before observed, joint tenants do not take by distinct halves; and by such grants the division and severalty of the estate is so plainly expressed, that it is impossible they should take a joint interest in the whole of the tenants.

But a devise to two persons to hold jointly and severally, is a joint tenancy; because that is necessarily implied in the word "jointly," the word "severally," perhaps, only implying the power of partition: and an estate given to A and B, equally to be divided between them, though in deeds it hath been said to be a joint tenancy (for it implies no more than the law has annexed to that estate, viz., divisibility), yet in wills it is certainly a tenancy in common; because the devisor may be presumed to have meant what is most beneficial to both the devisees, though his meaning is imperfectly expressed.

This nicety in the wording of grants makes it the most usual as well as the safest way, when a tenancy in common is meant to be created, to add express words of exclusion as well as description, and limit the estate to A and B, to hold as tenants in common, and not as joint tenants.

⚖ INCIDENTS OF TENANCIES IN COMMON — As to the incidents attending a tenancy in common: tenants in common (like joint tenants) are compellable by the statutes to make partition of their lands; which they were not at common law. They have no entirety of interest; and therefore there is no survivorship between tenants in common. Their other incidents are such as merely arise from the unity of possession; and are therefore the same as appertain to joint tenants merely upon that account: such as being liable to reciprocal actions of waste, and of account, by the statute of Westminster (1285), and (Joint Tenants, 1705).

For by the common law no tenant in common was liable to account with his companion for embezzling the profits of the estate; though if one actually turns the other out of possession, an action of ejectment will lie against him. But, as for other incidents of joint tenants, which arise from the privity of title, or the union and entirety of interest (such as joining or being joined in actions, unless in the case where some entire or indivisible thing is to be recovered), these are not applicable to tenants in common, whose interests are distinct, and whose titles are not joint but several.

⚖ DISSOLUTION OF TENANCIES IN COMMON — Estates in common can only be dissolved two ways: 1. By uniting all the titles and interests in one tenant, by purchase or otherwise; which brings the whole to one severalty: 2. By making partition between the several tenants in common, which gives them all respective severalties. For indeed tenancies differ in nothing from sole estates, but merely in the blending and unity of possession. And this finishes our inquiries with respect to the nature of estates.

TITLE TO THINGS REAL, IN GENERAL

⚖ TITLE TO THINGS REAL — The foregoing chapters having been principally employed in defining the nature of things real, in describing the tenures by which they may be holden, and in distinguishing the several kinds of estates or interest that may be had therein, I come now to consider, lastly, the title to things real, with the manner of acquiring and losing it.

⚖ DEFINITION OF TITLE — A title is the legal ground of possessing that which is our own; or, it is the means whereby the owner of lands hath the just possession of his property. There are several stages or degrees requisite to form a complete title to lands and tenements. We will consider them in a progressive order.

⚖ MERE POSSESSION — The lowest and most imperfect degree of title consists in the mere naked possession, or actual occupation of the estate; without any apparent right, or any shadow or pretense of right, to hold and continue such possession. This may happen, when one man invades the possession of another, and by force or surprise turns him out of the occupation of his lands; which is termed a disseisin, being a deprivation of that actual seisin, or corporal freehold of the lands, which the tenant before enjoyed. Or it may happen that after the death of the ancestor and before the entry of the heir or after the death of a particular tenant and before the entry of him in remainder or reversion, a stranger may contrive to get possession of the vacant land, and hold out him that had a right to enter.

In all which cases, and many others that might be here suggested, the wrongdoer has only a mere naked possession, which the rightful owner may put an end to; by a variety of legal remedies, as will more fully appear in the third book of these Commentaries. But in the meantime, till some act be done by the rightful owner to divest this possession and assert his title, such actual possession is evidence of a legal title in the possessor; and it may by length of time and negligence of him who hath the right, by degrees ripen into a perfect and indefeasible title. At all events, without such actual possession no title can be completely good.

☙ RIGHT OF POSSESSION — The next step to a good and perfect title is the right of possession, which may reside in one man, while the actual possession is not in himself but in another. For if a man be disseised, or otherwise kept out of possession, by any of the means before mentioned, though the actual possession be lost, yet he has still remaining in him the right of possession; and may exert it whenever he thinks proper, by entering upon the disseisor, and turning him out of that occupancy which he has so illegally gained.

But this right of possession is of two sorts: an apparent right of possession, which may be defeated by proving a better; and an actual right of possession, which will stand the test against all opponents. Thus, if the disseisor, or other wrongdoer, dies possessed of the land whereof he so became seised by his own unlawful act, and the same descends to his heir; now by the common law the heir hath obtained an apparent right, though the actual right of possession resides in the person disseised; and it shall not be lawful for the person disseised to divest this apparent right by mere entry or other act of his own, but only by an action at law. For, until the contrary be proved by legal demonstration, the law will rather presume the right to reside in the heir, whose ancestor died seised, than in one who has no such presumptive evidence to urge in his own behalf.

This doctrine in some measure arose from the principles of the feudal law, which, after feuds became hereditary, much favored the right of descent; in order that there might be a person always upon the spot to perform the feudal duties and services: therefore, when a feudatory died in battle, or otherwise, it presumed always that his children were entitled to the feud, till the right was otherwise determined by his fellow-soldiers and fellow-tenants, the peers of the feudal court. But if he, who has the actual right of possession, puts in his claim and brings his action within a reasonable time, and can prove by what unlawful means the ancestor became seised, he will then by sentence of law recover that possession, to which he hath such actual right. Yet, if he omits to bring this his possessory action within a competent time, his adversary may imperceptibly gain an actual right of possession, in consequence of the other's negligence. By this, and certain other means, the party kept out of possession may have nothing left in him, but what we are next to speak of:

⚖️   MERE RIGHT OF PROPERTY — The mere right of property without either possession or even the right of possession is frequently spoken of in our books under the name of the mere right; and the estate of the owner is in such cases said to be totally divested, and put to a right.

A person in this situation may have the true ultimate property of the lands in himself; but by the intervention of certain circumstances, either by his own negligence, the solemn act of his ancestor, or the determination of a court of justice, the presumptive evidence of that right is strongly in favor of his antagonist; who has thereby obtained the absolute right of possession.

As, in the first place, if a person disseised, or turned out of possession of his estate, neglects to pursue his remedy within the time limited by law: by this means the disseisor or his heirs gain the actual right of possession: for the law presumes that either he had a good right originally, in virtue of which he entered on the lands in question, or that since such his entry he has procured a sufficient title; and therefore, after so long an acquiescence, the law will not suffer his possession to be disturbed without inquiring into the absolute right of property. Yet, still, if the person disseised or his heir hath the true right of property remaining in himself, his estate is indeed said to be turned into a mere right; but, by proving such his better right, he may at length recover the lands.

If a tenant in tail discontinues his estate-tail, by alienating the lands to a stranger in fee, and dies; here the issue in tail hath no right of possession, independent of the right of property: for the law presumes that the ancestor would not disinherit, or attempt to disinherit, his heir, unless he had power so to do; and therefore, as the ancestor had in himself the right of possession, and has transferred the same to a stranger, the law will not permit that possession now to be disturbed, unless by showing the absolute right of property to reside in another person. The heir, therefore, in this case has only a mere right, and must be strictly held to the proof of it, in order to recover the lands.

Lastly, if by accident, neglect, or otherwise, judgment is given for either party in any possessory action (that is, such wherein the right of possession only, and not that of property, is contested), and the other party hath indeed in himself the right of property, this is now turned to a mere right; and upon proof thereof in a subsequent action, denominated a writ of right, he shall recover his seisin of the lands.

⚖️   TITLE BY LIMITATION — Thus, if a disseisor turns me out of possession of my lands, he thereby gains a mere naked possession, and I still retain the right of possession and right of property. If the disseisor dies, and the lands descend to his son, the son gains an apparent right of possession; but I still retain the actual right both of possession and property. If I acquiesce for thirty years, without bringing any action to recover possession of the lands, the son gains the actual right of possession, and I retain nothing but the mere right of property. Even this right of property will fail, or at least it will be without a remedy, unless I pursue it within the space of sixty years.

So, also, if the father be tenant in tail, and aliens the estate-tail to a stranger in fee, the alienee thereby gains the right of possession, and the son hath only the mere right or right of property. And hence it will follow that one man may have the possession, another the right of possession, and the third the right of property. For if tenant in tail enfeoffs A in fee simple, and dies, and B disseises A; now B will have the possession, A the right of possession, and the issue in tail the right of property: A may recover the possession against B; and afterwards the issue in tail may evict A, and unite in himself the possession, the right of possession, and also the right of property.

COMPLETE TITLE — It is an ancient maxim of the law, that no title is completely good, unless the right of possession be joined with the right of property; which right is then denominated a double right. When to this double right the actual possession is also united, then, and then only, is the title completely legal.

TITLE BY DESCENT

⚖ MODES OF ACQUIRING AND LOSING TITLE — The several gradations and stages, requisite to form a complete title to lands, tenements, and hereditaments, having been briefly stated in the preceding chapter, we are next to consider the several manners, in which this complete title may be reciprocally lost and acquired: whereby the dominion of things real is either continued, or transferred from one man to another. And here we must first of all observe, that by whatever method one man gains an estate, by that same method or its correlative some other man has lost it.

As where the heir acquires by descent, the ancestor has first lost or abandoned his estate by his death: where the lord gains land by escheat, the estate of the tenant is first of all lost by the natural or legal extinction of all his hereditary blood: where a man gains an interest by occupancy, the former owner has previously relinquished his right of possession: where one man claims by prescription or immemorial usage, another man has either parted with his right by an ancient and now forgotten grant, or has forfeited it by the supineness or neglect of himself and his ancestors for ages; and so, in case of forfeiture, the tenant by his own misbehavior or neglect has renounced his interest in the estate; whereupon it devolves to that person who by law may take advantage of such default: and, in alienation by common assurances, the two considerations of loss and acquisition are so interwoven, and so constantly contemplated together, that we never hear of a conveyance, without at once receiving the ideas as well of the grantor as the grantee.

⚖ DESCENT AND PURCHASE — The methods, therefore, of acquiring on the one hand, and of losing on the other, a title to estates in things real, are reduced by our law to two: descent, where the title is vested in a man by the single operation of law; and purchase, where the title is vested in him by his own act or agreement.

⚖️ DESCENT, OR HEREDITARY SUCCESSION — Descent, or hereditary succession, is the title whereby a man on the death of his ancestor acquires his estate by right of representation, as his heir at law. An heir, therefore, is he upon whom the law casts the estate immediately on the death of the ancestor; and an estate so descending to the heir is in law called the inheritance.

The doctrine of descents, or law of inheritances in fee simple, is a point of the highest importance; and is indeed the principal object of the laws of real property in England. All the rules relating to purchases, whereby the legal course of descents is broken and altered, perpetually refer to this settled law of inheritance, as a first principle universally known, and upon which their subsequent limitations are to work.

Thus a gift in tail, or to a man and the heirs of his body, is a limitation that cannot be perfectly understood without a previous knowledge of the law of descents in fee simple. One may well perceive that this is an estate confined in its decent to such heirs only of the donee, as have sprung or shall spring from his body; but who those heirs are, whether all his children both male and female, or the male only, and (among the males) whether the eldest, youngest, or other son alone, or all the sons together, shall be the heir; this is a point, that we must result back to the standing law of descents in fee simple to be informed of.

⚖️ DESCENT AT COMMON LAW — In order, therefore, to treat a matter of this universal consequence the more clearly, I shall endeavor to lay aside such matters as will only tend to breed embarrassment and confusion in our inquiries, and shall confine myself entirely to this one object. I shall therefore decline considering at present who are, and who are not, capable of being heirs; reserving that for the chapter of escheats.

I shall also pass over the frequent division of descents, in those by custom, statute, and common law: for descents by particular custom, as to all the sons in gavelkind, and to the youngest in borough-English, have already been often hinted at, and may also be incidentally touched upon again; but will not make a separate consideration by themselves, in a system so general as the present: and descents by statute, or in fees-tail (by the form of the gift) in pursuance of the statute of Westminster the Second have also been already copiously handled; and it has been seen that the descent in tail is restrained and regulated according to the words of the original donation, and does not entirely pursue the common-law doctrine of inheritance; which, and which only, it will now be our business to explain.

As this depends not a little on the nature of kindred, and the several degrees of consanguinity, it will be previously necessary to state, as briefly as possible, the true notion of this kindred or alliance in blood.

⚖ CONSANGUINITY — Consanguinity, or kindred, is defined by the writers on these subject to be the connection or relation of persons descended from the same stock or common ancestor. This consanguinity is either lineal or collateral.

⚖ LINEAL CONSANGUINITY — Lineal consanguinity is that which subsists between persons, of whom one is descended in a direct line from the other, as between John Stiles (the propositus in the table of consanguinity) and his father, grandfather, great-grandfather, and so upwards in the direct ascending line; or between John Stiles and his son, grand-son, great-grandson, and so downwards in the direct descending line.

Every generation, in this lineal direct consanguinity, constitutes a different degree, reckoning either upwards or downwards: the father of John Stiles is related to him in the first degree, and so likewise is his son; his grandsire and grandson in the second; his great grandsire, and great-grandson in the third. This is the only natural way of reckoning the degrees in the direct line, and therefore universally obtains, as well in the civil, and canon, as in the common law.

The doctrine of lineal consanguinity is sufficiently plain and obvious; but it is at the first view astonishing to consider the number of lineal ancestors which every man has, within no very great number of degrees: and so many different bloods, is a man said to contain in his veins, as he hath lineal ancestors.

Of these he hath two in the first ascending degree, his own parents; he hath four in the second, the parents of his father and the parents of his mother; he hath eight in the third, the parents of his two grandfathers and two grandmothers; and by the same rule of progression, he hath an hundred and twenty-eight in the seventh; a thousand and twenty-four in the tenth; and the twentiety degree, or the distance of twenty generations, every man hath above a million of ancestors, as common arithmetic will demonstrate. This consanguinity, we may observe, falls strictly within the definition of the connection of persons from a common ancestor; since lineal relations are such as descend one from the other, and both of course from the same common ancestor.

⚖ COLLATERAL CONSANGUINITY — Collateral kindred answers to the same description: collateral relations agreeing with the lineal in this, that they descend from the same stock or ancestor; but differing in this, that they do not descend one from the other. Collateral kinsmen are such then as lineally spring from one and the same ancestor, who is the stirps, or root, the trunk, or common stock, from whence these relations are branched out. As if John Stiles hath two sons, who have each a numerous issue; both these issues are lineally descended from John Stiles as their common ancestor; and they are collateral kinsmen to each other, because they are all descended from this common ancestor, and all have a portion of his blood in their veins, which denominates them blood relations.

We must be careful to remember that the very being of collateral consanguinity consists in this descent from one and the same common ancestor. Thus Titius and his brother are related. Why? Because both are derived from one father. Titius and his first cousin are related. Why? Because both descend from the same grandfather; and his second cousin's claim to consanguinity is this, that they both are derived from one and the same great-grandfather. In short, as many ancestors as a man has, so many common stocks he has, from which collateral kinsmen may be derived. As we are taught by Holy Writ that there is one couple of ancestors belonging to us all, from whom the whole race of mankind is descended, the obvious and undeniable consequence is, that all men are in some degree related to each other.

For, indeed, if we only suppose each couple of our ancestors to have left, one with another, two children; and each of those children on an average to have left two more (and, without such a supposition, the human species must be daily diminishing); we shall find that all of us have now subsisting near two hundred and seventy millions of kindred in the fifteenth degree, at the same distance from the several common ancestors as ourselves are; besides those that are one or two descents nearer to or further from the common stock, who may amount to as many more. If this calculation should appear incompatible with the number of inhabitants on the earth, it is because, by intermarriages among the several descendants from the same ancestor, a hundred or a thousand modes of consanguinity may be consolidated in one person, or he may be related to us a hundred or a thousand different ways.

☙☙ COMPUTATION OF DEGREES — The method of computing these degrees in the canon law, which our law has adopted, is as follows: We begin at the common ancestor, and reckon downwards; and in whatsoever degree the two persons, or the most remote of them, is distant from the common ancestor, that is the degree in which they are related to each other. Thus Titius and his brother are related in the first degree; for from the father to each of them is counted only one; Titius and his nephew are related in the second degree; for the nephew is two degrees removed from the common ancestor; viz., his own grandfather, the father of Titius.

⚖ RULES OF DESCENT — The nature and degrees of kindred being thus in some measure explained, I shall next proceed to lay down a series of rules, or canons of inheritance, according to which estates are transmitted from the ancestor to the heir; together with an explanatory comment, remarking their original and progress, the reasons upon which they are founded, and in some cases their agreement with the laws of other nations.

⚖ FIRST RULE — The first rule is, that inheritances shall lineally descend to the issue of the person last actually seised; but shall never lineally ascend.

⚖ HEIRS APPARENT AND PRESUMPTIVE — To explain the more clearly both this and the subsequent rules, it must be still observed, that by law no inheritance can vest, nor can any person be the actual complete heir of another, till the ancestor is previously dead. Before that time the person who is next in the line of succession is called an heir apparent, or heir presumptive.

Heirs apparent are such, whose right of inheritance is indefeasible, provided they outlive the ancestor; as the eldest son or his issue, who must be the course of the common law be heirs to the father whenever he happens to die. Heirs presumptive are such who, if the ancestor should die immediately, would in the present circumstances of things be his heirs; but whose right of inheritance may be defeated by the contingency of some nearer heir being born: as a brother, or nephew, whose presumptive succession may be destroyed by the birth of a child; or a daughter, whose present hopes may be hereafter cut off by the birth of a son. Nay, even if the estate hath descended, by the death of the owner, to such brother, or nephew, or daughter; in the former cases, the estate shall be divested and taken away by the birth of a posthumous child; and, in the latter, it shall also be totally divested by the birth of a posthumous son.

⚖ SEISIN NECESSARY IN ANCESTOR — We must also remember that no person can be properly such an ancestor, as that an inheritance of lands or tenements can be derived from him, unless he hath had actual seisin of such lands, either by his own entry, or by the possession of his own or his ancestor's lessees for years, or by receiving rent from the lessee of a freehold: or unless he hath had what is equivalent to corporal seisin in hereditaments that are incorporeal; such as the receipt of rent, a presentation to the church in case of an advowson, and the like. But he shall not be accounted an ancestor, who hath only a bare right or title to enter or be otherwise seised.

Therefore all the cases which will be mentioned in the present chapter are upon the supposition that the deceased (whose inheritance is now claimed) was the last person actually seised thereof. For the law requires this notoriety of possession, as evidence that the ancestor had that property in himself, which is now to be transmitted to his heir. Which notoriety hath succeeded in the place of the ancient feudal investiture, whereby, while feuds were precarious, the vassal on the descent of lands was formerly admitted in the lord's court (as is still the practice in Scotland) and there received his seisin, in the nature of a renewal of his ancestors' grant, in the presence of the feudal peers: till at length, when the right of succession became indefeasible, an entry on any part of the lands, within the country (which if disputed was afterwards to be tried by those peers) or other notorious possession, was admitted as equivalent to the formal grant of seisin, and made the tenant capable of transmitting his estate by descent.

The seisin, therefore, of any person, thus understood, makes him the root or stock, from which all future inheritancy by right of blood must be derived.

༄༅ DESCENT FROM FATHER TO SON — When, therefore a person dies so seised, the inheritance first goes to his issue: as if there be Geoffrey, John, and Matthew, grandfather, father, and son; and John purchases land, and dies; his son Matthew shall succeed him as heir, and not the grandfather Geoffrey; to whom the lands shall never ascend, but shall rather escheat to the lord.

༄༅ EXCLUSION OF LINEAL ASCENT — This rule, so far as it is affirmative and relates to lineal descents, is almost universally adopted by all nations; and it seems founded on a principle of natural reason, that (whenever a right of property transmissible to representatives is admitted) the possessions of the parents should go, upon their decease, in the first place to their children, as those to whom they have given being, and for whom they are therefore bound to provide. But the negative branch, or total exclusion of parents and all lineal ancestors from succeeding to the inheritance of their offspring, is peculiar to our own laws, and such as have been deduced from the same original.

For, by the Jewish law, on failure of issue, the father succeeded to the son, in exclusion of brethren, unless one of them married the widow and raised up see to his brother. And, by the laws of Rome, in the first place the children or lineal descendants were preferred; and, on failure of these, the father and mother or lineal ascendants succeeded together with the brethren and sisters; though by the law of the twelve tables the mother was originally, on account of her sex, excluded. Hence this rule of our laws has been censured and declaimed against, as absurd and derogating from the maxims of equity and natural justice. Yet that there is nothing unjust or absurd in it, but that, on the contrary, it is founded upon very good reason, may appear from considering as well the nature of the rule itself as the occasion of introducing it into our laws.

We are to reflect, in the first place, that all rules of succession to estates are creatures of the civil polity, and of positive law merely. The right of property, which is gained by occupancy, extends naturally no further than the life of the present possessor: after which the land by the law of nature would again become common, and liable to be seized by the next occupant: but society, to prevent the mischiefs that might ensue from a doctrine so productive of contention, has established conveyances, wills, and successions; whereby the property originally gained by possession is continued, and transmitted from one man to another, according to the rules which each state has respectively thought proper to prescribe. There is certainly, therefore, no injustice done to individuals, whatever be the path of descent marked out by the municipal law.

If we next consider the time and occasion of introducing this rule into our law, we shall find it to have been grounded upon very substantial reasons. I think there is no doubt to be made, but that it was introduced at the same time with, and in consequence of, the feudal tenures. For it was an express rule of the feudal law, the nature of feudal succession is such that those in the ascending line do not inherit; and the same maxim obtains also in the French law to this day. For if the feud, of which the son died seised, was really an ancient fee, or one descended to him from his ancestors, the father could not possibly succeed to it, because it must have passed him in the course of descent, before it could come to the son: unless it were a maternal fee, or one descended from his mother, and then for other reasons which will appear hereafter, the father could in no wise inherit it. If it were a new fee, or one newly acquired by the son, then only the descendants from the body of the feudatory himself could succeed, by the known maxim of the early feudal constitutions; which was founded as well upon the personal merit of the vassal, which might be transmitted to his children but could not ascend to his progenitors, as also upon this consideration of military policy, that the decrepit grandsire of a vigorous vassal would be but indifferently qualified to succeed him in his feudal services.

Nay, even if this nee fee were held by the son as an ancient fee, or with all the qualities annexed of a feud descended from his ancestors, such feud must in all respects have descended as if it had been really an ancient feud, the father must have been dead before it could have come to the son.

⚖ SECOND RULE — A second general rule is, that the male issue shall be admitted before the female.

Thus sons shall be admitted before daughters; or, as our male lawgivers have somewhat uncomplaisantly expressed it, the worthiest of blood shall be preferred. As if John Stiles hath two sons, Mathew and Gilbert, and two daughters, Margaret and Charlotte, and dies; first Mathew, and in case of his death without issue, then Gilbert, shall be admitted to the succession in preference to both the daughters.

This preference of males to females is entirely agreeable to the law of succession among the Jews, and also among the states of Greece, or at least among the Athenians; but was totally unknown to the laws of Rome (such of them, I mean, as are at present extant), wherein brethren and sisters were allowed to succeed to equal portions of the inheritance.

Our present preference to males to females seems to have arisen entirely from the feudal law. For though our British ancestors, the Welsh, appear to have given a preference to males, yet our subsequent Danish predecessors seem to have made no distinction of sexes, but to have admitted all the children at once to the inheritance. But the feudal law of the Saxons on the Continent (which was probably brought over hither, and first altered by the law of King Canute) gives an evident preference of the male to the female sex. The father or mother at their death shall leave their inheritance to their son, not to their daughter. If a man at his death leave no sons, but only daughters, then the whole inheritance shall belong to them.

It is possible, therefore, that this preference might be a branch of that imperfect system of feuds, which obtained here before the Conquest; especially as it subsists among the customs of gavelkind, and as, in the charter of King Henry the First, it is not like many Norman innovations, given up, but rather enforced. The true reason of preferring the males must be deduced from feudal principles: for, by the genuine and original policy of that constitution, no female could ever succeed to a proper feud, inasmuch as they were incapable of performing those military services, for the sake of which that system was established.

But our law does not extend to a total exclusion of females, as the Salic law, and others, where feuds were most strictly retained: it only postpones them to males; for, though daughters are excluded by sons, yet they succeed before any collateral relations: our law, like that of the Saxon feudists before mentioned, thus steering a middle course, between the absolute rejection of females, and the putting them on a footing with males.

⚖ THIRD RULE — A third rule, or canon of descent, is this; that there are two or more males in equal degree, the eldest only shall inherit; but the females all together.

As if a man hath two sons, Matthew and Gilbert, and two daughters, Margaret and Charlotte, and dies; Matthew, his eldest son, shall alone succeed to his estate, in exclusion of Gilbert, the second son, and both the daughters; but, if both the sons die without issue before the father, the daughters Margaret and Charlotte shall both inherit the estate as coparceners.

⚖ ORIGIN OF PRIMOGENITURE — This right of primogeniture in males seems anciently to have only obtained among the Jews, in whose constitution the eldest son had a double portion of the inheritance; in the same manner as with us, by the laws of King Henry the First, the eldest son had the capital fee or principal feud of his father's possessions, and no other pre-eminence; and as the eldest daughter had afterwards the principal mansion, when the estate descended in coparcenary.

The Greeks, the Romans, the Britons, the Saxons, and even originally the feudists, divided the lands equally; some among all the children at large, some among the males only. This is certainly the most obvious and natural way; and has the appearance, at least in the opinion of younger brothers, of the greatest impartiality and justice. But when the emperors began to create honorary feuds, or titles of nobility, it was found necessary (in order to preserve their dignity) to make them impartible, or indivisible fees, and in consequence descendible to the eldest son alone.

This example was further enforced by the inconveniences that attended the splitting of estates; namely, the division of the military services, the multitude of infant tenants incapable of performing any duty, the consequential weakening of the strength of the kingdom, and the inducing younger sons to take up with the business and idleness of a country life, instead of being serviceable to themselves and the public, by engaging in mercantile, in military, in civil, or in ecclesiastical employments. These reasons occasioned an almost total change in the method of feudal inheritances abroad; so that the eldest male began universally to succeed to the whole of the lands in all military tenures: and in this condition the feudal constitution was established in England by William the Conqueror.

⚖ PRIMOGENITURE IN SOCAGE ESTATES — Yet we find that socage estates frequently descended to all the sons equally, so lately as the reign of Henry the Second; and it is mentioned as a part of our ancient constitution, that knights' fees should descend to the eldest son, and socage fees should be partible among the male children. However, in Henry the Third's time we find that socage lands, in imitation of lands in chivalry, had almost entirely fallen into the right of succession by primogeniture, as the law now stands: except in Kent, where they gloried in the preservation of their ancient gavelkind tenure, of which a principal branch was the joint inheritance of all the sons; and except in some particular manors and townships, where their local customs continued the descent, sometimes to the youngest son only, or in other more singular methods of succession.

⚖ DESCENT AS AMONG FEMALES — As to the females, they are still left as they were by the ancient law: for they were all equally incapable of performing any personal service: and therefore one main reason of preferring the eldest ceasing, such preference would have been injurious to the rest; and the other principal purpose, the prevention of the two minute subdivisions of estates, was left to be considered and provided for by the lords, who had the disposal of these female heiresses in marriage. However, the succession by primogeniture, even among females, took place as to the inheritance of the crown; wherein the necessity of a sole and determinate succession is as great in the one sex as the other.

The right of sole succession, though not of primogeniture, was also established with respect to female dignities and titles of honor. If a man holds an earldom to him and the heirs of his body, and dies, leaving only daughters; the eldest shall not, of course, be countess, but the dignity is in suspense or abeyance till the king shall declare his pleasure; for he, being the fountain of honor, may confer it on which of them he pleases. In which disposition is preserved a strong trace of the ancient law of feuds, before their descent by primogeniture even among the males was established; namely, that the lord might bestow them on which of the sons he thought proper.

⚖ FOURTH RULE — A fourth rule, of descents is this; that the lineal descendants, in infinitum, of any person deceased shall represent their ancestor; that is, shall stand in the same place as the person himself would have done, had he been living.

Thus the child, grandchild, or great-grandchild (either male or female) of the eldest son succeeds before the younger son, and so in infinitum. These representatives shall take neither more nor less, but just so much as their principals would have done. As if there be two sisters, Margaret and Charlotte; and Margaret dies, leaving six daughters; and then John Stiles, the father of the two sisters, dies, without other issue: these six daughters shall take among them exactly the same as their mother Margaret would have done, had she been living; that is, a moiety of the lands of John Stiles in coparcenary: so that, upon partition made, if the land be divided into twelve parts, thereof Charlotte, the surviving sister, shall have six, and her six nieces, the daughters of Margaret, one apiece.

⚖ CALLED SUCCESSION IN STIRPES — This taking by representation is called succession in stirpes, according to the roots; since all the branches inherit the same share that their root, whom they represent, would have done. And in this manner also was the Jewish succession directed.

⚖ REASON FOR RULE OF SUCCESSION IN STIRPES — This mode of representation is a necessary consequence of the double preference given by our law, first to the male issue and next to the first born among the males. For if all the children of three sisters were in England to claim per capita in their own right as next of kin to the ancestor, without any respect to the stocks from whence they sprung, and those children were partly male and partly female; then the eldest male among them would exclude not only his own brethren and sisters, but all the issue of the other two daughters; or else the law in this instance must be inconsistent with itself, and depart from the preference which it constantly gives to the males, and the firstborn, among persons in equal degree. Whereas, by dividing the inheritance according to the roots, or stirpes, the rule of descent is kept uniform and steady: the issue of the eldest son excludes all other pretenders, as the son himself (if living) would have done; but the issue of two daughters divide the inheritance between them provided their mothers (if living) would have done the same: and among these several issue, or representatives of the respective roots, the same preference to males and the same right of primogeniture obtain, as would have obtained at the first among the roots themselves, the sons or daughters of the deceased.

If a man hath two sons, A and B, and A dies leaving two sons, and then the grandfather dies; now the eldest son of A shall succeed to the whole of his grandfather's estate; and if A had left only two daughters, they should have succeeded also to equal moieties of the whole, in exclusion of B and his issue. But if a man hath only three daughters, C, D, and E; and C dies leaving two sons, D leaving two daughters, and E leaving a daughter and a son who is younger than his sister: here when the grandfather dies, the eldest son of C shall succeed to one-third, in exclusion of the younger; the two daughters of D to another third in exclusion of his elder sister. The same right of representation, guided and restrained by the same rules of descent, prevails downwards in infinitum.

༄ FIFTH RULE — A fifth rule is, that on failure of lineal descendants, or issue, of the person last seised, the inheritance shall descend to the blood of the first purchases; subject to the three preceding rules.

Thus, if Geoffrey Stiles purchases land, and it descends to John Stiles, his son, and John dies seised thereof without issue; whoever succeeds to this inheritance must be of the blood of Geoffrey, the first purchases of this family. The first purchases is he who first acquired the estate to his family, whether the same was transferred to him by sale, or by gift, or by any other method, except only that of descent.

༄ SIXTH RULE — A sixth rule or canon therefore is, that the collateral heir of the person last seised must be his next collateral kinsman, of the whole blood.

First, he must be his next collateral kinsman, either personally or by right of representation; which proximity is reckoned according to the canonical degrees of consanguinity before mentioned. Therefore, the brother being in the first degree, he and his descendants shall exclude the uncle and his issue, who is only in the second. Herein consists the true reason of the different methods of computing the degrees of consanguinity, on the civil law on the one hand, and in the canon law and common law on the other.

The civil law regards consanguinity principally with respect to successions, and therein very naturally considers only the person deceased, to whom the relation is claimed: it therefore counts the degrees of kindred according to the number of persons through whom the claim must be derived from him; and makes not only his great-nephew but also his first cousin to be both related to him in the fourth degree; because there are three persons between him and each of them.

The canon law regards consanguinity principally with a view to prevent incestuous marriages, between those who have a large portion of the same blood running in their respective veins; and therefore looks up to the author of that blood, or the common ancestor, reckoning the degrees from him: so that the great-nephew is related in the third canonical degree to the person proposed, and the first cousin in the second; the former being distant three degrees from the common ancestor, and therefore deriving only one-fourth of his blood from the same fountain.

The common law regards consanguinity principally with respect to descents; and, having therein the same object in view as the civil, it may seem as if it ought to proceed according to the civil computation. But as it also respects the purchasing ancestor, from whom the estate was derived, it therein resembles the canon law, and therefore counts its degrees in the same manner. Indeed, the designation of person (in seeming for the next of kin) will come to exactly the same end (though the degrees will be differently numbered), whichever method of computation we suppose the law of England to use; since the right of representation (of the father by the son, etc.) is allowed to prevail in infinitum.

This allowance was absolutely necessary, else there would have frequently been many claimants in exactly the same degree of kindred, as (for instance) uncles and nephews of the deceased; which multiplicity though no inconvenience in the Roman law of partible inheritances, yet would have been productive of endless confusion where the right of sole succession, as with us, is established. The issue of descendants, therefore, of John Stiles' brothers are all of them in the first degree of kindred with respect to inheritances, as their father also, when living, was: those of his uncle in the second, and so on, and are severally called to the succession in right of such their representative proximity.

The right of representation being thus established, the former part of the present rule amounts to this; that on failure of issue of the person last seised, the inheritance shall descend to the issue of his next immediate ancestor. Thus, if John Stiles dies without issue, his estate shall descend to Francis, his brother, who is lineally descended from Geoffrey Stiles, his next immediate ancestor, or father. On failure of brethren, or sisters, and their issue, it shall descend to the uncle of John Stiles, the lineal descendant of his grandfather George, and so on infinitum.

⚖ LINEAL ANCESTORS ARE THE COMMON STOCKS — Now, here it must be observed, that the lineal ancestors, though (according to the first rule) incapable themselves of succeeding to the estate, because it is supposed to have already passed them, are yet the common stocks from which the next successor must spring. In the Jewish law, which in this respect entirely corresponds with ours, the father or other lineal ancestor is himself said to be the heir, though long since dead, as being represented by the persons of his issue; who are held to succeed not in their own rights, as brethren, uncles, etc., but in right of representation, as the offspring of the father, grandfather, etc., of the deceased.

But, though the common ancestor be thus the root of the inheritance, yet with us it is not necessary to name him in making out the pedigree or descent. For the descent between two brothers is held to be an immediate descent: and therefore title may be made by one brother or his representatives to or through another, without mentioning their common father. If Geoffrey Stiles hath two sons, John and Francis, Francis may claim as heir to John, without naming their Father Geoffrey; and so the son of Francis may claim as cousin and heir to Matthew, the son of John, without naming the grandfather; viz., as son of Francis, who was the brother of John, who was the father of Matthew. But though the common ancestors are not named in deducing the pedigree, yet the law still respects them as the fountains of inheritable blood: and therefore in order to ascertain the collateral heir of John Stiles, it is in the first place necessary to recur to his ancestors in the first degree; and if they have left any other issue besides John, that issue will be his heir.

On default of such, we must ascend one step higher to the ancestors in the second degree, and then to those in the third, and fourth, and so upwards in infinitum; till some ancestors be found, who have other issue descending from them besides the deceased, in a parallel or collateral line. From these ancestors the heir of John Stiles must derive his descent; and in such derivation the same rules must be observed, with regard to sex, primogeniture, and representation, that have before been laid down with regard to lineal descents from the person of the last proprietor.

⚖ EXCLUSION OF THE HALF BLOOD — But, secondly, the heir need not be nearest kinsman absolutely, but only in a particular way, that is, he must be the nearest kinsman of the whole blood; for, if there be a much nearer kinsman of the half blood, a distant kinsman of the whole blood shall be admitted, and the other entirely excluded.

A kinsman of the whole blood is he that is derived, not only from the same ancestor, but from the same couple of ancestors. For, as every man's own blood is compounded of the bloods of his respective ancestors, he only is properly of the whole or entire blood with another, who hath (so far as the distance of degrees will permit) all the same ingredients in the composition of his blood that the other hath. Thus, the blood of John Stiles being composed of those of Geoffrey Stiles, his father, and Lucy Baker, his mother, therefore his brother Francis, being descended from both the same parents, hath entirely the same blood with John Stiles; or he is his brother of the whole blood.

If, after the death of Geoffrey, Lucy Baker, the mother, marries a second husband, Lewis Gay, and hath issue by him; the blood of this issue, being compounded of the blood of Luch Baker on the one part, but that of Lewis Gay (instead of Geoffrey Stiles) on the other part, it hath therefore only half the same ingredients with that of John Stiles; so that he is only his brother of the half blood, and for that reason they shall never inherit to each other. So also, if the father has two sons, A and B, by different wives; now these two brethren are not brethren of the whole blood, and therefore shall never inherit to each other, but the estate shall rather escheat to the lord. Nay, even if the father dies, and his lands descend to this eldest son A, who enters thereon, and dies seised without issue; still B shall not be heir to this estate; because he is only of the half blood to A, the person last seised: but, had A died without entry, then B might have disinherited; not as heir to A, his half-brother, but as heir to their common father, who was the person last actually seised.

REASON FOR EXCLUDING HALF BLOOD — This total exclusion of the half blood from the inheritance, being almost peculiar to our own law, is looked upon as a strange hardship by such as are unacquainted with the reasons on which it is grounded. But these censures arise from a misapprehension of the rule, which is not so much to be considered in the light of a rule of descent, as of a rule of evidence; an auxiliary rule, to carry a former into execution. Here we must again remember, that the great and most universal principle of collateral inheritances being this, that an heir to a feudum antiquum must be of the blood of the first feudatory or purchases, that is, derived in a lineal descent from him; it was originally requisite, as upon gifts in tail it still is, to make out the pedigree of the heir from the first donee or purchases, and to show that such heir was his lineal representative.

But when, by length of time and a long course of descents, it came (in those rude and unlettered ages) to be forgotten who was really the first feudatory or purchaser, and thereby the proof of an actual descent from him became impossible: then the law substituted a reasonable, in the stead of an impossible, proof: for it remits the proof of an actual descent from the first purchaser; and only requires in lieu of it, that the claimant be next of the whole blood to the person last in possession (or derived from the same couple of ancestors); which will probably answer the same end as if he could trace his pedigree in a direct line from the first purchaser.

For he who is my kinsman of the whole blood can have no ancestors beyond or higher than the common stock, but what are equally my ancestors also; and mine are vice versa his: he therefore is very likely to be derived from that unknown ancestor of mine, from whom the inheritance descended. But a kinsman of the half blood has but one-half of his ancestors above the common stock the same as mine; and therefore there is not the same probability of that standing requisite in the law, that he be derived from the blood of the first purchaser.

To illustrate this by example. Let there be John Stiles, and Francis, brothers by the same father and mother, and another son of the same mother by Lewis Gay a second husband. Now, if John dies seised of lands, but it is uncertain whether they descended to him from his father or mother; in this case his brother Francis, of the whole blood, is qualified to be his heir; for he is sure to be in the line of descent from the first purchaser, whether it were the line of the father or the mother. But if Francis should die before John, without issue, the mother's son by Lewis Gay (or brother of the half blood) is utterly incapable of being heir; for he cannot prove his descent from the first purchaser, who is unknown, nor has he that fair probability which the law admits as presumptive evidence, since he is to the full as likely, not to be descended from the line of the first purchaser, as to be descended: and therefore the inheritance shall go to the nearest relation possessed of this presumptive proof, the whole blood.

As this is the case in ancient fees, where there really did once exist a purchasing ancestor, who is forgotten; it is also the case where the purchasing ancestor is merely ideal, and never existed but only in fiction of law. Of this nature are all grants of lands in fee simple at this day, which are inheritable as if they descended from some uncertain indefinite ancestor, and therefore any of the collateral kindred of the real modern purchaser (and not his own offspring only) may inherit them, provided they be of the whole blood; for all such are, in judgment of law, likely enough to be derived from this indefinite ancestor: but those of the half blood are excluded, for want of the same probability.

Nor should this be thought hard, that a brother of the purchaser, though only of the half blood, must be disinherited, and a more remote relation of the whole blood admitted, merely upon a supposition and fiction of law; since it is only upon a like supposition and fiction, that brethren of purchasers (whether of the whole or half blood) are entitled to inherit at all: for we have seen that in fees strictly new neither brethren nor any other collaterals were admitted.

Perhaps by this time the exclusion of the half blood does not appear altogether so unreasonable as at first sight it is apt to do. It is certainly a very fine-spun and subtle nicety: but, considering the principles upon which our law is founded, it is not an injustice, nor always a hardship; since even the succession of the whole blood was originally a beneficial indulgence, rather than the strict right of collaterals: and, though that indulgence is not extended to the demi-kindred, yet they are rarely abridged of any right which they could possibly have enjoyed before. The doctrine of the whole blood was calculated to supply the frequent impossibility of proving a descent from the first purchaser, without some proof of which (according to our fundamental maxim) there can be no inheritance allowed of. This purpose it answers, for the most part effectually enough.

I speak with these restrictions, because it does not, neither can any other method, answer this purpose entirely. For though all the ancestors of John Stiles, above the common stock, are also the ancestors of his collateral kinsman of the whole blood; yet, unless that common stock be in the first degree (that is, unless they have the same father and mother), there will be intermediate ancestors below the common stock, that may belong to either of them respectively, from which the other is not descended, and therefore can have none of their blood. Thus, though John Stiles and his brother of the whole blood can each have no other ancestors than what are in common to them both; yet with regard to his uncle, where the common stock is removed one degree higher (that is, the grandfather and grandmother), one-half of John's ancestors will not be the ancestors of his uncle: his father's brother, derives not his descent from John's maternal ancestors; nor his mother's brother, from those in the paternal line.

Here, then, the supply of proof is deficient, and by no means amounts to a certainty: and, the higher the common stock is removed, the more will even the probability decrease. But it must be observed, that (upon the same principles of calculation) the half blood have always a much less chance to be descended from an unknown indefinite ancestor of the deceased, than the whole blood in the same degree. As, in the first degree, the whole brother of John Stiles is sure to be descended from that unknown ancestor; his half-brother has only an even chance, for half John's ancestors are not his. So, in the second degree, John's uncle of the whole blood has an even chance; but the chances are three to one against his uncle of the half blood, for three-fourths of John's ancestors are not his.

In like manner, in the third degree, the chances are three to one against John's great-uncle of the whole blood, but they are seven to one against his great-uncle of the half blood, for seven-eighths of John's ancestors have no connection in blood with him. Therefore, the much less probability of the half blood's descent from the first purchaser, compared with that of the whole blood, in the several degrees, has occasioned a general exclusion of the half blood in all.

⚖ UNJUST EXTENSION OF RULE EXCLUDING HALF BLOOD — But, while I thus illustrate the reason of excluding the half blood in general I must be impartial enough to own, that, in some instances, the practice is carried further than the principle upon which it goes will warrant. Particularly, when a kinsman of the whole blood in a remoter degree, as the uncle or great-uncle, is preferred to one of the half blood in a nearer degree, as the brother: for the half-brother hath the same chance of being descended from the purchasing ancestor as the uncle; and a thrice better chance than the great-uncle, or kinsman in the third degree. It is also more especially overstrained, when a man has two sons by different venters, and the estate on his death descends from him to the eldest, who enters, and dies without issue; in which case the younger son cannot inherit this estate, because he is not of the whole blood to the last proprietor.

This, it must be owned, carried a hardship with it, even upon feudal principles: for the rule was introduced only to supply the proof of a descent from the first purchaser; but here, as this estate notoriously descended from the father, and as both the brothers confessedly sprung from him, it is demonstrable that the half-brother must be of the blood of the first purchaser, who was either the father or some of the father's ancestors. When therefore, there is actual demonstration of the thing to be proved, it is hard to exclude a man by a rule substituted to supply that proof when deficient. So far as the inheritance can be evidently traced back, there seems no need of calling in this presumptive proof, this rule of probability, to investigate what is already certain.

It is, moreover, worthy of observation, that by our law, as it now stands, the crown (which is the highest inheritance in the nation) may descend to the half blood of the preceding sovereign, so as it be the blood of the first monarch, purchaser (or in the feudal language), conqueror, of the reigning family. Thus it actually did descend from King Edward VI to Queen Mary, and from her to Queen Elizabeth, who were respectively of the half blood of each other. The royal pedigree being always a matter of sufficient notoriety, there is no occasion to call in the aid of this presumptive rule of evidence, to render probable the descent from the royal stock, which was formerly King William the Norman, and is now by act of parliament the Princess Sophia of Hanover. Hence also it is, that in estates-tail, where the pedigree from the first donee must be strictly proved, half blood is no impediment to the descent: because, when the lineage is clearly made out, there is no need of this auxiliary proof.

⚖ SUMMARY OF REASONS FOR RULE — The rule, then, together with its illustration, amounts to this: that, in order to keep the estate of John Stiles as nearly as possible in the line of his purchasing ancestor, it must descend to the issue of the nearest couple of ancestors that have left descendants behind them; because the descendants of one ancestor only are not so likely to be in the line of that purchasing ancestor, as those who are descended from two.

But here another difficulty arises. In the second, third, fourth, and every superior degree, every man has many couples of ancestors, increasing according to the distances in a geometrical progression upwards, the descendants of all which respective couples are representatively related to him in the same degree. Thus in the second degree, the issue of George and Cecilia Stiles and of Andrew and Esther Baker, the two grandsires and grandmothers of John Stiles, are each in the same degree of propinquity; in the third degree, the respective issues of Walter and Christian Stiles, of Luke and Frances Kempe, of Herbert and Hannah Baker, and of James and Emma Thorpe, are (upon the extinction of the two inferior degrees) all equally entitled to call themselves the next kindred of the whole blood to John Stiles. To which, therefore, of these ancestors must we first resort, in order to find out descendants to be preferably called to the inheritance? The answer is found in the last or Seventh Rule.

⚖ SEVENTH RULE — The seventh and last rule or canon is, that in collateral inheritances the male stock shall be preferred to the female, that is, kindred derived from the blood of the male ancestors shall be admitted before those from the blood of the female, unless where the lands have, in fact, descended from a female.

Thus, the relations on the father's side are admitted in infinitum, before those on the mother's side are admitted at all; and the relations of the father's father, before those of the father's mother; and so on.

REASONS FOR RULE PREFERRING MALE STOCKS — However, I am inclined to think, that this rule of our law does not owe its immediate original to any view of conformity to those which I have just now mentioned; but was established in order to effectuate and carry into execution the fifth rule or canon before laid down; that every heir must be of the blood of the first purchaser. For, when such first purchaser was not easily to be discovered after a long course of descents, the lawyers not only endeavored to investigate him by taking the next relation of the whole blood to the person last in possession; but also considering that a preference had been given to males (by virtue of the second canon) through the whole course of lineal descent from the first purchaser to the present time, they judged it more likely that the lands should have descended to the last tenant from his male than from his female ancestors; from the father (for instance) rather than from the mother; from the father's father, rather than the father's mother: and therefore they hunted back the inheritance (if I may be allowed the expression) through the male line; and gave it to the next relations on the side of the father, the father's father, and so upwards; imagining with reason that this was the most probable way of continuing it in the line of the first purchaser.

Whenever the lands have notoriously descended to a man from his mother's side, this rule is totally reversed, and no relation of his by the father's side, as such, can ever be admitted to them; because he cannot possibly be of the blood of the first purchaser. So, if the lands descended from the father's side, no relation of the mother, as such, shall ever inherit. So, also, if they in fact descended to John Stiles from his father's mother, Cecilia Kempe; here not only the blood of Lucy Baker, his mother, but also of George Stiles, his father's father, is perpetually excluded. In like manner, if they be known to have descended from Frances Holland, the mother of Cecilia Kempe, the line not only of Lucy Baker, and of George Stiles, but also of Luke Kempe, the father of Cecilia, is excluded. Whereas, when the side from which they descended is forgotten, or never known (as in the case of an estate newly purchased), here the right of inheritance first runs up all the father's side, with a preference to the male stocks in every instance; and, if it finds no heirs there, it then, and then only, resorts to the mother's side; leaving no place untried, in order to find heirs that may be possibly derived from the original purchaser. The greatest possibility of finding such was among those descended from the male ancestors; but, upon failure of issue there, they may possibly be found among those derived from the females.

⚖ TRACING A PEDIGREE — Before we conclude this branch of our inquiries, it may not be amiss to exemplify these rules by a short sketch of the manner in which we must search for the heir of a person, as John Stiles, who dies seised of land which he acquired, and which therefore he held as a feud of indefinite antiquity.

In the first place succeeds the eldest son, Matthew Stiles, or his issue: (1) — If his line be extinct, then Gilbert Stiles and the other sons, respectively, in order of birth, or their issue; (2) — In default of these, all the daughters together, Margaret and Charlotte Stiles, or their issue; (3) — on failure of the descendants of John Stiles himself, the issue of Geoffrey and Luch Stiles, his parents, is called in: Viz., first, Francis Stiles, the eldest brother of the whole blood, or his issue; (4) — then Oliver Stiles, and the other whole brothers, respectively, in order of birth or their issue; (5) — then the sisters of the whole blood all together, Bridget and Alice Stiles, or their issue; (6) — in defect of these, the issue of George and Cecilia Stiles, his father's parents; respect being still had to their age and sex; (7) — then the issue of Walter and Christian Stiles, the parents of his paternal grandfather; (8) — then the issue of Richard and Anne Stiles, the parents of his paternal grandfather's father; (9) — and so on in the paternal grandfather's paternal line, or blood of Walter Stiles, in infinitum.

In defect of these, the issue of William and Jane Smith, the parents of his paternal grandfather's mother: (10) — and so on in the paternal grandfather's maternal line, or blood of Christian Smith, in infinitum; till both the immediate bloods of George Stiles, the paternal grandfather are spent. Then we must resort to the issue of Luke and Frances Kempe, the parents of John Stiles' paternal grandmother: (11) — then to the issue of Thomas and Sarah Kempe, the parents of his paternal grandmother's father: (12) — and so on in the paternal grandmother's paternal line, or blood of Luke Kempe, in infinitum. In default of which we must call in the issue of Charles and Mary Holland, the parents of his paternal grandmother's mother: (13) — and so on in the paternal grandmother's maternal line, or blood of Frances Holland, in infinitum; till both the immediate bloods of Cecilia Kempe, the paternal grandmother, are also spent. Whereby the paternal blood of John Stiles entirely failing, recourse must then, and not before, be had to his maternal relations; or the blood of the Bakers (No. 14, 15, 16), Willis's (No. 17), Thorpes (No. 18, 19), and Whites (No. 20); in the same regular successive order as in the paternal line.

TITLE BY PURCHASE

⚖ DEFINITION OF PURCHASE — Purchase, taken in its largest and most
extensive sense, is the possession of lands and tenements, which a man
hath by his own act or agreement, and not by descent from any of his
ancestors or kindred. In this sense it is contradistinguished from acquisition by right of blood, and includes every other method of coming to
an estate, but merely that by inheritance: Wherein the title is vested in a
person, not be his own act or agreement, but by the single operation of
law.

⚖ LEGAL CONCEPTION OF PURCHASE — Purchase, indeed, in its vulgar
and confined acceptation, is applied only to such acquisitions of land,
as are obtained by way of bargain and sale, for money, or some other valuable consideration. But this falls far short of the legal idea of purchase:
for, if I give land freely to another, he is in the eye of the law a purchaser;
for he comes to the estate by his own agreement, that is, he consents to
the gift. A man who has his father's estate settled upon him in tail, before
he was born, is also a purchaser; for he takes quite another estate than the
law of descents would have given him. Nay, even if the ancestor devises
his estate to his heir at law by will, with other limitations or in any other
shape then the course of descents would direct, such heir shall take by
purchase.

But if a man, seised in fee, devises his whole estate to his heir at
law, so that the heir takes neither a greater nor a less estate by the devise
than he would have done without it, he shall be adjudged to take by descent, even though it be charged with encumbrances, for the benefit of
creditors, and others, who have demands on the estate of the ancestor.

If a remainder be limited to the heirs of Sempronius, here Sempronius himself takes nothing; but, if he dies during the continuance of the
particular estate, his heirs shall take as purchasers. But, if an estate be
made to A for life, remainder to his right heirs, in fee, his heirs shall take

by descent: for it is an ancient rule of law, that wherever the ancestor takes an estate for life, the heir cannot by the same conveyance take an estate in fee by purchase, but only by descent. And, if A dies before entry, still his heir shall take by descent, and not by purchase; for, where the heir takes anything that might have vested in the ancestor, he takes by way of descent. The ancestor, during his life, beareth in himself all his heirs; and therefore, when once he is or might have been seised of the lands, the inheritance so limited to his heirs vests in the ancestor himself: and the word "heirs" in this case is not esteemed a word of purchase, but a word of limitation, inuring so as to increase the estate of the ancestor from a tenancy for life to a fee simple. And, had it been otherwise, had the heir (who is uncertain till the death of the ancestor) been allowed to take as a purchaser originally nominated in the deed, as must have been the case if the remainder had been expressly limited to Matthew or Thomas by name; then, in the times of strict feudal tenure, the lord would have been defrauded by such a limitation of the fruits of his seigniory, arising from a descent to the heir.

⚖ "CONQUEST" OF THE FEUDISTS — What we call purchase, the feudists call conquest: both denoting any means of acquiring an estate out of the common course of inheritance. And this is still the proper phrase in the law of Scotland: as it was among the Norman Jurists, who styled the purchaser (that is, he who brought the estate into the family which at present owns it) the conqueror.

⚖ DIFFERENCES BETWEEN DESCENT AND PURCHASE — The difference, in effect, between the acquisition of an estate by descent and by purchase, consists principally in these two points: 1. That by purchase the estate acquires a new inheritable quality, and is descendible to the owner's blood in general, and not the blood only of some particular ancestor. For, when a man takes an estate by purchase, he takes it not as a fee paternal or maternal, which would descend only to the heirs by the father's or the mother's side: but he take it as an ancient fee, as a feud of indefinite antiquity; whereby it becomes inheritable to his heirs general, first of the paternal, and then of the maternal line.

2. An estate taken by purchase will not make the heir answerable for the acts of the ancestor, as an estate by descent will. For, if the ancestor by any deed, obligation, covenant, or the like, bindeth himself and his heirs, and he dieth; this deed, obligation, or covenant, shall be binding upon the heirs so far forth only as he had any estate of inheritance vested in him (or in some other in trust for him) by descent from that

ancestor, sufficient to answer the charge; whether he remains in possession, or hath aliened it before action brought; which sufficient estate is in the law called assets; from the French word "assez," enough. Therefore, if a man covenants, for himself and his heirs to keep my house in repair, I can then (and only then) compel his heir to perform this covenant, when he has an estate sufficient for this purpose, or assets, by descent from the covenantor: for though the covenant descends to the heir, whether he inherits any estate or no, it lies dormant, and is not compulsory, until he has assets by descent.

⚖️ FIVE MODES OF ACQUIRING TITLE BY PURCHASE — This is the legal signification of the word purchase; and in this sense it includes the five following methods of acquiring a title to estates: 1. Escheat. 2. Occupancy. 3. Prescription. 4. Forfeiture. 5. Alienation.

⚖️ ESCHEAT — Escheat, we may remember, was one of the fruits and consequences of feudal tenure. The word itself is originally French or Norman, in which language it signifies chance or accident; and with us it denotes an obstruction of the course of descent, and a consequent determination of the tenure, by some unforeseen contingency: in which case the land naturally results back, by a kind of reversion, to the original grantor or lord of the fee.

⚖️ REQUISITES OF ESCHEAT — Escheat, therefore, being a title frequently vested in the lord by inheritance, as being the fruit of a seigniory to which he was entitled by descent (for which reason the lands escheated shall attend the seigniory, and be inheritable by such only of his heirs as are capable of inheriting the other), it may seem in such cases to fall more properly under the former general head of acquiring title to estates, viz., by descent (being vested in him by act of law, and not by his own act or agreement), than under the present, by purchase.

But it must be remembered that, in order to complete this title by escheat, it is necessary that the lord perform an act of his own, by entering on the lands and tenements so escheated, or suing out a writ of escheat: on failure of which, or by doing any act that amounts to an implied waiver of his right, as by accepting homage or rent of a stranger who usurps the possession, his title by escheat is barred. It is therefore in some respects a title acquired by his own act, as well as by act of law.

⚖️ PRINCIPLE OF ESCHEAT — The law of escheats is founded upon this single principle, that the blood of the person last seised in fee simple is, by some means or other, utterly extinct and gone: and, since none can inherit his estate but such as are of his blood and consanguinity, it follows as a regular consequence that when such blood is extinct, the inheritance itself must fail; the land must become what the feudal writers denominate an open fee; and must result back again to the lord of the fee, by whom, or by those whose estate he hath, it was given.

⚖️ FAILURE OF HEREDITARY BLOOD — Escheats are frequently divided into those "through failure of issue" and those "through the fault of the tenant": the one sort, if the tenant dies without heirs; the other, if his blood be attainted. But both these species may well be comprehended under the first denomination only; for he that is attainted suffers an extinction of his blood, as well as he that dies without relations. The inheritable quality is expunged in one instance, and expires in the other; or, as the doctrine of escheats is very fully expressed: the chief lord of the fee is accounted heir whenever the blood of the tenant is extinct either by failure of issue or corruption.

⚖️ CASES OF FAILURE OF HEREDITARY BLOOD — Escheats, therefore, arising merely upon the deficiency of the blood, whereby the descent is impeded, their doctrine will be better illustrated by considering the several cases wherein hereditary blood may be deficient, than by any other method whatsoever.

⚖️ TENANT DYING; (1) WITHOUT ANY RELATIONS AT ALL; (2) WITHOUT RELATIONS REPRESENTING ANCESTOR FROM WHOM ESTATE DESCENDED; (3) WITHOUT RELATIONS OF WHOLE BLOOD — The first three cases, wherein inheritable blood is wanting, may be collected from the rules of descent laid down and explained in the preceding chapter, and therefore will need very little illustration or comment. First, when the tenant dies without any relations on the part of any of his ancestors: secondly, when he dies without any relations on the part of those ancestors from whom his estate descended: thirdly when he dies without any relations of the whole blood.

In two of these cases the blood of the first purchaser is certainly, in the other it is probably, at an end; and therefore in all of them the law directs that the land shall escheat to the lord of the fee: for the lord would be manifestly prejudiced, if, contrary to the inherent condition tacitly annexed to all feuds, any person should be suffered to succeed to the lands, who is not of the blood of the first feudatory, to whom for his personal merit the estate is supposed to have been granted.

⚖️ MONSTERS — A monster, which hath not the shape of mankind, but in any part evidently bears the resemblance of the brute creation, hath no inheritable blood, and cannot be heir to any land, albeit it be brought forth in marriage: but, although it hath deformity in any part of its body, yet if it hath human shape, it may be heir. This is a very ancient rule in the land of England; and its reason is too obvious, and too shocking, to bear a minute discussion. But our law will not admit a birth of this kind to be such an issue as shall entitle the husband to be tenant by the courtesy; because it is not capable of inheriting. Therefore, if there appears no other heir than such a prodigious birth, the land shall escheat to the lord.

⚖ BASTARDS — Bastards are incapable of being heirs. Bastards, by our law, are such children as are not born either in lawful wedlock, or within a competent time after its determination. Such are held to be the sons of nobody: for the maxim of law is "those who are the offspring of an illicit connection are not reckoned as children." Being thus the sons of nobody, they have no blood in them, at least no inheritable blood; consequently, none of the blood of the first purchaser; and therefore, if there be no other claimant than such illegitimate children, the land shall escheat to the lord.

The civil law differs from ours in this point, and allows a bastard to succeed to an inheritance, if after its birth the mother was married to the father; and also, if the father had no lawful wife or child, then, even if the concubine was never married to the father, yet she and her bastard son were admitted each to one-twelfth of the inheritance: and a bastard was likewise capable of succeeding to the whole of his mother's estate, although she was never married; the mother being sufficiently certain, though the father is not. But our law, in favor of marriage, is much less indulgent to bastards.

⚖ ALIENS — Aliens also are incapable of taking by descent, or inheriting: for they are not allowed to have any inheritable blood in them; rather, indeed, upon a principle of national or civil policy, than upon reasons strictly feudal. Though, if lands had been suffered to fall into their hands who owe no allegiance to the crown of England, the design of introducing our feuds, the defense of the kingdom, would have been defeated. Wherefore if a man leaves no other relations but aliens, his land shall escheat to the lord.

As aliens cannot inherit, so far they are on a level with bastards; but as they are also disabled to hold by purchase, they are under still greater disabilities. As they can neither hold by purchase nor by inheritance, it is almost superfluous to say that they can have no heirs, since they can have nothing for an heir to inherit; but so it is expressly holden, because they have not in them any inheritable blood.

☙ DENIZENS — Further, if an alien be made a denizen by the king's letters patent, and then purchases lands (which the law allows such a one to do), his son, born before his denization, shall not (by the common law) inherit those lands; but a son born afterwards may, even though his elder brother be living; for the father, before denization, had no inheritable blood to communicate to his eldest son; but by denization it acquires an hereditary quality, which will be transmitted to his subsequent posterity. Yet, if he had been naturalized by act of parliament, such eldest son might then have inherited; for that cancels all defects, and is allowed to have a retrospective energy, which simple denization has not.

☙ DIRECT DESCENT BETWEEN BROTHERS — It is now held for law, that the sons of an alien, born here, may inherit to each other. And reasonably enough upon the whole; for, as (in common purchases) the whole of the supposed descent from indefinite ancestors is but fictitious, the law may as well suppose the requisite ancestor as suppose the requisite descent.

☙ DESCENT THROUGH AN ALIEN — It is also enacted, by statute (Aliens, 1700), that all persons, being natural-born subjects of the king, may inherit and make their titles by descent from any of their ancestors, lineal or collateral; although their father, or mother, or other ancestor, by, from, through, or under whom they derive their pedigrees, were born out of the king's allegiance.

But inconveniences were afterwards apprehended, in case persons should thereby gain a future capacity to inherit, who did not exist at the death of the person last seised. As, if Francis, the elder brother of John Stiles, be an alien, and Oliver, the younger, be a natural-born subject, upon John's death without issue his lands will descend to Oliver, the younger brother: now, if afterwards Francis has a child born in England, it was feared that, under the statute of King William, this new-born child might defeat the estate of his uncle, Oliver. Wherefore it is provided, by the statute (Title by Descent, 1751), that no right of inheritance shall accrue by virtue of the former statute to any persons whatsoever, unless they are in being and capable to take as heirs at the death of the person last seised:—with an exception, however, to the case, where lands shall descend to the daughter of an alien; which descent shall be divested in favor of an after-born brother, or the inheritance shall be divided with an after-born sister or sisters, according to the usual rule of descents by the common law.

⚜ ATTAINDER — By attainder, also, for treason or other felony, the blood of the person attainted is so corrupted as to be rendered no longer inheritable.

Great care must be taken to distinguish between forfeiture of lands to the king, and this species of escheat to the lord; which, by reason of their similitude in some circumstances, and because the crown is very frequently the immediate lord of the fee, and therefore entitled to both, have been often confounded together. Forfeiture of lands, and of whatever else the offender possessed, was the doctrine of the old Saxon law, as a part of punishment for the offense; and does not at all relate to the feudal system, nor is the consequence of any seigniory or lordship paramount: but, being a prerogative vested in the crown, was neither superseded nor diminished by the introduction of the Norman tenures; a fruit and consequence of which, escheat must undoubtedly be reckoned. Escheat therefore operates in subordination to this more ancient and superior law of forfeiture.

⚜ DOCTRINE OF ESCHEAT UPON ATTAINDER — The doctrine of escheat upon attainder, taken singly, is this: that the blood of the tenant, by the commission of any felony (under which denomination all treasons were formerly comprised), is corrupted and stained, and the original donation of the feud is thereby determined, it being always granted to the vassal on the implied condition whilst he shall have conducted himself well. Upon the thorough demonstration of which guilt, by legal attainder, the feudal covenant and mutual bond of fealty are held to be broken, the estate instantly falls back from the offender to the lord of the fee, and the inheritable quality of his blood is extinguished and blotted out forever.

In this situation the law of feudal escheat was brought into England at the Conquest; and in general superadded to the ancient law of forfeiture. In consequence of which corruption and extinction of hereditary blood, the land of all felons would immediately revert in the lord, but that the superior law of forfeiture intervenes, and intercepts it in its passage; in case of treason, forever; in case of other felony, for only a year and a day, after which time it goes to the lord in a regular course of escheat, as it would have done to the heir of the felon in case the feudal tenures had never been introduced.

As a consequence of this doctrine of escheat, all lands of inheritance immediately revesting in the lord, the wife of the felon was liable to lose her dower, till the statue (Dower, 1547) enacted, that albeit any person be attainted of misprison of treason, murder, or felony, yet his wife shall enjoy her dower. But she has not this indulgence where the ancient law of forfeiture operates, for it is expressly provided by the statute (Treason, 1551), that the wife of one attaint of high treason shall not be endowed at all.

If, therefore, a father be seised in fee, and the son commits treason and is attainted, and then the father dies: here the land shall escheat to the lord; because the son, by the corruption of his blood, is incapable to be heir, and there can be no other heir during his life: but nothing shall be forfeited to the king, for the son never had any interest in the lands to forfeit. In this case the escheat operates, and not the forfeiture; but in the following instance the forfeiture works, and not the escheat. As where a new felony is created by act of parliament, and it is provided as is frequently the case, that it shall not extend to corruption of blood: here the lands of the felon shall not escheat to the lord, but yet the profits of them shall be forfeited to the king so long as the offender lives.

There is yet a further consequence of the corruption and extinction of hereditary blood, which is this: that the person attainted shall not only be incapable himself of inheriting, or transmitting his own property by heirship, but shall also obstruct the descent of lands or tenements to his posterity, in all cases where they are obliged to derive their title through him from any remoter ancestor. The channel, which conveyed the hereditary blood from his ancestors to him, is not only exhausted for the present, but totally dammed up and rendered impervious for the future.

This is a refinement upon the ancient law of feuds, which allowed that the grandson might be heir to his grandfather, though the son in the intermediate generation was guilty of felony. But, by the law of England, a man's blood is so universally corrupted by attainder, that his sons can neither inherit to him nor to any other ancestor, at least on the part of their attainted father.

This corruption of blood cannot be absolutely removed but by authority of parliament. The king may excuse the public punishment of an offender; but cannot abolish the private right, which has accrued or may accrue to individuals as a consequence of the criminal's attainder. He may remit a forfeiture, in which the interest of the crown is alone concerned: but he cannot wipe away the corruption of blood; for therein a third person hath an interest, the lord who claims by escheat. If, therefore, a man hath a son, and is attainted, and afterwards pardoned by the king; this son can never inherit to his father, or father's ancestors; because his paternal blood being once thoroughly corrupted by his father's attainder, must continue so: but if the son had been born after the pardon, he might inherit; because by the pardon the father is made a new man, and may convey new inheritable blood to his after-born children.

Herein there is, however, a difference between aliens and persons attainted. Of aliens, who could never by any possibility be heirs, the law takes no notice: and therefore we have seen that an alien elder brother shall not impede the descent to a natural-born younger brother. But in attainders it is otherwise: for if a man hath issue a son, and is attainted, and afterwards pardoned, and then hath issue a second son, and dies; here the corruption of blood is not removed from the eldest, and therefore he cannot be heir: neither can the youngest be heir, for he hath an elder brother living, of whom the law takes notice, as he once had a possibility of being heir; and therefore the younger brother shall not inherit, but the land shall escheat to the lord: though had the elder died without issue in the life of the father, the younger son born after the pardon might well have inherited, for he hath no corruption of blood.

So if a man hath issue two sons, and the elder in the lifetime of the father hath issue, and then is attainted and executed, and afterwards the father dies, the lands of the father shall not descend to the younger son: for the issue of the elder, which had once a possibility to inherit, shall impede the descent to the younger, and the land shall escheat to the lord.

Upon the whole it appears that a person attainted is neither allowed to retain his former estate, nor to inherit any future one, nor to transmit any inheritance to his issue, either immediately from himself, or mediately through himself from any remoter ancestor; for his inheritable blood, which is necessary either to hold, to take, or to transmit any feudal property, is blotted out, corrupted, and extinguished forever: the consequence of which is, that estates, thus impeded in their descent, result back and escheat to the lord.

This corruption of blood, thus arising from feudal principles, but perhaps extended further than even those principles, will warrant, has been long looked upon as a peculiar hardship: because the oppressive parts of the feudal tenures being now in general abolished, it seems unreasonable to reserve one of their most inequitable consequences; namely, that the children should not only be reduced to present poverty (which, however severe, is sufficiently justified upon reasons of public policy), but also be laid under future difficulties of inheritance, on account of the guilt of their ancestors. Therefore in most (if not all) of the new felonies created by parliament since the reign of Henry the Eighth, it is declared that they shall not extend to any corruption of blood: and by statute it is enacted, that no attainder for treason shall extend to the disinheriting any heir, nor the prejudice of any person, other than the offender himself: which provisions have indeed carried the remedy farther than was required by the hardship above complained of; which is only the future obstruction of descents, where the pedigree happens to be deduced through the blood of an attainted ancestor.

❧❧ EXCEPTION TO RULE OF ESCHEAT: CORPORATIONS — Before I conclude this head of escheat, I must mention one singular instance in which lands held in fee simple are not liable to escheat to the lord, even when their owner is no more, and hath left no heirs to inherit them. This is the case of a corporation; for if that comes by any accident to be dissolved, the donor or his heirs shall have the land again in reversion, and not the lord by escheat; which is perhaps the only instance where a reversion can be expectant on a grant in fee-simple absolute.

But the law, we are told, doth tacitly annex a condition to every such gift or grant, that if the corporation be dissolved, the donor or grantor shall re-enter; for the cause of the gift or grant faileth. This is indeed founded upon the self-same principle as the law of escheat: the heirs of the donor being only substituted instead of the chief lord of the fee: which was formerly very frequently the case in subinfeudations, or alienations of lands by a vassal to be holden as of himself; till that practice was restrained by statute (1290), to which this very singular instance still in some degree remains an exception.

TITLE BY OCCUPANCY

✼✼ OCCUPANCY — Occupancy is the taking possession of those things which before belonged to nobody. This, as we have seen, is the true ground and foundation of all property, or of holding those things in severalty, which by the law of nature, unqualified by that of society, were common to all mankind. But, when once it was agreed that everything capable of ownership should have an owner, natural reason suggested, that he who could first declare his intention of appropriating anything to his own use, and, in consequence of such intention, actually took it into possession, should thereby gain the absolute property of it; according to that rule of the law of nations; "that which belongs to no one, is by natural reason granted the the occupant thereof."

✼✼ OCCUPANCY OF ESTATE PER AUTER VIE — This right of occupancy, so far as it concerns real property (for of personal chattel I am not in this place to speak), hath been confined by the laws of England within a very narrow compass; and was extended only to a single instance: namely, where a man was tenant per auter vie, or had an estate granted to himself only (without mentioning his heirs) for the life of another man, and died during the life of cestuy que vie, or him by whose life it was holden: in this case he, that could first enter on the land, might lawfully retain the possession so long as cestuy que vie lived, by right of occupancy.

✼✼ COMMON AND SPECIAL OCCUPANT — This seems to have been recurring to first principles, and calling in the law of nature to ascertain the property of the land, when left without a legal owner. For it did not revert to the grantor, though formerly held so to do; for he had parted with all his interest, so long as cestuy que vie lived: it did not escheat to the lord of the fee; for all escheats must be of the absolute entire fee, and not of any particular estate carved out of it; much less of so minute a remnant as this; it did not belong to the grantee; for he was dead:

it did not descend to his heirs; for there were no words of inheritance in the grant: nor could it vest in his executors; for no executors could succeed to a freehold.

Belonging, therefore, to nobody, the law left it open to be seized and appropriated by the first person that could enter upon it, during the life of cestuy que vie, under the name of an occupant. But there was no right of occupancy allowed, where the king had the reversion of the lands; for the reversioner hath an equal right with any other man to enter upon the vacant possession, and where the king's title and a subject's concur, the king's shall be always preferred: against the king, therefore, there could be no prior occupant, because time runs not against the king.

Even in the case of a subject, had the estate pur auter vie, being granted to a man and his heirs during the life of cestuy que vie, there the heir might, and still may, enter and hold possession, and is called in law a special occupant; as having a special exclusive right, by the terms of the original grant, to enter upon and occupy during the residue of the estate granted: though some have thought him so called with no very great propriety; and that such estate is rather a descendible freehold.

COMMON OCCUPANCY ABOLISHED: SPECIAL OCCUPANCY DEVISABLE —

But the title of common occupancy is now reduced almost to nothing by two statutes: the one (Statute of Frauds, 1677), which enacts (according to the ancient rule of law) that where there is no special occupant, in whom the estate may vest, the tenant pur auter vie may devise it by will, or it shall go to the executors or administrators and be assets in their hands for payment of debts: the other (Common Recoveries, 1740), which enacts that the surplus of such estate pur auter vie, after payment of debts, shall go in a course of distribution like a chattel interest.

By these two statutes the title of common occupancy is utterly extinct and abolished: though that of special occupancy by the heir at law continues to this day; such heir being held to succeed to the ancestor's estate, not by descent, for then he must take an estate of inheritance, but as an occupant, specially marked out and appointed by the original grant. But, as before the statutes there could no common occupancy be had of incorporeal hereditaments, as of rents, tithes, advowsons, commons, or the like (because, with respect to them, there could be no actual entry made, or corporal seisin had; and therefore by the death of the grantee per auter vie a grant of such hereditaments was entirely determined), so now, I apprehend, notwithstanding these statutes, such grant would be determined likewise; and the hereditaments would not be devisable, nor vest in the executors, nor go in a course of distribution.

For these statutes must not be construed so as to create any new estate, or keep that alive which by the common law was determined, and thereby to defer the grantor's reversion; but merely to dispose of an interest in being, to which by law there was no owner, and which, therefore, was left open to the first occupant. When there is a residue left, the statutes give it to the executors and administrators, instead of the first occupant; but they will not create a residue on purpose to give it to either. They only meant to provide an appointed instead of a casual, a certain instead of an uncertain, owner, of lands which before were nobody's; and thereby to supply this omitted case, and render the disposition of law in all respects entirely uniform: this being the only instance wherein a title to a real estate could ever be acquired by occupancy.

This, I say, was the only instance; for I think there can be no other case devised wherein there is not some owner of the land appointed by the law. In the case of a sole corporation, as a parson of a church, when he dies or resigns, though there is no actual owner of the land till a successor be appointed, yet there is a legal, potential ownership, subsisting in contemplation of law; and when the successor is appointed, his appointment shall have a retrospect and relation backwards, so as to entitle him to all the profits from the instant that the vacancy commenced. In all other instances, when the tenant dies intestate, and no other owner of the lands is to be found in the common course of descents, there the law vests an ownership in the king, or in the subordinate lord of the fee by escheat.

ISLANDS: ALLUVION: DERELICTION — So, also, in some cases, where the laws of other nations give a right by occupancy, as in lands newly created, by the rising of an island in a river, or by the alluvion or dereliction of the sea; in these instances the law of England assigns them an immediate owner.

If an island arise in the middle of a river, it belongs in common to those who have lands on each side thereof; but if it be nearer to one bank than the other, it belongs only to him who is proprietor of the nearest shore: which is agreeable to, and probably copied from, the civil law.

Yet this seems only to be reasonable, where the soil of the river is equally divided between the owners of the opposite shores: for if the whole soil is the freehold of any one man, as it must be whenever a several fishery is claimed, there it seems just that little islands, arising in any part of the river, shall be the property of him who owneth the piscary and the soil. However, in case a new island rise in the sea, though the civil law gives it to the first occupant, yet ours gives it to the king.

As to lands gained from the sea, either by alluvion, by the washing up of sand and earth, so as in time to make terra firma; or by dereliction, as when the sea shrinks back below the usual water-mark; in these cases the law is held to be, that if this gain be by little and little, by small imperceptible degrees, it shall go to the owner of the land adjoining. For the law takes not cognizance of small things: and, besides, these owners being often losers by the breaking in of the sea, or at charges to keep it out, this possible gain is therefore a reciprocal consideration for such possible charge or loss.

But, if the alluvion or dereliction be sudden and considerable, in this case it belongs to the king; for, as the king is lord of the sea, and so owner of the soil while it is covered with water, it is but reasonable he should have the soil when the water has left it dry. So that the quantity of ground gained, and the time during which it is gaining, are what make it either the king's or the subject's property.

In the same manner if a river, running between two lordships by degrees gains upon the one, and thereby leaves the other dry; the owner who loses his ground thus imperceptibly has no remedy: but if the course of the river be changed by a sudden and violent flood, or other hasty means, and thereby a man loses his ground, he shall have what the river has left in any other place, as a recompense for this sudden loss.

This law of alluvions and derelictions, with regard to rivers, is nearly the same in the imperial law; from whence indeed these our determinations seem to have been drawn and adopted: but we ourselves, as islanders, have applied them to marine increases; and have given our sovereign the prerogative he enjoys, as well upon the particular reasons before mentioned, as upon this other ground of prerogative, which was formerly remarked, that whatever hath no other owner is vested by law in the king.

TITLE BY PRESCRIPTION

✢✢   PRESCRIPTION — A third method of acquiring real property by purchase is that by prescription; as when a man can show no other title to what he claims than that he, and those under whom he claims, have immemorially used it to enjoy it. Concerning customs, or immemorial usages, in general, with the several requisites and rules to be observed, in order to prove their existence and validity, we inquired at large in the preceding part of these Commentaries. At present, therefore, I shall only, first, distinguish between custom, strictly taken, and prescription; and then show, what sort of things may be prescribed for.

✢✢   DISTINCTION BETWEEN CUSTOM AND PRESCRIPTION — First, the distinction between custom and prescription is this; that custom is properly a local usage, and not annexed to any person: such as a custom in the manor of Dale that lands shall descend to the youngest son: prescription is merely a personal usage; as, that Sempronius, and his ancestors, or those whose estate he hath, have used time out of mind to have such an advantage or privilege. As for example: if there be a usage in the parish of Dale, that all the inhabitants of that parish may dance on a certain close, at all times, for their recreation; this is strictly a custom for it is applied to the place in general, and not to any particular persons: but if the tenant, who is seised of the manor of Dale in fee, alleges that he and his ancestors, or all those whose estate he hath in the same manor, have used time out of mind to have common of pasture in such a close, this is properly called a prescription; for this is a usage annexed to the person of the owner of this estate.

All prescription must be either in a man and his ancestors, or in a man and those whose estate he hath; which last is called prescribing in a que estate. Formerly a man might, by the common law, have prescribed for a right which had been enjoyed by his ancestors or predecessors at any distance of time, though his or their enjoyment of it has been suspended for an indefinite series of years. But by the statute of limitations (Prescription, 1540), it is enacted, that no person shall make any prescription by the seisin or possession of his ancestor or predecessor, unless such seisin or possession hath been within three-score years next before such prescription made.

⚖ RULES GOVERNING PRESCRIPTION — INCORPOREAL HEREDITAMENTS — Secondly, as to the several species of things which may, or may not, be prescribed for: we may in the first place observe that nothing but incorporeal hereditaments can be claimed by prescription; as a right of way, a common, etc., but that no prescription can give a title to lands, and other corporeal substances, of which more certain evidence may be had. For no man can be said to prescribe that he and his ancestors have immemorially used to hold the castle of Arundel: for this is clearly another sort of title; a title of corporal seisin and inheritance, which is more permanent, and therefore more capable of proof, than that of prescription. But, as to a right of way, a common, or the like, a man may be allowed to prescribe; for of these there is no corporal seisin, the enjoyment will be frequently by intervals, and therefore the right to enjoy them can depend on nothing else but immemorial usage.

⚖ IN TENANT OF THE FEE — A prescription must always be laid in him that is tenant of the fee. A tenant for life for years, at will, or a copyholder, cannot prescribe, by reason of the imbecility of their estates, for, as prescription is usage beyond time of memory, it is absurd that they should pretend to prescribe, whose estates commenced within the remembrance of man. And therefore the copyholder must prescribe under cover of the tenant in fee simple.

As, if tenant for life of a manor would prescribe for a right of common as appurtenant to the same, he must prescribe under cover of the tenant in fee simple; and must plead that John Stiles and his ancestors had immemorially used to have this right of common, appurtenant to the said manor, and that John Stiles demised the said manor, with its appurtenances, to him, the said tenant, for life. .

⚖ PRESCRIPTION PRESUPPOSES A GRANT — A prescription cannot be for a thing which cannot be raised by grant. For the law allows prescription only in supply of the loss of a grant, and therefore every prescription presupposes a grant to have existed. Thus the lord of a manor cannot prescribe to raise a tax or toll upon strangers; for, as such claim could never have been good by any grant, it shall not be good by prescription.

⚖️ NO PRESCRIPTION IN MATTER OF RECORD — A fourth rule is, that what is to arise by matter of record cannot be prescribed for, but must be claimed by grant, entered on record; such as, for instance, the royal franchises of deodands, felons' goods, and the like. These, not being forfeited till the matter on which they arise is found by the inquisition of a jury, and so made a matter of record, the forfeiture itself cannot be claimed by any inferior title. But the franchises of treasure-trove, waifs, estrays, and the like may be claimed by prescription; for they arise from private contingencies, and not from any matter of record.

⚖️ PRESCRIPTION IN A QUE ESTATE — Among things incorporeal, which may be claimed by prescription, a distinction must be made with regard to the manner of prescribing; that is, whether a man shall prescribe in a que estate, or in himself and his ancestors. For, if a man prescribes in a que estate (that is, in himself and those whose estate he holds), nothing is claimable by this prescription, but such things as are incident, appendant, or appurtenant to lands; for it would be absurd to claim anything as the consequence, or appendix, of an estate, with which the thing claimed has no connection: but, if he prescribes in himself and his ancestors, he may prescribe for anything whatsoever that lies in grant; not only things that are appurtenant, but also as may be in gross.

Therefore a man may prescribe that he, and those whose estate he hath in the manor; but if he would prescribe for a common ingross, he must prescribe in himself and his ancestors.

⚖️ DESCENT OF ESTATES PRESCRIBED — Lastly, we may observe that estates gained by prescription are not, of course, descendible to the heirs general, like other purchased estates, but are an exception to the rule. For, properly speaking, the prescription is rather to be considered as an evidence of a former acquisition, than as an acquisition de novo: and therefore, if a man prescribes for a right of way in himself and his ancestors, it will descend only to the blood of that line of ancestors, in whom he so prescribes; the prescription in this case being indeed a species of descent. But if he prescribes for it in a que estate, it will follow the nature of that estate in which the prescription is laid, and be inheritable in the same manner, whether that were acquired by descent or purchase: for every accessory followeth the nature of its principal.

TITLE BY FORFEITURE

⚙ FORFEITURE — Forfeiture is a punishment annexed by law to some illegal act, or negligence, in the owner of lands, tenements, or hereditaments; whereby he loses all his interests therein, and they go to the party injured, as a recompense for the wrong which either he alone, or the public together with himself hath sustained.

⚙ CAUSES OF FORFEITURE — Land, tenements, and hereditaments may be forfeited in various degrees and by various means: 1. By crimes and misdemeanors.   2. By alienation contrary to law.   3. By nonpresentation of a benefice, when the forfeiture is denominated a lapse.   4. By simony.   5. By nonperformance of condition. 6. By waste.   7. By breach of copyhold customs.   8. By bankruptcy.

⚙ FORFEITURES FOR CRIMES AND MISDEMEANORS — The foundation and justice of forfeitures for crimes and misdemeanors, and the several degrees of those forfeitures, proportioned to the several offenses, have been hinted at in the preceding volume; but will be more properly considered, and more at large, in the fourth book of these Commentaries. At present I shall only observe in general that the offenses which induce a forfeiture of lands and tenements to the crown are principally the following six: 1. Treason.   2. Felony.   3. Misprision of treason.   4. Praemunire.   5. Drawing a weapon on a judge, or striking anyone in the presence of the king's principal courts of justice.   6. Popish recusancy, or nonobservance of certain laws enacted in restraint of papists. But at what time they severally commence, how far they extend, and how long they endure, will with greater propriety be reserved as the object of our future inquiries.

⚙ FORFEITURE FOR ALIENATION CONTRARY TO LAW — Lands and tenements may be forfeited by alienation, or conveying them to another, contrary to law. This is either alienation in mortmain, alienation to an alien, or alienation by particular tenants; in the two former of which cases the forfeiture arises from the incapacity of the alienee to take; in the latter from the incapacity of the alienor to grant.

⚖　ALIENATION IN MORTMAIN — Alienation in mortmain, (in dead-hand), is an alienation of lands or tenements to any corporation, sole or aggregate, ecclesiastical or temporal. But these purchases having been chiefly made by religious houses, in consequence whereof the lands became perpetually inherent in one dead-hand, this hath occasioned the general appellation of mortmain to be applied to such alienations, and the religious houses themselves to be principally considered in forming the statutes of mortmain: in deducing the history of which statutes it will be matter of curiosity to observe the great address and subtle contrivance of the ecclesiastics in eluding from time to time the laws in being, and the zeal with which successive parliaments have pursued them through all their finesses: how new remedies were still the parents of new evasions; till the legislature at last, though with difficulty, hath obtained a decisive victory.

⚖　LICENSES IN MORTMAIN — By the common law any man might dispose of his lands to any other private man at his own discretion, especially when the feudal restraints of alienation were torn away. Yet in consequence of these it was always, and is still, necessary for corporations to have a license in mortmain from the crown, to enable them to purchase lands: for as the king is the ultimate lord of every fee, he ought not, unless by his own consent, to lose his privilege of escheats and other feudal profits, by the vesting of lands in tenants that can never be attainted or die.

But, besides this general license from the king, as lord paramount of the kingdom, it was also requisite, whenever there was a mesne or intermediate lord between the king and the alienor, to obtain his license also (upon the same feudal principles) for the alienation of the specific land. If no such license was obtained, the king or other lord might respectively enter on the lands so aliened in mortmain as a forfeiture. The necessity of this license from the crown was acknowledged by the constitutions of Clarendon, in respect of advowsons, which the monks always greatly coveted, as being the groundwork of subsequent appropriations.

⚖　EVASIONS OF RULE BY CLERGY — Yet such were the influence and ingenuity of the clergy, that (notwithstanding this fundamental principle) we find that the largest and most considerable dotations of religious houses happened within less than two centuries after the Conquest. And (when a license could not be obtained) their contrivance seems to have been this that, as the forfeiture for such alienations accrued in the first place to the immediate lord of the fee, the tenant who meant to alienate first conveyed his lands to the religious house, and instantly took them back again, to hold as tenant to the monastery; which kind of instantaneous seisin was probably held not to occasion any forfeiture: and then, by pretext of some other forfeiture, surrender, or escheat, the society entered into those lands in right of such their newly acquired seigniory, as immediate lords of the fee.

⚖ PROHIBITION IN MAGNA CARTA — But, when these dotations began to grow numerous, it was observed that the feudal services, ordained for the defense of the kingdom, were every day visibly withdrawn; that the circulation of landed property from man to man began to stagnate; and that the lords were curtailed of the fruits of their seigniories, their escheats, wardships, reliefs, and the like: and therefore, in order to prevent this, it was ordained by the second of King Henry III's great charters, and afterwards by that printed in our common statute-books that all such attempts should be void, and the land forfeited to the lord of such fee.

But, as this prohibition extended only to religious houses, bishops and other sole corporations were not included therein: and the aggregate ecclesiastical bodies (who, Sir Edward Coke observes, in this were to be commended, that they ever had of their counsel the best learned men that they could get) found many means to creep out of this statute, by buying in lands that were bona fide holden of themselves as lords of the fee, and thereby evading the forfeiture; or by taking long leases for years, which first introduced those extensive terms, for a thousand or more years, which are now so frequent in conveyances.

⚖ STATUTE DE RELIGIOSIS — This produced the statute de religiosis (of religious persons) (1279); which provided, that no person, religious or other whatsoever, should buy, or sell, or receive, under pretense of a gift, or term of years, or any other title whatsoever, nor should by any act or ingenuity appropriate to himself, any lands or tenements in mortmain; upon pain that the immediate lord of the fee, or, on his default for one year, the lords paramount, and, in default of all of them, the king, might enter thereon as a forfeiture.

⚖ COMMON RECOVERIES — This seemed to be a sufficient security against all alienations in mortmain: but as these statutes extended only to gifts and conveyances between the parties, the religious houses now began to set up a fictitious title to the land, which it was intended they should have, and to bring an action to recover it against the tenant; who, by fraud and collusion made no defense, and thereby judgment was given for the religious house, which then recovered the land by sentence of law upon a supposed prior title. Thus they had the honor of inventing those fictitious adjudications of right which are since become the great assurance of the kingdom, under the name of common recoveries.

But upon this the statute (Mortmain, 1285), enacted, that in such cases a jury shall try the true right of the demandants or plaintiffs to the land, and if the religious house or corporation be found to have it, they shall still recover seisin; otherwise it shall be forfeited to the immediate lord of the fee, or else to the next lord, and finally to the king, upon the immediate or other lord's default. Like provision was made by the succeeding chapter, in case the tenants set up crosses upon their lands (the badges of knights templars and hospitalers) in order to protect them from the feudal demands of their lords, by virtue of the privileges of those religious and military orders.

To prevent any future evasions, when the statute of quia emptores (1290), abolished all subinfeudations, and gave liberty for all men to alienate their lands to be holden of their next immediate lord, a proviso was inserted that this should not extend to authorize any kind of alienation in mortmain. When afterwards the method of obtaining the king's license by writ of ad quod damnum (at what loss) was marked out, by statute (1298), it was further provided by statute (1306), that no such license should be effectual, without the consent of the mesne or intermediate lords.

⚖ INVENTION OF USES — Yet still it was found difficult to set bounds to ecclesiastical ingenuity: for when they were driven out of all their former holds, they devised a new method of conveyance, by which the lands were granted, not to themselves directly, but to nominal feoffees to the use of the religious houses; thus distinguishing between the possession and the use, and receiving the actual profits, while the seisin of the lands remained in the nominal feoffee; who was held by the courts of equity (then under the direction of the clergy) to be bound in conscience to account to his cestuy que use (he who benefits by the use) for the rents and emoluments of the estate.

It is to these inventions that our practicers are indebted for the introduction of uses and trusts, the foundation of modern conveyancing. But, unfortunately for the inventors themselves, they did not long enjoy the advantage of their new device; for the statute (Mortmain, 1391), enacts that the lands which had been so purchased to uses should be amortized by license from the crown, or else be sold to private persons; and that for the future, uses shall be subject to the statutes of mortmain, and forfeitable like the lands themselves. Whereas the statutes had been eluded by purchasing large tracts of land, adjoining to churches, and consecrating them by the name of churchyards, each subtle imagination is also declared to be within the compass of the statutes of mortmain.

Civil or lay corporations, as well as ecclesiastical, are also declared to be within the mischief, and of course within the remedy provided by those salutary laws. Lastly, as during the times of popery lands were frequently given to superstitious uses, though not to any corporate bodies; or were made liable in the hands of heirs and devisees to the charge of obits, chanteries, and the like, which were equally pernicious in a well-governed state as actual alienations in mortmain; therefore, at the dawn of the Reformation, the statute (Mortmain, 1531), declares, that all future grants of lands for any of the purposes aforesaid, if granted for any longer term than twenty years, shall be void.

POWER OF CROWN TO REMIT FORFEITURES — But, during all this time, it was in the power of the crown, by granting a license of mortmain, to remit the forfeiture, so far as related to its own rights; and to enable any spiritual or other corporation to purchase and hold any lands or tenements in perpetuity: which prerogative is declared and confirmed by the statute (Mortmain, 1344). But, as doubts were conceived at the time of the revolution how far such license was valid, since the king had no power to dispense with the statutes of mortmain and as, by the gradual declension of mesne seigniories through the long operation of the statute of quia emptores (1290) the rights of intermediate lords were reduced to a very small compass; it was therefore provided by the statute (Mortmain, 1696), that the crown for the future at its own discretion may grant licenses to alien or take in mortmain, of whomsoever the tenements may be holden.

SUSPENSION OF STATUTES OF MORTMAIN — After the dissolution of monasteries under Henry VIII, though the policy of the next popish successor affected to grant a security to the possessors of abby lands, yet, in order to regain so much of them as either the zeal or timidity of their owners might induce them to part with, the statutes or mortmain were suspended for twenty years by the statute (Mortmain, 1554), and, during that time, any lands or tenements were allowed to be granted to any spiritual corporation without any license whatsoever. And, long afterwards, for a much better purpose, the augmentation of poor livings, it was enacted by the statute (Mortmain, 1665), that appropriators may annex the great tithes to the vicarages; and that all benefices under £100 per annum may be augmented by the purchase of lands, without license of mortmain in either case.

⚖️ CHARITABLE USES — It hath also been held, that the statute (Mortmain, 1531), before mentioned did not extend to anything but superstitious uses; and that therefore a man may give lands for the maintenance of a school, an hospital, or any other charitable uses. But as it was apprehended from recent experience that persons on their death-beds might make large and improvident dispositions even for these good purposes, and defeat the political ends of the statutes of mortmain; it is therefore enacted by the statute (Charitable Uses, 1736), that no lands or tenements, or money to be laid out thereon, shall be given for or charged with any charitable uses whatsoever, unless by deed indented, executed in the presence of two witnesses twelve calendar months before the death of the donor, and enrolled in the court of chancery within six months after its execution (except stocks in the public funds, which may be transferred within six months previous to the donor's death), and unless such gift be made to take effect immediately, and be without power of revocation: and that all other gifts shall be void.

⚖️ ALIENATION TO AN ALIEN — Secondly, alienation to an alien is also a cause of forfeiture to the crown of the lands so alienated; not only on account of his incapacity to hold them, which occasions him to be passed by in descents of land, but likewise on account of his presumption in attempting, by an act of his own, to acquire any real property; as was observed in the preceding volume.

⚖️ TORTIOUS ALIENATION BY PARTICULAR TENANTS — Lastly, alienations by particular tenants, when they are greater than the law entitles them to make, and divest the remainder or reversion, are also forfeitures to him whose right is attacked thereby. As, if tenant for his own life aliens by feoffment or fine for the life of another, or in tail, or in fee; these being estates, which either must or may last longer than his own, the creating them is not only beyond his power, and inconsistent with the nature of his interest, but is also a forfeiture of his own particular estate to him in remainder or reversion. For which there seem to be two reasons.

First, because such alienation amounts to a renunciation of the feudal connection and dependence; it implies a refusal to perform the due renders and services to the lord of the fee, of which fealty is constantly one; and it tends in its consequence to defeat and divest the remainder or reversion expectant: as, therefore, that is put in jeopardy, by such act of the particular tenant, it is but just that, upon discovery, the particular estate should be forfeited and taken from him who has shown so manifest an inclination to make an improper use for it.

The other reason is, because the particular tenant, by granting a larger estate than his own, has by his own act determined and put an entire end to his own original interest; and on such determination the next taker is entitled to enter regularly, as in his remainder or reversion. The same law, which is thus laid down with regard to tenants for life, holds also with respect to all tenants of the mere discontinuance (as it is called) of the estates-tail, which the issue may afterwards avoid by due course of law: for he in remainder or reversion hath only a very remote and barely possible interest therein, until the issue in tail is extinct.

But, in case of such forfeitures by particular tenants, all legal estates by them before created, as if tenant for twenty years grants a lease for fifteen, and all charges by him lawfully made on the lands, shall be good and available in law. For the law will not hurt an innocent lessee for the fault of his lessor; nor permit the lessor, after he has granted a good and lawful estate, by his own act to avoid it, and defeat the interest which he himself has created.

DISCLAIMER OF TENURE — Equivalent, both in its nature and its consequences, to an illegal alienation by the particular tenant, is the civil crime of disclaimer; as where a tenant, who holds of any lord, neglects to render him the due services, and, upon an action brought to recover them, disclaims to hold of his lord. Which disclaimer of tenure in any court of record is a forfeiture of the lands to the lord, upon reasons most apparently feudal. And so, likewise, if in any court of record the particular tenant does any act which amounts to a virtual disclaimer; if he claims any greater estate than was granted him at the first to tenants of a superior class; if he affirms the reversion to be in a stranger, by accepting his fine, attorning as his tenant, collusive pleading, and the like; such behavior amounts to a forfeiture of his particular estate.

RIGHT OF LAPSE — Lapse is a species of forfeiture, whereby the right of presentation to a church accrues to the ordinary by neglect of the patron to present, to the metropolitan by neglect of the ordinary, and to the king by neglect of the metropolitan. For it being for the interest of religion, and the good of the public, that the church should be provided with an officiating minister, the law has therefore given this right of lapse, in order to quicken the patron; who might otherwise, by suffering the church to remain vacant, avoid paying his ecclesiastical dues, and frustrate the pious intentions of his ancestors.

This right of lapse was first established about the time (though not by the authority) of the council of Lateran, which was in the reign of our Henry II when the bishops first began to exercise universally the right of institution to churches. Therefore where there is no right of institution, there is no right of lapse: so that no donative can lapse to the ordinary unless it hath been augmented by the queen's bounty. But no right of lapse can accrue, when the original presentation is in the crown.

The term, in which the title to present by lapse accrues from the one to the other successively, is six calendar months (following in this case the computation of the church, and not the usual one of the common law); and this exclusive of the day of the avoidance.

⚖ SIMONY — By simony, the right of presentation to a living is forfeited and vested pro hac vice (for this occasion) in the crown. Simony is the corrupt presentation of anyone to an ecclesiastical benefice for money, gift, or reward. It is so called for the resemblance it is said to bear to the sin of Simon Magus, though the purchasing of holy orders seems to approach nearer to his offense. It was by the canon law a very grievous crime: and is so much the more odious, because it is ever accompanied with perjury; for the presentee is sworn to have committed no simony. However, it was not an offense punishable in a criminal way at the common law; it being thought sufficient to leave the clerk to ecclesiastical censures. But as these did not affect the simoniacal patron, nor were efficacious enough to repel the notorious practice of the thing, divers acts of parliament have been made to restrain it by means of civil forfeitures; which the modern prevailing usage, with regard to spiritual preferments, calls aloud to be put in execution.

⚖ BREACH OF CONDITION — The next kind of forfeitures are those by breach or nonperformance of a condition annexed to the estate, either expressly by deed at its original creation, or impliedly by law from a principle of natural reason. Both which we considered at large in a former chapter.

⚖ WASTE — I therefore now proceed to another species of forfeiture, viz., by waste. Waste, is a spoil or destruction in houses, gardens, trees, or other corporeal herditaments, to the disherison of him that hath the remainder or reversion in fee simple or fee-tail.

⚖ ACTS CONSTITUTING WASTE — Waste is either voluntary, which is a crime of commission, as by pulling down a house; or it is permissive, which is a matter of omission only, as by suffering it to fall for want of necessary reparations. Whatever does a lasting damage to the freehold or inheritance is waste. Therefore, removing wainscot, floors, or other things once fixed to the freehold of a house, is waste.

If a house be destroyed by tempest, lightning, or the like, which is the act of Providence, it is no waste: but otherwise, if the house be burnt by the carelessness or negligence of the lessee; though now by the statute (Apprehension of Housebreakers, 1706), no action will lie against a tenant for an accident of this kind. Waste may also be committed in ponds, dovehouses, warrens, and the like; by so reducing the number of the creatures therein, that there will not be sufficient for the reversioner when he comes to the inheritance. Timber also is part of the inheritance. But underwood the tenant may cut down at any seasonable time that he pleases; and may take sufficient estovers (which is usual) by particular covenants or exceptions.

The conversion of land from one species to another is waste. To convert wood, meadow, or pasture, into arable; meadow, or pasture, into woodland; or to turn arable or woodland into meadow or pasture; are all of them waste. To open the land to search for mines of metal, coal, etc., is waste; for this is a detriment to the inheritance; but, if the pits or mines were open before, it is no waste for the tenant to continue digging them for his own use; for it is now become the mere annual profit of the land.

These three are the general heads of waste, viz., in houses, in timber, and in land. Though, as was before said, whatever else tends to the destruction, or depreciating the value of the inheritance, is considered by the law as waste.

⚖ WHO LIABLE FOR WASTE — By the feudal law, feuds being originally granted for life only, we find that the rule was general for all vassals or feudatories: "If a vassal shall have wasted the fee, or lessened its value by any notorious injury, he shall be deprived of it."

But in our ancient common law the rule was by no means so large: for not only he that was seised of an estate of inheritance might do as he pleased with it, but also waste was not punishable in any tenant, save only in three persons; guardian in chivalry, tenant in dower, and tenant by the curtesy; and not in tenant for life or years. The reason of the diversity was, that the estate of the three former was created by the act of the law itself, which therefore gave a remedy against them; but tenant for life, or for years, came in by the demise and lease of the owner of the fee, and therefore he might have provided against the committing of waste by his lessee; and if he did not, it was his own default. But, in favor of the owners of the inheritance, the statutes of Marlbridge and Gloucester provided, that the writ of waste shall not only lie against tenants by the law of England (or curtesy), and those in dower, but against any farmer or other that holds in any manner for life or years.

So that, for above five hundred years past, all tenants merely for life, or for any less estate (except tenants by statute merchant, statute staple, recognizance, or elegit, against whom the debtor may set off the damages in account) have been punishable or liable to be impeached for waste, both voluntary and permissive; unless their leases be made, as sometimes they are, without impeachment of waste; that is, with a provision or protection that no man shall sue him, for waste committed.

⚖️ PUNISHMENT FOR WASTE — The punishment for waste committed was, by common law and the statute of Marlbridge, only single damages; except in the case of a guardian, who also forfeited his wardship by the provisions of the great charter: but the statute of Gloucester directs that the other four species of tenants shall lose and forfeit the place wherein the waste is committed, and also treble damages, to him that hath the inheritance. The expression of the statute is, "he shall forfeit the thing which he hath wasted," and it hath been determined, that under these words the place is also included.

If waste be done here and there, all over a wood, the whole wood shall be recovered; or if in several rooms of a house, the whole house shall be forfeited; because it is impracticable for the reversioner to enjoy only the identical places wasted, when lying interspersed with the other. But if waste be done only in one end of a wood (or perhaps in one room of a house, if that can be separated from the rest), that part only is the thing wasted, and that only shall be forfeited to the reversioner.

⚖️ FORFEITURE OF COPYHOLDS BY BREACH OF CUSTOM — A seventh species of forfeiture is that of copyhold estates, by breach of the customs of the manor. Copyhold estates are not only liable to the same forfeitures as those which are held in socage, for treason, felony, alienation, and waste; whereupon the lord may seize them without any presentment by the homage; but also to peculiar local customs of certain particular manors.

We may observe that, as these tenements were originally holden by the lowest and most abject vassals, the marks of feudal dominion continue much the strongest upon this mode of property. Most of the offenses, which occasioned a resumption of the fief of the feudal law, and were denominated felonies, by which the vassal would lose his fee, still continue to be causes of forfeiture in many of our modern copyholds. As, by subtraction of suit and service; by disclaiming to hold of the lord, or swearing himself not his copyholder; by neglect to be admitted tenant by contumacy in not appearing in court after three proclamations; or by refusing, when sworn of the homage, to present the truth according to his oath.

In these, and a variety of other cases, which it is impossible here to enumerate, the forfeiture does not accrue to the lord till after the offenses are presented by the homage, or jury of the lord's court-baron. No soldier shall be removed from the possession of his benefice, unless convicted of some offense, which must be pronounced by the judgment of his peers.

⚖️ BANKRUPTCY — The eighth and last method, whereby lands and tenements may become forfeited, is that of bankruptcy, or the act of becoming a bankrupt: which unfortunate person may from the several descriptions given of him in our statute law be thus defined; a trader, who secretes himself, or does certain other acts, tending to defraud his creditors.

Who shall be such a trader, or what acts are sufficient to denominate him a bankrupt, with the several connected consequences resulting from that unhappy situation, will be better considered in a subsequent chapter; when we shall endeavor more fully to explain its nature, as it most immediately relates to personal goods and chattels. I shall only here observe the manner in which the property of lands and tenements are transferred, upon the supposition that the owner of them is clearly and indisputably a bankrupt, and that a commission of bankrupt is awarded and issued against him.

By the statute (Bankruptcy, 1571), the commissioners for that purpose, when a man is declared a bankrupt, shall have full power to dispose of all his lands and tenements, which he had in his own right at the time when he became a bankrupt, or which shall descend or come to him at any time afterwards, before his debts are satisfied or agreed for; and all lands and tenements which were purchased by him jointly with his wife or children to his own use (or such interest therein as he may lawfully part with), or purchased with any other person upon secret trust for his own use; and to cause them to be appraised to their full value, and to sell the same by deed indented and enrolled, or divide them proportionably among the creditors.

This statute expressly included not only free, but customary and copyhold, lands: but did not extend to estates-tail further than for the bankrupt's life; nor to equities of redemption on a mortgaged estate, wherein the bankrupt has no legal interest, but only an equitable reversion. Whereupon the statute (Bankruptcy, 1623), enacts, that the commissioners shall be empowered to sell or convey, by deed indented and enrolled, any lands or tenements of the bankrupt, wherein he shall be seised of an estate-tail in possession, remainder, or reversion, unless the remainder or reversion thereof shall be in the crown; and that such sale shall be good against all such issues in tail, remaindermen, and reversioners, whom the bankrupt himself might have barred by a common recovery, or other means: and that all equities of redemption upon mortgaged estates shall be at the disposal of the commissioners; for they shall have power to redeem the same, as the bankrupt himself might have done, and after the redemption to sell them. Also, all fraudulent conveyances to defeat the intent of these statutes are declared void; but that no purchaser bona fide, for a good or valuable consideration, shall be affected by the bankrupt laws, unless the commission be sued forth within five years after the act of bankruptcy committed.

By virtue of these statutes a bankrupt may lose all his real estates; which may at once be transferred by his commissioners to their assignees, without his participation or consent.

TITLE BY ALIENATION

⚖️ ACQUISITION OF TITLE BY CONVEYANCE OR ALIENATION — The most usual and universal method of acquiring a title to real estates is that of alienation, conveyance, or purchase in its limited sense: under which may be comprised any method wherein estates are voluntarily resigned by one man and accepted by another: whether that be effected by sale, gift, marriage settlement, devise, or other transmission of property by the mutual consent of the parties.

⚖️ FORMER RESTRICTIONS ON ALIENATION — This means of taking estates, by alienation, is not of equal antiquity in the law of England with that of taking them by descent. For we may remember that, by the feudal law, a pure and genuine feud could not be transferred from one feudatory to another without the consent of the lords; lest thereby a feeble or suspicious tenant might have been substituted and imposed upon him to perform the feudal services, instead of one on whose abilities and fidelity he could depend.

Neither could the feudatory then subject the land to his debts; for, if he might, the feudal restraint of alienation would have been easily frustrated, and evaded. As he could not alien it in his lifetime, so neither could he by will defeat the succession, by devising his feud to another family; nor even alter the course of it, by imposing particular limitations, or prescribing an unusual path of descent. Nor, in short, could he alien the estate, even with the consent of the lord, unless he had also obtained the consent of his own next apparent or presumptive heir.

On the other hand, as the feudal obligation was looked upon to be reciprocal, the lord could not alien or transfer his seigniory, without the consent of his vassal: for it was esteemed unreasonable to subject a feudatory to a new superior, with whom he might have a deadly enmity, without his being thoroughly apprised of it, that he might know with certainty to whom his renders and services were due, and be able to distinguish a lawful distress for rent from a hostile seizing of his cattle by the lord of a neighboring clan. This consent of the vassal was expressed by what was called attorning, or professing to become the tenant of the new lord: which doctrine of attornment was afterwards extended to all lessees for life or years. For if one bought an estate with any lease for life or years standing out thereon, and the lessee or tenant refused to attorn to the purchaser, and to become his tenant, the grant or contract was in most cases void, or at least incomplete: which was also an additional clog upon alienations.

⚶ FREEDOM OF ALIENATION — But by degrees this feudal severity is worn off, and experience hath shown, that property best answers the purposes of civil life, especially in commercial countries, when its transfer and circulation are totally free and unrestrained. The road was cleared, in the first place, by a law of King Henry I, which allowed a man to sell and dispose of lands which he himself had purchased; for over these he was thought to have more extensive power than over what had been transmitted to him in a course of descent from his ancestors: a doctrine which is countenanced by the feudal constitutions themselves: but he was not allowed to sell the whole of his own acquirements, so as totally to disinherit his children, any more than he was at liberty to alien his paternal estate.

Afterwards a man seems to have been at liberty to part with all his own acquisitions, if he had previously purchased to him and his assigns by name; but, if his assigns were not specified in the purchase deed, he was not empowered to alien. Also he might part with one-fourth of the inheritance of his ancestors without the consent of his heir. By the great charter of Henry III, no subinfeudation was permitted or part of the land, unless sufficient was left to answer the services due to the superior lord, which sufficiency was probably interpreted to be one-half or moiety of the land. But these restrictions were in general removed by the statute of Quoa emptores, whereby all persons, except the king's tenants in capite (in chief, i.e., directly of the king), were left at liberty to alien all or any part of their lands at their own discretion. Even these tenants in capite were by statute (Sale of Land, 1326), permitted to alien, on paying a fine to the king. By the temporary statutes (Soldiers' privileges, 1491, and 1511), all persons attending the king in his wars were allowed to alien their lands without license, and were relieved from other feudal burdens. Lastly, these very fines for alienations were, in all cases of freehold tenure, entirely abolished by statute (Military Tenures, 1660).

As to the power of charging lands with the debts of the owner, this was introduced so early as statute Westm. 2, which subjected a moiety of the tenant's lands to executions, for debts recovered by law; as the whole of them was likewise subjected to be pawned in a statute merchant by statute (1353), and in other similar recognizances by statute (Recognizances for Debt, 1531). And now, the whole of them is not only subject to be pawned for the debts of the owner, but likewise to be absolutely sold for the benefit of trade and commerce by the several statutes of bankruptcy.

The restraint of devising lands by will, except in some places by particular custom lasted longer; that not being totally removed, till the abolition of the military tenures. The doctrine of attornments continued still later than any of the rest, and became extremely troublesome, though many methods were invented to evade them: till at last, they were made no longer necessary, by statutes (Attornment, 1705), and (Distress for Rent, 1737).

In examining the nature of alienation, let us first inquire, briefly, who may alien and to whom; and then, more largely, how a man may alien, or the several modes of conveyance.

⚖ WHO MAY ALIEN: WHO MAY PURCHASE — Who may alien, and to whom: or in other words, who is capable of conveying and who of purchasing. Herein we must consider rather the incapacity, than capacity, of the several parties: for all persons in possession are prima facie, capable both of conveying and purchasing, unless the law has laid them under any particular disabilities. But, if a man has only in him the right of either possession or property, he cannot convey it to any other, lest pretended titles might be granted to great men, whereby justice might be trodden down, and the weak oppressed.

Yet reversions and vested remainders may be granted; because the possession of the particular tenant is the possession of him in reversion or remainder: but contingencies, and mere possibilities, though they may be released, or devised by will, or may pass to the heir or executor, yet cannot (it hath been said) be assigned to a stranger, unless coupled with some present interest.

⚖ PERSONS ATTAINTED — Persons attainted of treason, felony, and praemunire, are incapable of conveying, from the time of the offense committed, provided attainder follows: for such conveyance by them may tend to defeat the king of his forfeiture, or the lord of his escheat. But they may purchase for the benefit of the crown, or the lord of the fee, though they are disabled to hold; the lands so purchased, if after attainder, being subject to immediate forfeiture; if before, to escheat as well as forfeiture, according to the nature of the crime. So, also, corporations, religious or others, may purchase lands: yet, unless they have a license to hold in mortmain, they cannot retain such purchase; but it shall be forfeited to the lord of the fee.

⚖ IDIOTS, INSANE, INFANTS, PERSONS UNDER DURESS — Idiots and persons of nonsane memory, infants, and persons under duress, are not totally disabled either to convey or purchase, but submodo (to a certain extent) only. For their conveyances and purchases are voidable, but not actually void. The king indeed, on behalf of an idiot, may avoid his grants or other acts. But it hath been said, that a non compos himself, though he be afterwards brought to a right mind, shall not be permitted to allege his own insanity in order to avoid such grant: for that no man shall be allowed to stultify himself, or plead his own disability.

The progress of this notion is somewhat curious. In the time of Edward I, non compos was a sufficient plea to avoid a man's own bond: and there is a writ in the register for the alien or himself to recover lands aliened by him during his insanity: and, afterwards, a defendant in assize having pleaded a release by the plaintiff since the last continuance, to which the plaintiff replied (ore tenus—by word of mouth—as the manner then was) that he was out of his mind when he gave it, the court adjourned the assize; doubting, whether as the plaintiff was sane both then and at the commencement of the suit, he should be permitted to plead an intermediate deprivation of reason; and the question was asked, how he came to remember the release, if out of his senses when he gave it.

Under Henry VI this way of reasoning (that a man shall not be allowed to disable himself, by pleading his own incapacity, because he cannot know what he did under such a situation) was seriously adopted by the judges in argument; upon a question, whether the heir was barred of his right of entry by the feoffment of his insane ancestor. And from these loose authorities, the maxim that a man shall not stultify himself hath been handed down as settled law: though later opinions, feeling the inconvenience of the rule, have in many points endeavored to restrain it. Clearly, the next heir, or other person interested, may, after the death of the idiot or non compos, take advantage of his incapacity and avoid the grant. And so, too, if he purchases under this disability, and does not afterwards upon recovering his senses agree to the purchase, his heir may either waive or accept the estate at his option.

In like manner, an infant may waive such purchase or conveyance, when he comes to full age; or, if he does not then actually agree to it, his heirs may waive it after him. Persons, also, who purchase or convey under duress, may affirm or avoid such transactions, whenever the duress is ceased. For all these are under the protection of the law; which will not suffer them to be imposed upon, through the imbecility of their present condition; so that their acts are only binding, in case they be afterwards agreed to, when such imbecility ceases.

Yet the guardians or committees of a lunatic, by statute (Lunacy, 1770), are empowered to renew in his right under the directions of the court of chancery any lease for lives or years, and apply the profits of such renewal for the benefit of such lunatic, his heirs, or executors.

⚖ FEME COVERT — The case of a feme covert is somewhat different. She may purchase an estate without the consent of her husband, and the conveyance is good during the coverture, till he avoids it by some act declaring his dissent. And, though he does nothing to avoid it, or even if he actually consents, the feme covert herself may, after the death of her husband, waive or disagree to the same: nay, even her heirs may waive it after her, if she dies before her husband, or if in her widowhood she does nothing to express her consent or agreement. But the conveyance or other contract of a feme covert (except by some matter of record) is absolutely void, and not merely voidable; and therefore cannot be affirmed or made good by any subsequent agreement.

⚖ ALIENS — The case of an alien born is also peculiar. For he may purchase anything; but after purchase he can hold nothing, except a lease for years of a house for convenience of merchandise, in case he be an alien friend; all other purchases (when found by an inquest of office) being immediately forfeited to the king.

⚖ PAPISTS — Papists, lastly, and persons professing the popish religion, are by statute (Popery, 1699, and 1700), disabled to purchase any lands, rents, or hereditaments; and estates made to their use, or in trust for them, are void. But this statute is construed to extend only to papists above the age of eighteen; such only being absolutely disabled to purchase: Yet the next Protestant heir of a papist under eighteen shall have the profits, during his life; unless he renounces his errors within the time limited by law.

⚖ MODES OF CONVEYING — We are next to consider the several modes of conveyance.

In consequence of the admission of property, or the giving a separate right by the law of society to those things which by the law of nature were in common, there was necessarily some means to be devised, whereby that separate right or exclusive property should be originally acquired; which, we have more than once observed, was that of occupancy or first possession. But this possession, when once gained, was also necessarily to be continued; or else, upon one man's dereliction of the thing he had seized, it would again become common, and all those mischiefs and contentions would ensue, which property was introduced to prevent.

For this purpose, therefore, of continuing the possession, the municipal law has established descents and alienations: the former to continue the possession in the heirs of the proprietor, after his involuntary dereliction of it by his death; the latter to continue it in those persons, to whom the proprietor, by his own voluntary act, shall choose to relinquish it in his lifetime.

A transaction, or transfer, of property being thus admitted by law, it becomes necessary that this transfer should be properly evidenced: in order to prevent disputes, either about the fact, as whether there was any transfer at all; or concerning the persons, by whom and to whom it was transferred; or with regard to the subject matter, as what the thing transferred consisted of; or, lastly, with relation to the mode and quality of the transfer, as for what period of time (or, in other words, for what estate and interest) the conveyance was made.

The legal evidences of this translation of property are called the common assurances of the kingdom; whereby every man's estate is assured to him, and all controversies, doubts, and difficulties are either prevented or removed.

⚖ COMMON ASSURANCES — These common assurances are of four kinds:

1. By matter in pais, or deed; which is an assurance transacted between two or more private persons in pais, in the country; that is (according to the old common law) upon the very spot to be transferred. 2. By matter of record, or an assurance transacted only in the king's public courts of record. 3. By special custom, obtaining in some particular places, and relating only to some particular species of property. Which three are such as take effect during the life of the party conveying or assuring. 4. The fourth takes no effect, till after his death; and that is by devise, contained in his last will and testament. We shall treat of each in its order.

ALIENATION BY DEED

⚖ DEEDS — In treating of deeds I shall examine, first, what a deed is; secondly, its requisites; and, thirdly, how it may be avoided.

⚖ GENERAL NATURE OF DEEDS — First, then, a deed is a writing sealed and delivered by the parties. It is sometimes called a charter, from its materials; but most usually, when applied to the transactions of private subjects, it is called a deed, in Latin factum, because it is the most solemn and authentic act that a man can possibly perform, with relation to the disposal of his property; and therefore a man shall always be estopped by his own deed, or not permitted to aver or prove anything in contradiction to what he has once so solemnly and deliberately avowed.

If a deed be made by more parties than one, there ought to be regularly as many copies of it as there are parties and each should be cut or indented (formerly in acute angles, like teeth, or serrated), but at present in a waving line on the top or side, to tally or correspond with the other; which deed, so made, is called an indenture. Formerly, when deeds were more concise than at present, it was usual to write both parts on the same piece of parchment, with some word or letters of the alphabet written between them; through which the parchment was cut, either in a straight or indented line, in such a manner as to leave half the word on one part and half on the other. When the several parts of an indenture are interchangeably executed by the several parties, that part or copy which is executed by the grantor is usually called the original, the rest are counterparts: though of late it is most frequent for all the parties to execute every part; which renders them all originals. A deed made by one party only is not indented, but polled or shaved quite even; and therefore called a deed poll, or a single deed.

⚖ REQUISITES OF A DEED — We are in the next place to consider the requisites of a deed.

The first of which is, that there be persons able to contract and be contracted with, for the purposes intended by the deed; and also a thing, or subject matter to be contracted for; all which must be expressed by sufficient names. So as in every grant there must be a grantor, a grantee, and a thing granted; in every lease a lessor, a lessee, and a thing demised.

⚖ CONSIDERATION — Secondly; the deed must be founded upon good and sufficient consideration. Not upon an usurious contract; nor upon fraud or collusion, either ot deceive purchasers bona fide, or just and lawful creditors; any of which bad considerations will vacate the deed, and subject such persons, as put the same in use, to forfeitures, and often to imprisonment.

A deed also, or other grant, made without any consideration, is, as it were, of no effect; for it is construed to inure, or to be effectual, only to the use of the grantor himself.

The consideration may be either a good or a valuable one. A good consideration is such as that of blood, or of natural love and affection, when a man grants an estate to a near relation; being founded on motives of generosity, prudence, and natural duty: a valuable consideration is such as money, marriage, or the like, which the law esteems an equivalent given for the grant; and is therefore founded in motives of justice. Deeds made upon good consideration only, are considered as merely voluntary, and are frequently set aside in favor of creditors, and bona fide purchasers.

⚖ WRITING — Thirdly, the deed must be written, or I presume, printed, for it may be in any character or any language, but it must be upon paper or parchment. For if it be written on stone, board, linen, leather, or the like, it is no deed. Wood or stone may be more durable, and linen less liable to rasures; but writing on paper or parchment unites in itself, more perfectly than any other way, both those desirable qualities: for there is nothing else so durable, and at the same time so little liable to alteration; nothing so secure from alteration, that is at the same time so durable. It must also have the regular stamps, imposed on it by the several statutes for the increase of the public revenue; else it cannot be given in evidence.

Formerly many conveyances were made by parol, or word of mouth only, without writing; but this giving a handle to a variety of frauds, the statute (Statute of Frauds, 1677), enacts, that no lease or estate in lands, tenements, or hereditaments (except leases, not exceeding three years from the making, and whereon the reserved rent is at least two-thirds of the real value) shall be looked upon as of greater force than a lease or estate at will; unless put in writing, and signed by the party granting, or his agent lawfully authorized in writing.

FORMAL AND ORDERLY PARTS — Fourthly; the matter written must be legally and orderly set forth; that is, there must be words sufficient to specify the agreement and bind the parties: which sufficiency must be left to the courts of law to determine. For it is not absolutely necessary in law to have all the formal parts that are usually drawn out in deeds, so as there be sufficient words to declare clearly and legally the party's meaning. But, as these formal and orderly parts are calculated to convey that meaning in the clearest, distinctest, and most effectual manner, and have been well considered and settled by the wisdom of successive ages, it is prudent not to depart from them without good reason or urgent necessity; and therefore I will here mention them in their usual order.

PREMISES — The premises may be used to set forth the number and names of the parties, with their additions or titles. They also contain the recital, if any, of such deeds, agreements, or matters of fact as are necessary to explain the reasons upon which the present transaction is founded: and herein also is set down the consideration upon which the deed is made. And then follows the certainty of the grantor, grantee, and thing granted.

HABENDUM — Next come the habendum and tenendum. The office of the habendum is probably to determine what estate or interest is granted by the deed: though this may be performed, and sometimes is performed, in the premises. In which case the habendum may lessen, enlarge, explain, or qualify, but not totally contradict or be repugnant to, the estate granted in the premises. As if a grant be "to A and the heirs of his body," in the premises, habendum "to him and his heirs forever," or vice versa: Here A has an estate-tail, and a fee simple expectant thereon. But, had it been in the premises "to him and his heirs," habendum "to him for life," the habendum would be utterly void; for an estate of inheritance is vested in him before the habendum comes, and shall not afterwards be taken away, or divested, by it.

TENENDUM — The tenendum, "and to hold," is now of very little use, and is only kept in by custom. It was sometimes formerly used to signify the tenure, by which the estate granted was to be holden; viz., to hold by military service, in burgage, in free socage. But all these being now reduced to free and common socage, the tenure is never specified.

REDDENDUM — Next follow the terms of stipulation, if any upon which the grant is made: the first of which is the reddendum or reservation, whereby the grantor doth create or reserve some new thing to himself out of what he had before granted. As "rendering, therefore, yearly the sum of ten shillings, or a pepper corn, or two days' plowing, or the like." Under the pure feudal system, this render, return or rent, consisted in chivalry principally of military services; in villeinage, of the most slavish offices; and in socage, it usually consists of money, though it may consist of services still, or of any other certain profit.

To make a reddendum good, if it be of anything newly created by the deed, the reservation must be to the grantors, or some, or one of them, and not to any stranger to the deed. But if it be of ancient services or the like, annexed to the land, then the reservation may be to the lord of the fee.

⚖ CONDITIONS — Another of the terms upon which a grant may be made is a condition: which is a clause of contingency, on the happening of which the estate granted may be defeated; and "provided always, that if the mortgagor shall pay the mortgagee 500£, upon such a day, the whole estate granted shall determine"; and the like.

⚖ WARRANTIES: IMPLIED AND EXPRESS — Next may follow the clause of warranty; whereby the grantor doth, for himself and his heirs, warrant and secure to the grantee the estate so granted. By the feudal constitution, if the vassal's title to enjoy the feud was disputed, he might vouch, or call, the lord or donor to warrant or insure his gift; which if he failed to do, and the vassal was evicted, the lord was bound to give him another feud of equal value in recompense.

And so, by our ancient law, if before the statute of quia emptores a man enfeoffed another in fee, by the feudal verb dedi (I have given), to hold of himself and his heirs by certain services; the law annexed a warranty to this grant, which bound the feoffor and his heirs, to whom the services (which were the consideration and equivalent for the gift) were originally stipulated to be rendered. Or if a man and his ancestors had immemorially holden land of another and his ancestors by the service of homage this also bound the lord to warranty; the homage being an evidence of such a feudal grant.

Upon a similar principle, in case, after a partition or exchange of lands of inheritance, either party or his heirs be evicted of his share, the other and his heirs are bound to warranty, because they enjoy the equivalent. So, even at this day, upon a gift in tail or lease for life, rendering rent, the donor or lessor and his heirs (to whom the rent is payable) are bound to warrant the title. But in a feoffment in fee by the verb dedi, since the statute of quia emptores (1290), the feoffor only is bound to the implied warranty, and not his heirs; because it is a mere personal contract on the part of the feoffor, the tenure (and of course the ancient services) resulting back to the superior lord of the fee.

In other forms of alienation, gradually introduced since that statute, no warranty whatsoever is implied; they bearing no sort of analogy to the original feudal donation. Therefore in such cases it became necessary to add an express clause of warranty, to bind the grantor and his heirs; which is a kind of covenant real, and can only be created by the verb warrantizo or warrant.

⚖ ORIGIN OF EXPRESS WARRANTIES — These express warranties were introduced, even prior to the statute of quia emptores, in order to evade the strictness of the feudal doctrine of nonalienation without the consent of the heir. For, though he, at the death of his ancestor, might have entered on any tenements that were aliened without his concurrence, yet, if a clause of warranty was added to the ancestor's grant, this covenant descending upon the heir insured the grantee; not so much by confirming his title, as by obliging such heir to yield him a recompense in lands of equal value: the law, in favor of alienations, supposing that no ancestor would wantonly disinherit his next of blood; and therefore presuming that he had received a valuable consideration, either in land, or in money which had purchased land, and that this equivalent descended to the heir together with the ancestor's warranty. So that when either an ancestor, being the rightful tenant of the freehold, conveyed the land to a stranger, and his heirs, or released the right in fee simple to one who was already in possession, and superadded a warranty to his deed, it was held that such warranty not only bound the warrantor himself to protect and assure the title of the warrantee, but it also bound his heir: and this, whether the warranty was lineal, or collateral to the title of the land.

⚖ LINEAL AND COLLATERAL WARRANTIES — Lineal warranty was where the heir derived or might by possibility have derived, his title to the land warranted, either from or through the ancestor who made the warranty: as where a father, or an elder son in the life of the father, released to the disseisor of either themselves or the grandfather, with warranty, this was lineal to the younger son.

Collateral warranty was where the heir's title to the land neither was, nor could have been, derived from the warranting ancestor; as where a younger brother released to his father's disseisor, with warranty, this was collateral to the elder brother. But where the very conveyance, to which the warranty was annexed, immediately followed a disseisin, or operated itself as such (as, where a father tenant for years, with remainder to his son in fee, aliened in fee simple with warranty) this, being in its original manifestly founded on the tort or wrong of the warrantor himself, was called a warranty commmencing by disseisin; and, being too palpably injurious to be supported, was not binding upon any heir of such tortious warrantor.

⚖   EFFECT OF WARRANTIES — In both lineal and collateral warranty, the obligation of the heir (in case the warrantee was evicted, to yield him other lands in their stead) was only on condition that he had other sufficient lands by descent from the warranting ancestor. But though, without assets, he was not bound to insure the title of another, yet, in case of lineal warranty, whether assets descended or not, the heir was perpetually barred from claiming the land himself; for, if he could succeed in such claim, he would then gain assets by descent (if he had them not before) and must fulfill the warranty of his ancestor: and the same rule was with less justice adopted also in respect of collateral warranties, which likewise (though no assets descended) barred the heir of the warrantor from claiming the land by any collateral title; upon the presumption of law that he might hereafter have assets by descent either from or through the same ancestor.

⚖   RESTRAINED BY STATUTES — The inconvenience of this latter branch of the rule was felt very early, when tenants by the curtesy took upon them to alien their lands with warranty; which collateral warranty of the father descending upon his son (who was the heir of both his parents) barred him from claiming his maternal inheritance: to remedy which the statute of Gloucester (1278), declared, that such warranty should be no bar to the son, unless assets descend from the father.

It was afterwards attempted (1376) to make the same provision universal, by enacting that no collateral warranty should be a bar, unless where assets descended from the same ancestor; but it then proceeded not to effect. However, by the statute (Recovery, 1495), notwithstanding any alienation with warranty by tenant in dower, the heir of the husband is not barred, though he be also heir to the wife. And by statute (1705), all warranties by any tenant for life shall be void against those in remainder or reversion; and all collateral warranties by any ancestor who has no estate of inheritance in possession shall be void against his heir.

By the wording of which last statute it should seem that the legislature meant to allow, that the collateral warranty of tenant in tail, descending (though without assets) upon a remainderman or reversioner, should still bar the remainder or reversion. For though the judges, in expounding the statute de donis, held that, by analogy to the statute of Gloucester, a lineal warranty by the tenant in tail without assets should not bar the issue in tail, yet they held such warranty with assets to be a sufficient bar; which was therefore formerly mentioned as one of the ways whereby an estate-tail might be destroyed; it being indeed nothing more in effect than exchanging the lands entailed for others of equal value. They also held that collateral warranty was not within the statue de donis; as that act was principally intended to prevent the tenant in tail from disinheriting his own issue: and therefore collateral warranty (though without assets) was allowed to be, as at common law, a sufficient bar of the estate-tail and all remainders and reversions expectant thereon.

And so it still continues to be, notwithstanding the statute of Queen Anne, if made by tenant in tail in possession: who therefore may now, without the forms of a fine or recovery, in some cases make a good conveyance in fee simple, by super-adding a warranty to his grant; which is accompanied with assets, bars his own issue, and without them bars such of his heirs as may be in remainder or reversion.

COVENANTS — After warranty usually follow covenants, or conventions, which are clauses of agreement contained in a deed, whereby either party may stipulate for the truth of certain facts, or may bind himself to perform, or give, something to the other. Thus the grantor may covenant that he hath a right to convey; or for the grantee's quiet enjoyment; or the like: the grantee may covenant to pay his rent, or keep the premises in repair, etc. If the covenantor covenants for himself and his heirs, it is then a covenant real, and descends upon the heirs; who are bound to perform it, provided they have assets by descent, but not otherwise: if he covenants also for his executors and administrators, his personal assets, as well as his real, are likewise pledged for the performance of the covenant; which makes such covenant a better security than any warranty, and it has therefore in modern practice totally superseded the other.

CONCLUSION OF THE DEED — Lastly, comes the conclusion, which mentions the execution and date of the deed, or the time of its being given or executed, either expressly, or by reference to some day and year before mentioned. Not but a deed is good, although it mention no date: or hath a false date; or even if it hath an impossible date, as the thirtieth of February; provided the real day of its being dated or given, that is, delivered, can be proved.

⚖⚖   READING OF THE DEED — I proceed now to the fifth requisite for making a good deed; the reading of it. This is necessary, whenever any of the parties desire it; and, if it be not done on his request, the deed is void as to him. If he can, he should read it himself: if he be blind or illiterate, another must read it to him. If it be read falsely it will be void; at least for so much as is misrecited: unless it be agreed by collusion that the deed shall be read false, on purpose to make it void; for in such case it shall bind the fraudulent party.

⚖⚖   SIGNING AND SEALING — Sixthly, it is requisite that the party, whose deed it is, should seal, and in most cases I apprehend should sign it also. The use of seals, as a mark of authenticity to letters and other instruments in writing, is extremely ancient. We read of it among the Jews and Persians in the earliest and most sacred records of history. And in the book of Jeremiah there is a very remarkable instance, not only of an attestation by seal, but also of the other usual formalities attending a Jewish purchase.

In the civil law, also, seals were the evidence of truth; and were required, on the part of the witnesses at least, at the attestation of every testament. But in the times of our Saxon ancestors, they were not much in use in England. The method of the Saxons was for such as could write to subscribe their names, and, whether they could write or not, to affix the sign of the cross; which custom our illiterate vulgar do, for the most part to this day keep up; by signing a cross for their mark, when unable to write their names. And indeed this inability to write, and therefore making a cross in its stead, is honestly avowed by Caedwalla, a Saxon King, at the end of one of his charters.

In a like manner, and for the same unsurmountable reason, the Normans, a brave but illiterate nation, at their first settlement in France, used the practice of sealing only, without writing their names: which custom continued, when learning made its way among them, though the reason for doing it had ceased; and hence the charter of Edward the Confessor to Westminster Abbey, himself being brought up in Normandy, was witnessed only by his seal, and is generally thought to be the oldest sealed charter of any authenticity in England.

At the Conquest, the Norman lords brought over into this kingdom their own fashions; and introduced waxen seals only, instead of the English method of writing their names, and signing with the sign of the cross. The impressions of these seals were sometimes a knight on horseback, sometimes other devices: but coats of arms were not introduced into seals, nor indeed into any other use, till about the reign of Richard I, who brought them from the crusade in the holy land; where they were first invented and painted on the shields of the knights, to distinguish the variety of persons of every Christian nation who resorted thither, and who could not, when clad in complete steel, be otherwise known or ascertained.

This neglect of signing, and resting only upon the authenticity of seals, remained very long among us; for it was held in all our books that sealing alone was sufficient to authenticity of seals, remained very long among us; for it was held in all our books that sealing alone was sufficient to authenticate a deed: and so the common form of attesting deeds, "sealed and delivered," continues to this day; notwithstanding the statute (Statute of Frauds, 1677), before mentioned, revives the Saxon custom, and expressly directs the signing, in all grants of lands, and many other species of deeds; in which, therefore, signing seems to be now as necessary as sealing, though it hath been sometimes held that the one includes the other.

⚖ DELIVERY OF THE DEED — A seventh requisite to a good deed is that it be delivered, by the party himself or his certain attorney: which, therefore, is also expressed in the attestation, "sealed and delivered." A deed takes effect only from this tradition or delivery; for if the date be false or impossible, the delivery ascertains the time of it. And if another person seals the deed, yet if the party delivers it himself, he thereby adopts the sealing, and by a parity of reason the signing also, and makes them both his own.

A delivery may be either absolute, that is, to a party or grantee himself; or to a third person, to hold till some conditions be performed on the part of the grantee; in which last case it is not delivered as a deed, but as an escrow; that is, as a scroll or writing, which is not to take effect as a deed till the conditons be performed; and then it is a deed to all intents and purposes.

⚖ ATTESTATION OR EXECUTION — The last requisite to the validity of a deed is the attestation, or execution of it in the presence of witnesses: though this is necessary, rather for preserving the evidence than for constituting the essence of the deed. Our modern deeds are in reality nothing more than an improvement or amplification of the witnessed memoranda mentioned by the feudal writers; which were written memorandums, introduced to perpetuate the tenor of the conveyance and investiture when grants by parol only became the foundation of frequent dispute and uncertainty. To this end they registered in the deed the persons who attended as witnesses, which was formerly done without their signing their names, that not being always in their power, but they only heard the deed read; and then the clerk or scribe added their names, in a sort of memorandum; thus "Witness John Moore, Jacob Smith and others, for this purpose assembled." This like all other solemn transactions, was originally done only before the peers, and frequently when assembled in the court-baron, hundred, or county court: which was then expressed in the attestation, witness the county, hundred, etc.

Afterwards the attestation of other witnesses was allowed, the trial in case of a dispute being still reserved to the peers; with whom the witnesses (if more than one) were associated and joined in the verdict: till that also was abrogated by the statute of York (1318). And in this manner, with some such clause are all old deeds and charters, particularly Magna Carta, witnessed. But in the king's common charters, writs, or letters patent, the style is now altered: for at present the king is his own witness, and attests his letters patent thus: "witness, ourself at Westminster, etc.," a form which was introduced by Richard I, but not commonly used till about the beginning of the fifteenth century, which was also the era of discontinuing it in the deeds of subjects, learning being then revived, and the faculty of writing more general; and therefore ever since that time the witnesses have subscribed their attestation, either at the bottom, or on the back of the deed.

⚖ DEEDS HOW AVOIDED — We are next to consider how a deed may be avoided, or rendered of no effect. And from what has been before laid down it will follow, that if a deed wants any of the essential requisites before mentioned; either, 1. Proper parties, and a proper subject matter: 2. A good and sufficient consideration: 3. Writing, on paper or parchment, duly stamped: 4. Sufficient and legal words, properly disposed: 5. Reading, if desired, before the execution: 6. Sealing; and, by the statute, in many cases signing also: or, 7. Delivery, it is a void deed ab initio (from the beginning).

It may also be avoided by matter ex post facto (after the fact): as, 1. By rasure, interlining, or other alteration in any material part; unless a memorandum be made thereof at the time of the execution and attestation. 2. By breaking off, or defacing the seal. 3. By delivering it up to be canceled; that is, to have lines drawn over it in the form of lattice work or cancelli; though the phrase is now used figuratively for any manner of obliteration or defacing it. 4. By the disagreement of such, whose concurrence is necessary, in order for the deed to stand: as, the husband, where a feme covert is concerned; an infant, or person under duress, when those disabilities are removed; and the like. 5. By the judgment or decree of a court of judicature. This was anciently the province of the court of Star Chamber, and now of the chancery: when it appears that the deed was obtained by fraud, force, or other foul practice; or is proved to be an absolute forgery. In any of these cases the deed may be voided, either in part or totally, according as the cause of avoidance is more or less extensive.

⚖ THE SEVERAL SPECIES OF DEEDS — And, having thus explained the general nature of deeds, we are next to consider their several species, together with their respective incidents. And herein I shall only examine the particulars of those, which, from long practice and experience of their efficacy, are generally used in the alienation of real estates: for it would be tedious, nay infinite, to descant upon all the several instruments made use of in personal concerns, but which fall under our general definition of a deed; that is, a writing sealed and delivered. The former, being principally such as serve to convey the property of lands and tenements from man to man, are commonly denominated conveyances: which are either conveyances at common law, or such as receive their force and efficacy by virtue of the statute of uses.

⚖ CONVEYANCES AT COMMON LAW — Of conveyances by the common law, some may be called original, or primary conveyances; which are those by means whereof the benefit or estate is created or first arises: others are derivative or secondary; whereby the benefit or estate, originally created, is enlarged, restrained, transferred, or extinguished.

⚖ ORIGINAL CONVEYANCES — Original conveyances are the following: 1. Feoffment; 2. Gift; 3. Grant; 4. Lease; 5. Exchange: 6. Partition.

Derivative are, 7. Release; 8. Confirmation; 9. Surrender; 10. Assignment; 11. Defeasance.

⚖ FEOFFMENT OR GRANT — A feoffment is a substantive derived from the vert, to enfeoff, to give one a feud, and therefore feoffment is properly donatio feudi (the gift of a fee). It is the most ancient method of conveyance, the most solemn and public, and therefore the most easily remembered and proved. It may properly be defined, the gift of any corporeal hereditament to another. He that so gives, or enfeoffs, is called the feoffor; and the person enfeoffed is denominated the feoffee.

This is plainly derived from, or is indeed itself the very mode of the ancient feudal donation; for though it may be performed by the word, "enfeoff" or "grant," yet the aptest word of feoffment is "do or dedi." And it is still directed and governed by the same feudal rules; insomuch that the principal rule relating to the extent and effect of the feudal grant, "it is the condition or tenor of the deed which gives validity to a fee," is, in other words, become the maxim of our law with relation to feoffments, "measure gives validity to the grant." Therefore as in pure feudal donations the lord, from whom the feud moved, must expressly limit and declare the continuance or quantity of estate which he meant to confer "lest anyone be presumed to have given more than is expressed in the donation"; so, if one grants by feoffment lands or tenements to another, and limits or expresses no estate, the grantee (due ceremonies of law being performed), hath barely an estate for life.

For, as the personal abilities of the feoffee were originally presumed to be the immediate or principal inducements to the feoffment, the feoffee's estate ought to be confined to his person and subsist only for his life: unless the feoffer, by express provision in the creation and constitution of the estate, hath given it a longer continuance. These express provisions are indeed generally made; for this was for ages the only conveyance, whereby our ancestors were wont to create an estate in fee simple, by giving the land to the feoffee, to hold to him and his heirs forever; though it serve equally well to convey any other estate or freehold.

FEUDAL INVESTITURE — But by the mere words of the deed the feoffment is by no means perfected; there still remains a very material ceremony to be performed, called livery of seisin; without which the feoffee has but a mere estate at will. This livery of seisin is no other than the pure feudal investiture, or delivery of corporal possession of the land or tenement; which was held absolutely necessary to complete the donation, and an estate was then only perfect, when, there is a conjunction of law and seisin.

INVESTITURES — In their original rise, were probably intended to demonstrate in conquered countries the actual possession of the lord; and that he did not grant a bare litigious right, but a peaceable and firm possession. At a time when writing was seldom practiced, a mere oral gift, at a distance from the spot that was given, was not likely to be either long or accurately retained in the memory of bystanders, who were very little interested in the grant. Afterwards they were retained as a public and notorious act, that the country might take notice of and testify the transfer of the estate; and that such, as claimed title by other means, might know against whom to bring their actions.

So, also, even in descents of lands, by our law, which are cast on the heir by act of the law itself, the heir has not full and complete ownership, till he had made an actual corporal entry into the lands: for if he dies before entry made, his heir shall not be entitled to take the possession, but the heir of the person who was last actually seised. It is not, therefore, only a mere right to enter, but the actual entry, that makes a man complete owner; so as to transmit the inheritance to his own heirs.

⚬ SYMBOLICAL DELIVERY OF POSSESSION — Yet, the corporal tradition of lands being sometimes inconvenient, a symbolical delivery of possession was in many cases anciently allowed; by transferring something near at hand, in the presence of credible witnesses, which by agreement should serve to represent the very thing designed to be conveyed; and an occupancy of this sign or symbol was permitted as equivalent to occupancy of the land itself.

Among the Jews we find the evidence of a purchase thus defined in the book of Ruth: "Now this was the manner in former time in Israel, concerning redeeming and concerning changing, for to confirm all things: a man plucked off his shoe, and gave it to his neighbor; and this was a testimony in Israel."

With our Saxon ancestors the delivery of a turf was a necessary solemnity, to establish the conveyance of lands. And, to this day, the conveyance of our copyhold estates is usually made from the seller to the lord or his steward by delivery of a rod or verge, and then from the lord to the purchaser, by redelivery of the same in the presence of a jury of tenants.

⚬ CONVEYANCES IN WRITING — Conveyances in writing were the last and most refined improvement. The very delivery of possession, either actual or symbolical, depending on the ocular testimony and remembrance of the witnesses, was liable to be forgotten or misrepresented, and became frequently incapable of proof. Besides the new occasions and necessities, introduced by the advancement of commerce, required means to be devised of charging and encumbering estates, and of making them liable to a multitude of conditions and minute designations for the purposes of raising money, without an absolute sale of the land; and sometimes the like proceedings were found useful in order to make a descent and competent provision for the numerous branches of a family, and for other domestic views. None of which could be effected by a mere, simple, corporal transfer of the soil from one man to another, which was principally calculated for conveying an absolute unlimited dominion. Written deeds were therefore introduced, in order to specify and perpetuate the peculiar purposes of the party who conveyed: yet still, for a very long series of years, they were never made use of, but in company with the more ancient and notorious method of transfer, by delivery of corporal possession.

⚖ LIVERY OF SEISIN — Livery of seisin, by the common law, is necessary to be made upon every grant of an estate of freehold in hereditaments corporeal, whether of inheritance or for life only. In hereditaments incorporeal it is impossible to be made; for they are not the object of the senses: and in leases for years, or other chattel interests, it is not necessary. In leases for years, indeed, an actual entry is necessary, to vest the estate in the lessee: for the bare lease gives him only a right to enter, which is called his interest in the term, and, when he enters in pursuance of that right, he is then and not before in possession of his term, and complete tenant for years.

This entry by the tenant himself serves the purpose of notoriety, as well as livery of seisin from the grantor could have done; which it would have been improper to have given in this case, because that solemnity is appropriated to the conveyance of a freehold. This is one reason why freeholds cannot be made to commence in futuro (at a future day), because they cannot (at the common law) be made but by livery of seisin; which livery, being an actual manual tradition of the land, must take effect in proesenti (immediately), or not at all.

On the creation of a freehold remainder, at one and the same time with a particular estate for years, we have before seen that at the common law livery must be made to the particular tenant. But if such a remainder be created afterwards, expectant on a lease for years now in being, the livery must not be made to the lessee for years, for then it operates nothing; "for what is once mine cannot be mine more fully," but it must be made to the remainderman himself, by consent of the lessee for years: for without his consent no livery of the possession can be given; partly because such forcible livery would be an ejectment of the tenant from his term, and partly for the reasons before given for introducing the doctrine of attornments.

⚖ LIVERY IN DEED — Livery of seisin is either in deed, or in law. Livery in deed is thus performed. The feoffer, lessor, or his attorney, together with the feoffee, lessee, or his attorney (for this may as effectually be done by deputy or attorney, as by the principals themselves in person) come to the land, or to the house; and there, in the presence of witnesses, declare the contents of the feoffment or lease, on which livery is to be made. Then the feoffor, if it be of land, doth deliver to the feoffee, all other persons being out of the ground, a clod or turf, or a twig or bough there growing, with words to this effect. "I deliver these to you in the name of seisin of all the lands and tenements contained in this deed." But if it be of a house, the feoffor must take the ring, or latch of the door, the house being quite empty, and deliver it to the feoffee in the same manner; and then the feoffee must enter alone, and shut the door, and then open it, and let in the others.

If the conveyance of feoffment be of divers lands, lying scattered in one and the same county, then in the feoffor's possession, livery of seisin of any parcel, in the name of the rest, sufficeth for all; but if they be in several counties, there must be as many liveries as there are counties. For, if the title to these lands comes to be disputed, there must be as many trials as there are counties, and the jury of one county are no judges of the notoriety of a fact in another. Besides, anciently this seisin was obliged to be delivered before the peers or freeholders of the neighborhood, who attested such delivery in the body or on the back of the deed; according to the rule of the feudal law, (the peers, and no others, should be present at the investiture of the fee): for which this reason is expressly given; because the peers or vassals of the lord, being bound by their oath of fealty, will take care that no fraud be committed to his prejudice, which strangers might be apt to connive at. Though, afterwards, the ocular attestation of the pares was held unnecessary, and livery might be made before any credible witnesses, yet the trial, in case it was disputed (like that of all other attestations), was still reserved to the pares or jury of the county.

Also, if the lands be out on lease, though all lie in the same county, there must be as many liveries as there are tenants: because no livery can be made in this case, but by the consent of the particular tenant; and the consent of one will not bind the rest. In all these cases it is prudent, and usual, to indorse the livery of seisin on the back of the deed, specifying the manner, place, and time of making it; together with the names of the witnesses. And thus much for livery in deeds.

⚖️   LIVERY IN LAW — Livery in law is where the same is not made on the land, but in sight of it only; the feoffor saying to the feoffee, "I give you yonder land; enter and take possession." Here, if the feoffee enters during the life of the feoffor, it is a good livery, but not otherwise; unless he dares not enter, through fear of his life or bodily harm: and then his continual claim, made yearly, in due form of law, as near as possible to the lands, will suffice without an entry. This livery in law cannot, however, be given or received by attorney, but only by the parties themselves.

⚖️   GIFTS — The conveyance by gift, donatio, is properly applied to the creation of an estate-tail, as feoffment is to that of an estate in fee, and lease to that of an estate for life or years. It differs in nothing from a feoffment, but in the nature of the estate passing by it: for the operative words of conveyance in this case are do or dedi; and gifts in tail are equally imperfect without livery of seisin, as feoffments in fee simple. In common acceptation gifts are frequently confounded with the next species of deeds: which are,

⚖️   GRANTS — Grants, the regular method by the common law of transferring the property of incorporeal hereditaments, or such things whereof no livery can be had. For which reason all corporeal hereditaments, as lands and houses, are said to lie in livery; and the others, as advowsons, commons, rents, reversions, etc., to lie in grant. The reason in livery is merely the transferring from one person to another, from one hand to another, or the induction into possession of a corporeal hereditament; but an incorporeal hereditament, which is the right itself to a thing, or inherent in the person, does not admit of delivery. These, therefore, pass merely by the delivery of the deed.

⚖️   LEASES — A lease is properly a conveyance of any lands or tenements (usually in consideration of rent or other annual recompense) made for life, for years or at will, but always for a less time than the lessor hath in the premises: for if it be for the whole interest, it is more properly an assignment than a lease. The usual words of operation in it are, "demise, grant, and to farm let" farm, or feorme, is an old Saxon word signifying provisions: and it came to be used instead of rent or render, because anciently the greater part of rents were reserved in provisions; in corn, in poultry, and the like; till the use of money became more frequent. So that a farmer was one who held his lands upon payment of a rent or feorme: though at present, by a gradual departure from the original sense, the word "farm" is brought to signify the very estate or lands so held upon farm or rent.

By this conveyance an estate for life, for years, or at will, may be created, either in corporeal or incorporeal hereditaments; though livery of seisin is indeed incident and necessary to one species of leases, viz., leases for life of corporeal hereditaments; but to no other.

☟☟ RIGHT TO MAKE LEASES — Whatever restriction, by the severity of the feudal law, might in times of very high antiquity be observed with regard to leases; yet by the common law, as it has stood for many centuries, all persons seised of any estate might let leases to endure so long as their own interest lasted, but no longer. Therefore, tenant in fee simple might let leases of any duration; for he hath the whole interest: but tenant in tail, or tenant for life, could make no leases which should bind the issue in tail or reversioner; nor could a husband, seised in right of his wife, make a firm or valid lease for any longer term than the joint lives of himself and his wife, for then his interest expired.

☟☟ EXCHANGE — An exchange is a mutual grant of equal interests, the one in consideration of the other. The word "exchange" is so individually requisite and appropriated by law to this case, that it cannot be supplied by any other word or expressed by any circumlocution. The estates exchanged must be equal in quality; not of value, for that is immaterial, but of interest; as fee simple for fee simple, a lease for twenty years for a lease for twenty years, and the like. The exchange may be of things that lie either in grant or in livery. But no livery of seisin, even in exchanges of freehold, is necessary to perfect the conveyance: for each party stands in the place of the other and occupies his right, and each of them hath already had corporal possession of his own land. But entry must be made on both sides; for, if either party die before entry, the exchange is void, for want of sufficient notoriety. If, after an exchange of lands or other hereditaments, either party be evicted of those which were taken by him in exchange, through defect of the other's title; he shall return back to the possession of his own, by virtue of the implied warranty contained in all exchanges.

☟☟ PARTITION — A partition is when two or more joint tenants, coparceners, or tenants in common, agree to divide the lands so held among them in severalty, each taking a distinct part. Here, as in some instances there is a unity of interest, and in all a unity of possession, it is necessary that they all mutually convey and assure to each other the several estates, which they are to take and enjoy separately. By the common law coparceners, being compellable to make partition, might have made it by parol only; but joint tenants and tenants in common must have done it by deed: and in both cases the conveyance must have been perfected by livery of seisin. But the statute of frauds (1677), hath now abolished this distinction, and make a deed in all cases necessary.

SECONDARY OR DERIVATIVE CONVEYANCES — These are the several species of primary, or original conveyances. Those which remain are of the secondary, or derivative sort; which presuppose some other conveyance precedent, and only serve to enlarge, confirm, alter, restrain, restore, or transfer the interest granted by such original conveyance. As,

RELEASES — Releases; which are a discharge or conveyance of a man's right in lands or tenements, to another that hath some former estate in possession. The words generally used therein are "remised, released, and forever quitclaimed." And these releases may inure either, 1. By way of enlarging as estate, as, if there be tenant for life or years, remainder to another in fee, and he in remainder releases all his right to the particular tenant and his heirs, this gives him the estate in fee. But in this case the relessee must be in possession of some estate, for the release to work upon; for if there be lessee for years, and before he enters and is in possession, the lessor releases to him all his right in the reversion, such release is void for want of possession in the relessee.

2. By way of passing an estate, as when one of two coparceners releaseth all her right to the other, this passeth the fee simple of the whole. And in both these cases there must be a privity of estate between the relessor and relessee; that is, one of their estates must be so related to the other, as to make but one and the same estate in law.

3. By way of passing a right as if a man be disseised, and releaseth to his disseisor all his right; hereby the disseisor acquires a new right, which changes the quality of his estate, and renders that lawful which before was tortious.

4. By way of extinguishment: as if my tenant for life makes a lease to A for life, remainder to B and his heirs, and I release to A; this extinguishes my right to the reversion, and shall inure to the advantage of B's remainder as well as of A's particular estate.

5. By way of entry and feoffment: as if there be two joint disseisors, and the disseisee releases to one of them, he shall be sole seised, and shall keep out his former companion: which is the same in effect as if the

disseisee had entered, and thereby put an end to the disseisin, and afterwards had enfeoffed one of the disseisors in fee.

Hereupon we may observe that when a man has in himself the possession of lands, he must at the common law convey in the freehold by feoffment and livery; which makes a notoriety in the country; but if a man has only a right or a future interest, he may convey that right or interest by a mere release to him that is in possession of the land: for the occupancy of the relessee is a matter of sufficient notoriety already.

CONFIRMATION — A confirmation is of a nature nearly allied to a release. Sir Edward Coke defines it to be a conveyance of an estate or right in esse, whereby a voidable estate is made sure and unavoidable, or whereby a particular estate is increased: and the words of making it are these, "have given, granted, ratified, approved, and confirmed." An instance of the first branch of the definition is, if tenant for life leaseth for forty years, and dieth during that term; here the lease for years is voidable by him in reversion: yet, if he hath confirmed the estate of the lessee for years, before the death of tenant for life, it is no longer voidable but sure. The latter branch, or that which tends to the increase of a particular estate, is the same in all respects with that species of release, which operates by way of enlargement.

SURRENDER — A surrender, or rendering up, is of a nature directly opposite to a release; for, as that operates by the greater estate's descending upon the less, a surrender is the falling of a less estate into a greater. It is defined, a yielding up of an estate for life or years to him that hath the immediate reversion or remainder, wherein the particular estate may merge or drown, by mutual agreement between them. It is done by these words, "hath surrendered, granted, and yielded up." The surrenderor must be in possession; and the surrenderee must have a higher estate, in which the estate surrendered may merge: therefore, tenant for life cannot surrender to him in remainder for years.

In a surrender there is no occasion for livery of seisin; for there is a privity of estate between the surenderor, and the surrenderee; the one's particular estate and the other's remainder are one and the same estate; and livery having been once made at the creation of it, there is no necessity for having it afterwards. For the same reason, no livery is required on a release or confirmation in fee to tenant for years or at will, though a freehold thereby passes: since the reversion of the relessee, or confirmee, are one and the same estate: and where there is already a possession, derived from such a privity of estate, any further delivery of possession would be vain and nugatory.

⚖ ASSIGNMENT — An assignment is properly a transfer, or making over to another, of the right one has in any estate; but it is usually applied to an estate for life or years. It differs from a lease only in this; that by a lease one grants an interest less than his own, reserving to himself a reversion; in assignments he parts with the whole property, and the assignee stands to all intents and purposes in the place of the assignor.

⚖ DEFEASANCE — A defeasance is a collateral deed, made at the same time with a feoffment or other conveyance, containing certain conditions, upon the performance of which the estate then created may be defeated or totally undone. And in this manner mortgages were in former times usually made; the mortgagor enfeoffing the mortgagee, and he at the same time executing a deed of defeasance, whereby the feoffment was rendered void on repayment of the money borrowed at a certain day. This, when executed at the same time with the original feoffment, was considered as part of it by the ancient law; and, therefore only, indulged: no subsequent secret revocation of a solemn conveyance, executed by livery of seisin, being allowed in those days of simplicity and truth; though, when uses were afterwards introduced, a revocation of such uses was permitted by the courts of equity. But things that were merely executory, or to be completed by matter subsequent (as rents, of which no seisin could be had till the time of payment; and so, also, annuities, conditions, warranties, and the like), were always liable to be recalled by defeasances made subsequent to the time of their creation.

⚖ CONVEYANCES UNDER THE STATUTE OF USES — There yet remain to be spoken of some few conveyances, which have their force and operation by virtue of the Statute of Uses.

⚖ USES AND TRUSTS — Uses and trusts are in their original of a nature very similar, or rather exactly the same: answering more to the trust than the usufruct of the civil law; which latter was the temporary right of using a thing, without having the ultimate property or full dominion of the substance. But the trust which usually was created by will, was the disposal of an inheritance to one, in confidence that he should convey it or dispose of the profits at the will of another. It was the business of a particular magistrate (trust praetor), instituted by Augustus, to enforce the observance of this confidence. So that the right thereby given was looked upon as a vested right, and entitled to a remedy from a court of justice; which occasioned that known division of rights by the

Roman law, into a legal right, which was remedied by the ordinary course of law; a right in trust, for which there was a remedy in conscience; and a right in curtesy, for which the remedy was only by entreaty or request.

In our law, a use might be ranked under the rights of the second kind; being a confidence reposed in another who was tenant of the land, that he should dispose of the land according to the intentions of cestuy que use, or him to whose use it was granted, and suffer him to take the profits. As, if a feoffment was made to A and his heirs, to the use of (or in trust for) B and his heirs; here at the common law A the terre-tenant, had the legal property and possession of the land, but B, the cestuy que use, was in conscience and equity to have the profits and disposal of it.

The notion was transplanted into England from the civil law, about the close of the reign of Edward III, by means of the foreign ecclesiastics; who introduced it to evade the statutes of Mortmain, by obtaining grants of lands, not to their religious houses directly, but to the use of the religious houses: which the clerical chancellors of those times held to be fideicommissa (trusts), and binding in conscience; and therefore assumed the jurisdiction, which Augustus had vested in his praetor, of compelling the execution of such trust in the chancery. As it was most easy to obtain such grants from dying persons, a maxim was established, that though by law the lands themselves were not devisable, yet if a testator had enfeoffed another to his own use and so was possessed of the use only, such use was devisable by will. But we have seen how this evasion was crushed in its infancy, by statute (Mortmain, 1391), with respect to religious houses.

Yet, the idea being once introduced, however fraudulently, it afterwards continued to be often innocently, and sometimes very laudably, applied to a number of civil purposes: particularly as it removed the restraint of alienations by will, and permitted the owner of lands in his lifetime to make various designations of their profits, as prudence, or justice, or family convenience, might from time to time require. Till at length, during our long wars in France and the subsequent civil commotions between the houses of York and Lancaster, uses grew almost universal; through the desire that men had (when their lives were continually in hazard) of providing for their children by will, and of securing their estates from forfeitures; when each of the contending parties, as they became uppermost, alternately attainted the other. Wherefore about the reign of Edward IV (before whose time, Lord Bacon remarks, there are not six cases to be found relating to the doctrine of uses), the courts of equity began to reduce them to something of a regular system.

⚖ DOCTRINE OF USES — Originally it was held that the chancery could give no relief, but against the very person himself intrusted for cestuy que use, and not against his heir or alienee. This was altered in the reign of Henry VI with respect to the heir; and afterwards the same rule, by a parity of reason, was extended to such alienees as had purchased either without a valuable consideration, or with an express notice of the use. But a purchaser for a valuable consideration, without notice, might hold the land discharged of any trust or confidence. Also it was held that neither the king or queen, on account of their dignity royal, nor any corporation aggregate, on account of its limited capacity, could be seised to any use but their own; that is, they might hold the lands, but were not compellable to execute the trust. If the feoffee to uses died without heir, or committed a forfeiture or married, neither the lord who entered for his escheat or forfeiture, nor the husband who retained the possession as tenant by the curtesy, nor the wife to whom the dower was assigned, were liable to perform the use; because they were not parties to the trust, but came in by act of law; though doubtless their title in reason was no better than that of the heir.

On the other hand, the use itself, or interest of cestuy que use, was learnedly refined upon with many elaborate distinctions. 1. It was held that nothing could be granted to a use, whereof the use is inseparable from the possession; as annuities, ways, commons, and authorities, which are consumed by the use itself: or whereof the seisin could not be instantly given. 2. A use could not be raised without a sufficient consideration. For where a man makes a feoffment to another without any consideration, equity presumes that he meant it to the use of himself: unless he expressly declares it to be to the use of another, and then nothing shall be presumed contrary to his own expressions. But, if either a good or a valuable consideration appears, equity will immediately raise a use correspondent to such consideration. 3. Uses were descendible according to the rules of the common law, in the case of inheritances in possession; for in this and many other respects equity follows the law, and cannot establish a different rule of property from that which the law has established. 4. Uses might be assigned by secret deeds between the parties, or be devised by last will and testament: for, as the legal estate in the soil was not transferred by these transactions, no livery of seisin was necessary: and as the intention of the parties was the leading principle in this species of property, any instrument declaring that intention was allowed to be binding in equity. But, cestuy que use could not at common law alien the legal interest of the lands, without the concurrence of his feoffee; to whom he was accounted by law to be only tenant at sufferance.   5. Uses were not liable to any of the feudal burdens; and particularly did not escheat for felony or other defect of blood; for escheats, etc., are the consequences of tenure, and uses are held of nobody; but the land itself was liable to escheat, whenever the blood of the feoffee to uses was extinguished by crime or by defect; and the lord (as was before observed) might hold it discharged of the use.   6. No wife could be endowed, or husband have his curtesy, of a use: for no trust was declared for their benefit, at the original grant of the estate. And therefore it became customary, when most estates were put in use, to settle before marriage some joint estate to the use of the husband and wife for their lives; which was the original of modern jointures.   7. A use could not be extended by writ or elegit, or other legal process, for the debts of cestuy que use. For, being merely a creature of equity, the common law, which looked no further than to the person actually seised of the land, could award no process against it.

It is impracticable, upon our present plan, to pursue the doctrine of uses through all the refinements and niceties, which the ingenuity of the times (abounding in subtle disquisitions) deduced from this child of imagination; when once a departure was permitted from the plain, simple rules of property established by the ancient law. These principal outlines will be fully sufficient to show the ground of Lord Bacon's complaint, that this course of proceeding "was turned to deceive many of their just and reasonable rights. A man, that had cause to sue for land, knew not against whom to bring his action, or who was the owner of it. The wife was defrauded of her thirds; the husband of his curtesy; the lord of his wardship, relief, heriot, and escheat; the creditor of his extent for debt; and the poor tenant of his lease."

To remedy these inconveniences abundance of statutes were provided, which made the lands liable to be extended by the creditors of cestuy que use; allowed actions for the freehold to be brought against him, if in the actual pernancy or enjoyment of the profits; made him liable to actions of waste; established his conveyances and leases made without the concurrence of his feoffees; and gave the lord the wardship of his heir, with certain other feudal perquisites.

⚖️ STATUTE OF USES — These provisions all tended to consider cestuy que use as the real owner of the estate; and at length that idea was carried into full effect by the statute (Statute of Uses, 1535), which is usually called the statute of uses, or, in conveyances and pleadings, the "statute for transferring uses into possession." The hint seems to have been derived from what was done at the accession of King Richard III; who having, when Duke of Gloucester, been frequently made a feoffee to uses, would upon the assumption of the crown (as the law was then understood) have been entitled to hold the lands discharged of the use. But, to obviate so notorious an injustice, an act of Parliament was immediately passed, which ordained that, where he had been so enfeoffed jointly with other persons, the land should vest in the other feoffees, as if he had never been named; and that, where he stood solely enfeoffed, the estate itself should vest in cestuy que use in like manner as he had the use. The statute thus executes the use as our lawyers term it; that is, it conveys the possession to the use, and transfers the use into possession: thereby making cestuy que use complete owner of the lands and tenements, as well at law as in equity.

⚖️ DECISIONS OF COMMON-LAW COURTS — The statute having thus, not abolished the conveyance to uses, but only anihilated the intervening estate of the feoffee, and turned the interest of cestuy que use into a legal instead of an equitable ownership; the courts of common law began to take cognizance of uses, instead of sending the party to seek his relief in chancery. Considering them now as merely a mode of conveyance, many of the rules before established in equity were adopted with improvements by the judges of the common law. The same persons only were held capable of being seised to a use, the same considerations were necessary for raising it, and it could only be raised of the same hereditaments, as formerly.

But, as the statute, the instant it was raised, converted it into an actual possession of the land, a great number of the incidents, that formerly attended it in its fiduciary state, were now at an end. The land could not escheat or be forfeited by the act or defect of the feoffee, nor be aliened to any purchaser discharged of the use, nor be liable to dower or curtesy on account of the seisin of such feoffee; because the legal estate never rests in him for a moment, but is instantaneously transferred to cestuy que use, as soon as the use is declared. As the use and the land were now convertible terms, they became liable to dower, curtesy and escheat, in consequence of the seisin of cestuy que use, who was now become the terre-tenant also; and they likewise were no longer devisable by will.

The various necessities of mankind induced also the judges very soon to depart from the rigor and simplicity of the rules of the common law, and to allow a more minute and complex construction upon conveyances to uses than upon others. Hence it was adjudged that the use need not always be executed the instant the conveyance is made: but, if it cannot take effect at that time, the operation of the statute may wait till the use shall arise upon some future contingency, to happen within a reasonable time; and in the meanwhile the ancient use shall remain in the original grantor: as, when lands are conveyed to the use of A and B, after a marriage shall be had between them, or to the use of A and his heirs till B shall pay him a sum of money, and then to the use of B and his heirs. Which doctrine, when devises by will were again introduced, and considered as equivalent in point of construction to declarations of uses, was also adopted in favor of executory devises.

But herein these, which are called contingent or springing uses, differ from an executory devise; in that there must be a person siesed to such uses at the time when the contingency happens, else they can never be executed by the statute; and therefore, if the estate of the feoffee to such use be destroyed by alienation or otherwise, before the contingency arises, the use is destroyed forever: whereas by an executory devise the freehold itself is transferred to the future devisee. In both these cases, a fee may be limited to take effect after a fee: because though that was forbidden by the common law in favor of the lord's escheat, yet, when the legal estate was not extended beyond one fee simple, such subsequent uses (after a use in fee) were before the statute permitted to be limited in equity; and then the statute executed the legal estate in the same manner as the use before subsisted.

It was also held that a use, though executed, may change from one to another by circumstances ex post facto (after the fact); as, if A makes a feoffment to the use of his intended wife and her eldest son for their lives, upon the marriage the wife takes the whole use in severalty; and, upon the birth of a son, the use is executed jointly in them both. This is sometimes called a secondary, sometimes a shifting, use. And, whenever the use limited by the deed expires, or cannot vest, it returns back to him who raised it, after such expiration or during such impossibility, and is styled a resulting use. As, if a man makes a feoffment to the use of his intended wife for life, with remainder to the use of her first-born son in tail: here, till he marries, the use results back to himself; after marriage, it is executed in the wife for life; and, if she dies without issue, the whole results back to him in fee.

It was likewise held, that the uses originally declared may be revoked at any future time, and new uses be declared of the land, provided the grantor reserved to himself such a power at the creation of the estate; whereas the utmost that the common law would allow, was a deed of defeasance coeval with the grant itself (and therefore esteemed a part of it) upon events specifically mentioned. In case of such a revocation, the old uses were held instantly to cease, and the new ones to become executed in their stead. This was permitted, partly to indulge the convenience and partly the caprice of mankind; who (as Lord Bacon observes) have always affected to have the disposition of their property revocable in their own time, and irrevocable ever afterwards.

✂ DECISIONS OF THE COURT OF CHANCERY — By this equitable train of decisions in the courts of law, the power of the court of chancery over landed property was greatly curtailed and diminished. But one or two technical scruples, which judges found it hard to get over, restored it with tenfold increase. They held, in the first place, that "no use could be limited on a use," and that when a man bargains and sells his land for money, which raises a use by implication to the bargainee, the limitation of further use to another person is repugnant, and therefore void. Therefore, on a feoffment to A and his heirs, to the use of B and his heirs, in trust for C and his heirs, they held that the statute executed only the first use, and that the second was a mere nullity: not adverting. that the instant the first use was executed in B, he became seised to the use of C, which second use the statute might as well be permitted to execute as it did the first; and so the legal estate might be instantaneously transmitted down, through a hundred uses upon uses, till finally executed in the last cestuy que use.

Again; as the statute mentions only such persons as were seised to the use of others, this was held not to extend to terms of years, or other chattel interests, whereof the termor is not seised, but only possessed; and therefore, if a term of one thousand years be limited to A, to the use of (or in trust for) B, the statute does not execute this use, but leaves it as at common law. And lastly (by more modern resolutions), where lands are given to one and his heirs in trust to receive and pay over the profits to another, this use is not executed by the statute:

for the land must remain in the trustee to enable him to perform the trust.

☙ MODERN LAW OF TRUSTS — Of the two more ancient distinctions the courts of equity quickly availed themselves. In the first case it was evident that B was never intended by the parties to have any beneficial interest; and, in the second, the cestuy que use of the term was expressly driven into the court of chancery to seek his remedy: and therefore that court determined, that though these were not uses, which the statute could execute, yet still they were trusts in equity, which in conscience ought to be performed. To this the reason of mankind assented, and the doctrine of uses was revived, under the denomination of trusts: and thus, by this strict construction of the courts of law, a statute made upon great deliberation, and introduced in the most solemn manner, has had little other effect than to make a slight alteration in the formal words of a conveyance.

However, the courts of equity, in the exercise of this new jurisdiction, have wisely avoided in a great degree those mischiefs which made uses intolerable. They now consider a trust estate (either when expressly declared or resulting by necessary implication) as equivalent to the legal ownership, governed by the same rules of property, and liable to every charge in equity, which the other is subject to in law: and, by a long series of uniform determinations, for now near a century past, with some assistance from the legislature, they have raised a new system of rational jurisprudence, by which trusts are made to answer in general all the beneficial ends of uses, without their inconvenience or frauds. The trustee is considered as merely the instrument of conveyance, and can in no shape affect the estate, unless by alienation for a valuable consideration to a purchaser without notice; which, as cestuy que is generally in possession of the land, is a thing that can rarely happen.

The trust will descend, may be aliened, is liable to debts, to forfeiture, to leases and other encumbrances, nay even to the curtesy of the husband, as if it was an estate at law. It has not yet indeed been subjected to dower, more from a cautious adherence to some hasty precedents, than from any well-grounded principle. It hath also been held not liable to escheat to the lord, in consequence of attainder or want of heirs: because the trust could never be intended for his benefit. But let us now return to the statute of uses.

The only service, as was before observed, to which this statute is now consigned, is in giving efficacy to certain new and secret species of conveyances; introduced in order to render transactions of this sort as private as possible, and to save the trouble of making livery of seisin, the only ancient conveyance of corporeal freeholds: the security and notoriety of which public investiture abundantly overpaid the labor of going to the land, or of sending an attorney in one's stead. But this now has given way to

⚖ COVENANT TO STAND SEISED TO USES — A twelfth species of conveyance, called a covenant to stand seised to uses; by which a man, seised of lands, covenants in consideration of blood or marriage that he will stand seised of the same to the use of his child, wife or kinsman; for life, in tail, or in fee. Here the statute executes at once the estate; for the party intended to be benefited, having thus acquired the use, is thereby put at once into corporal possession of the land, without ever seeing it, by a kind of parliamentary magic. But this conveyance can only operate, when made upon such weighty and interesting considerations as those of blood or marriage.

⚖ BARGAIN AND SALE — A thirteenth species of conveyance, introduced by this statute, is that of a bargain and sale of lands, which is a kind of a real contract, whereby the bargainor for some pecuniary consideration bargains and sells, that is, contracts to convey, the land to the bargainee; and then the statute of uses completes the purchase: or, as it hath been well expressed, the bargain first vests the use, and then the statute vests the possession. But as it was foreseen that conveyances, thus made, would want all those benefits of notoriety, which the old common-law assurances were calculated to give; to prevent, therefore, clandestine conveyances of freeholds, it was enacted in the same session of parliament by statute (Enrollments, 1536), that such bargains and sales should not inure to pass a freehold, unless the same be made by indenture, and enrolled within six months in one of the courts of Westminster Hall, or with the Keeper of the Rolls of the county.

Clandestine bargains and sales of chattel interests, or leases for years, were thought not worth regarding, as such interests were very precarious till about six years before; which also occasioned them to be overlooked in framing the statute of uses: and therefore such bargains and sales are not directed to be enrolled. But how impossible it is to foresee, and provide against, all the consequences of innovations! This omission has given rise to.

⚖   LEASE AND RELEASE — A fourteenth species of conveyance, viz., by lease and release; first invented by Sergeant Moore, soon after the statute of uses, and now the most common of any. It is thus contrived. A lease, or rather bargain and sale, upon some pecuniary consideration, for one year, is made by the tenant of the freehold to the lessee or bargainee the use of the term for a year; and then the statute immediately annexes the possession. He therefore being thus in possession, is capable of receiving a release of the freehold and reversion; which, we have seen before, must be made to a tenant in possession: and accordingly, the next day, a release is granted to him. This is held to supply the place of livery of seisin; and so a conveyance by lease and release is said to amount to a feoffment.

⚖   DEEDS TO LEAD OR DECLARE USES — To these may be added deeds to lead or declare the uses of other more direct conveyances, as feoffments, fines, and recoveries; of which we shall speak in the next chapter: and,

⚖   DEEDS OF REVOCATION OF USES — Deeds of revocation of uses, hinted at in a former page, and founded in a previous power, reserved at the raising of the uses, to revoke such as were then declared; and to appoint others in their stead, which is incident to the power of revocation. And this may suffice for a specimen of conveyances founded upon the statute of uses; and will finish our observations upon such deeds as serve to transfer real property.

⚖   DEEDS TO CHARGE AND DISCHARGE LANDS — Before we conclude, it will not be improper to subjoin a few remarks upon such deeds as are used not to convey, but to charge or encumber lands, and discharge them again: of which nature are, obligations or bonds, recognizances, and defeasances upon them both.

⚖   OBLIGATION OR BOND — An obligation or bond, is a deed whereby the obligor obliges himself, his heirs, executors, and administrators, to pay a certain sum of money to another at a day appointed. If this be all, the bond is called a single one, simplex obligatio (single bond, i.e., bond without a condition); but there is generally a condition added, that if the obligor does some particular act, the obligation shall be void, or else shall remain in full force: as, payment of rent; performance of covenants in a deed; or repayment of a principal sum of money borrowed of the obligee, with interest, which principal sum is usually one-half of the penal sum specified in the bond. In case this condition is not performed, the bond becomes forfeited, or absolute at law, and charges the obligor while living; and after his death the obligation descends upon his heir, who (on defect of personal assets) is bound to discharge it, provided he has real assets by descent as a recompense. So that it may be called, though not a direct, yet a collateral, charge upon the lands. How it affects the personal property of the obligor, will be more properly considered hereafter.

If the condition of a bond be impossible at the time of making it, or be to do a thing contrary to some rule of law that is merely positive, or be uncertain, or insensible, the condition alone is void, and the bond shall stand single and unconditional: for it is the folly of the obligor to enter into such an obligation, from which he can never be released. If it be to do a thing that is malum in se (wrong in itself), the obligation itself is void: for the whole is an unlawful contract, the obligee shall take no advantage from such a transaction.

If the condition be possible at the time of making it, and afterwards becomes impossible by the act of God, the act of law, or the act of the obligee himself, there the penalty of the obligation is saved: for no prudence or foresight of the obligor could guard against such a contingency. On the forfeiture of a bond, or its becoming single, the whole penalty was formerly recoverable at law; but here the courts of equity interposed, and would not permit a man to take more than in conscience he ought; viz., his principal, interest, and expenses, in case the forfeiture accrued by nonpayment of money borrowed; the damages sustained, upon nonperformance of covenants; and the like.

The like practice having gained some footing in the courts of law, the statute (1705), at length enacted, in the same spirit of equity, that in case of a bond, conditioned for the payment of money, the payment or tender of the principal sum due, with interest, and costs, even though the bond be forfeited and a suit commenced thereon, shall be a full satisfaction and discharge.

⚖ RECOGNIZANCE — A recognizance is an obligation of record, which a man enters into before some court of record or magistrate duly authorized, with condition to do some particular act, as to appear at the assizes, to keep the peace, to pay a debt, or the like. It is in most respects like another bond: the difference being chiefly this: that the bond is the creation of a fresh debt or obligation de novo, the recognizance is an acknowledgment of a former debt upon record; the form whereof is "that A B doth acknowledge to owe to our lord the king, to the plaintiff, to

C D or the like, the sum of ten pounds," with condition to be void on performance of the thing stipulated: in which case the king, the plaintiff, C D, etc., is called the cognizee, "is cui cognoscitur (he to whom it is acknowledged)"; as he that enters into the recognizance is called the cognizor, "is qui cognoscit (he who acknowledges)." This, being either certified to, or taken by the officer of some court, is witnessed only by the record of that court, and not by the party's seal: so that it is not in strict propriety a deed, though the effects of it are greater than a common obligation; being allowed a priority in point of payment, and binding the lands of the cognizor, from the time of enrollment on record.

There are also other recognizances, of a private kind, in nature of a statute staple, by virtue of the statute (Recognizances for Debt, 1531), which have been already explained, and shown to be a charge upon real property.

☙☙ DEFEASANCE — A defeasance, on a bond, or recognizance, or judgment recovered, is a condition which, when performed, defeats or undoes it, in the same manner as a defeasance of an estate before mentioned. It differs only from the common condition of a bond, in that the one is always inserted in the deed or bond itself, the other is made between the same parties by a separate, and frequently a subsequent deed. This, like the condition of a bond, when performed discharges and disencumbers the estate of the obligor.

☙☙ QUESTION OF REGISTERING DEEDS — These are the principal species of deeds or matter in pais, by which estates may be either conveyed or at least affected. Among which the conveyances to uses are by much the most frequent of any; though in these there is certainly one palpable defect, the want of sufficient notoriety: so that purchases or creditors cannot know with any absolute certainty what the estate, and the title to it, in reality are, upon which they are to lay out or to lend their money.

In the ancient feudal method of conveyance (by giving corporal seisin of the lands) this notoriety was in some measure answered; but all the advantages resulting from thence are now totally defeated by the introduction of death-bed devises and secret conveyances: and there has never been yet any sufficient guard provided against fraudulent charges and encumbrances; since the disuse of the old Saxon custom of transacting all conveyances at the county court, and entering a memorial of them in the chartulary or ledger-book of some adjacent monastery; and the failure of the general register established by King Richard the First, for the starrs or mortgages made to Jews, in the capitula de Judaeis, of which Hoveden has preserved a copy. How far the establishment of a like general register, for deeds, and wills, and other acts affecting real property, would remedy this inconvenience, deserves to be well considered.

In Scotland every act and event, regarding the transmission of property, is regularly entered on record. And some of our own provincial divisions, particularly the extended county of York, and the populous county of Middlesex, have prevailed with the legislature to erect such registers in their several districts. But, however plausible these provisions may appear in theory, it hath been doubted by very competent judges, whether more disputes have not arisen in those counties by the inattention and omissions of parties, than prevented by the use of registers.

ALIENATION BY MATTER OF RECORD

ASSURANCES BY MATTER OF RECORD — Assurances by matter of record are such as do not entirely depend on the act or consent of the parties themselves: but the sanction of a court of record is called in to substantiate, preserve, and be a perpetual testimony of, the transfer of property from one man to another; or of its establishment, when already transferred. Of this nature are, 1. Private acts of parliament. 2. The king's grants. 3. Fines. 4. Common recoveries.

PRIVATE ACTS OF PARLIAMENT — Private acts of parliament are, especially of late years, become a very common mode of assurance. For it may sometimes happen, that by the ingenuity of some, and the blunders of other practitioners, an estate is most grievously entangled by a multitude of contingent remainders, resulting trusts, springing uses, executory devises, and the like artificial contrivances (a confusion unknown to the simple conveyances of the common law); so that it is out of the power of either courts of law or equity to relieve the owner. Or it may sometimes happen, that by the strictness or omission of family settlements, the tenant of the estate is abridged of some reasonable power (as letting leases, making a jointure for a wife, or the like), which power cannot be given him by the ordinary judges either in common law or equity. Or it may be necessary, in settling an estate, to secure it against the claims of infants or other persons under legal disabilities; who are not bound by any judgments or decrees of the ordinary courts of justice.

In these, or other cases of the like kind, the transcendent power of parliament is called in, to cut the Gordian knot; and by a particular law, enacted for this very purpose, to unfetter an estate; to give its tenant reasonable powers; or to assure it to a purchaser, against the remote or latent claims of infants or disabled persons, by settling a proper equivalent in proportion to the interest so barred.

This practice was carried to a great length in the year succeeding the restoration; by setting aside many conveyances alleged to have been made by constraint, or in order to screen the estates from being forfeited during the usurpation. At last it proceeded so far, that, as the noble historian expresses it, every man had raised an equity in his own imagination, that he thought was entitled to prevail against any descent, testament, or act of law, and to find relief in parliament: which occasioned the king at the close of the session to remark that the good old rules of law are the best security; and to wish that men might now have too much cause to fear, that the settlements which they make of their estates shall be too easily unsettled when they are dead, by the power of parliament.

Acts of this kind are, however, at present carried on, in both houses, with great deliberation and caution; particularly in the house of lords they are usually referred to two judges to examine and report the facts alleged, and to settle all technical forms. Nothing, also, is done without the consent, expressly given, of all parties in being and capable of consent, that have the remotest interest in the matter; unless such consent shall appear to be perversely and without any reason withheld. And, as was before hinted, an equivalent in money or other estate is usually settled upon infants, or persons not in esse, or not of capacity to act for themselves, who are to be concluded by this act. A general saving is constantly added, at the close of the bill, of the right and interest of all persons whatsoever; except those whose consent is so given or purchased, and who are therein particularly named.

A law, thus made, though it binds all parties to the bill, is yet looked upon rather as a private conveyance, than as the solemn act of the legislature. It is not therefore allowed to be a public, but a mere private statute; it is not printed or published among the other laws of the session; it hath been relieved against, when obtained upon fraudulent suggestions; and no judge or jury is bound to take notice of it, unless the same be specially set forth and pleaded to them. It remains, however, enrolled among the public records of the nation, to be forever preserved as a perpetual testimony of the conveyance or assurance so made or established.

⚖ THE KING'S GRANTS — The king's grants are also matter of public record. For the king's excellency is so high in the law, that no freehold may be given to the king, nor derived from him, but by matter of record. To this end a variety of offices are erected, communicating in a regular subordination one with another through which all the king's grants must pass, and be transcribed, and enrolled; that the same may be narrowly inspected by his officers, who will inform him if anything contained therein is improper, or unlawful to be granted.

These grants, whether of lands, honors, liberties, franchises, or aught besides, are contained in charters, or letters patent, that is, open letters: so called because they are not sealed up, but exposed to open view, with the great seal pendant at the bottom; and are usually directed or addressed by the king to all his subjects at large. Therein they differ from certain other letters of the king, sealed also with his great seal, but directed to particular persons, and for particular purposes: which, therefore, not being proper for public inspection, are closed up and sealed on the outside, and are thereupon called writs close and are recorded in the close-rolls, in the same manner as the others are in the patent-rolls.

THE PRACTICE IN ROYAL GRANTS — Grants or Letters patent must first pass by bill: which is prepared by the attorney and solicitor general, in consequence of a warrant from the crown; and is then signed, that is, superscribed at the top, with the king's own sign manual, and sealed with his privy signet, which is always in the custody of the principal secretary of state; and then sometimes it immediately passes under the great seal, in which case the patent is subscribed in these words, "per ipsum regem (by the king himself)."

CONSTRUCTION OF ROYAL GRANTS — The manner of granting by the king does not more differ from that by a subject, than the construction of his grants, when made. 1. A grant made by the king, at the suit of the grantee, shall be taken most beneficially for the king, and against the party: whereas the grant of a subject is construed most strongly against the grantor. Wherefore it is usual to insert in the king's grants, that they are made, not at the suit of the grantee, but "by the special favor, certain knowledge, and mere motion of the king"; and then they have a more liberal construction.

2. A subject's grant shall be construed to include many things, besides what are expressed, if necessary for the operation of the grant. Therefore, in a private grant of the profits of land for one year, free ingress, egress, and regress, to cut and carry away those profits, are also inclusively granted: and if a feoffment of land was made by a lord to his villein, this operated as a manumission; for he was otherwise unable to hold it. But the king's grant shall not inure to any other intent than that which is precisely expressed in the grant. As, if he grants land to an alien, it operates nothing; for such grant shall not also inure to make him a denizen, that so he may be capable of taking by grant.

3. When it appears, from the face of the grant, that the king is mistaken, or deceived, either in matter of fact or matter of law, as in case of false suggestion, misinformation, or misrecital of former grants; or if his own title to the thing granted be different from what he supposes; or if the grant be informal; or if he grants an estate contrary to the rules of law; in any of these cases the grant is absolutely void.

For instance; if the king grants lands to one and his heirs male, this is merely void: for it shall not be an estate-tail, because they want words of procreation, to ascertain the body, out of which the heirs shall issue; neither is it a fee simple, as in common grants it would be; because it may reasonably be supposed, that the king meant to give no more than an estate-tail: the grantee is therefore (if anything) nothing more than tenant at will. To prevent deceits of the king, with regard to the value of the estate granted, it is particularly provided by the statute (Petitions to the King for Lands, 1399), that no grant of his shall be good, unless, in the grantee's petition for them, express mention be made of the real value of the lands.

⚖ NATURE OF A FINE — A fine is sometimes said to be a feoffment of record: though it might with more accuracy be called, an acknowledgment of a feoffment on record. By which is to be understood, that it has at least the same force and effect with a feoffment, in the conveying and assuring of land: though it is one of those methods of transferring estates of freehold by the common law, in which livery of seisin is not necessary to be actually given; the supposition and acknowledgment thereof in a court of record, however fictitious, inducing an equal notoriety.

But, more particularly, a fine may be described to be an amicable composition or agreement of a suit, either actual or fictitious, by leave of the king or his justices; whereby the lands in question become, or are acknowledged to be, the right of one of the parties. In its original it was founded on an actual suit, commenced at law for recovery of the possession of land or other hereditaments; and the possession thus gained by such composition was found to be so sure and effectual, that fictitious actions were, and continue to be, every day commenced, for the sake of obtaining the same security.

A fine is so called because it puts an end, not only to the suit thus commenced, but also to all other suits and controversies concerning the same matter. Or, as it is expressed in an ancient record of parliament (Fines, 1290), "there is no greater or more common security provided in the kingdom of England, or by which a person can acquire a surer title, than by a fine levied in the king's court: nor can any testimony be produced more customary for confirming a title. It is called a fine because it is finis, that is, the end and consummation of all suits; and for this purpose it was provided."

Fines indeed are of equal antiquity with the first rudiments of the law itself; are spoken of in the reigns of Henry II and Henry III, as things then well known and long-established; and instances have been produced of them even before the Norman invasion. So that the statute called modus levandi fines (in manner of levying fines), did not give them original, but only declared and regulated the manner in which they should be levied or carried on. And that is as follows:

⚖ MODE OF LEVYING FINES — WRIT OF PRAECIPE — The party, to whom the land is to be conveyed or assured, commences an action or suit at law against the other, generally an action or covenant: the foundation of which is a supposed agreement or covenant, that the one shall convey the lands to the other; on the breach of which agreement the action is brought. On this writ there is due to the king, by ancient prerogative, a primer fine, or a noble for every five marks of land sued for; that is, one-tenth of the annual value. The suit being thus commenced, then follows,

⚖ LICENTIA CONCORDANDI — The licentia concordandi, or leave to agree the suit. For, as soon as the action is brought, the defendant, knowing himself to be in the wrong, is supposed to make overtures of peace and accommodation to the plaintiff. Who, accepting them, but having, upon suing out the writ, given pledges to prosecute his suit, which he endangers if he now deserts it without license, he therefore applies to the court for leave to make the matter up. This leave is readily granted, but for it there is also another fine due to the king by his prerogative which is an ancient revenue of the crown, and is called the king's silver, or sometimes the post fine, with respect to the primer fine before mentioned. It is as much as the primer fine, and half as much more, or ten schillings for every five marks of land; that is, three-twentieths of the supposed annual value.

⚖ CONCORD OR AGREEMENT — Next comes the concord, or agreement itself, after leave obtained from the court; which is usually an acknowledgment from the deforciants (or those who keep the other out of possession) that the lands in question are the right of the complainant. From this acknowledgment, or recognition of right, the party levying the fine is called the cognizor, and he to whom it is levied the cognizee. This acknowledgment must be made either openly in the court of common pleas, or before one of the judges of that court, or else before commissioners in the country, empowered by a special authority, called a writ of dedimus potestatem (we have given power); which judges and commissioners are bound by statute (Fines, 1290), to take care that the cognizors be of full age, sound memory, and out of prison. If there be any feme covert among the cognizors, she is privately examined whether she does it willingly and freely, or by compulsion of her husband.

By these acts all the essential parts of a fine are completed: and, if the cognizor dies the next moment after the fine is acknowledged, provided it be subsequent to the day on which the writ is made turnable, still the fine shall be carried on in all its remaining parts.

NOTE OF THE FINE — The note of the fine: which is only an abstract of the writ of covenant, and the concord; naming the parties, the parcels of land, and the agreement. This must be enrolled or recorded in the proper office, by direction of statute (Fines, 1403).

THE FOOT OF THE FINE — The fifth part or the foot of the fine, or conclusion of it: which includes the whole matter, reciting the parties, day, year, and place, and before whom it was acknowledged or levied. Of this there are indentures made, or engrossed, at the chirographer's office, and delivered to the cognizor and the cognizee; usually beginning thus: "this is the final agreement," and then reciting the whole proceeding at length. And thus the fine is completely levied at common law.

FORCE AND EFFECT OF A FINE — We are next to consider the force and effect of a fine. These principally depend, at this day, on the common law, and the two statutes (Fines, 1488, and Fines, 1540). The ancient common law, with respect to this point, is very forcibly declared by statute (1290), in these words: "And the reason, why such solemnity is required in the passing of a fine, is this; because the fine is so high a bar, and of so great force, and of a nature so powerful in itself, that it precludes not only those which are parties and privies to the fine, and their heirs, but all other persons in the world, who are of full age, out of prison, of sound memory, and within the four seas the day of the fine levied; unless they put in their claim on the foot of the fine within a year and a day."

But this doctrine, of barring the right of nonclaim, was abolished for a time by a statute made (Fines, 1360), which admitted persons to claim, and falsify a fine, at any indefinite distance: whereby, as Sir Edward Coke observes, great contention arose, and few men were sure of their possessions, till the parliament (1488), reformed that mischief, and excellently moderated between the latitude given by the statute and the rigor of the common law. For the statute, then made, restored the doctrine of nonclaim; but extended the time of claim.

So that now, by that statute, the right of all strangers whatsoever is bound, unless they make claim, by way of action or lawful entry, not within one year and a day, as by the common law, but within five years after proclamations made: except feme coverts, infants, prisoners, persons beyond the seas, and such as are not of whole mind; who have five years allowed to them and their heirs, after the death of their husbands, their attaining full age, recovering their liberty, returning into England, or being restored to their right mind.

It seems to have been the intention of that politic prince, King Henry VII, to have covertly by this statute extended fines to have been a bar of estates-tail, in order to unfetter the more easily the estates of his powerful nobility, and lay them more open to alienations; being well aware that power will always accompany property. But doubts have arisen whether they could, by mere implication, be adjudged a sufficient bar (which they were expressly declared not to be by the statute de donis), the statute (Fines, 1540), was thereupon made; which removes all difficulties, by declaring that a fine levied by any person of full age, to whom or to whose ancestors lands have been entailed, shall be a perpetual bar to them and their heirs claiming by force of such entail: unless the fine be levied by a woman after the death of her husband, of lands which were, by the gift of him or his ancestor, assigned to her in tail for her jointure; or unless it be of lands entailed by act of parliament or letters patent, and whereof the reversion belongs to the crown.

From this view of the common law, regulated by these statutes, it appears, that a fine is a solemn conveyance on record from the cognizor to the cognizee, and that the persons bound by a fine are parties, privies, and strangers.

⚖ PARTIES TO A FINE — The parties are either the cognizors, or cognizees; and these are immediately concluded by the fine, and barred of any latent right they might have, even though under the legal impediment of coverture. Indeed, as this is almost the only act that a feme covert, or married woman, is permitted by law to do (and that because she is privately examined as to her voluntary consent, which removes the general suspicion of compulsion by her husband), it is therefore the usual and almost the only safe method, whereby she can join in the sale, settlement, or encumbrance, of any estate.

⚖ PRIVIES TO A FINE — Privies to a fine are such as are any way related
to the parties who levy the fine, and claim under them by any right of blood, or other right of representation. Such as are the heirs general of the cognizor, the issue in tail since the statute of Henry the Eighth, the vendee, the devisee, and all others who must make title by the persons who levied the fine. For the act of the ancestor shall bind the heir, and the act of the principal his substitute, or such as claim under any conveyance made by him subsequent to the fine as levied.

⚖ STRANGERS TO A FINE — Strangers to a fine are all other persons in
the world, except only parties and privies. These are also bound by a fine, unless, within five years after proclamations are made, they interpose their claim; provided they are under no legal impediments, and have then a present interest in the estate. The impediments, as hath before been said, are coverture, infancy, imprisonment, insanity, and absence beyond sea: and persons, who are thus incapacitated to prosecute their rights, have five years allowed them to put in their claims after such impediments are removed. Persons also that have not a present, but a future interest only, as those in remainder or reversion, have five years allowed them to claim in, from the time that such right accrues. And if within that time they neglect to claim, or (by the statute Fines, 1705), if they do not bring an action or try the right, within one year after making such claim, and prosecute the same with effect, all persons whatsoever are barred of whatever right they may have, by force of the statute of nonclaim.

⚖ FREEHOLD INTEREST ESSENTIAL TO A FINE — But, in order to make a
fine of any avail at all, it is necessary that the parties should have some interest or estate in the lands to be affected by it. Else it were possible that two strangers, by a mere confederacy, might without any risk defraud the owners by levying fines of their lands; for if the attempt be discovered, they can be no sufferers, but must only remain in status quo (in the same condition as before): whereas if a tenant for life levies a fine, it is an absolute forfeiture of his estate to the remainderman or reversioner, if claimed in proper time. It is not, therefore, to be supposed that such tenants will frequently run so great a hazard; but if they do, and the claim is not duly made within five years after their respective terms expire, the estate is forever barred by it. Yet where a stranger, whose presumption cannot thus be punished, officiously inter-

feres in an estate which in no wise belongs to him, his fine is of no effect; and may at any time be set aside.

⚖ COMMON RECOVERY — The fourth species of assurance, by matter of record, is a common recovery. Concerning the original of which, it was formerly observed, that common recoveries were invented by the ecclesiastics to elude the statutes of mortmain; and afterwards encouraged by the finesse of the courts of law (1472), in order to put an end to all fettered inheritances, and bar not only estates-tail, but also all remainders and reversions expectant thereon. I am now, therefore, only to consider, first, the nature of a common recovery; and secondly, its force and effect.

⚖ NATURE OF A COMMON RECOVERY — A common recovery is so far like a fine that it is a suit or action, either actual or fictitious: and in it the lands are recovered against the tenant of the freehold; which recovery, being a supposed adjudication of the right, binds all persons, and vests a free and absolute fee simple in the recoverer. A recovery, therefore, being in the nature of an action at law, not immediately compromised like a fine, but carried on through every regular stage of proceeding, I am greatly apprehensive that its form and method will not be easily understood by the student, who is not yet acquainted with the course of judicial proceedings; which cannot be thoroughly explained, till treated at large in the third book of these Commentaries. However, I shall endeavor to state its nature and progress, as clearly and concisely as I can; avoiding, as far as possible, all technical terms, and phrases not hitherto interpreted.

⚖ SINGLE VOUCHER — Let us, in the first place, suppose David Edwards to be tenant of the freehold, and desirous to suffer a common recovery, in order to bar all entails, remainders, and reversions, and to convey the same in fee simple to Francis Golding. To effect this, Golding is to bring an action against him for the lands; and he accordingly sues out a writ, called a praecipe quod reddat (command him to restore), because those were its initial or most operative words, when the law proceedings were in Latin.

In this writ the demandant Golding alleges, that the defendant Edwards (here called the tenant) has no legal title to the land; but that he came into possession of it after one Hugh Hunt had turned the demandant out of it. The subsequent proceedings are made up into a record or recovery roll, in which the writ and complaint of the demandant are first recited: whereupon the tenant appears, and calls upon one

Jacob Morland, who is supposed, at the original purchase, to have warranted the title to the tenant; and thereupon he prays, that the said Jacob Morland may be called in to defend the title which he so warranted. This is called the voucher (vocatio), or calling of Jacob Morland to warranty; and Morland is called the vouchee. Upon this, Jacob Morland, the vouchee, appears, is impleaded, and defends the title. Whereupon, Golding, the demandant, desires leave of the court to impart, or confer with the vouchee in private; which is (as usual) allowed him.

Soon afterwards the demandant, Golding, returns to court, but Morland the vouchee disappears, or makes default. Whereupon judgment is given for the demandant, Golding, now called the recoverer, to recover the lands in question against the tenant, Edwards, who is now the recoveree; and Edwards has judgment to recover of Jacob Morland lands of equal value, in recompense for the lands so warranted by him, and now lost by his default; which is agreeable to the doctrine of warranty mentioned in the preceding chapter. This is called the recompense, or recovery in value. But Jacob Morland having no lands of his own, being usually the crier of the court (who, from being frequently thus vouches, is called the common vouchee), it is plain that Edwards has only a nominal recompense for the lands so recovered against him by Golding; which lands are now absolutely vested in the said recoverer by judgment of law, and seisin thereof is delivered by the sheriff of the county. So that this collusive recovery operates merely in the nature of a conveyance in fee simple, from Edwards the tenant in tail, to Golding the purchaser.

⚖️ DOUBLE VOUCHER — The recovery, here described, is with a single voucher only; but sometimes it is with double, treble, or further voucher, as the exigency of the case may require, and indeed it is now usual always to have a recovery with double voucher at the least: by first conveying as estate of freehold to any indifferent person, against whom the praecipe is brought; and then he vouches the tenant in tail, who vouches over the common vouchee. For, if a recovery be had immediately against tenant in tail, it bars only such estate in the premises of which he is then actually seised; whereas, if the recovery be had against another person, and the tenant in tail be vouched, it bars every latent right and interest which he may have in the lands recovered.

If Edwards, therefore, be tenant of the freehold in possession, and John Barker be tenant in tail in remainder, here Edwards doth first vouch Barker, and then Barker vouches Jacob Morland, the common vouchee; who is always the last person vouched, and always makes default; whereby the demandant Golding recovers the land against the tenant Edwards, and Edwards recovers a recompense of equal value against Barker, the first vouchee; who recovers the like against Morland, the common vouchee, against whom such ideal recovery in value is always ultimately awarded.

⚖ SUPPOSED RECOMPENSE FROM THE COMMON VOUCHEE — This supposed recompense in value is the reason why the issue in tail is held to be barred by a common recovery. For, if the recoveree should obtain a recompense in lands from the common vouchee (which there is a possibility in contemplation of law, though a very improbable one, of his doing), these lands would supply the place of those so recovered from him by collusion, and would descend to the issue in tail. This reason will also hold with equal force, as to most remaindermen and reversioners; to whom the possibility will remain and revert, as a full recompense for the reality, which they were otherwise entitled to; but it will not always hold; and therefore the judges have been cunning in inventing other reasons to maintain the authority of recoveries. In particular, it hath been said, that, though the estate-tail is gone from the recoveree, yet it is not destroyed, but only transferred; and still subsists, and will ever continue to subsist (by construction of law) in the recoverer, his heirs and assigns: and, as the estate-tail so continues to subsist forever, the remainders or reversions expectant on the determination of such estate-tail can never take place.

⚖ IMPROVEMENTS DESIRABLE — To such awkward shifts, such subtle refinements, and such strange reasoning, were our ancestors obliged to have recourse, in order to get the better of that stubborn statute de donis. The design, for which these contrivances were set on foot, was certainly laudable; the unriveting the fetters of estates-tail, which were attended with a legion of mischiefs to the commonwealth: but, while we applaud the end, we cannot but admire the means. Our modern courts of justice have indeed adopted a more manly way of treating the subject; by considering common recoveries in no other light than as the formal mode of conveyance, by which tenant in tail is enabled to alien his lands.

But, since the ill consequences of fettered inheritances are now generally seen and allowed, and of course the utility and expedience of setting them at liberty are apparent, it hath often been wished, that the process of this conveyance was shortened, and rendered less subject to niceties, by either totally repealing the statute de donis; which, perhaps, by reviving the old doctrine of conditional fees, might give birth to many litigations: or by vesting in every tenant in tail of full age the same absolute fee simple at once, which now he may obtain whenever he pleases, by the collusive fiction of a common recovery; though this might possibly bear hard upon those in remainder or reversion, by abridging the chances they would otherwise frequently have, as no recovery can be suffered in the intervals between term and term, which sometimes continue for near five months together: or, lastly, by empowering the tenant in tail to bar the estate-tail by a solemn deed, to be made in term time and enrolled in some court of record; which is liable to neither of the other objections, and is warranted not only by the usage of our American colonies, but by the precedent of the statute (Bankruptcy, 1623), which, in case of a bankrupt tenant in tail, empowers his commissioners to sell the estate at any time, by deed indented and enrolled.

⚖ FORCE AND EFFECT OF COMMON RECOVERIES — The force and effect of common recoveries may appear, from what has been said, to be an absolute bar not only of all estates-tail, but of remainders and reversions. But, by statute (Fines and Recoveries, 1543), no recovery had against tenant in tail, of the king's gift, whereof the remainder or reversion is in the king, shall bar such estate-tail, or the remainder or reversion of the crown. By the statute (Bar of Entail, 1495), no woman, after her husband's death, shall suffer a recovery of lands settled on her by her husband or settled on her husband and her by any of his ancestors. By statute (Recoveries, 1572), no tenant for life, of any sort, can suffer a recovery, so as to bind them in remainder or reversion. For which reason, if there be tenant for life, with remainder in tail, and other remainders over, and the tenant for life is desirous to suffer a valid recovery; either he, or the tenant to the praecipe by him made, must vouch the remainder-man in tail, otherwise the recovery is void: but if he does vouch such remainderman, and if he appears and vouches the common vouchee, it is then good; for if a man be vouched and appears, and suffers the recovery to be had, it is as effectual to bar the estate-tail as if he himself were the recoveree.

⚖ RECOVEREE MUST BE SEISED OF THE FREEHOLD — In all recoveries it is necessary that the recoveree, or tenant to the praecipe, as he is usually called, be actually seised of the freehold, else the recovery is void. For all actions, to recover the seisin of lands, must be brought against the actual tenant of the freehold, else the suit will lose its effect; since the freehold cannot be recovered of him who has it not. Though these recoveries are in themselves fabulous and fictitious, yet it is necessary that there be actors fabulae (actors of the fiction), properly qualified.

☙☙ DEEDS TO LEAD OR DECLARE USES — Before I conclude this head, I must add a word concerning deeds to lead, or to declare, the uses of fines, and of recoveries. For if they be levied or suffered without any good consideration, and without any uses declared, they, like other conveyances, inure only to the use of him who levies or suffers them.

ALIENATION BY DEVISE

⚕️ CONVEYANCE BY DEVISE — The last method of conveying real property is by devise, or disposition contained in a man's last will and testament. And, in considering this subject, I shall not at present inquire into the nature of wills and testaments, which are more properly the instruments to convey personal estates; but only into the original and antiquity of devising real estates by will, and the construction of the several statutes upon which that power is now founded.

⚕️ FEUDAL RESTRAINTS ON POWER TO DEVISE — It seems sufficiently clear, that, before the Conquest, lands were devisable by will. But, upon the introduction of the military tenures, the restraint of devising lands naturally took place, as a branch of the feudal doctrine of non-alienation without the consent of the lord. Some have questioned, whether this restraint was not founded upon truer principles of policy than the power of wantonly disinheriting the heir by will, and transferring the estate, through the dotage or caprice of the ancestor, from those of his blood to utter strangers. For this, it is alleged, maintained the balance of property, and prevented one man from growing too big or powerful for his neighbors; since it rarely happens that the same man is heir to many others, though by art and management he may frequently become their devisee.

Thus the ancient law of the Athenians directed that the estate of the deceased should always descend to his children; or, on failure of lineal descendants, should go to the collateral relations: which had an admirable effect in keeping up equality and preventing the accumulations of estates. But when Solon made a slight alteration, by permitting them (though only on failure of issue) to dispose of their lands by testament, and devise away estates from the collateral heir, this soon produced an excess of wealth in some, and of poverty in others: which, by a natural progression, first produced popular tumults and dissensions; and these at length ended in tyranny, and the utter extinction of liberty; which was quickly followed by a total subversion of their state and union.

On the other hand, it would now seem hard, on account of some abuses (which are the natural consequence of free agency, when coupled with human infirmity) to debar the owner of lands from distributing them after his death, as the exigence of his family affairs, or the justice due to his creditors, may perhaps require. This power, if prudently managed, has with us a pecular propriety; by preventing the very evil which resulted from Solon's institution, the too great accumulation of property: which is the natural consequence of our doctrine of succession by primogeniture, to which the Athenians were strangers. Of this accumulation the ill effects were severely felt even in the feudal times: but it should always be strongly discouraged in a commercial country, whose welfare depends on the number of moderate fortunes engaged in the extension of trade.

However this be, we find that, by the common law of England since the Conquest, no estate, greater than for term of years, could be disposed of by testament; except only in Kent, and in some ancient burghs, and a few particular manors, where their Saxon immunities by special indulgence subsisted. Though the feudal restraint on alienations by deed vanished very early, yet this on wills continued for some centuries after; from an apprehension of infirmity and imposition on the testator in extremis (in his last moments), which made such devises suspicious. Besides, in devises there was wanting that general notoriety, and public designation of the successor, which in descents is apparent to the neighborhood, and which the simplicity of the common law always required in every transfer and new acquisition of property.

⚖ DEVISE OF THE USE: STATUTE OF WILLS — But when ecclesiastical ingenuity had invented the doctrine of uses, as a thing distinct from the land, uses began to be devised very frequently, and the devisee of the use could in chancery compel its execution. For it is observed by Gilbert, that, as the popish clergy then generally sat in the court of chancery, they considered that men are most liberal when they can enjoy their possessions no longer: and therefore at their death would choose to dispose of them to those who, according to the superstition of the times, could intercede for their happiness in another world. But, when the statute of uses had annexed the possession to the use, these uses, being now the very land itself, became no longer devisable: which might have occasioned a great revolution in the law of devises, had not the statute of wills been made about five years after, viz. (Wills, 1540), which enacted that all persons being seised in fee simple (except feme coverts, infants, idiots and persons of nonsane memory) might by will and testament in writing devise to any other person, but not to bodies corporate, two-thirds of their lands, tenements and heriditament, held in chivalry, and the whole of those held in socage: which now, through the alteration of tenures by the statute of Charles the Second, amounts to the whole of their landed property, except their copyhold tenements.

☙ DEVISES TO CORPORATIONS FOR CHARITABLE USES — Corporations were excepted in these statutes, to prevent the extension of gifts in mortmain; but now, by construction of the statute (Charitable Gifts, 1601), it is held, that a devise to a corporation for a charitable use is valid, as operating in the nature of an appointment, rather than of a bequest. Indeed the piety of the judges hath formerly carried them great lengths in supporting such charitable uses; it being held that the statute of Elizabeth, which favors appointments to charities, supersedes and repeals all former statutes, and supplies all defects of assurances: and therefore not only a devise to a corporation, but a devise by a copyhold tenant without surrendering to the use of his will, and a devise (nay, even a settlement) by tenant in tail without either fine or recovery, if made to a charitable use, are good by way of appointment.

☙ STATUTE OF FRAUDS — With regard to devises in general, experience soon showed how difficult and hazardous a thing it is, even in matters of public utility, to depart from the rules of the common law; which are so nicely constructed and so artificially connected together, that the least breach in any one of them disorders for a time the texture of the whole. Innumerable frauds and perjuries were quickly introduced by this parliamentary method of inheritance: for so loose was the construction made upon this act by the courts of law, that bare notes in the handwriting of another person were allowed to be good wills within the statute. To remedy which, the statute of frauds and perjuries (1677), directs, that all devises of lands and tenements shall not only be in writing, but signed by the testator, or some other person in his presence, and by his express direction; and be subscribed, in his presence, by three or four credible witnesses. A solemnity nearly similar is requisite for revoking a devise.

☙ SIGNING, WITNESSES — In the construction of this last statute, it has been adjudged that the testator's name, written with his own hand, at the beginning of his will, as, "I, John Mills, do make this my last will and testament," is a sufficient signing, without any name at the bottom; though the other is the safer way. It has also been determined, that though the witnesses must all see the testator sign, or at least acknowledge the signing, yet they may do it at different times. But they must all subscribe their names as witnesses in his presence, lest by any possibility they should mistake the instrument.

In one case determined by the court of king's bench, the judges were extremely strict in regard to the credibility, or rather the competency, of the witnesses: for they would not allow any legatee, or by consequence a creditor, where the legacies and debts were charged on the real estate, to be a competent witness to the devise, as being too deeply concerned in interest not to wish the establishment of the will; for, if it were established, he gained a security for his legacy or debt from the real estate, whereas otherwise he had no claim but on the personal assets. This determination, however, alarmed many purchases and creditors and threatened to shake most of the titles in the kingdom, that depended on devises by will. For, if the will was attested by a servant to whom wages were due, by the apothecary or attorney whose very attendance made them creditors, or by the minister of the parish who had any demand for tithes or ecclesiastical dues (and these are the persons most likely to be present in the testator's last illness), and if in such case the testator had charged his real estate with the payment of his debts, the whole will, and every disposition therein, so far as related to real property, were held to be utterly void.

This occasioned the statute (Legatees, 1751), which restored both the competency and the credit of such legatees, by declaring void all legacies given to witnesses, and thereby removing all possibility of their interest affecting their testimony. The same statute likewise established the competency of creditors, by directing the testimony of all such creditors to be admitted, but leaving their credit (like that of all other witnesses) to be considered, on a view of all the circumstances, by the court and jury before whom such will shall be contested.

☙ SPECIALTY CREDITORS — Another inconvenience was found to attend this new method of conveyance by devise; in that creditors by bond and other specialties, which affected the heir provided he had assets by descent, were now defrauded of their securities, not having the same remedy against the devisee of their debtor. To obviate which, the statute (Wills, 1691), hath provided, that all wills, and testaments, limitations, dispositions, and appointments of real estates, by tenants in fee simple or having power to dispose by will, shall (as against such creditors only) be deemed to be fraudulent and void: and that such creditors may maintain their actions jointly against both the heir and the devisee.

⚖ DISTINCTION BETWEEN WILLS OF LAND AND OF CHATTELS — A will of lands, made by the permission and under the control of these statutes, is considered by the courts of law not so much in the nature of a testament, as of a conveyance declaring the uses to which the land shall be subject: with this difference, that in other conveyances the actual subscription of the witnesses is not required by law, though it is prudent for them so to do, in order to assist their memory when living and to supply their evidence when dead; but in devises of lands such subscription is now absolutely necessary by statute, in order to identify a conveyance, which in its nature can never be set up till after the death of the devisor.

And upon this notion, that a devise affecting lands is merely a species of conveyance, is founded this distinction between such devises and testaments of personal chattels; that the latter will operate upon whatever the testator dies possessed of, the former only upon such real estates as were his at the time of executing and publishing his will. Wherefore no after-purchased lands will pass under such devise, unless, subsequent to the purchase or contract, the devisor republishes his will.

⚖ RULES AND MAXIMS FOR CONSTRUING CONVEYANCES — We have now considered the several species of common assurances, whereby a title to lands and tenements may be transferred and conveyed from one man to another. But, before we conclude this head, it may not be improper to take notice of a few general rules and maxims, which have been laid down by courts of justice, for the construction and exposition of them all. These are:

⚖ FAVORABLE TO APPARENT INTENT — That the construction be favorable, and as near the minds and apparent intents of the parties as the rules of law will admit. For the maxims of law are, that "words would be subservient to the intention"; and "We interpret deeds favorably on account of the ignorance of the laity." And therefore the construction must also be reasonable, and agreeable to common understanding.

⚖ WORDS TAKEN IN ORDINARY SENSE — Where there is no ambiguity in the words, they should be construed according to their obvious meaning: but, that, where the intention is clear, too minute a stress be not laid on the strict and precise signification of words; for he who confines himself to the letter, goes but halfway. Therefore, by the grant of a remainder a reversion may well pass and e converso. And another maxim of law is, that bad grammar does not vitiate a deed; neither false English nor bad Latin will destroy a deed. Which perhaps a classical critic may think to be no unnecessary caution.

⚖ EFFECT TO EVERY PART — That the construction be made upon the entire deed, and not merely upon disjointed parts of it. "For a deed is best interpreted by the bearing of all its parts." And therefore that every part of it, be (if possible) made to take effect; and no word but what may operate in some shape or other. "For words should be understood with an effect that may tend more to strengthen than destroy the subject matter."

⚖ TAKEN MOST STRONGLY AGAINST MAKER — That the deed be taken most strongly against him that is the agent or contractor, and in favor of the other party. "Words should be taken most strongly against him who uses them." As, if tenant in fee simple grants to anyone an estate for life, generally, it shall be construed an estate for the life of the grantee. For the principle of self-preservation will make men sufficiently careful, not to prejudice their own interest by the too extensive meaning of their words: and thereby all manner of deceit in any grant is avoided; for men would always affect ambiguous and intricate expressions, provided they were afterwards at liberty to put their own construction upon them.

But here a distinction must be taken between an indenture and a deed poll: for the words of an indenture, executed by both parties, are to be considered as the words of them both; for, though delivered as the words of one party, yet they are not his words only, but the other party hath given his consent to every one of them. But in a deed poll, executed only by the grantor, they are the words of the grantor only, and shall be taken most strongly against him. In general, this rule being a rule of some strictness and rigor, is the last to be resorted to, and is never to be relied upon, but where all other rules of exposition fail.

⚖ VALIDITY PREFERRED — That, if the words will bear two senses, one agreeable to, and the other against, Law; that sense be preferred, which is most agreeable thereto. As if tenant in tail lets a lease for life generally, it shall be construed for his own life only, for that stands with the law; and not for the life of the lessee, which is beyond his power to grant.

⚖ WHERE CLAUSES REPUGNANT — That, in a deed, if there be two clauses so totally repugnant to each other, that they cannot stand together, the first shall be received and the latter rejected: wherein it differs from a will; for there, of two such repugnant clauses the latter shall stand. Which is owing to the different natures of the two instruments; for the first deed, and the last will are always most available in law. Yet in both cases we should rather attempt to reconcile them.

THE DEVISOR'S INTENTION TO BE ATTAINED — That a devise be most favorably expounded, to pursue, if possible, the will of the devisor, who for want of advice or learning may have omitted the legal or proper phrases. Therefore many times the law dispenses with the want of words in devises, that are absolutely requisite in all other instruments. Thus a fee may be conveyed without words of inheritance; and an estate-tail without words of procreation.

By a will, also, an estate may pass by mere implication, without any express words to direct its course. As, where A devises lands to his heir at law, after the death of his wife: here, though no estate is given to the wife in express terms, yet she shall have an estate for life by implication; for the intent of the testator is clearly to postpone the heir till after her death; and, if she does not take it, nobody else can. In general, where any implications are allowed, they must be such as are necessary (or at least highly probable) and not merely possible implication. Herein there is no distinction between the rules of law and of equity; for the will, being construed in both courts in the light of a limitation of uses, is construed in each with equal favor and benignity, and expounded rather on its own particular circumstances, than by any general rules of positive law.

RECAPITULATION OF SUBJECT OF COMMON ASSURANCES — Thus we have taken the transient view, in this and the three preceding chapters, of a very large and diffusive subject, the doctrine of common assurances: which concludes our observations on the title to things real, or the means by which they may be reciprocally lost and acquired.

We have before considered the estates which may be had in them, with regard to their duration or quantity of interest, the time of their enjoyment, and the number and connections of the persons entitled to hold them: we have examined the tenures, both ancient and modern, whereby those estates have been, and are now, holden: and have distinguished the object of all these inquiries, namely, things real, into the corporeal or substantial, and incorporeal or ideal kind; and have thus considered the rights of real property in every light wherein they are contemplated by the laws of England. A system of laws that differs much from every other system, except those of the same feudal origin, in its notions and regulations of landed estates; and which therefore could in this particular be very seldom compared with any other.

The subject, which has thus employed our attention, is of very extensive use, and of as extensive variety. Yet, I am afraid, it has offered the student less amusement and pleasure in the pursuit, than the matters discussed in the preceding volume. To say the truth, the vast alterations which the doctrine of real property has undergone from the Conquest to the present time; the infinite determinations upon points that continually arise, and which have been heaped one upon another for a course of seven centuries, without any order or method; and the multiplicity of acts of parliament which have amended, or sometimes only altered the common law: these causes have made the study of this branch of our national jurisprudence a little perplexed and intricate. It hath been my endeavor principally to select such parts of it, as were of the most general use, where the principles were the most simple, the reasons of them the most obvious, and the practice the least embarrassed.

Yet I cannot presume that I have always been thoroughly intelligible to such of my readers, as were before strangers even to the very terms of art, which I have been obliged to make use of: though, whenever those have first ocurred, I have generally attempted a short explication of their meaning. Therefore I shall close this branch of our inquiries with the words of Sir Edward Coke: "Albeit the student shall not at any one day, do what he can, reach to the full meaning of all that is here laid down, yet let him no way discourage himself but proceed; for on some other day, in some other place" (or perhaps upon a second perusal of the same), "his doubts will be probably removed."

THINGS PERSONAL

✪   THINGS PERSONAL — Under the name of things personal are included all sorts of things movable, which may attend a man's person wherever he goes; and therefore, being only the objects of the law while they remain within the limits of its jurisdiction, and being also of a perishable quality, are not esteemed of so high a nature, nor paid so much regard to by the law, as things that are in their nature more permanent and immovable, as lands, and houses, and the profits issuing thereout. These being constantly within the reach, and under the protection of the law, were the principal favorites of our first legislators: who took all imaginable care in ascertaining the rights, and directing the disposition, of such property as they imagined to be lasting, and which would answer to posterity the trouble and pains that their ancestors employed about them; but at the same time entertained a very low and contemptuous opinion of all personal estate, which they regarded only as a transient commodity.

The amount of it indeed was, comparatively, very trifling, during the scarcity of money and the ignorance of luxurious refinements, which prevailed in the feudal ages. Hence it was, that a tax of the fifteenth, tenth, or sometimes a much larger proportion, of all the movables of the subject, was frequently laid without scruple, and is mentioned with much unconcern by our ancient historians, though now it would justly alarm our opulent merchants and stockholders. Hence likewise may be derived the frequent forfeitures inflicted by the common law, of all a man's goods and chattels, for misbehaviors and inadvertencies that at present hardly seem to deserve so severe a punishment. Our ancient law books, which are founded upon the feudal provisions, do not, therefore, often condescend to regulate this species of property.

✪   MODERN IMPORTANCE OF THINGS PERSONAL — But of later years, since the introduction and extension of trade and commerce, which are entirely occupied in this species of property, and have greatly augmented its quantity and of course its value, we have learned to conceive different ideas of it. Our courts now regard a man's personality in a light nearly, if not quite, equal to his realty: and have adopted a more enlarged and less technical mode of considering the one than the other; frequently drawn from the rules which they found already established by the Roman Law, wherever those rules appeared to be well-grounded and opposite to the case in question, but principally from reason and convenience, adopted to the circumstances of the times; preserving with a due regard to ancient usages, and a certain feudal tincture, which is still to be found in some branches of personal property.

⚖ MEANING OF THINGS PERSONAL, OR CHATTELS — But things personal, by our law, do not only include things movable, but also something more: the whole of which is comprehended under the general name of chattels, which Sir Edward Coke says is a French word, signifying goods. The appellation is in truth derived from the technical Latin word "catalla"; which primarily signified only beasts of husbandry, or (as we still call them) cattle, but in its secondary sense was applied to all movables in general.

In the grand coustumier of Normandy a chattel is described as a mere movable, but at the same time it is set in opposition to a fief or feud: so that not only goods, but whatever was not a feud, were accounted chattels. It is in this latter, more extended, negative sense, that our law adopts it: the idea of goods, or movables only, being not sufficiently comprehensive to take in everything that the law considers as a chattel interest. For since, as the commentator on the coustumier observes, there are two requisites to make a fief or heritage, duration as to time, and immobility with regard to place; whatever wants either of these qualities is not, according to the Normans, an heritage or fief; or, according to us, is not a real estate: the consequence of which in both laws is, that it must be a personal estate, or chattel.

Chattels, therefore, are distributed by law into two kinds: chattels real, and chattels personal.

⚖ CHATTELS REAL — Chattels real, saith Sir Edward Coke, are such as concern, or savor of, the realty; as terms for years of land, wardships in chivalry (while the military tenures subsisted) the next presentation to a church, estates by statute-merchant, statute-staple, elegit, or the like; of all which we have already spoken. These are called real chattels, as being interests issuing out of, or annexed to, real estate: of which they have one quality, viz., immobility, which denominates them real; but want the other, viz., a sufficient, legal, indeterminate duration: and this want it is that constitutes then chattels. The utmost period for which they can last is fixed and determinate, either for such a space of time certain, or till such a particular sum of money be raised out of such a particular income; so that they are not equal in the eye of the law to the lowest estate of freehold, a lease for another's life: their tenants were considered upon feudal principles, as merely bailiffs or farmers; and the tenant of the freehold might at any time have destroyed their interest, till the reign of Henry VIII.

A freehold, which alone is a real estate, and seems (as has been said) to answer to the fief in Normandy, is conveyed by corporal investiture and livery of seisin; which gives the tenant so strong a hold of the land, that it never after can be wrested from him during his life, but by his own act, of voluntary transfer or of forfeiture; or else by the happening of some future contingency, as in estates pur auter vie, and the determinable freeholds mentioned in a former chapter. Even these, being of an uncertain duration, may by possibility last for the owner's life; for the law will not presuppose the contingency to happen before it actually does, and till then the estate is to all intents and purposes a life estate, and therefore a freehold, interest. On the other hand, a chattel interest in lands, which the Normans put in opposition to fief, and we to freehold, is conveyed by no seisin or corporal investiture, but the possession is gained by the mere entry of the tenant himself; and it will certainly expire at a time prefixed and determined, if not sooner.

Thus a lease for years must necessarily fail at the end and completion of the term; the next presentation to a church is satisfied and gone the instant it comes into possession, that is, by the first avoidance and presentation to the living; the conditional estates by statutes and elegit are determined as soon as the debt is paid; and so guardianships in chivalry expired, of course, the moment that the heir came of age. If there be any other chattel real, it will be found to correspond with the rest in this essential quality, that its duration is limited to a time certain, beyond which it cannot subsist.

⚜ CHATTELS PERSONAL — Chattels personal are, properly and strictly speaking, things movable; which may be annexed to or attendant on the person of the owner, and carried about with him from one part of the world to another. Such are animals, household stuff, money, jewels, corn, garments, and everything else that can properly be put in motion, and transferred from place to place. Of this kind of chattels it is that we are principally to speak in the remainder of this book; having been unavoidably led to consider the nature of chattels real, and their incidents, in the former chapters which were employed upon real estates: that kind of property being of a mongrel amphibious nature, originally endowed with one of the characteristics of each species of things; the immobility of things real, and the precarious duration of things personal.

Chattel interests being thus distinguished and distributed, it will be proper to consider, first, the nature of that property, or dominion, to which they are liable; which must be principally, nay solely, referred to personal chattels: and, secondly, the title to that property, or how it may be lost and acquired. Of each of these in its order.

PROPERTY IN THINGS PERSONAL

☙ PROPERTY IN POSSESSION — Property, in chattels personal, may be
either in possession; which is where a man hath not only the right
to enjoy, but hath the actual enjoyment of, the thing: or else it is in action; where a man hath only a bare right, without any occupation or enjoyment. Of these the former, or property in possession, is divided into
two sorts: an absolute and a qualified property.

☙ ABSOLUTE PROPERTY — First, then, of property in possession absolute;
which is where a man hath, solely and exclusively, the right, and also
the occupation of any movable chattels; so that they cannot be transferred from him, or cease to be his, without his own act or default.
Such may be all inanimate things, as goods, plate, money, jewels, implements of war, garments, and the like: such, also, may be all vegetable
productions, as the fruit or other parts of a plant, when severed from the
body of it; or the whole plant itself when severed from the ground; none
of which can be moved out of the owner's possession without his own act
or consent, or at least without doing him an injury, which it is the business of the law to prevent or remedy. Of these, therefore, there remains little to be said.

☙ PROPERTY IN ANIMALS — But with regard to animals, which have in
themselves a principle and power of motion, and (unless particularly
confined) can convey themselves from one part of the world to another,
there is a great difference made with respect to their several classes, not
only in our law, but in the law of nature and of all civilized nations.

☙ TAME ANIMALS — They are distinguished into such as are domitae,
and such as are ferae naturae: some being of a tame and others of a
wild disposition. In such as are of a nature tame and domestic (as horses,
kine, sheep, poultry, and the like), a man may have as absolute a property as in any inanimate beings; because these continue perpetually in
his occupation, and will not stray from his house or person, unless by

accident or fraudulent enticement, in either of which cases the owner does not lose his property. The stealing, or forcible abduction, of such property as this, is also felony; for these are things of intrinsic value, serving for the food of man, or else for the use of husbandry. But in animals ferae naturae a man can have no absolute property.

Of all tame and domestic animals, the brood belongs to the owner of the dam or mother; the English law agreeing with the civil, that "the offspring follows the condition of the mother" in the brute creation, though for the most part in the human species it disallows that maxim. Therefore in the laws of England, as well as Rome, "if my mare be with foal by your horse, the offspring is not yours but mine." For this, a sensible reason: not only because the male is frequently unknown; but also because the dam, during the time of her pregnancy, is almost useless to the proprietor, and must be maintained with greater expense and care: wherefore, as her owner is the loser by her pregnancy, he ought to be the gainer by her brood. An exception to this rule is in case of young cygnets; which belong equally to the owner of the cock and hen, and shall be divided between them. But here the reasons of the general rule cease, and "the reason ceasing, the law itself ceases": for the male is well known, by his constant association with the female; and for the same reason the owner of the one doth not suffer more disadvantage, during the time of pregnancy and nurture, than the owner of the other.

QUALIFIED PROPERTY — Other animals, that are not of a tame and domestic nature, are either not the objects of property at all, or else fall under our other division, namely, that of qualified, limited, or special property: which is such as is not in its nature permanent, but may sometimes subsist, and at other times not subsist. In discussing which subject I shall, in the first place, show how this species of property may subsist in such animals as are ferae naturae, or of a wild nature; and then, how it may subsist in any other things, when under particular circumstances.

PROPERTY IN WILD ANIMALS — First, then, a man may be invested with a qualified, but not an absolute, property, in all creatures that are ferae naturae, either per industriam, propter impotentian, or propter privilegium (by the industry of man, on account of the inability of the animal, or by reason of privilege).

PROPERTY IN WILD ANIMALS PER INDUSTRIAM — A qualified property may subsist in animals ferae naturae, per industriam hominis (by the industry of man): by a man's reclaiming and making them tame by art, industry, and education; or by so confining them within his own immediate power, that they cannot escape and use their natural liberty. Under this head some writers have ranked all the former species of animals we have mentioned, apprehending none to be originally and naturally tame, but only made so by art and custom: as horses, swine, and other cattle; which if originally left to themselves, would have chosen to rove up and down, seeking food at large, and are made domestic only by use and familiarity; and are therefore tame, as accustomed to the hand.

But however well this notion may be founded, abstractedly considered, our law apprehends the most obvious distinction to be, between such animals as we generally see tame, and are therefore seldom, if ever, found wandering at large, which it calls domitae naturae; and such creatures as are usually found at liberty, which are therefore supposed to be more emphatically ferae naturae, though it may happen that the latter shall be sometimes tamed and confined by the art and industry of man. Such as are deer in a park, hares or rabbits in an inclosed warren, doves in a dovehouse, pheasants or partridges in a mew, hawks that are fed and commanded by their owner, and fish in a private pond or in trunks. These are no longer the property of a man, than while they continue in his keeping or actual possession: But if at any time they regain their natural liberty, his property instantly ceases; unless they have aninum revertendi (the intention of returning), which is only to be known by their usual custom of returning.

The law therefore extends this possession further than the mere manual occupation; for my tame hawk that is pursuing his quarry in my presence, though he is at liberty to go where he pleases, is nevertheless my property; for he hath animum revertendi. So are my pigeons, that are flying at a distance from their home (especially of the carrier kind), and likewise the deer that is chased out of my park or forest, and is instantly pursued by the keeper or forester: all which remain still in my possession, and I still preserve my qualified property in them. But if they stray without my knowledge, and do not return in the usual manner, it is then lawful for any stranger to take them.

But if a deer, or any wild animal reclaimed, hath a collar or other mark put upon him, and goes and returns at his pleasure; or if a wild swan is taken, and marked and turned loose in the river, the owner's property in him still continues, and it is not lawful for anyone else to take him: but otherwise, if the deer has been long absent without returning, or the swan leaves the neighborhood. Bees also are ferae naturae; but, when hived and reclaimed, a man may have a qualified property in them, by the law of nature, as well as by the civil law. To the same purpose not to say in the same words, with the civil law, speaks Bracton: occupation, that is, having or including them, gives the property in bees; for, though a swarm lights upon my tree, I have no more property in them till I have hived them, than I have in the birds which make their nest thereon; and therefore if another hives them, he shall be their proprietor: but a swarm, which fly from and out of my hive, are mine as long as I can keep them in sight, and have power to pursue them; and in these circumstances no one else is entitled to take them. But it hath been also said, that with us the only ownership in bees is ratione soli (on account of the soil); and the charter of the forest, which allows every freeman to be entitled to the honey found within his own woods, affords great countenance to this doctrine, that a qualified property may be had in bees, in consideration of the property of the soil whereon they are found.

But while they thus continue my qualified or defeasible property, they are as much under the protection of the law, as if they were absolutely and indefeasibly mine: and an action will lie against any man that detains them from me, or unlawfully destroys them. It is also as much felony by common law to steal such of them as are fit for food, as it is to steal tame animals: but not so, if they are only kept for pleasure, curiosity, or whim, as dogs, bears, cats, apes, parrots, and singing birds; because their value is not intrinsic, but depending only on the caprice of the owner: though it is such an invasion of property as may amount to a civil injury, and be redressed by a civil action.

Yet to steal a reclaimed hawk is felony both by common law and statute; which seems to be a relic of the tyranny of our ancient sportsmen. Among our elder ancestors, the ancient Britons, another species of reclaimed animals, viz., cats, were looked upon as creatures of intrinsic value; and the killing or stealing of one was a grievous crime, and subjected the offender to a fine; especially if it belonged to the king's household.

⚖ PROPERTY IN WILD ANIMALS PROPTER IMPOTENTIAM — A qualified property may also subsist with relation to animals ferae naturae, ratione, impotentiae, on account of their own inability. As when hawks, herons, or other birds build in my trees, or conies or other creatures make their nests or burrows in my land, and have young ones there; I have a qualified property in those young ones till such time as they can fly or run away, and then my property expires: but, till then, it is in some cases trespass, and in others, felony, for a stranger to take them away. For here, as the owner of the land has it in his power to do what he pleases with them, the law therefore vests a property in him of the young ones, in the same manner as it does of the old ones if reclaimed and confined: for these cannot through weakness, any more than the others through restraint, use their natural liberty and forsake him.

⚖ PROPERTY IN WILD ANIMALS PROPTER PRIVILEGIUM — A man may, lastly, have a qualified property in animals ferae naturae, propter privilegium: that is, he may have the privilege of hunting, taking, and killing them, in exclusion of other persons. Here he has a transient property in these animals, usually called game, so long as they continue within his liberty; and may restrain any stranger from taking them therein: but the instant they depart into another liberty, this qualified property ceases. The manner in which this privilege is acquired will be shown in a subsequent chapter.

⚖ PROPERTY IN AIR, LIGHT, AND WATER — Many other things may also be the objects of qualified property. It may subsist in the very elements, of fire or light, of air, and of water. A man can have no absolute permanent property in these, as he may in the earth and land; since these are of a vague and fugitive nature, and therefore can admit only of a precarious and qualified ownership, which lasts so long as they are in actual use and occupation, but no longer.

If a man disturbs another, and deprives him of the lawful enjoyment of these; if one obstructs another's ancient windows, corrupts the air of his house or gardens, fouls his water, or unpens and lets it out, or if he diverts an ancient watercourse that used to run to the other's mill or meadow; the law will animadvert hereon as an injury, and protect the party injured in his possession. But the property in them ceases the instant they are out of possession: for, then no man is engaged in their actual occupation, they become again common, and every man has an equal right to appropriate them to his own use.

⚖ QUALIFIED PROPERTY ARISING FROM CIRCUMSTANCES — These kinds of qualification in property depend upon the peculiar circumstances of the subject matter, which is not capable of being under the absolute dominion of any proprietor. But property may also be of a qualified or special nature, on account of the peculiar circumstances of the owner, when the thing itself is very capable of absolute ownership. As in the case of bailment, or delivery, of goods to another person for a particular use; as to a carrier to convey to London, to an innkeeper to secure in his inn, or the like. Here there is no absolute property in either the bailor or the bailee, the person delivering, or him to whom it is delivered: for the bailor hath only the right, and not the immediate possession, the bailee hath the possession, and only a temporary right. But it is a qualified property in them both; and each of them is entitled to an action, in case the goods be damaged or taken away: the bailee on account of his immediate possession; the bailor, because the possession of the bailee is, mediately, his possession also.

So, also, in case of goods pledged or pawned upon condition, either to repay money or otherwise; both the pledgor and the pledgee have a qualified, but neither of them an absolute, property therein: the pledgor's property is conditional, and depends upon the performance of the condition of repayment, etc.; and so, too, is that of the pledgee, which depends upon its nonperformance. The same may be said of goods distrained for rent, or other case of distress: which are in the nature of a pledge, and are not, at the first taking, the absolute property of either the distrainor or party distrained; but may be redeemed, or else forfeited, by the subsequent conduct of the latter.

But a servant, who hath the care of his master's goods or chattels, as a butler of plate, a shepherd of sheep, and the like, hath not any property or possession either absolute or qualified, but only a mere charge or oversight.

⚖ PROPERTY IN ACTION: CHOSES IN ACTION — We will proceed next to take a short view of the nature of property in action, or such where a man hath not the occupation, but merely a bare right to occupy the thing in question; the possession whereof may, however, be recovered by suit or action at law: from whence the thing so recoverable is called a thing, or chose, in action. Thus money due on a bond is a chose in action; for a property in the debts vests at the time of forfeiture mentioned in the obligation, but there is no possession till recovered by course of law. If a man promises, or covenants with me, to do any act, and fails in it, whereby I suffer damage, the recompense for this damage is a chose in action: for though a right to some recompense vests in me, at the time of the damage done, yet what and how large such recompense shall be, can only be ascertained by verdict; and the possession can only be given me by legal judgment and execution.

In the former of these cases the student will observe that the property, or right of action, depends upon an express contract or obligation to pay a stated sum: and in the latter it depends upon an implied contract, that if the covenantor does not perform the act he engaged to do, he shall pay me the damages I sustain by this breach of covenant. Hence it may be collected, that all property in action depends entirely upon contracts, either express or implied; which are the only regular means of acquiring a chose in action, and of the nature of which we shall discourse at large in a subsequent chapter.

At present we have only to remark, that upon all contracts or promises, either express or implied, and the infinite variety of cases into which they are and may be spun out, the law gives an action of some sort or other to the party injured in case of nonperformance; to compel the wrongdoer to do justice to the party with whom he has contracted, and, on failure of performing the identical thing he engaged to do, to render a satisfaction equivalent to the damage sustained. But while the thing, or its equivalent, remains in suspense, and the injured party has only the right and not the occupation, it is called a chose in action; being a thing rather in potentia (in possibility) than in esse (in being): though the owner may have an absolute property in, and be as well entitled to, such things in action, as to things in possession.

TIME OF ENJOYMENT OF PERSONAL PROPERTY — Having thus distinguished the different degree or quantity of dominion of property to which things personal are subject, we may add a word or two concerning the time of their enjoyment, and the number of their owners.

First, as to the time of enjoyment. By the rules of the ancient common law, there could be no future property, to take place in expectancy, created in personal goods and chattels; because, being things transitory, and by many accidents subject to be lost, destroyed, or otherwise impaired, and the exigencies of trade requiring also a frequent circulation thereof, it would occasion perpetual suits and quarrels, and put a stop to the freedom of commerce, if such limitations in remainder were generally tolerated and allowed. But yet in last wills and testaments such limitations of personal goods and chattels, in remainder after a bequest for life, were permitted: though originally that indulgence was only shown, when merely the use of the goods, and not the goods themselves, was given to the first legatee; the property being supposed to continue all the time in the executor of the devisor. But now that distinction is disregarded: and therefore if a man either by deed or will limits his books or furniture to A for life, with remainder over to B, this remainder is good. But where an estate-tail in things personal is given to the first or any subsequent possessor, it vests in him the total property, and no remainder over shall be permitted on such a limitation. For this, if allowed, would tend to a perpetuity, as the devisee or grantee in tail of a chattel has no method of barring the entail: and therefore the law vests in him at once the entire dominion of the goods, being analogous to the fee simple which a tenant in tail may acquire in a real estate.

⚖ NUMBER OF OWNERS OF PERSONAL PROPERTY — Next, as to the number of owners. Things personal may belong to their owners, not only in severalty, but also in joint tenancy, and in common, as well as real estates. They cannot, indeed, be bested incoparcenary; because they do not descend from the ancestor to the heir, which is necessary to constitute coparceners. But if a horse, or other personal chattel, be given to two or more, absolutely, they are joint tenants hereof; and, unless the jointure be severed, the same doctrine of survivorship shall take place as in estates of lands and tenements.

In like manner, if the jointure be severed, as by either of them selling his share, the vendee and the remaining part owner shall be tenants in common, without any survivorship. So, also if 100 pounds be given by will to two or more, equally to be divided between them, this makes them tenants in common; as we have formerly seen, the same words would have done, in regard to real estates. But, for the encouragement of husbandry and trade, it is held that a stock on a farm, though occupied jointly, and also a stock used in a joint undertaking, by way of partnership in trade, shall always be considered as common and not as joint property; and there shall be no survivorship therein.

TITLE TO THINGS PERSONAL BY OCCUPANCY

THE MODES OF ACQUIRING THINGS PERSONAL — We are next to consider the title to things personal, or the various means of acquiring, and of losing, such property as may be had therein: both which considerations of gain and loss shall be blended together in one and the same view, as was done in our observations upon real property; since it is for the most part impossible to contemplate the one, without contemplating the other also. These methods of acquisition or loss are principally twelve: 1. By occupancy. 2. By prerogative. 3. By forfeiture. 4. By Custom. 5. By succession. 6. By marriage. 7. By judgment. 8. By Gift, or Grant. 9. By contract. 10. By Bankruptcy. 11. By Testament. 12. By administration.

TITLE BY OCCUPANCY — First, a property in goods and chattels may be acquired by occupancy: which, we have more than once remarked, was the original and only primitive method of acquiring any property at all; but which has since been restrained and abridged, by the positive laws of society, in order to maintain peace and harmony among mankind. For this purpose, by the laws of England, gifts, and contracts, testaments, legacies, and administrations have been introduced and countenanced, in order to transfer and continue that property and possession in things personal, which has once been acquired by the owner. Where such things are found without any other owner, they for the most part belong to the king by virtue of his prerogative; except in some few instances, wherein the original and natural right of occupancy is still permitted to subsist, and which we are now to consider.

GOODS OF ALIEN ENEMY — Thus, in the first place, it hath been said, that anybody may seize to his own use such goods as belong to an alien enemy. For such enemies, not being looked upon as members of our society, are not entitled during their state of enmity to the benefit or protection of the laws; and therefore every man that has opportunity is permitted to seize upon their chattels, without being compelled as in other cases to make restitution or satisfaction to the owner. But this, however generally laid down by some of our writers, must in reason and justice be restrained to such captors as are authorized by the public authority of the state, residing in the crown; and to such goods as are brought into this country by an alien enemy, after a declaration of war, without a safe-conduct or passport. Therefore where a foreigner is resident in England, and afterwards a war breaks out between his country and ours, his goods are not liable to be seized.

It hath also been adjudged, that if an enemy take the goods of an Englishman, which are afterwards retaken by another subject of this kingdom, the former owner shall lose his property therein, and it shall be indefeasibly vested in the second taker; unless they were retaken the same day, and the owner before sunset puts in his claim of property. Which is agreeable to the law of nations, as understood in the time of Grotius, even with regard to captures made at sea, which were held to be the property of the captors after a possession of twenty-four hours; though the modern authorities require that before the property can be changed, the goods must have been brought into port, and have continued a night in a place of safe custody, so that all hope of recovering them was lost.

As in the goods of an enemy, so also in his person, a man may acquire a sort of qualified property, by taking him a prisoner in war; at least till his ransom be paid. This doctrine seems to have been extended to Negro servants, who are purchased, when captives, of the nations with whom they are at war, and are therefore supposed to continue in some degree the property of their masters who buy them: though, accurately speaking, that property (if it indeed continues) consists rather in the perpetual service, than in the body or person of the captive.

TREASURE-TROVE — Thus again, whatever movables are found upon the surface of the earth, or in the sea, and are unclaimed by any owner, are supposed to be abandoned by the last proprietor; and, as such, are returned into the common stock and mass of things: and therefore they belong, as in a state of nature, to the first occupant or fortunate finder, unless they fall within the description of waifs, or estrays, or wreck, or hidden treasure; for these, we have formerly seen, are vested by law in the king, and form a part of the ordinary revenue of the crown.

⚖️ LIGHT, AIR, AND WATER — Thus, too, the benefit of the elements, the
      light, the air, and the water can only be appropriated by occupancy.
If I have an ancient window overlooking my neighbor's ground, he may
not erect any blind to obstruct the light: but if I build my house close to
his wall, which darkens it, I cannot compel him to demolish his wall; for
there the first occupancy is rather in him, than in me. If my neighbor
makes a tanyard, so as to annoy and render less salubrious the air of
my house or gardens, the law will furnish me with a remedy; but if
he is first in possession of the air, and I fix my habitation hear him, the
nuisance is my own seeking, and may continue. If a stream be unoc-
cupied, I may erect a mill thereon, and detain the water; yet not so
as to injure my neighbor's prior mill, or his meadow; for he hath by
the first occupancy acquired a property in the current.

⚖️ WILD ANIMALS — With regard likewise to animals ferae naturae, all
      mankind had by the original grant of the Creator a right to pursue and
take any fowl or insect of the air, any fish or inhabitant of the waters,
and any beast or reptile of the field: and this natural right still continues
in every individual, unless where it is restrained by the civil laws of the
country. When a man has once so seized them, they become while living
his qualified property, or, if dead, are absolutely his own: so that to
steal them, or otherwise invade this property, is, according to their respective values, sometimes a criminal offense, sometimes only a civil injury.

   The restrictions which are laid upon this right, by the laws of England, relate principally to royal fish, as whale and sturgeon, and such
terrestrial, aerial, or aquatic animals as go under the denomination of
game; the taking of which is made the exclusive right of the prince,
and such of his subjects to whom he has granted the same royal privilege.
But those animals, which are not expressly so reserved, are still liable
to be taken and appropriated by any of the king's subjects, upon their own
territories; in the same manner as they might have taken even game
itself, till these civil prohibitions were issued: there being in nature no
distinctions between one species of wild animals and another, between
the right of acquiring property in a hare or a squirrel, in a partridge or
a butterfly: but the difference, at present made, arises merely from the
positive municipal law.

⚖️ EMBLEMENTS — To this principle of occupancy also must be referred
      the method of acquiring a special personal property in corn growing
on the ground, or other emblements, by any possessor of the land who
hath sown or planted it, whether he be owner of the inheritance in fee

or in tail, or be tenant for life, for years, or at will: which emblements are distinct from the real estate in the land, and subject to many, though not all, the incidents attending personal chattels. They were devisable by testament before the statute of wills, and at the death of the owner shall vest in his executor and not his heir; they are forfeitable by outlawry in a personal action: and by (Distress for Rent, 1737), though not by the common law, they may be distrained for rent arrear. The reason for admitting the acquisition of this special property, by tenants who have temporary interest, was formerly given; and it was extended to tenants in fee, principally for the benefit of their creditors: and therefore, though the emblements are assets in the hands of the executor, are forfeitable upon outlawry, and distrainable for rent, they are not in other respects considered as personal chattels; and particularly they are not the object of larceny, before they are severed from the ground.

ACCESSION — The doctrine of property arising from accession is also grounded on the right of occupancy. By the Roman law, if any given corporeal substance received afterwards an accession by natural or by artificial means, as by the growth of vegetables, the pregnancy of animals, the embroidering of cloth, or the conversion of wood or metal into vessels and utensils, the original owner of the thing was entitled by his right of possession to the property of it under such its state of improvement: but if the thing itself, by such operation, was changed into a different species, as by making wine, oil, or bread, out of another's grapes, olives, or wheat, it belonged to the new operator; who was only to make a satisfaction to the former proprietor for the materials, which he had so converted.

It hath even been held, that if one takes away another's wife or son, and clothes them, and afterwards the husband or father retakes them back, the garments shall cease to be the property of him who provided them, being now annexed to the person of the child or woman.

CONFUSION — But in the case of confusion of goods, where those of two persons are so intermixed, that the several portions can be no longer distinguished, the English law partly agrees with, and partly differs from, the civil. If the intermixture be by consent, I apprehend that in both laws the proprietors have an interest in common, in proportion to their respective shares. But, if one willfully intermixes his money, corn, or hay, with that of another man, without his approbation or knowledge, or casts gold in like manner into another's melting pot or crucible, the civil law, though it gives the sole property of the whole to him who has not interfered in the mixture, yet allows a satisfaction to the other for what he has so improvidently lost. But our law, to guard against fraud, allows no remedy in such a case; but gives the entire property, without any account, to him, whose original dominion is invaded, and endeavored to be rendered uncertain, without his own consent.

COPYRIGHT — There is still another species of property, which (if it subsists) being grounded on labor and invention, is more properly reducible to the head of occupancy than any other; since the right of occupancy itself is supposed by Mr. Locke, and many others, to be founded on the personal labor of the occupant. This is the right, which an author may be supposed to have in his own original literary compositions: so that no other person without his leave may publish or make profit of the copies.

When a man by the exertion of his rational powers has produced an original work, he has clearly a right to dispose of that identical work as he pleases, and any attempt to take it from him, or vary the disposition he has made of it, is an invasion of his right of property. Now, the identity of a literary composition consists entirely in the sentiment and the language; the same conceptions, clothed in the same words, must necessarily be the same composition: and whatever method be taken of conveying that composition to the ear or the eye of another, by recital, by writing, or by printing, in any number of copies or at any period of time, it is always the identical work of the author which is so conveyed; and no other man (it hath been thought) can have a right to convey or transfer it without his consent, either tacitly or expressly given. This consent may perhaps be tacitly given, when an author permits his work to be published, without any reserve of right, and without stamping on it any marks of ownership: it is then a present to the public, like the building of a church, or the laying out of a new highway: but, in case of a bargain for a single impresson, or a total sale or gift of the copyright, in the one case the reversion hath been supposed to continue in the original proprietor; in the other the whole property, with all its exclusive rights, to be perpetually transferred to the grantee.

On the other hand, it is urged, that though the exclusive property of the manuscript, and all which it contains, undoubtedly belongs to the author, before it is printed or published; yet from the instant of publication, the exclusive right of an author or his assigns to the sole communication of his ideas immediately vanishes and evaporates; as being a right of too subtile and unsubstantial a nature to become the subject of property at the common law, and only capable of being guarded by positive statutes and special provisions of the magistrate.

The Roman law adjudged, that if one man wrote anything, though never so elegantly, on the paper or parchment of another, the writing should belong to the original owner of the materials on which it was written: meaning certainly nothing more thereby than the mere mechanical operation of writing, for which it directed the scribe to receive a satisfaction; especially as in works of genius and invention, such as a picture painted on another man's canvas, the same law gave the canvas to the painter.

We find no other mention in the civil law of any property in the works of the understanding, though the sale of literary copies, for the purposes of recital or multiplication, is certainly as ancient as the times of Terence, Martial, and Statius. Neither with us in England hath there been (till very lately) any final determination upon the right of authors at the common law.

But whatever inherent copyright might have been supposed to subsist by the common law, the statute (Copyright, 1709) (amended by statute Copyright, 1774), hath now declared that the author and his assigns shall have the sole liberty of printing and reprinting his works for the term of fourteen years, and no longer; and hath also protected that property by additional penalties and forfeitures: directing, further, that if, at the end of that term, the author himself be living, the right shall then return to him for another term of the same duration: and a similar privilege is extended to the inventors of prints and engravings, for the term of eight and twenty years, by the statutes. All which parliamentary protections appear to have been suggested by the exception in the statute of monopolies (1623), which allows a royal patent of privilege to be granted for fourteen years to any inventor of a new manufacture, for the sole working or making of the same; by virtue whereof it is held that a temporary property therein becomes vested in the king's patentee.

TITLE BY PREROGATIVE, AND FORFEITURE

🙖 TITLE BY PREROGATIVE — A second method of acquiring property in personal chattels is by the king's prerogative: whereby a right may accrue either to the crown itself, or to such as claim under the title of the crown, as by grant or by prescription.

🙖 TAXES AND CUSTOMS — Such, in the first place, are all tributes, taxes, and customs; whether constitutionally inherent in the crown, as flowers of the prerogative and branches of the ancient royal revenue, or whether they be occasionally created by authority of parliament.

In these the king acquires and the subject loses a property the instant they become due: if paid, they are a chose in possession; if unpaid, a chose in action. Hither also may be referred all forfeitures, fines, and amercements due to the king, which accrue by virtue of his ancient prerogative, or by particular modern statutes: which revenues created by statute do always assimilate, or take the same nature, with the ancient revenues; and may therefore be looked upon as arising from a kind of artificial or secondary prerogative. In either case, the owner of the thing forfeited, and the person fined or amerced, lose and part with the property of the forfeiture, fine, or amercement, the instant the king or his grantee acquires it.

🙖 KING CANNOT BE JOINT OWNER — In these several methods of acquiring property by prerogative there is also this peculiar quality, that the king cannot have a joint property with any person in one entire chattel, or such a one as is not capable of division or separation; but where the titles of the king and a subject concur, the king shall have the whole: in like manner as the king can, neither by grant nor contract, become a joint tenant of a chattel real with another person; but by such grant or contract shall become entitled to the whole in severalty.

Thus, if a horse be given to the king and a private person, the king shall have the sole property: if a bond be made to the king and a subject, the king shall have the whole penalty; the debt or duty being one single chattel; and, so if two persons have the property of a horse between them, or have a joint debt owing them on bond, and one of them assigns his part to the king, or is attainted, whereby his moiety is forfeited to the crown; the king shall have the entire horse, and entire debt. For, as it is not consistent with the dignity of the crown to be partner with a subject, so neither does the king ever lose his right in any instance; but, where they interfere, he is always preferred to that of another person: from which two principles it is a necessary consequence, that the innocent, though unfortunate, partner must lose his share in both the debt and the horse, or in any other chattel in the same circumstances.

KING'S SPECIAL PROPERTY — This doctrine has no opportunity to take place in certain other instances of title by prerogative, that remain to be mentioned: as the chattels thereby vested are originally and solely vested in the crown, without any transfer or derivative assignment either by deed or law from any former proprietor. Such is the acquisition of property in wreck, in treasure-trove, in waifs, in estrays, in royal fish, in swans and the like; which are not transferred to the sovereign from any former owner, but are originally inherent in him by the rules of law, and are derived to particular subjects, as royal franchises, by his bounty. These are ascribed to him, partly upon the particular reasons mentioned in the former book; and partly upon the general principle of their being bona vacantia (goods having no claimant), and therefore vested in the king, as well to preserve the peace of the public, as in trust to employ them for the safety and ornament of the commonwealth.

PREROGATIVE COPYRIGHT — There is also a kind of prerogative copyright subsisting in certain books, which is held to be vested in the crown upon different reasons. Thus   1. The king, as the executive magistrate, has the right of promulging to the people all acts of state and government. This gives him the exclusive privilege of printing, at his own press, or that of his grantees, all acts of parliament, proclamations, and orders of council.   2. As supreme head of the church, he hath a right to the publication of all liturgies and books of divine service.   3. He is also said to have a right by purchase to the copies of such law books, grammars, and other compositions, as were compiled or translated at the expense of the crown.

Upon these two last principles, combined, the exclusive right of printing the translation of the Bible is founded.

ꙮ   PROPERTY IN GAME — There still remains another species of prerogative property, founded upon a very different principle from any that have been mentioned before; the property of such animals ferae naturae, as are known by the denomination of game, with the right of pursuing, taking, and destroying them: which is vested in the king alone, and from him derived to such of his subjects as have received the grants of a chase, a park, a free-warren, or free fishery. This may lead us into an inquiry concerning the original of these franchises, or royalties, on which we touched a little in a former chapter; the right itself being an incorporeal hereditament, though the fruits and profits of it are of a personal nature.

In the first place, then, we have already shown, and indeed it cannot be denied, that by the law of nature every man from the prince to the peasant has an equal right of pursuing, and taking to his own use, all such creatures as are ferae naturae, and therefore the property of nobody, but liable to be seized by the first occupant. So it was held by the imperial law, even so late as Justinian's time: "Therefore, wild beasts and birds, and all animals which are produced in air, sea, or earth, when taken by anyone, immediately become his property by the law of nations. For that which belongs to none, belongs by natural reason to the taker." But it follows from the very end and constitution of society, that this natural right, as well as many others belonging to man as an individual, may be restrained by positive laws enacted for reasons of state, or for the supposed benefit of the community.

This restriction may be either with respect to the place in which this right may, or may not, be exercised; with respect to the animals that are the subject of this right; or with respect to the persons allowed or forbidden to exercise it. In consequence of this authority, we find that the municipal laws of many nations have exerted such power of restraint; have in general forbidden the entering on another man's grounds, for any cause without the owner's leave; have extended their protection to such particular animals as are usually the objects of pursuit; and have invested the prerogative of hunting and taking such animals in the sovereign of the state only, and such as he shall authorize.

Many reasons have concurred for making these constitutions: as, 1. For the encouragement of agriculture and improvement of lands, by giving every man an exclusive dominion over his own soil. 2. For preservation of the several species of these animals, which would soon be extirpated by a general liberty. 3. For prevention of idleness and dissipation in husbandmen, artificers, and others of lower rank; which would be the unavoidable consequence of universal license. 4. For prevention of popular insurrections and resistance to the government, by disarming the bulk of the people: which last is a reason oftener meant, than avowed, by the makers of forest or game laws. Nor, certainly, in these prohibitions is there any natural injustice, as some have weakly enough supposed: since, as Puffendorf observes, the law does not hereby take from any man his present property, or what was already his own, but barely abridges him of one means of acquiring a future property, that of occupancy; which indeed the law of nature would allow him, but of which the laws of society have in most instances very justly and reasonably deprived him.

FREE FISHERY AND FREEWARREN — As to all inferior species of game, called beasts and fowls of warren, the liberty of taking or killing them is another franchise or royalty, derived likewise from the crown, and called freewarren; a word, which signifies preservation or custody: as the exclusive liberty of taking and killing fish in a public stream or river is called a free fishery; of which, however, no new franchise can at present be granted, by the express provision of Magna Carta. The principal intention of granting to anyone these franchises or liberties was in order to protect the game, by giving the grantee a sole and exclusive power of killing it himself, provided he prevented other persons. No man, but he who has a chase or freewarren, by grant from the crown, or prescription which supposes one, can justify hunting or sporting upon another man's soil; nor indeed, in thorough strictness of common law, either hunting or sporting at all.

TITLE BY FORFEITURE — I proceed now to a third method, whereby a title to goods and chattels may be acquired and lost, viz., by forfeiture; as a punishment for some crime or misdemeanor in the party forfeiting, and as a compensation for the offense and injury committed against him to whom they are forfeited. Of forfeitures, considered as the means whereby real property might be lost and acquired, we treated in a former chapter. It remains, therefore, in this place only to mention by what means or for what offenses goods and chattels become liable to forfeiture.

FORFEITURE FOR OFFENSES — In the variety of penal laws with which the subject is at present encumbered, it were a tedious and impracticable task to reckon up the various forfeitures, inflicted by special statutes, for particular crimes and misdemeanors: some of which are male in se, or offenses against the divine law, either natural or revealed; but by far the greatest part are mala prohibita, or such as derive their guilt merely from their prohibiton by the laws of the land: such as is the forfeiture of 40 pounds per month by the statute (Artificers and Apprentices, 1562), for exercising a trade without having served seven years as an apprentice thereto; and the forfeiture of 10 pounds (1710), for printing an almanac without a stamp. I shall therefore confine myself to those offenses only, by which all the goods and chattels of the offenders are forfeited. Indeed, as most of these forfeitures belong to the crown, they may seem as if they ought to have been referred to the preceding method of acquiring personal property, namely, by prerogative. But as, in the instance of partial forfeitures, a moiety often goes to the informer, the poor, or sometimes to other persons; and as one total forfeiture, namely, that by a bankrupt who is guilty of felony by concealing his effects, accrues entirely to his creditors, I have therefore made it a distinct head of transferring property.

☙ FORFEITURE FOR TREASON AND FELONY — Goods and chattels, then, are totally forfeited by conviction of high treason, or misprision of treason; of petit treason; of felony in general, and particularly of felony de se, and of manslaughter; nay, even by conviction of excusable homicide; by outlawry for treason or felony; by conviction of petit larceny; by flight in treason or felony, even though the party be acquitted of the fact; by standing mute, when arraigned of felony; by drawing a weapon on a judge, or striking anyone in the presence of the king's courts; by praemunire: by pretended prophecies, upon a second conviction; by owling; by the residing abroad of artificers; and by challenging to fight on account of money won at gaming. All these offenses, as will more fully appear in the fourth book of these Commentaries, induce a title forfeiture of goods and chattels.

Their forfeiture commences from the time of conviction, not the time of committing the fact, as in forfeitures of real property. For chattels are of so vague and fluctuating a nature, that to affect them by any relation back, would be attended with more inconvenience than in the case of landed estates: and part, if not the whole of them, must be expended in maintaining the delinquent, between the time of committing the fact and his conviction. Yet a fraudulent conveyance of them, to defeat the interest of the crown, is made void by statute (Fraudulent Conveyances, 1571).

TITLE BY CUSTOM

🦋 TITLE BY CUSTOM — A fourth method of acquiring property in things personal, or chattels, is by custom; whereby a right vests in some particular persons, either by the local usage of some particular place, or by the almost general and universal usage of the kingdom: I shall therefore content myself with making some observations on three sorts of customary interests, which obtain pretty generally throughout most parts of the nation, and are therefore of more universal concern; viz., heriots, mortuaries, and heirlooms.

🦋 HERIOTS — Heriots, which were slightly touched upon in a former chapter, are usually divided into two sorts: heriot service and heriot custom. The former are such as are due upon a special reservation in a grant or lease of lands, and therefore amount to little more than a mere rent: the latter arise upon no special reservation whatsoever, but depend merely upon immemorial usage and custom. Of these, therefore, we are here principally to speak: and they are defined to be a customary tribute of goods and chattels, payable to the lord of the fee on the decease of the owner of the land.

🦋 HERIOTS OF DANISH ORIGIN — The first establishment, if not introduction, of compulsory heriots into England, was by the Danes: and we find in the laws of King Canute the several heriots specified, which were then exacted by the king on the death of divers of his subjects, according to their respective dignities; from the highest down to the most inferior landholder. These, for the most part, consisted in arms, horses, and habiliments of war; which the word itself, according to Sir Henry Spelman, signifies. These were delivered up to the sovereign on the death of the vassal, who could no longer use them, to be put into other hands for the service and defense of the country. Upon the plan of this Danish establishment did William the Conqueror fashion his law of reliefs, when he ascertained the precise relief to be taken of every tenant in chivalry, and, contrary to the feudal custom and the usage of his own Duchy of Normandy, required arms and implements of war to be paid instead of money.

The Danish compulsive heriots, being thus transmuted into reliefs, underwent the same several vicissitudes as the feudal tenures, and in socage estates do frequently remain to this day, in the shape of a double rent payable at the death of the tenant: the heriots which now continue among us, and preserve that name, seeming rather to be of Saxon parentage, and at first to have been merely discretionary. These are now for the most part confined to copyhold tenures, and are due by custom only, which is the life of all estates by copy; and perhaps are the only instance where custom has favored the lord. For this payment was originally a voluntary donation, or gratuitous legacy of the tenant; perhaps in acknowledgment of his having been raised a degree above villeinage, when all his goods and chattels were quite at the mercy of the lord: and custom which has on the one hand confirmed the tenant's interest in exclusion of the lord's will, has on the other hand established this discretional piece of gratitude into a permanent duty.

An heriot may also appertain to free land, that is held by service and suit of court; in which case it is most commonly a copyhold enfranchised, whereupon the heriot is still due by custom. Bracton speaks of heriots as frequently due on the death of both species of tenants: "There is indeed another presentation, which is called a heriot; where a tenant at his death, whether a freeman or a slave, acknowledges the lord of whom he held, by giving his best beast or the second best, according to the custom of the place." This, he adds, "is more a matter of favor than of right"; in which Fleta and Britton agree: thereby plainly intimating the original of this custom to have been merely voluntary, as a legacy from the tenant; though now the immemorial usage has established it as of right in the lord.

⚖ HERIOTS ALWAYS PERSONAL CHATTELS — This heriot is sometimes the best live beast, which the tenant dies possessed of (which is particularly denominated the villein's relief in the twenty-ninth law of King William the Conqueror), sometimes the best inanimate good, under which a jewel or piece of plate may be included: but it is always a personal chattel, which immediately on the death of the tenant who was the owner of it, being ascertained by the option of the lord, becomes vested in him as his property; and is no charge upon the lands, but merely on the goods and chattels.

The tenant must be the owner of it, else it cannot be due; and therefore on the death of a feme covert no heriot can be taken; for she can have no ownership in things personal. In some places there is a customary composition in money, as ten or twenty shillings in lieu of a heriot, by which the lord and tenant are both bound, if it be an indisputably ancient custom: but a new composition of this sort will not bind the representatives of either party; for that amounts to the creation of a new custom, which is now impossible.

⚖ MORTUARIES — Mortuaries are a sort of ecclesiastical heriots being a customary gift claimed by and due to the minister in very many parishes on the death of his parishioners. They seem originally to have been, like lay heriots, only a voluntary bequest to the church; being intended, as Lyndewode informs us from a constitution of Archbishop Langham, as a kind of expiation and amends to the clergy for the personal tithes, and other ecclesiastical duties, which the laity in their lifetime might have neglected or forgotten to pay. For this purpose, after the Lord's heriot or best good was taken out, the second best chattel was reserved to the church as a mortuary. It was anciently usual in this kingdom to bring the mortuary to church along with the corpse when it came to be buried.

⚖ HEIRLOOMS — Heirlooms are such goods and personal chattels, as, contrary to the nature of chattels, shall go by special custom to the heir along with the inheritance, and not to the executor of the last proprietor. The termination, loom, is of Saxon origin; in which language it signifies a limb or member; so that an heirloom is nothing else, but a limb or member of the inheritance. They are generally such things as cannot be taken away without damaging or dismembering the freehold: otherwise the general rule is, that no chattel interest whatsoever shall go to the heir, notwithstanding it be expressly limited to a man and his heirs, but shall vest in the executor. But deer in a real authorized park, fishes in a pond, doves in a dovehouse, etc., though in themselves personal chattels, yet they are so annexed to and so necessary to the well-being of the inheritance, that they shall accompany the land wherever it vests, by either descent or purchase. For this reason, also, I apprehend it is, that the ancient jewels of the crown are held to be heirlooms; for they are necessary to maintain the state, and support the dignity, of the sovereign for the time being. Charters likewise, and deeds, court rolls, and other evidences of the land, together with the chests in which they are contained, shall pass together with the land to the heir in the nature of heirlooms, and shall not go to the executor.

By special custom also, in some places, carriages, utensils, and other household implements, may be heirlooms; but such custom must be strictly proved. On the other hand by almost general custom, whatever is strongly affixed to the freehold or inheritance, and cannot be severed from thence without violence or damage, whatever is not easily severed from houses, is become a member of the inheritance, and shall thereupon pass to the heir; as chimney-pieces, pumps, old fixed or dormant tables, benches.

Other personal chattels there are, which also descend to the heir in the nature of heirlooms as a monument or tombstone in a church, or the coat-armor of his ancestor there hung up, with the pennons and other ensigns of honor, suited to his degree. In this case, albeit the freehold of the church is in the parson, and these are annexed to that freehold, yet cannot the parson or any other take them away or deface them, but is liable to an action from the heir.

Pews in the church are somewhat of the same nature, which may descend by custom immemorial (without any ecclesiastical concurrence) from the ancestor to the heir. But though the heir has a property in the monuments and escutcheons of his ancestors, yet he has none in their bodies or ashes; nor can he bring any civil action against such as indecently at least, if not impiously, violate and disturb their remains, when dead and buried. The parson, indeed, who has the freehold of the soil, may bring an action of trespass against such as dig and disturb it: and, if anyone in taking up a dead body steals the shroud or other apparel, it will be felony, for the property thereof remains in the executor, or whoever was at the charge of the funeral.

But to return to heirlooms: these, though they be mere chattels, yet cannot be devised away from the heir by will; but such a devise is void, even by a tenant in fee simple. For, though the owner might during his life have sold or disposed of them, as he might of the timber of the estate, since, as the inheritance was his own, he might mangle or dismember it as he pleased; yet, they being at his death instantly vested in the heir, the devise (which is subsequent, and not to take effect till after his death) shall be postponed to the custom, whereby they have already descended.

TITLE BY SUCCESSION, MARRIAGE, AND JUDGMENT

In the present chapter we shall take into consideration three other species of title to goods and chattels.

⚖ TITLE BY SUCCESSION — The fifth method, therefore, of gaining a property in chattels, either personal or real, is by succession: which is, in strictness of law, only applicable to corporations aggregate of many, as dean and chapter, mayor and commonalty, master and fellows, and the like; in which one set of men may, by succeeding another set, acquire a property in all the goods, movables, and other chattels of the corporation. The true reason whereof is, because in judgment of law a corporation never dies; and therefore the predecessors, who lived a century ago, and their successors now in being, are one and the same body corporate. Which identity is a property so inherent in the nature of a body politic, that, even when it is meant to give anything to be taken in succession by such a body, that succession need not be expressed: but the law will of itself imply it. So that a gift to such a corporation, either of lands or of chattels, without naming their successors, vests an absolute property in them so long as the corporation subsists. Thus a lease for years, an obligation, a jewel, a flock of sheep, or other chattel interest, will vest in the successors, by succession, as well as in the identical members, to whom it was originally given.

⚖ DISTINCTION AS TO SOLE CORPORATIONS — But with regard to sole corporations, a considerable distinction must be made. For if such sole corporation be the representative of a number of persons; as the master of an hospital, who is a corporation for the benefit of the poor brethren; an abbot, or prior, by the old law before the Reformation, who represented the whole convent; or the dean of some ancient cathedral, who stands in the place of, and represents in his corporate capacity, the chapter; such sole corporations as these have in this respect the same powers, as corporations aggregate have, to take personal property or chattels in succession. Therefore a bond of such a master, abbot, or dean, and his successors, is good in law; and the successor shall have the advantage of it, for the benefit of the aggregate society, of which he is in law the representative. Whereas as the case of sole corporations, which represent no others but themselves, as bishops, parsons, and the like, no chattel interest can regularly go in succession: and therefore, if a lease for years be made to the bishop of Oxford and his successors, in such case his executors or administrators, and not his successors, shall have it.

For the word "successors," when applied to a person in his political capacity, is equivalent to the word "heirs" in his natural; and as such a lease for years, if made to John and his heirs, would not vest in his heirs, but his executors; so if it be made to John, Bishop of Oxford, and his successors, who are the heirs of his body politic, it shall still vest in his executors and not in such his successors. The reason of this is obvious: for, besides that the law looks upon goods and chattels as of too low and perishable a nature to be limited either to heirs, or such successors as are equivalent to heirs; it would also follow, that if any such chattel interest (granted to a sole corporation and his successors) were allowed to descend to such successor, the property thereof must be in abeyance from the death of the present owner until the successor be appointed; and this is contrary to the nature of a chattel interest, which can never be in abeyance or without an owner; but a man's right therein, when once suspended, is gone forever.

This is not the case in corporations aggregate, where the right is never in suspense; nor in the other sole corporations before mentioned, who are rather to be considered as heads of an aggregate body, than subsisting merely in their own right: the chattel interest, therefore, in such a case, is really and substantially vested in the hospital, convent, chapter, or other aggregate body; though the head is the visible person in whose name every act is carried on, and in whom every interest is therefore said (in point of form) to vest. But the general rule, with regard to corporations merely sole, is this, that no chattel can go or be acquired by right of succession.

Yet to this rule there are two exceptions. One in the case of the king, in whom a chattel may vest by a grant of it formerly made to a preceding king and his successors. The other exception is, where, by a particular custom, some particular sole corporations have acquired a power of taking particular chattel interests in succession. This custom, being against the general tenor of the common law, must be strictly interpreted, and not extended to any other chattel interests than such immemorial usage will strictly warrant. Thus the chamberlain of London, who is a sole corporation, may by the custom of London take bonds and recognizances to himself and his successor, for the benefit of the orphan's fund: but it will not follow from thence, that he has a capacity to take a lease for years to himself and his successors for the same purpose; for the custom extends not to that: nor that he may take a bond to himself and his successors, for any other purpose than the benefit of the orphan's fund; for that also is not warranted by the custom.

Wherefore, upon the whole, we may close this head with laying down this general rule; that such right of succession to chattel is universally inherent by the common law in all aggregate corporations, in the king, and in such single corporations as represent a number of persons; and may, by special custom, belong to certain other sole corporations for some particular purposes: although, generally, in sole corporations no such right can exist.

⚖️ TITLE BY MARRIAGE — A sixth method of acquiring property in goods and chattels is by marriage; whereby those chattels, which belonged formerly to the wife, are by act of law vested in the husband, with the same degree of property and with the same powers, as the wife, when sole, had over them.

This depends entirely on the notion of a unity of person between the husband and wife; it being held that they are one person in law, so that the very being and existence of the woman is suspended during the coverture, or entirely merged or incorporated in that of the husband. Hence it follows, that whatever personal property belonged to the wife, before marriage, is by marriage absolutely vested in the husband. In a real estate, he only gains a title to the rents and profits during coverture: for that, depending upon feudal principles, remains entire to the wife after the death of her husband, or to her heirs, if she dies before him; unless by the birth of a child, he becomes tenant for life by the curtesy. But, in chattel interests, the sole and absolute property vests in the husband, to be disposed of at his pleasure, if he chooses to take possession of them: for unless he reduces them to possession, by exercising some act of ownership upon them, no property vests in him, but they shall remain to the wife, or to her representatives, after the coverture is determined.

⚖ DIFFERENCE BETWEEN CHATTELS REAL AND PERSONAL — There is therefore a very considerable difference in the acquisition of this species of property by the husband, according to the subject matter; viz., whether it be a chattel real, or a chattel personal; and, of chattels personal, whether it be in possession, or in action only.

A chattel real vests in the husband, not absolutely, but sub modo. As in case of a lease for years, the husband shall receive all the rents and profits of it, and may, if he pleases, sell, surrender, or dispose of it during the coverture: if he is liable to execution for his debts: and, if he survives his wife, it is to all intents and purposes his own. Yet, if he has made no disposition thereof in his lifetime, and dies before his wife, he cannot dispose of it by will: for, the husband having made no alteration in the property during his life, it never was transferred from the wife; but after his death she shall remain in her ancient possession, and it shall not go to his executors.

So it is also of chattels personal (or choses) in action; as debts upon bond, contracts, and the like: these the husband may have if he pleases; that is, if he reduces them into possession by receiving or recovering them at law. Upon such receipt or recovery, they are absolutely and entirely his own; and shall go to his executors or administrators, or as he shall bequeath them by will, and shall not revest in the wife. But, if he dies before he has recovered or reduced them into possession, so that at his death they still continue choses in action, they shall survive to the wife; for the husband never exerted the power he had of obtaining an exclusive property in them. So, if an estray comes into the wife's franchise, and the husband seizes it, it is absolutely his property: but, if he dies without seizing it, his executors are not now at liberty to seize it, but the wife or her heirs; for the husband never exerted the right he had, which right determined with the coverture.

Thus in both these species of property the law is the same, in case the wife survives the husband; but, in case the husband survives the wife, the law is very different with respect to chattels real and choses in action: for he shall have the chattel real by survivorship, but not the chose in action; except in the case of arrears of rent, due to the wife before her coverture, which in case of her death are given to the husband by statute (Administration of Estates, 1540).

The reason for the general law is this: that the husband is in absolute possession of the chattel real during the coverture, by a kind of joint tenancy with the wife; wherefore the law will not wrest it out of his hands, and give it to her representatives; though, in case he had died first, it would have survived to the wife, unless he thought proper in his lifetime to alter the possession. But a chose in action shall not survive to him, because he never was in possession of it at all, during the coverture; and the only method he had to gain possession of it, was by suing in his wife's right: but, as after her death, he cannot (as husband) bring an action in her right, because they are no longer one and the same person in law, therefore he can never (as such) recover the possession. But he still will be entitled to be her administrator; and may, in that capacity, recover such things in action as become due to her before or during the coverture.

Thus, and upon these reasons, stands the law between husband and wife, with regard to chattels real, and choses in action: but, as to chattels personal (or choses) in possession, which the wife hath in her own right, as ready money, jewels, household goods, and the like, the husband hath therein an immediate and absolute property, devolved to him by the marriage, not only potentially but in fact, which never can again revest in the wife or her representative.

⚖ PARAPHERNALIA — As the husband may thus generally acquire a property in all the personal substance of the wife, so in one particular instance the wife may acquire a property in some of her husband's goods; which shall remain to her after his death, and not go to his executors. These are called her paraphernalia, which is a term borrowed from the civil law, and is derived from the Greek language, signifying something over and above her dower. Our law uses it to signify the apparel and ornaments of the wife, suitable to her rank and degree: which she becomes entitled to at the death of her husband, over and above her jointure or dower, and preferably to all other representatives: and her jewels of a peeress, usually worn by her, have been held to be paraphernalia. Neither can the husband devise by his will such ornaments and jewels of his wife; though during his life perhaps he hath the power (if unkindly inclined to exert it) to sell them or give them away. But if she continues in the use of them till his death, she shall afterwards retain them against his executors and administrators, and all other persons, except creditors, where there is a deficiency of assets. Her necessary apparel is protected even against the claim of creditors.

⚖ TITLE BY JUDGMENT — A judgment, in consequence of some suit or action in a court of justice, is frequently the means of vesting the right and property of chattel interests in the prevailing party. Here we must be careful to distinguish between property, the right of which is before vested in the party, and of which only possession is recovered by suit or action; and property, to which a man before had no determinate title or certain claim, but he gains as well the right as the possession by the process and judgment of the law. Of the former sort are all debts and choses in action; as if a man gives bond for 20 pounds and agrees to buy a horse at a stated sum, or takes up goods of a tradesman upon an implied contract to pay as much as they are reasonably worth: in all these cases the right accrues to the creditor, and is completely vested in him, at the time of the bond being sealed, or the contract or agreement made; and the law only gives him a remedy to recover the possession of that right, which already in justice belongs to him.

But there is also a species of property to which a man has not any claim or title whatsoever, till after suit commenced and judgment obtained in a court of law: where the right and the remedy do not follow each other, as in common cases, but accrue at one and the same time; and where, before judgment had, no man can say that he has an absolute property, either in possession or in action. Of this nature are:

PENALTIES — Such penalties as are given by particular statutes, to be recovered on an action popular; or, in other words, to be recovered by him or them that will sue for the same. Such as the penalty of 500 pounds, which those persons are by several acts of parliament made liable to forfeit, that, being in particular offices or situations in life, neglect to take the oaths to the government: which penalty is given to him or them that will sue for the same.

Now, here it is clear that no particular person, A or B, has any right, claim, or demand, in or upon this penal sum, till after action brought; for he that brings his action, and can bona fide obtain judgment first, will undoubtedly secure a title to it, in exclusion of everybody else. He obtains an inchoate imperfect degree of property, by commencing his suit: but it is not consummated till judgment; for, if any collusion appears, he loses the priority he had gained. But, otherwise, the right so attaches in the first informer, that the king (who before action brought shall grant a pardon which shall be a bar to all the world) cannot after suit commenced remit anything but his own part of the penalty. For by commencing the suit the informer has made the popular action his own private action, and it is not in the power of the crown, or of anything but parliament to release the informer's interest. This, therefore, is one instance, where a suit and judgment at law are not only the means of recovering, but also of acquiring, property.

What is said of this one penalty is equally true of all others, that are given thus at large to a common informer, or to any person that will sue for the same. They are placed, as it were, in a state of nature, accessible by all the king's subjects, but the acquired right of none of them: open, therefore, to the first occupant, who declares his intention to possess them by bringing his action; and who carries that intention into execution, by obtaining judgment to recover them.

DAMAGES — Another species of property that is acquired and lost by suit and judgment at law, is that of damages given to a man by a jury, as a compensation and satisfaction for some injury sustained; as for a battery, for imprisonment, for slander, or for trespass. Here the plaintiff has no certain demand till after verdict; but, when the jury has assessed his damages, and judgment is given thereupon, whether they amount to twenty pounds or twenty shillings, he instantly acquires, and the defendant loses at the same time, a right to that specific sum. It is true, that this is not an acquisition so perfectly original as in the former instance: for here the injured party has unquestionably a vague and indeterminate right to some damages or other, the instant he received the injury; and the verdict of the jurors, and judgment of the court thereupon, do not in this case so properly vest a new title in him, as fix and ascertain the old one; they do not give, but define, the right.

But, however, though strictly speaking the primary right to a satisfaction for injuries is given by the law of nature, and the suit is only the means of as ascertaining and recovering that satisfaction; yet, as the legal proceedings are the only visible means of this acquisition of property, we may fairly enough rank such damages, or satisfaction assessed, under the head of property acquired by suit and judgment at law.

COSTS — Hither also may be referred, upon the same principle, all title to costs and expenses of suit; which are often arbitrary, and rest entirely on the determination of the court, upon weighing all circumstances, both as to the quantum (amount), and also (in the courts of equity especially, and upon motions in the courts of law) whether there shall be any costs at all. These costs, therefore, when given by the court to either party, may be looked upon as an acquisition made by the judgment of law.

TITLE BY GIFT,
GRANT AND CONTRACT

We are now to proceed, according to the order marked out, to the discussion of two of the remaining methods of acquiring a title to property in things personal, which are much connected together, and answer in some measure to the conveyances of real estates; being those by gift or grant, and by contract: whereof the former vests a property in possession, the latter a property in action.

⚖️ TITLE BY GIFT OR GRANT — CHATTELS REAL — Gifts, then, or grants, which are the eighth method of transferring personal property, are thus to be distinguished from each other, that gifts are always gratuitous, grants are upon some consideration or equivalent: and they may be divided; with regard to their subject matter, into gifts or grants of chattels real, and gifts or grants of chattels personal.

Under the head of gifts or grants of chattels real, may be included all leases for years of land, assignments, and surrenders of those leases; and all the other methods of conveying an estate less than freehold; which were heretofore considered in the present book, and therefore need not be here again repeated; though these very seldom carry the outward appearance of a gift, however freely bestowed; being usually expressed to be made in consideration of blood, or natural affection, or of five or ten shillings nominally paid to the grantor; and in case of leases, always reserving a rent, though it be but a peppercorn: any of which considerations will, in the eye of the law, convert the gift, if executed, into a grant; if not executed, into a contract.

⚖️ CHATTELS PERSONAL — Grants or gifts, of chattels personal, are the act of transferring the right and the possession of them; whereby one man renounces, and another man immediately acquires, all title and interest therein: which may be done either in writing, or by word of mouth attested by sufficient evidence, of which the delivery of possession is the strongest and most essential. But this conveyance, when merely voluntary, is somewhat suspicious; and is usually construed to be fraudulent, if creditors or others become sufferers thereby. Particularly, by statute (Fraudulent Deeds of Gift, 1487), all deeds of gift of goods, made in trust to the use of the donor, shall be void; because otherwise persons might be tempted to commit treason or felony, without danger of forfeiture; and the creditors of the donor might also be defrauded of their rights.

By (Fraudulent Conveyance, 1571), every grant or gift of chattels, as well as lands, with intent to defraud creditors or others, shall be void as against such persons to whom such fraud would be prejudicial; but, as against the grantor himself, shall stand good and effectual: and all persons partakers in, or privy to, such fraudulent grants, shall forfeit the whole value of the goods, on moiety to the king, and another moiety to the party grieved: and also on conviction shall suffer imprisonment for half a year.

A true and proper gift or grant is always accompanied with delivery of possession, and takes effect immediately: as if A gives to B 100 pounds or a flock of sheep, and puts him in possession of them directly, it is then a gift executed in the donee; and it is not in the donor's power to retract it, though he did it without any consideration or recompense: unless it be prejudicial to creditors; or the donor were under any legal incapacity, as infancy, coverture, duress, or the like; or if he were drawn in, cirumvented, or imposed upon, by false pretenses, ebriety, or surprise. But if the gift does not take effect, by delivery of immediate possession, it is then not properly a gift, but a contract: and this a man cannot be compelled to perform, but upon good and sufficient consideration; as we shall see under our next division.

⚖ TITLE BY CONTRACT — A contract, which usually conveys an interest merely in action, is thus defined: "an agreement, upon sufficient consideration, to do or not to do a particular thing." From which definition there arise three points to be contemplated in all contracts; 1. The agreement. 2. The consideration: and 3. The thing to be done or omitted, or the different species of contracts.

⚖ AGREEMENT — First, then it is an agreement, a mutual bargain or convention; and therefore there must at least be two contracting parties, of sufficient ability to make a contract: as where A contracts with B to pay him 100 pounds and thereby transfers a property in such sum to B. Which property is, however, not in possession, but in action merely, and recoverable by suit at law; wherefore it could not be transferred to another person by the strict rules of the ancient common law: for no chose in action could be assigned or granted over, because it was thought to be a great encouragement to litigiousness if a man were allowed to make over to a stranger his right of going to law.

But this nicety is now disregarded: though, in compliance with the ancient principle, the form of assigning a chose in action is in the nature of a declaration of trust, and an agreement to permit the assignee to make use of the name of the assignor, in order to recover the possession. Therefore, when in common acceptation a debt or bond is said to be assigned over, it must still be sued in the original creditor's name; the person, to whom it is transferred, being rather an attorney than an assignee.

The king is an exception to this general rule; for he might always either grant or receive a chose in action by assignment: and our courts of equity, considering that in a commerical country almost all personal property must necessarily lie in contract, will protect the assignment of a chose in action, as much as the law will that of a chose in possession.

EXPRESS AND IMPLIED CONTRACTS — This contract or agreement may be either expressed or implied. Express contracts are where the terms of the agreement are openly uttered and avowed at the time of the making, as to deliver an ox, or ten loads of timber, or to pay a stated price for certain goods. Implied are such as reason and justice dictate, and which therefore the law presumes that every man undertakes to perform. As, if I employ a person to do any business for me, or perform any work; the law implies that I undertook, or contracted to pay him as much as his labor deserves. If I take up wares from a tradesman, without any agreement of price, the law concludes that I contracted to pay their real value.

There is also one species of implied contracts, which runs through and is annexed to all other contracts, conditions, and covenants, viz., that if I fail in my part of the agreement, I shall pay the other party such damages as he has sustained by my neglect or refusal. In short, almost all the rights of personal property (when not in actual possession) do in great measure depend upon contracts of one kind or other, or at least might be reduced under some of them: which indeed is the method taken by the civil law; it having referred the greatest part of the duties and rights, which it treats of, to the head of obligations ex contractu (arising from a contract) and quasi ex contractu (from something in the nature of a contract).

⚖ EXECUTED AND EXECUTORY CONTRACTS — A contract may also be either executed, as if A agrees to change horses with B, and they do it immediately; in which case the possession and the right are transferred together: or it may be executory, as if they agree to change next week; here the right only vests, and their reciprocal property in each other's horse is not in possession but in action; for a contract executed (which differs nothing from a grant) conveys a chose in possession; a contract executory conveys only a chose in action.

⚖ CONSIDERATION — Having thus shown the general nature of a contract, we are, secondly, to proceed to the consideration upon which it is founded; or the reason which moves the contracting party to enter into the contract. "It is an agreement, upon sufficient consideration." The civilians hold, that in all contracts, either express or implied, there must be something given in exchange, something that is mutual or reciprocal. This thing, which is the price or motive of the contract, we call the consideration: and it must be a thing lawful in itself, or else the contract is void.

A good consideration, we have before seen, is that of blood or natural affection between near relations; the satisfaction accruing from which the law esteems an equivalent for whatever benefit may move from one relation to another. This consideration may sometimes, however, be set aside, and the contract become void, when it tends in its consequences to defraud creditors or other third persons of their just rights.

But a contract for any valuable consideration, as for marriage, for money, for work done, or for other reciprocal contract, can never be impeached at law; and, if it be of sufficient adequate value, is never set aside in equity: for the person contracted with has been given an equivalent in recompense, and is therefore as much an owner, or a creditor, as any other person.

⚖ CONSIDERATION IN THE CIVIL LAW — These valuable considerations are divided by the civilians into four species: 1. Do ut des (I give that you may give): as when I give money or goods, on a contract that I shall be repaid money or goods for them again. Of this kind are all loans of money upon bond, or promise of repayment; and all sales of goods, in which there is either an express contract to pay so much for them, or else the law implies a contract to pay so much as they are worth.

2. The second species is facio ut facias (I do that you may do): as when I agree with a man to do his work for him, if he will do mine for me; or if two persons agree to marry together: or to do any other

positive acts on both sides. Or, it may be to forbear on one side on consideration of something done on the other; as, that in consideration A, the tenant, will repair his house, B, the landlord, will not sue him for waste. Or, it may be for mutual forbearance on both sides; as, that in consideration that A will not trade to Lisbon, B will not trade to Marseilles: so as to avoid interfering with each other.

3. The third species of consideration is facio ut des (I do that you may give): when a man agrees to perform anything for a price, either specifically mentioned, or left to the determination of the law to set a value to it. When a servant hires himself to his master for certain wages or an agreed sum of money: here the servant contracts to do his master's service, in order to earn that specific sum. Otherwise, if he be hired generally; for then he is under an implied contract to perform this service for what it shall be reasonably worth.

4. The fourth species is do ut facias (I give that you may do): which is the direct counterpart of the other. As when I agree with the servant to give him such wages upon his performing such work: which, we see, is nothing else but the last species inverted; for the servant performs, that the heir may give and the heir gives, that the servant may perform.

⚖ NUDE PACTS — A consideration of some sort or other is so absolutely necessary to the forming of a contract, that a nudum pactum (nude pact) or agreement to do or pay anything on one side, without any compensation on the other, is totally void in law: and a man cannot be compelled to perform it. As if one man promises to give another 100 pounds, here there is nothing contracted for or given on the one side, and therefore there is nothing binding on the other. However, a man may or may not be bound to perform it, in honor or conscience, which the municipal laws do not take upon them to decide; certainly those municipal laws will not compel the execution of what he had no visible inducement to engage for: and therefore our law has adopted the maxim of the civil law, that ex nudo pacto non oritur actio (no action arises from a nude pact). But any degree of reciprocity will prevent the pact from being nude: nay, even if the thing be founded on a prior moral obligation (as a promise to pay a just debt, though barred by the statute of limitations), it is no longer nudum pactum. As this rule was principally established, to avoid the inconvenience that would arise from setting up mere verbal promises, for which no good reason could be assigned, it therefore does not hold in some cases, where such promise is authentically proved by written documents. For if a man enters into a voluntary bond, or gives a promissory note, he shall not be allowed to aver the want of a consideration in order to evade the payment: for every bond from a solemnity of the instrument, and every note from the subscription of the drawer, carries with it an internal evidence of a good consideration. Courts of justice will therefore support them both, as against the contractor himself; but not to the prejudice of creditors, or strangers to the contract.

⚖ THE SEVERAL SPECIES OF CONTRACT — We are next to consider, thirdly, the thing agreed to be done or omitted. "A contract is an agreement, upon sufficient consideration, to do or not to do a particular thing." The most usual contracts, whereby the right of chattels personal may be acquired in the laws of England, are: 1. That of sale or exchange. 2. That of bailment. 3. That of hiring and borrowing. 4. That of debt.

⚖ SALE OR EXCHANGE — Sale or exchange is a transmutation of property from one man to another, in consideration of some price or recompense in value: for there is no sale without a recompense; there must be quid pro quo (something for something). If it be a commutation of goods for goods, it is more properly an exchange; but, if it be a transferring of goods for money, it is called a sale: which is a method of exchange introduced for the convenience of mankind, by establishing a universal medium, which may be exchanged for all sorts of other property; whereas if goods were only to be exchanged for goods, by way of barter, it would be difficult to adjust the respective values, and the carriage would be intolerably cumbersome.

All civilized nations adopted, therefore, very early the use of money; for we find Abraham giving "four hundred shekels of silver, current money with the merchant," for the field of Machpelah: though the practice of exchanges still subsists among several of the savage nations. But, with regard to law of sales and exchanges, there is no difference. I shall therefore treat of them both under the denomination of sales only; and shall consider their force and effect, in the first place where the vendor hath in himself, and secondly where he hath not, the property of the thing sold.

⚖ SALE AFTER EXECUTION — Where the vendor hath in himself the property of the goods sold, he hath the liberty of disposing of them to whomever he pleases, at any time, and in any manner: unless judgment has been obtained against him for a debt or damages, and the writ of execution is actually delivered to the sheriff. For then, by the statute of frauds, the sale shall be looked upon as fraudulent, and the property of the goods shall be bound to answer the debt, from the time of delivering the writ. Formerly it was bound from the teste, or issuing, of the writ, and any subsequent sale was fraudulent; but the law was thus altered in favor of purchasers, though it still remains the same between the parties: and therefore if a defendant dies after the awarding and before the delivery of the writ, his goods are bound by it in the hands of his executors.

⚖ CONTRACT OF SALE WHEN COMPLETE — If a man agrees with another for goods at a certain price, he may not carry them away before he hath paid for them; for it is no sale without payment, unless the contrary be expressly agreed. Therefore, if the vendor says, the price of a beast is four pounds, and the vendee says he will give four pounds, the bargain is struck; and they neither of them are at liberty to be off, provided immediate possession be tendered by the other side. But if neither the money be paid, nor the goods delivered, nor tender made, nor any subsequent agreement be entered into, it is no contract, and the owner may dispose of the goods as he pleases. But if any part of the price is paid down, if it be but a penny, or any portion of the goods delivered by way of earnest (a token of a contract for purchase and sale), the property of the goods is absolutely bound by it: and the vendee may recover the goods by action, as well as the vendor may the price of them.

⚖ STATUTE OF FRAUDS, 1677 — Such regard does the law pay to earnest as an evidence of a contract, that no contract for the sale of goods, to the value of ten pounds or more, shall be valid, unless the buyer actually receives part of the goods sold, by way of earnest on his part; or unless he gives part of the price to the vendor by way of earnest to bind the bargain, or in part of payment; or unless some note in writing be made and signed by the party, or his agent, who is to be charged with the contract.

With regard to goods under the value of ten pounds no contract or agreement for the sale of them shall be valid, unless the goods are to be delivered within a year, or unless the contract be made in writing, and signed by the party who is to be charged therewith.

Anciently, among all the northern nations, shaking of hands was held necessary to bind the bargain; a custom which we still retain in many verbal contracts. A sale thus made was called hand-sale (a sale by the mutual joining of hands); till in process of time the same word was used to signify the price or earnest, which was given immediately after the shaking of hands, or instead thereof.

☙ WHEN TITLE PASSES — As soon as the bargain is struck, the property of the goods is transferred to the vendee, and that of the price to the vendor; but the vendee cannot take the goods, until he tenders the price agreed on. But if he tenders the money to the vendor, and he refuses it, the vendee may seize the goods, or have an action against the vendor for detaining them. By a regular sale, without delivery, the property is so absolutely vested in the vendee, that if A sells a horse to B for ten pounds and B pays him earnest, or signs a note in writing of the bargain; and afterwards, before the delivery of the horse or money paid, the horse dies in the vendor's custody; still he is entitled to the money, because by the contract, the property was in the vendee. Thus may property in goods be transferred by sale, where the vendor hath such property in himself.

☙ SALE BY NOT ONE OWNER — But property may also in some cases be transferred by sale, though the vendor hath none at all in the goods: for it is expedient that the buyer, by taking proper precautions, may at all events be secure of his purchase; otherwise all commerce between man and man must soon be at an end.

☙ MARKET OVERT — Therefore the general rule of law is, that all sales and contracts of anything vendible, in fairs or markets overt (that is, open), shall not only be good between the parties, but also be binding on all those that have any right or property therein. Our Saxon ancestors prohibited the sale of anything above the value of twenty pence, unless in open market, and directed every bargain and sale to be contracted in the presence of credible witnesses.

Market overt in the country is only held on the special days, provided for particular towns by charter or prescription; but in London every day, except Sunday, is a market day. The market place, or spot of ground set apart by custom for the sale of particular goods, is also in the country the only market overt; but in London every shop in which goods are exposed publicly to sale, is market overt, for such things only as the owner professes to trade in.

☙ STOLEN GOODS — But if my goods are stolen from me and sold, out of market overt, my property is not altered, and I may take them wherever I find them. It is expressly provided by statute (Broker, 1603), that the sale of any goods wrongfully taken, to any pawnbroker in London, or within two miles thereof, shall not alter the property: for this, being usually a clandestine trade, is therefore made an exception to the general rule. Even in market overt, if the goods be the property of the king, such sale (though regular in all other respects) will in no case bind him; though it binds infants, feme coverts, idiots, or lunatics, and men beyond sea or in prison: or if the goods be stolen from a common person, and then taken by the king's officer from the felon, and sold in open market; still, if the owner has used due diligence in prosecuting the thief to conviction, he loses not his property in the goods.

⚖ KNOWLEDGE OF DEFECTIVE TITLE — So, likewise, if the buyer knoweth the property not to be in the seller; or there be any other fraud in the transaction; if he knoweth the seller to be an infant, or feme covert not usually trading for herself; if the sale be not originally and wholly made in the fair or market, or not at the usual hours; the owner's property is not bound thereby. If a man buys his own goods in a fair or market, the contract of sale shall not bind him so as that he shall render the price, unless the property had been previously altered by a former sale. Notwithstanding any number of intervening sales, if the original vendor, who sold without having the property, comes again into possession of the goods, the original owner may take them, when found in his hands who was guilty of the first breach of justice. By which wise regulations the common law has secured the right of the proprietor in personal chattels from being divested, so far as was consistent with that other necessary policy, that purchasers, bona fide, in a fair, open and regular manner, should not be afterwards put to difficulties by reason of the previous knavery of the seller.

⚖ SALE OF HORSES — But there is one species of personal chattels, in which the property is not easily altered by sale, without the express consent of the owner, and those are horses. For a purchaser gains no property in a horse that has been stolen, unless it be bought in a fair or market overt, according to the directions of the statutes (Horses, Markets and Fairs, 1555, and 1588). By which it is enacted that the horse shall be openly exposed, in the time of such fair or market, for one whole hour together, between ten in the morning and sunset, in the public place used for such sales, and not in any private yard or stable; and afterwards brought by both the vendor and vendee to the bookkeeper of such fair or market: that toll be paid, if any be due; and if not, one penny to the bookkeeper, who shall enter down the price, color and marks of the horse, with the names, additions, and abode of the vendee and vendor; the latter being properly attested.

Nor shall such sale take away the property of the owner, if within six months after the horse is stolen he puts in his claim before some magistrate, where the horse shall be found; and, within forty days more, proves such his property by the oath of two witnesses, and tenders to the person in possession such price as he bona fide paid for him in market overt. But in case any one of the points before mentioned be not observed, such sale is utterly void; and the owner shall not lose his property, but at any distance of time may seize or bring an action for his horse, wherever he happens to find him.

⚖ WARRANTY — By the civil law an implied warranty was annexed to every sale, in respect to the title of the vendor: and so, too, in our law, a purchaser of goods and chattels may have a satisfaction from the seller, if he sells them as his own and the title proves deficient, without any express warranty for that purpose. But, with regard to the goodness of the wares so purchased, the vendor is not bound to answer; unless he expressly warrants them to be sound and good, or unless he knew them to be otherwise and hath used any art to disguise them, or unless they turn out to be different from what he represented to the buyer.

⚖ BAILMENT — Bailment, from the French bailler, to deliver, is a delivery of goods in trust, upon a contract expressed or implied, that the trust shall be faithfully executed on the part of the bailee. As if cloth be delivered, or (in our legal dialect) bailed, to a tailor to make a suit of clothes, he had it upon an implied contract to render it again when made, and that in a workmanly manner. If money or goods be delivered to a common carrier, to convey from Oxford to London, he is under a contract in law to pay, or carry, them to the person appointed. If a horse, or other goods, be delivered to an innkeeper or his servants, he is bound to keep them safely, and restore them when his guest leaves the house.

If a man takes in a horse, or other cattel, to graze and depasture in his grounds, which the law calls agistment, he takes them upon an implied contract to return them on demand of the owner. If a pawnbroker received plate or jewels as a pledge, or security, for the repayment of money lent thereon at a day certain, he has them upon an express contract or condition to restore them, if the pledgor performs his part by redeeming them in due time: for the due execution of which contract many useful regulations are made by statute (Obtaining Money by False Pretenses, 1756).

So if a landlord distrains goods for rent, or a parish officer for taxes, these for a time are only a pledge in the hands of the distrainors, and they are bound by an implied contract in law to restore them on payment of the debts, duty, and expenses, before the time of sale; or when sold, to render back the overplus. If a friend delivers anything to his friend to keep for him, the receiver is bound to restore it on demand; and it was formerly held that in the meantime he was answerable for any damage or loss it might sustain, whether by accident or otherwise; unless he expressly undertook to keep it only with the same care as his own goods, and then he should not be answerable for theft or other accidents. But now the law seems to be settled, that such a general bailment will not charge the bailee with any loss, unless it happens by gross neglect, which is an evidence of fraud; but, if he undertakes specially to keep the goods safely and securely, he is bound to take the same care of them as a prudent man would take of his own.

⚖️ BAILEE'S QUALIFIED PROPERTY — In all these instances there is a special qualified property transferred from the bailor to the bailee, together with the possession. It is not an absolute property, because of his contract for restitution; the bailor having still left in him the right to a chose in action, grounded upon such contract. On account of this qualified property of the bailee, he may (as well as the bailor) maintain an action against such as injure or take away these chattels. The tailor, the carrier, the innkeeper, the agisting farmer, the pawnbroker, the distrainor, and the general bailee, may all of them vindicate, in their own right, this their possessory interest, against any stranger or third person. For, being responsible to the bailor, if the goods are lost or damaged by his willful default or gross negligence, or if he do not deliver up the chattels on lawful demand, it is therefore reasonable that he should have a right of action against all other persons who may have purloined or injured them; that he may always be ready to answer the call of the bailor.

⚖️ HIRING AND BORROWING — Hiring and borrowing are also contracts by which a qualified property may be transferred to the hirer or borrower: in which there is only this difference, that hiring is always for a price, a stipend, or additional recompense; borrowing is merely gratuitous. But the law in both cases is the same. They are both contracts, whereby the possession and a transient property is transferred for a particular time or use, on condition to restore the goods so hired or borrowed, as soon as the time is expired or use performed; together with the price or stipend (in case of hiring) either expressly agreed on by the parties, or left to be implied by law according to the value of the service.

By this mutual contract, the hirer or borrower gains a temporary property in the thing hired, accompanied with an implied condition to use it with moderation and not abuse it; and the owner or lender retains a reversionary interest in the same, and acquires a new property in the price or reward. Thus if a man hires or borrows a horse for a month, he had the possession and a qualified property therein during that period; on the expiration of which his qualified property determines, and the owner becomes (in case of hiring) entitled also to the price, for which the horse was hired.

⚖ INTEREST — There is one species of this price or reward, the most usual of any, but concerning which many good and learned men have in former times very much perplexed themselves and other people, by raising doubts about its legality in foro conscientiae (in the forum of the conscience). That is, when money is lent on a contract to receive not only the principal sum again, but also an increase by way of compensation for the use; which generally is called interest by those who think it lawful, and usury by those who do not so. For the enemies to interest in general make no distinction between that and usury, holding any increase of money to be indefensibly usurious.

This they ground as well on the prohibition of it by the law of Moses among the Jews, as also upon what is said to be laid down by Aristotle, that money is naturally barren, and to make it breed money is preposterous, and a perversion of the end of its institution, which was only to serve the purposes of exchange, and not of increase. Hence the school divines have branded the practice of taking interest, as being contrary to the divine law both natural and revealed; and the canon law has prescribed the taking any, the least, increase for the loan of money as a mortal sin.

But, in answer to this, it may be observed, that the mosaical precept was clearly a political, and not a moral, precept. It only prohibited the Jews from taking usury from their brethren, the Jews: but in express words permitted them to take it of a stranger: which proves that the taking of moderate usury, or a reward for the use, for so the word signifies, is not malum in se, since it was allowed where any but an Israelite was concerned. As to the reason supposed to be given by Aristotle, and deduced from the natural barrenness of money, the same may with equal force be alleged of houses, which never breed houses; and twenty other things, which nobody doubts it is lawful to make profit of, by letting them to hire.

Though money was originally used only for the purposes of exchange, yet the laws of any state may be well justified in permitting it to be turned to the purposes of profit, if the convenience of society (the great end for which money was invented) shall require it. That the allowance of moderate interest tends greatly to the benefit of the public, especially in a trading country, will appear from that generally acknowledged principle, that commerce cannot subsist without mutual and extensive credit.

Unless money, therefore, can be borrowed, trade cannot be carried on: and if no premium were allowed for the hire of money, few persons would care to lend it; or at least the ease of borrowing at a short warning (which is the life of commerce) would be entirely at an end. Thus, in the dark ages of monkish superstition and civil tyranny, when interest was laid upon a total interdict, commerce was also at its lowest ebb, and fell entirely into the hands of the Jews and Lombards: but when men's minds began to be more enlarged, when true religion and real liberty revived, commerce grew again into credit; and again introduced with itself its inseparable companion, the doctrine of loans upon interest. As to any scruples of conscience, since all other conveniences of life may either be bought or hired, but money can only be hired, there seems to be no greater oppression in taking a recompense or price for the hire of this, than of any other convenience.

To demand an exorbitant price is equally contrary to conscience, for the loan of a horse, or the loan of a sum of money: but a reasonable equivalent for the temporary inconvenience, which the owner may feel by the want of it, and for the hazard of his losing it entirely, is not more immoral in one case than it is in the other. Indeed, the absolute prohibition of lending upon any, even moderate interest, introduces the very inconvenience which it seems meant to remedy. The necessity of individuals will make borrowing unavoidable. Without some profit allowed by law, there will be but few lenders: and those principally bad men, who will break through the law, and take a profit; and then will endeavor to indemnify themselves from the danger of the penalty, by making that profit exorbitant.

A capital distinction must therefore be made between a moderate and exorbitant profit; to the former of which we usually give the name of interest, to the latter the truly odious appellation of usury: the former is necessary in every civil state, if it were but to exclude the latter, which ought never to be tolerated in any well-regulated society. For, as the whole of this matter is well summed up by Grotius, "if the compensation allowed by law does no exceed the proportion of the hazard run, or the want felt, by the loan, its allowance is neither repugnant to the revealed nor the natural law; but if it exceeds those bounds, it is then oppressive usury; and though the municipal laws may give it impunity, they never can make it just."

We see that the exorbitance or moderation of interest, for money lent, depends upon two circumstances; the inconvenience of parting with it for the present, and the hazard of losing it entirely. The inconvenience to individual lenders can never be estimated by laws; the rate, therefore, of general interest must depend upon the usual or general inconvenience. This results entirely from the quantity of specie or current money in the kingdom; for, the more specie there is circulating in any nation, the greater superfluity there will be, beyond what is necessary to carry on the business of exchange and the common concerns of life.

In every nation or public community, there is a certain quantity of money thus necessary; which a person well skilled in political arithmetic might perhaps calculate as exactly, as a private banker can the demand for running cash in his own shop: all above this necessary quantity may be spared, or lent, without much inconvenience to the respective lenders; and the greater this national superfluity is, the more numerous will be the lenders, and the lower ought the rate of the national interest to be: but where there is not enough, or barely enough, circulating cash, to answer the ordinary uses of the public, interest will be proportionably high; for lenders will be but few, as few can submit to the inconvenience of lending.

So, also, the hazard of an entire loss has its weight in the regulation of interest: hence, the better the security, the lower will the interest be; the rate of interest being generally in a compound ratio, formed out of the inconvenience, and the hazard. As, if there were no inconvenience, there should be no interest but what is equivalent to the hazard, so if there were no hazard, there ought to be no interest, save only what arises from the mere inconvenience of lending. Thus, if the quantity of specie in a nation be such, that the general inconvenience of lending for a year is computed to amount to three per cent; a man that has money by him will perhaps lend it upon good personal security at five per cent, allowing two for the hazard run; he will lend it upon landed security or mortgage at four per cent, the hazard being proportionably less: but he will lend it to the state, on the maintenance of which all his property depends, at three per cent, the hazard being none at all.

But sometimes the hazard may be greater than the rate of interest allowed by law will compensate. This gives rise to the practice of

1. Bottomry, or respondentia.   2. Policies of insurance.   3. Annuities upon lives.

⚖ BOTTOMRY OR RESPONDENTIA — First, bottomry (which originally arose from permitting the master of a ship, in a foreign country, to hypothecate the ship in order to raise money to refit) is in the nature of a mortgage of a ship; when the owner takes up money to enable him to carry on his voyage, and pledges the keel or bottom of the ship (pars pro toto—a part for the whole) as a security for the repayment. In which case it is understood, that if a ship be lost, the lender loses also his whole money; but if it returns in safety, then he shall receive back his principal, and also the premium or interest agreed upon, however it may exceed the legal rate of interest. This is allowed to be a valid contract in all trading nations, for the benefit of commerce, and by reason of the extraordinary hazard run by the lender. In this case the ship and tackle, if brought home, are answerable (as well as the person of the borrower) for the money lent.

If the loan is not upon the vessel, but upon the goods and merchandise, which must necessarily be sold or exchanged in the course of the voyage, then only the borrower, personally, is bound to answer the contract; who therefore in this case is said to take up money at respondentia. These terms are also applied to contracts for the repayment of money borrowed, not on the ship and goods only, but on the mere hazard of the voyage itself; when a man lends a merchant 1,000 pounds to be employed in a beneficial trade, with condition to be repaid with extraordinary interest, in case such a voyage be safely performed: which kind of agreement is sometimes called faenus nauticum (naval usury), and sometimes usura maritima (maritime usury). But as this gave an opening for usurious and gaming contracts, especially upon long voyages, it was enacted by statute (Marine Insurance, 1745), that all moneys lent on bottomry or at respondentia, on vessels bound to or from the East Indies, shall be expressly lent only upon the ship or upon the merchandise; that the lender shall have the benefit of salvage; and that if the borrower has not on board effects to the value of the sum borrowed, he shall be responsible to the lender for so much of the principal as hath not been laid out, with legal interest and all other charges, though the ship and merchandise be totally lost.

⚖ INSURANCE — Secondly, a policy of insurance is a contract between A and B, that, upon A's paying a premium equivalent to the hazard run, B will indemnify or insure him against a particular event. This is founded upon one of the same principles as the doctrine of interest upon loans, that of hazard; but not that of inconvenience. For if I insure a ship to the Levant, and back again, at five per cent; here I calculate the chance that she performs her voyage to be twenty to one against her being lost; and, if she be lost, I lose 100 pounds and get 5 pounds.

Now, this is much the same as if I lend the merchant whose whole fortunes are embarked in this vessel, 100 pounds at the rate of eight per cent. For by a loan I should be immediately out of possession of my money, in inconvenience of which we have computed equal to three per cent: if, therefore, I had actually lent him 100 pounds I must have added 3 pounds on the score of inconvenience, to the 5 pounds allowed for the hazard, which together would have made 8 pounds. But, as upon an insurance, I am never out of possession of my money till the loss actually happens, nothing is therein allowed upon the principle of inconvenience, but all upon the principal of hazard. Thus, too, in a loan, if the chance of repayment depends upon the borrower's life, it is frequent (besides the usual rate of interest) for the borrower to have his life insured till the time of repayment; for which he is loaded with an additional premium, suited to his age and constitution.

LIFE INSURANCE — Thus, if Sempronius has only an annuity for his life, and would borrow 100 pounds of Titius for a year; the inconvenience and general hazard of this loan, we have seen, are equivalent to 5 pounds, which is therefore the legal interest: but there is also a special hazard in this case; for if Sempronius dies within the year, Titius must lose the whole of his 100 pounds. Suppose this chance to be as one to ten: it will follow that the extraordinary hazard is worth 10 pounds more, and therefore, that the reasonable rate of interest in this case would be fifteen per cent. But this the law, to avoid abuses, will not permit to be taken; Sempronius there gives Titius, the lender, only 5 pounds the legal interest; but applies to Gaius an insurer, and gives him the other 10 pounds to indemnify Titius against the extraordinary hazard.

In this manner may any extraordinary or particular hazard be provided against, which the established rate of interest will not reach; that being calculated by the state to answer only the ordinary and general hazard, together with the lender's inconvenience in parting with his specie for the time. But, in order to prevent these insurances from being turned into a mischievous kind of gaming, it is enacted by statute (Life Insurance, 1774), that no insurance shall be made on lives, or on any other event, wherein the party insured hath no interest; that in all policies the name of such interested party shall be inserted; and nothing more shall be recovered thereon than the amount of the interest of the insured.

⚖ MARINE INSURANCE — This doth not, however, extend to Marine insurances, which were provided for by a prior law of their own, and the learning relating to which hath of late years been greatly improved by a series of judicial decisions, which have now established the law in such a variety of cases, that (if well and judiciously collected) they would form a very complete title in a code of commercial jurisprudence. But, being founded on equitable principles, which chiefly result from the special circumstances of the case, it is not easy to reduce them to any general heads in mere elementary institutes. Thus much, however, may be said; that, being contracts, the very essence of which consists in observing the purest good faith and integrity, they are vacated by any the least shadow of fraud or undue concealment: and, on the other hand, being much for the benefit and extension of trade, by distributing the loss or gain among the number of adventures, they are greatly encouraged and protected by both common law and acts of parliament.

But, as a practice had obtained of insuring large sums without having any property on board, which were called insurances, interest or no interest; and also of insuring the same goods several times over; both of which were a species of gaming, without any advantage to commerce, and were denominated wagering policies: it is therefore enacted by the statute (Marine Insurance, 1745), that all insurances, interest or no interest, or without further proof of interest than the policy itself, or by way of gaming or wagering, or without benefit of salvage to the insurer (all of which had the same pernicious tendency), shall be totally null and void.

⚖ ANNUITIES — Thirdly, the practice of purchasing annuities for lives at a certain price or premium, instead of advancing the same sum on an ordinary loan, arises usually from the inability of the borrower to give the lender a permanent security for the return of the money borrowed, at any one period of time. He therefore stipulates to repay annually, during his life, some part of the money borrowed; together with legal interest for so much of the principal as annually remains unpaid, and an additional compensation for the extraordinary hazard run, of losing that principal entirely by the contingency of the borrower's death: all of which considerations, being calculated and blended together, will constitute the just proportion or quantum of the annuity grant. The real value of that contingency must depend on the age, constitution, situation, and conduct of the borrower; and therefore the price of such annuities cannot without the utmost difficulty be reduced to any general rules. So that if, by the terms of the contract, the lender's principal is bona fide (and not colorably) put in jeopardy, no inequality of price will make it an usurious bargain; though, under some circumstances of imposition, it may be relieved against in equity.

To throw, however, some check upon improvident transactions of this kind, which are usually carried on with great privacy, the statute (Grants of Life Annuities, 1776), has directed, that upon the sale of any life annuity of more than the value of ten pounds per annum (unless a sufficient pledge of lands in fee simple or stock in the public funds) the true consideration, which shall be in money only, shall be set forth and described in the security itself; and a memorial of the date of the security, of the names of the parties and witnesses, and of the consideration money, shall within twenty days after its execution be enrolled in the court of chancery; else the security shall be null and void.

In case of collusive practices respecting the consideration, the court, in which any action is brought or judgment obtained upon such collusive security, may order the same to be canceled, and the judgment (if any) to be vacated. All contracts for the purchase of annuities from infants shall remain utterly void, and incapable of confirmation after such infants arrive to the age of maturity. But, to return to the doctrine of common interest on loans:

⚖ RATES OF INTEREST — Upon the two principles of inconvenience and hazard, compared together, different nations have at different times established different rates of interest. The Romans at one time allowed one per cent monthly or twelve per cent per annum, to be taken for common loans; but Justinian reduced it to four per cent; but allowed higher interest to be taken of merchants, because there the hazard was greater. So, too, Grotius, informs us, that in Holland the rate of interest was then eight per cent in common loans, but twelve to merchants. Our law establishes one standard for all alike, where the pledge or security itself is not put in jeopardy; lest, under the general pretense of vague and indeterminate hazards, a door should be opened to fraud and usury: leaving specific hazards to be provided against by specific insurances, by annuities for lives, or by loans upon respondentia, or bottomry.

The rate of legal interest has varied and decreased for two hundred years past, according as the quantity of specie in the kingdom has increased by accessions of trade, the introduction of paper credit, and other circumstances. The statute (Usury, 1545), confined interest to ten per cent. But as the nation grew more wealthy the statute (Usury, 1660), to six; and lastly by statute (Usury, 1713), it was brought down to five per cent yearly, which is now the extremity of legal interest that can be taken. But yet, if a contract which carried interest be made in a foreign country, our courts will direct the payment of interest according to the law of that country in which the contract was made.

⚖️ DEBT — The last general species of contracts, which I have to mention, is that of debt; whereby a chose in action, or right to a certain sum of money, is mutually acquired and lost. This may be the counterpart of, and arise from, any of the other species of contracts. As, in case of a sale, where the price is not paid in ready money, the vendee becomes indebted to the vendor for the sum agreed on; and the vendor has a property in this price, as a chose in action, by means of this contract of debt. In bailment, if the bailee loses or detains a sum of money bailed to him for any special purpose, he becomes indebted to the bailor in the same numerical sum, upon his implied contract, that he should execute the trust reposed in him, or repay the money to the bailor.

Upon hiring or borrowing, the hirer or borrower, at the same time that he acquires a property in the thing lent, may also become indebted to the lender, upon his contract to restore the money borrowed, to pay the price or premium of the loan, the hire of the horse, or the like. Any contract, in short, whereby a determinate sum of money becomes due to any person, and is not paid but remains, in action merely, is a contract of debt. Taken in this light, it comprehends a great variety of acquisition; being usually divided into debts of record, debts by special, and debts by simple contract.

⚖️ DEBTS OF RECORD — A debt of record is a sum of money, which appears to be due by the evidence of a court of record. Thus, when any specific sum is adjudged to be due from the defendant to the plaintiff, on an action or suit at law; this is a contract of the highest nature, being established by the sentence of a court of judicature. Debts upon recognizance, are also a sum of money, recognized or acknowledged to be due to the crown or a subject, in the presence of some court or magistrate, with a condition that such acknowledgment shall be void upon the appearance of the party, his good behavior, or the like: and these, together with statutes merchant and statutes staple, etc., if forfeited by nonperformance of the condition, are also ranked among this first and principal class of debts, viz., debts of record; since the contract, on which they are founded, is witnessed by the highest kind of evidence, viz., by matter of record.

⚖️ DEBTS BY SPECIALTY — Debts by specialty, or special contract, are such whereby a sum of money becomes, or is acknowledged to be, due by deed or instrument under seal. Such as by deed of covenant, by deed of sale, by lease reserving rent, or by bond or obligation: which last we took occasion to explain in the twentieth chapter of the present book; and then showed that it is an acknowledgment or creation of a debt from the obligor to the obligee, unless the obligor performs a condition thereunto usually annexed, as the payment of rent or money borrowed, the observance of a covenant, and the like; on failure of which the bond becomes forfeited and the debt becomes due in law. These are looked upon as the next class of debts after those of record, being confirmed by special evidence, under seal.

⚖️ DEBTS BY SIMPLE CONTRACT — Debts by simple contract are such, where the contract upon which the obligation arises is neither ascertained by matter of record, nor yet by deed or special instrument, but by mere oral evidence, the most simple of any; or by notes unsealed, which are capable of a more easy proof, and (therefore only) better, than a verbal promise. It is easy to see into what a vast variety of obligations this last class may be branched out, through the numerous contracts for money, which are not only expressed by the parties, but virtually implied in law.

At present, by statute (Statute of Frauds, 1677), no executor or administrator shall be charged upon any special promise to answer damages out of his own estate, and no person shall be charged upon any promise to answer for the debt or default of another, or upon any agreement in consideration of marriage, or upon any contract or sale of any real estate, or upon any agreement that is not to be performed within one year from the making; unless the agreement or some memorandum thereof be in writing, and signed by the party himself or by his authority.

But there is one species of debts upon simple contract, which, being a transaction now introduced into all sorts of civil life, under the name of paper credit, deserves a more particular regard. These are debts by bills of exchange, and promissory notes.

⚖️ BILLS OF EXCHANGE — A bill of exchange is a security, originally invented among merchants in different countries, for the more easy remittance of money from the one to the other, which has since spread itself into almost all pecuniary transactions. It is an open letter of request from one man to another, desiring him to pay a sum named therein to a third person on his account; by which means a man at the most distant part of the world may have money remitted to him from any trading country.

If A lives in Jamaica, and owes B, who lives in England, 1,000 pounds, now if C be going from England to Jamaica, he may pay B this 1,000 pounds and take a bill of exchange drawn by B in England upon A in Jamaica, and receive it when he comes thither. Thus does B receive his debt, at any distance of place, by transferring it to C; who carries over his money in proper credit, without danger of robbery or loss.

This method is said to have been brought into general use by the Jews and Lombards, when banished for their usury and other vices; in order the more easily to draw their effects out of France and England, into those countries in which they had chosen to reside. But the invention of it was a little earlier: for the Jews were banished out of Guienne in 1287, and out of England in 1290; and in 1236 the use of paper credit was introduced into the Mogul empire in China.

In common speech such a bill is frequently called a draft, but a bill of exchange is the more legal as well as mercantile expression. The person, however, who writes this letter, is called in law the drawer, and he to whom it is written the drawee; and the third person, or negotiator, to whom it is payable (whether specially named, or the bearer generally) is called the payee.

⚖ FOREIGN AND INLAND BILLS — These bills are either foreign, or inland; foreign, when drawn by a merchant residing abroad upon his correspondent in England, or vice versa; and inland, when both the drawer and the drawee reside within the kingdom. Formerly foreign bills of exchange were much more regarded in the eye of the law than inland ones, as being thought of more public concern in the advancement of trade and commerce. But now by two statutes (Bill of Exchange, 1697), the other (Bill of Exchange, 1704), inland bills of exchange are put upon the same footing as foreign ones; what was the law and custom of merchants with regard to the one, and taken notice of merely as such, being by those statutes expressly enacted with regard to the other. So that there is now in law no manner of difference between them.

⚖ PROMISSORY NOTES — Promissory notes, or notes of hand, are a plain and direct engagement in writing, to pay a sum specified at the time therein limited to a person therein named, or sometimes to his order, or often to the bearer at large. These, also, by the same statute (Bill of Exchange, 1704), are made assignable and indorsable in like manner as bills of exchange. But, by statute (Negotiation of Notes and Bills, 1774), all promissory or other notes, bills of exchange, drafts, and undertakings in writing, being negotiable or transferable, for the payment of less than twenty shillings, are declared to be null and void: and it is made penal to utter or publish any such; they being deemed prejudicial to trade and public credit. By (Bill of Exchange, 1776), all such notes, bills, drafts, and undertakings, to the amount of twenty shillings and less than five pounds, are subjected to many other regulations and formalities; the omission of any one of which vacates the security, and is penal to him that utters it.

☙ NEGOTIABILITY OF BILLS AND NOTES — The payee, we may observe, either of a bill of exchange or promissory note, has clearly a property vested in him (not indeed in possession but in action) by the express contract of the drawer in the case of a promissory note, and, in the case of a bill of exchange, by his implied contract, viz., that, provided the drawee does not pay the bill, the drawer will: for which reason it is usual, in bills of exchange, to express that the value thereof hath been received by the drawer; in order to show the consideration, upon which the implied contract of repayment arises.

This property, so vested, may be transferred and assigned from the payee to any other man; contrary to the general rule of the common law, that no chose in action is assignable: which assignment is the life of paper credit. It may therefore be of some use to mention a view of the principal incidents attending this transfer or assignment, in order to make it regular, and thereby to charge the drawer with the payment of the debt to other persons than those with whom he originally contracted.

☙ INDORSEMENT — In the first place, then, the payee, or person to whom or whose order such bill of exchange or promissory note is payable, may by indorsement, or writing his name in dorso or on the back of it, assign over his whole property to the bearer, or else to another person by name, either of whom is then called the indorsee; and he may assign the same to another, and so on in infinitum. A promissory note, payable to A or bearer, is negotiable without any indorsement, and payment thereof may be demanded by any bearer of it.

☙ PRESENTATION AND ACCEPTANCE — In case of a bill of exchange, the payee, or the indorsee (whether it be a general or particular indorsement), is to go to the drawee, and offer his bill for acceptance; which acceptance (so as to charge the drawer with costs) must be in writing, under or on the back of the bill. If the drawee accepts the bill, either verbally or in writing, he then makes himself liable to pay it; this being now a contract on his side, grounded on an acknowledgment that the drawer has effects in his hands, or at least credit sufficient to warrant the payment.

If the drawee refuses to accept the bill, and it be of the value of 20 pounds, or upward, and expressed to be for value received, the payee or indorsee may protest it for nonacceptance: which protest must be made in writing, under a copy of such bill of exchange, by some notary public; or, if no such notary be resident in the place, then by any other substantial inhabitant in the presence of two credible witnesses; and notice of such protest must, within fourteen days after, be given to the drawer.

⚖ PROTEST FOR NONPAYMENT — In case such bill be accepted by the drawee, and after acceptance he fails or refuses to pay it within three days after it becomes due (which three days are called days of grace), the payee or indorsee is then to get it protested for nonpayment, in the same manner, and by the same persons who are to protest it in case of nonacceptance, and such protest must also be notified, within fourteen days after, to the drawer. He, on producing such protest, either of nonacceptance or nonpayment, is bound to make good to the payee, or indorsee, not only the amount of the said bills (which he is bound to do within a reasonable time after nonpayment, without any protest, by the rules of the common law), but also interest and all charges, to be computed from the time of making such protest.

If no protest be made or notified to the drawer, and any damages accrues by such neglect, it shall fall on the holder of the bill. The bill, when refused, must be demanded of the drawer as soon as conveniently may be: for though, when one draws a bill of exchange, he subjects himself to the payment, if the person on whom it is drawn refuses either to accept or pay, yet that is with this limitation, that if the bill be not paid, when due, the person to whom it is payable shall in convenient time give the drawer notice thereof; for otherwise the law will imply it paid: since it would be prejudicial to commerce, if a bill might rise up to charge the drawer at any distance of time; when in the meantime all reckonings and accounts may be adjusted between the drawer and drawee.

⚖ LIABILITY OF INDORSERS — If the bill be an indorsed bill, and the indorsee cannot get the drawee to discharge it, he may call upon either the drawer or the indorser, or if the bill has been negotiated through many hands, upon any of the indorsers; for each indorser is a warrantor for the payment of the bill, which is frequently taken in payment as much (or more) upon the credit of the indorser, as of the drawer. If such indorser, so called upon, has the names of one or more indorsers prior to his own, to each of whom he is properly an indorsee, he is also at liberty to call upon any of them to make him satisfaction; and so upward. But the first indorser has nobody to resort to but the drawer only.

What has been said of bills of exchange is applicable also to promissory notes, that are indorsed over, and negotiated from one hand to another: only that, in this case, as there is no drawee, there can be no protest for nonacceptance; or rather, the law considered a promissory note in the light of a bill drawn by a man upon himself, and accepted at the time of drawing. In case of nonpayment by the drawer, the several indorsees of a promissory note have the same remedy, as upon bills of exchange, against the prior indorsers.

TITLE BY BANKRUPTCY

The preceding chapter having treated pretty largely of the acquisition of personal property by several commercial methods, we from thence shall be easily led to take into our present consideration a tenth method of transferring property, which is that of

⚖ TITLE BY BANKRUPTCY — Bankruptcy; a title which we before lightly touched upon, so far as it related to the transfer of the real estate of the bankrupt. At present we are to treat of it more minutely, as it principally relates to the disposition of chattels, in which the property of persons concerned in trade more usually consists, than in lands or tenements. Let us therefore first of all consider, 1. Who may become a bankrupt: 2. What acts make a bankrupt: 3. The proceedings on a commission of bankrupt: and 4. In what manner an estate in goods and chattels may be transferred by bankruptcy.

⚖ WHO MAY BECOME A BANKRUPT — A bankrupt was before defined to be "a trader, who secretes himself, or does certain other acts, tending to defraud his creditors." He was formerly considered merely in the light of a criminal or offender. At present the laws of bankruptcy are considered as laws calculated for the benefit of trade, and founded on the principles of humanity as well as justice; and to that end they confer some privileges, not only on the creditors, but also on the bankrupt or debtor himself. On the creditors; by compelling the bankrupt to give up all his effects to their use, without any fradulent concealment: on the debtor; by exempting him from the rigor of the general law, whereby his person might be confined at the discretion of his creditor, though in reality he has nothing to satisfy the debt: whereas the law of bankrupts: taking into consideration the sudden and unavoidable accidents to which men in trade are liable, has given them the liberty of their persons, and some pecuniary emoluments, upon condition they surrender up their whole estate to be divided among the creditors.

⚖ ROMAN LAW — In this respect our legislature seems to have attended to the example of the Roman law. I mean not the terrible law of the twelve tables; whereby the creditors might cut the debtor's body into pieces, and each of them take his proportionable share: if indeed that law of cutting the debtor into pieces, is to be understood in so very butcherly a light; which many learned men have with reason doubted. Nor do I mean those less inhuman laws (if they may be called so, as their meaning is indisputably certain) of imprisoning the debtor's person in chains; subjecting him to stripes and hard labor, at the mercy of his rigid creditor; and sometimes selling him, his wife, and children, to perpetual foreign slavery trans Tiberim (beyond the Tiber): an oppression which produced so many popular insurrections and secessions to the mons sacer (the sacred mount). But I mean the law of cession, introduced by the Christian emporers; whereby, if a debtor ceded, or yielded up all his fortune to his creditors, he was secured from being dragged to a jail, all bodily torture being also removed. For, as the emperor justly observes, it was inhuman, being deprived of all his fortune, to be utterly ruined. Thus far was just and reasonable: but, as the departing from one extreme is apt to produce its opposite, we find it afterwards enacted, that if the debtor by any unforeseen accident was reduced to low circumstances, and would swear that he had not sufficient left to pay his debts, he should not be compelled to cede or give up even that which he had in his possession: a law, which under a false notion of humanity, seems to be fertile of perjury, injustice, and absurdity.

⚖ ONLY TRADERS WITHIN THE LAW OF ENGLAND — The laws of England, more wisely, have steered in the middle between both extremes; providing at once against the inhumanity of the creditor, who is not suffered to confine an honest bankrupt after his effects are delivered up; and at the same time taking care that all his just debts shall be paid, so far as the effects will extend. But still they are cautious of encouraging prodigality and extravagance by this indulgence to debtors; and therefore they allow the benefit of the laws of bankruptcy to none but actual traders; since that set of men are, generally speaking, the only persons liable to accidental losses, and to an inability of paying their debts, without any fault of their own.

If persons in other situations of life run in debt without the power of payment, they must take the consequences of their own indiscretion, even though they meet with sudden accidents that may reduce their fortunes: for the law holds it to be an unjustifiable practice, for any person but a trader to encumber himself with debts of any considerable value. If a gentleman, or one in a liberal profession, at the time of contracting his debts, has a sufficient fund to pay them, the delay of payment is a species of dishonesty, and a temporary injustice to his creditor: and if, at such time, he has no sufficient fund, the dishonesty and injustice is the greater. He cannot therefore murmur, if he suffers the punishment which he has voluntarily drawn upon himself. But in mercantile transactions the case is far otherwise. Trade cannot be carried on without mutual credit on both sides: the contracting of debts is therefore here not only justifiable, but necessary. If by accidental calamities, as by the loss of a ship in a tempest, the failure of brother traders, or by the nonpayment of persons out of trade, a merchant or trader becomes incapable of discharging his own debts, it is his misfortune and not his fault.

To the misfortunes, therefore, of debtors, the law has given a compassionate remedy, but denied it to their faults: since, at the same time that it provides for the security of commerce, by enacting that every considerable trader may be declared a bankrupt, for the benefit of his creditors as well as himself, it has also to discourage extravagance declared, that no one shall be capable of being made a bankrupt, but only a trader; nor capable of receiving the full benefit of the statutes, but only an industrious trader.

⚖️ FIRST BANKRUPT ACTS — The first statute made concerning any English bankrupts was (Bankruptcy, 1542), when trade began first to be properly cultivated in England: which has been almost totally altered by statute (Bankrupts, 1571), whereby bankruptcy is confined to such persons only as have used the trade of merchandise, in gross or by retail, by way of bargaining, exchange, re-change, bartering, chevisance, (that is making contracts) or otherwise; or have sought their living by buying and selling.

By statute (Bankrupts, 1623), persons using the trade and profession of a scrivener, receiving other men's moneys and estates into their trust and custody, are also made liable to the statutes of bankruptcy: and the benefits, as well as the penal parts of the law, are extended as well to aliens and denizens as to natural-born subjects; being intended entirely for the protection of trade, in which aliens are often as deeply concerned as natives.

By many subsequent statutes, but lastly by statute (Bankrupts, 1731), bankers, brokers, and factors, are declared liable to the statutes of bankruptcy; and this upon the same reason that scriveners are included by the statute of James I, viz., for the relief of their creditors; whom they have otherwise more opportunities of defrauding than any other set of dealers: and they are properly to be looked upon as traders, since they make merchandise of money, in the same manner as other merchants do of goods and other movable chattels.

By the same act, no farmer, grazier, or drover, shall (as such) be liable to be deemed a bankrupt: for though they buy and sell corn, and hay, and beasts, in the course of husbandry, yet trade is not their principal, but only a collateral, object; their chief concern being to manure and till the ground, and make the best advantage of its produce. Besides, the subjecting them to the laws of bankruptcy might be a means of defeating their landlords of the security which the law has given them above all others, for the payment of their reserved rents: wherefore, also, upon a similar reason, a receiver of the king's taxes is not capable, as such, of being a bankrupt; lest the king should be defeated of those extensive remedies against his debtors, which are put into his hands by the prerogative.

By the same statute, no person shall have a commission of bankrupt awarded against him, unless at the petition of some one creditor, to whom he owes 100 pounds; or of two, to whom he is indebted 150 pounds; or of more, to whom all together he is indebted 200 pounds. For the law does not look upon persons, whose debts amount to less, to be traders considerable enough, either to enjoy the benefit of the statutes, themselves, or to entitle the creditors, for the benefit of public commerce, to demand the distribution of their effects.

⚖ WHAT CONSTITUTES TRADING — In the interpretation of these several statutes it hath been held, that buying only, or selling only, will not qualify a man to be a bankrupt; but it must be both buying and selling, and also getting a livelihood by it. As, by exercising the calling of a merchant, a grocer, a mercer, or, in one general word, a chapman, who is one that buys and sells anything.

⚖ WHAT ARE ACTS OF BANKRUPTCY — We are to inquire, secondly, by what acts a man may become a bankrupt. A bankrupt is "a trader, who secretes himself, or does certain other acts, tending to defraud his creditors." We have hitherto been employed in explaining the former part of this description, "a trader"; let us now attend to the latter, "who secretes himself, or does certain other acts, tending to defraud his creditors." In general, whenever such a trader, as is before described, hath endeavored to avoid his creditors, or evade their just demands, this hath been declared by the legislature to be an act of bankruptcy, upon which a commission may be sued out. For in this extra-judicial method of proceeding, which is allowed merely for the benefit of commerce, the law is extremely watchful to detect a man, whose circumstances are declining, in the first instance, or at least as early as possible: that the creditors may receive as large a proportion of their debts as may be; and that a man may not go on wantonly wasting his substance, and then claim the benefit of the statutes, when he has nothing left to distribute.

To learn what the particular acts of bankruptcy are, which render a man a bankrupt, we must consult the several statutes, and the resolutions formed by the courts thereon. Among these may therefore be reckoned, 1. Departing from the realm, whereby a man withdraws himself from the jurisdiction and coercion of the law, with intent to defraud his creditors. 2. Departing from his own house, with intent to secrete himself, and avoid his creditors. 3. Keeping in his own house, privately, so as not to be seen or spoken with by his creditors, except for just and necessary cause; which is likewise construed to be an intention to defraud his creditors, by avoiding the process of the law. 4. Procuring or suffering himself willingly to be arrested, or outlawed, or imprisoned, without just and lawful cause; which is likewise deemed an attempt to defraud his creditors. 5. Procuring his money, goods, chattels, and effects to be attached or sequestered by any legal process; which is another plain and direct endeavor to disappoint his creditors of their security. 6. Making any fraudulent conveyance to a friend, or secret trustee, of his lands, tenements, goods, or chattels; which is an act of the same suspicious nature with the last. 7. Procuring any protection, not being himself privileged by parliament, in order to screen his person from arrests; which also is an endeavor to elude the justice of the law. 8. Endeavoring or desiring, by any petition to the king, or bill exhibited in any of the king's courts against any creditors, to compel them to take less than their just debts; or to procrastinate the time of payment, originally contracted for; which are an acknowledgment of either his poverty or his knavery. 9. Lying in prison for two months, or more, upon arrest or other detention for debts, without finding bail, in order to obtain his liberty. For the inability to procure bail argues a strong deficiency in his credit, owing either to his suspected poverty or ill character; and his neglect to do it, if able, can arise only from a fraudulent intention: in either of which cases it is high time for his creditors to look to themselves, and compel a distribution of his effects. 10. Escaping from prison after an arrest for a just debt of 100 pounds or upwards. For no man would break prison that was able and desirous to procure bail; which brings it within the reason of the last case.   11. Neglecting to make satisfaction for any just debt to the amount of 100 pounds within two months after service of legal process, for such debts, upon any trader having privilege of parliament.

⚖ CONSTRUCTION OF STATUTES — These are the several acts of bankruptcy, expressly defined by the statutes relating to this title: which being so numerous, and the whole law of bankrupts being an innovation on the common law, our courts of justice have been tender of extending or multiplying acts of bankruptcy by any construction, or implication.

Sir John Holt held, that a man's removing his goods privately to prevent their being seized in execution, was no act of bankruptcy. For the statutes mention only fraudulent gifts to third persons, and procuring them to be seized by sham process, in order to defraud creditors: but this, though a palpable fraud, yet falling within neither of those cases, cannot be adjudged an act of bankruptcy. So, also, it has been determined expressly, that a banker's stopping or refusing payment is no act of bankruptcy; for it is not within the description of any of the statutes, and there may be good reasons for his so doing, as suspicion of forgery, and the like: and if, in consequence of such refusal, he is arrested, and puts in bail, still it is no act of bankruptcy: but if he goes to prison, and lies there two months, then, and not before, is he become a bankrupt. Let us next consider,

⚖ PROCEEDINGS IN BANKRUPTCY — The proceedings on a commission of bankrupt; so far as they affect the bankrupt himself. These depend entirely on the several statutes of bankruptcy; all which I shall endeavor to blend together, and digest into a concise methodical order.

First, there must be a petition to the lord chancellor by one creditor to the amount of 100 pounds, or by two to the amount of 150 pounds, or by three or more to the amount of 200 pounds; upon which he grants a commission to such discreet persons as to him shall seem good, who are then styled commissioners of bankrupt. The petitioners, to prevent malicious applications, must be bound in a security of 200 pounds to make the party amends in case they do not prove him a bankrupt.

If, on the other hand, they receive any money of effects from the bankrupt, as a recompense for suing out the commission, so as to receive more than their ratable dividends of the bankrupt's estate, they forfeit not only what they shall have so received, but their whole debt. These provisions are made, as well to secure persons in good credit from being damnified by malicious petitions, as to prevent knavish combinations between the creditors and bankrupt, in order to obtain the benefit of a commission. When the commission is awarded and issued, the commissioners are to meet, at their own expense, and to take an oath for the due execution of their commission, and to be allowed a sum not exceeding 20 shillings, per diem each, at every sitting. No commission of bankrupt shall abate, or be void, upon any demise of the crown.

⚖ PROOF: FINDING: NOTICE: SURRENDER — When the commissioners have received their commission, they are first to receive proof of the person's being a trader, and having committed some act of bankruptcy; and then to declare him a bankrupt, if proved so; and to give notice thereof in the *Gazette,* and at the same time to appoint three meetings.

At one of these meetings an election must be made of assignees, or persons to whom the bankrupt's estate shall be assigned, and in whom it shall be vested for the benefit of the creditors; which assignees are to be chosen by the major part, in value, of the creditors who shall then have proved their debts; but may be originally appointed by the commissioners, and afterwards approved or rejected by the creditors: but no creditor shall be admitted to vote in the choice of assignees, whose debt on the balance of accounts does not amount to 10 pounds.

At the third meeting, at farthest, which must be the forty-second day after the advertisement in the *Gazette,* the bankrupt, upon notice also personally served upon him or left at his usual place of abode, must surrender himself personally to the commissioners, and must thenceforth in all respects conform to the directions of the statutes of bankruptcy; or, in default thereof, shall be guilty of felony without benefit of clergy, and shall suffer death, and his goods and estate shall be distributed among his creditors.

⚖ ARREST OF BANKRUPT — In case the bankrupt absconds, or is likely to run away, between the time of the commission issued, and the last day of surrender, he may by warrant from any judge or justice of the peace be apprehended and committed to the county jail, in order to be forthcoming to the commissioners; who are also empowered immediately to grant a warrant for seizing his goods and papers.

⚖ EXAMINATION OF BANKRUPT — When the bankrupt appears, the commissioners are to examine him touching all matters relating to his trade and effects. They may also summon before them, and examine, the bankrupt's wife and any other person whatsoever, as to all matters relating to the bankrupt's affairs. In case any of them shall refuse to answer, or shall not answer fully, to any lawful question, or shall refuse to subscribe such their examination, the commissioners may commit them to prison without bail, till they make and sign a full answer; the commissioners specifying in their warrant of commitment the question so refused to be answered. Any jailer, permitting such person to escape, or go out of prison, shall forfeit 500 pounds to the creditors.

The bankrupt, upon this examination, is bound upon pain of death to make a full discovery of all his estate and effects, as well in expectancy as possession, and how he has disposed of the same; together with all books and writings relating thereto; and is to deliver up all in his own power to the commissioners (except the necessary apparel of himself, his wife, and his children); or, in case he conceals or embezzles any effects to the amount of 20 pounds, or withholds any books or writings with intent to defraud his creditors, he shall be guilty of felony without benefit of clergy.

After the time allowed to the bankrupt for such discovery is expired, any other person voluntarily discovering any part of his estate, before unknown to the assignees, shall be entitled to five per cent out of the effects so discovered, and such further reward as the assignees and commissioners shall think proper. Any trustee willfully concealing the estate of any bankrupt, after the expiration of the two and forty days, shall forfeit 100 pounds and double the value of the estate concealed, to the creditors.

⚖ CERTIFICATE OF CONFORMITY — Hitherto everything is in favor of the creditors; and the law seems to be pretty rigid and severe against the bankrupt but in case he proves honest, it makes him full amends for all this rigor and severity. For if the bankrupt hath made an ingenuous discovery, hath conformed to the directions of the law, and hath acted in all points to the satisfaction of his creditors; and if they or four parts in five of them in number and value (but none of them creditors for less than 20 pounds), will sign a certificate to that purport; the commissioners are then to authenticate such certificate under their hands and seals, and to transmit it to the lord chancellor: and he, or two judges whom he shall appoint, on oath made by the bankrupt that such certificate was obtained without fraud, may allow the same; or disallow it, upon cause shown by any of the creditors of the bankrupt.

⚖ ALLOWANCE TO BANKRUPT — If no cause be shown to the contrary, the certificate is allowed of course; and then the bankrupt is entitled to a decent and reasonable allowance out of his effects, for his future support and maintenance, and to put him in a way of honest industry. This allowance is also in proportion to his former good behavior, in the early discovery of the decline of his affairs, and thereby giving his creditors a larger dividend.

If his effects will not pay one-half of his debts, or ten shillings in the pound, he is left to the discretion of the commissioners and assignees, to have a competent sum allowed him, not exceeding three per cent; but if they pay ten shillings in the pound, he is to be allowed five per cent; if twelve shillings and six-pence, then seven and a half per cent; and if fifteen shillings in the pound, then the bankrupt shall be allowed ten per cent: provided, that such allowance does not in the first case exceed 200£, in the second 250£, and in the third 300£.

DISCHARGE OF DEBTS — Besides this allowance, he has also an indemnity granted him, of being free and discharged forever from all debts owing by him at the time he became a bankrupt; even though judgment shall have been obtained against him, and he lies in prison upon execution for such debts; and, for that among other purposes, all proceedings on commission of bankrupt are, on petition, to be entered of record, as a perpetual bar against actions to be commenced on this account: though, in general, the production of the certificate property allowed shall be sufficient evidence of all previous proceedings. Thus the bankrupt becomes a clear man again; and, by the assistance of his allowance and his own industry, may become a useful member of the commonwealth: which is rather to be expected, as he cannot be entitled to these benefits, but by the testimony of his creditors themselves of his honest and ingenuous disposition; and unless his failures have been owing to misfortunes, rather than to misconduct and extravagance.

CONDITIONS OF ALLOWANCE AND DISCHARGE — No allowance or indemnity shall be given to a bankrupt, unless his certificate be signed and allowed, as before mentioned; and also, if any creditor produces a fictitious debt, and the bankrupt does not make discovery of it, but suffers the fair creditors to be imposed upon, he loses all title to these advantages. Neither can he claim them, if he has given with any of his children above 100 pounds for a marriage portion, unless he had at that time sufficient left to pay all his debts; or if he has lost at any one time 5 pounds, or in the whole 100 pounds, within a twelvemonth before he became bankrupt, by any manner of gaming or wagering whatsoever; or, within the same time has lost to the value of 100 pounds by stock-jobbing.

To prevent the too common practice of frequent and fraudulent or careless breaking, a mark is set upon such as have been once cleared by a commission of bankrupt, or have compounded with their creditors, or have been delivered by an act of insolvency: which is an occasional act, frequently passed by the legislature; whereby all persons whatsoever, who are either in too low a way of dealing to become bankrupts, or not being in a mercantile state of life are not included within the laws of bankruptcy, are discharged from all suits and imprisonment, upon delivering up all their estate and effects to their creditors upon oath, at the sessions or assizes; in which case their perjury or fraud is usually, as in case of bankrupts, punished with death. Persons who have been once cleared by this, or either of the other methods (of composition with their creditors, or bankruptcy), and afterwards become bankrupts again, unless they pay full fifteen shillings in the pound, are only thereby indemnified as to the confinement of their bodies; but any future estate they shall acquire remains liable to their creditors, excepting their necessary apparel, household goods, and the tools and implements of their trades.

⚖ EFFECT OF BANKRUPTCY ON PROPERTY — The method whereby a real estate, in lands, tenements, and hereditaments, may be transferred by bankruptcy, was shown under its proper head in a former chapter. At present, therefore, we are only to consider the transfer of things personal by this operation of law.

By virtue of the statutes before mentioned all the personal estate and effects of the bankrupt are considered as vested, by the act of bankruptcy, in the future assignees of these commissioners, whether they be goods in actual possession, or debts, contracts, and other choses in action; and the commissioners by their warrant may cause any house or tenement of the bankrupt to be broken open, in order to enter upon and seize the same. When the assignees are choses or approved by the creditors, the commissioners are to assign everything over to them; and the property of every part of the estate is thereby as fully vested in them, as it was in the bankrupt himself, and they have the same remedies to cover it.

⚖ ASSIGNEE'S TITLE — The property vested in the assignees is the whole that the bankrupt had in himself, at the time he committed the first act of bankruptcy, or that has been vested in him since, before his debts are satisfied or agreed for. Therefore, it is usually said, that once a bankrupt, and always a bankrupt: by which is meant, that a plain direct act of bankruptcy once committed cannot be purged, or explained away, by any subsequent conduct, as a dubious equivocal act may be; but that, if a commission is afterwards awarded, the commission and the property of the assignees shall have a relation, or reference, back to the first and original act of bankruptcy. Insomuch that all transactions of the bankrupt are from that time absolutely null and void, either with regard to the alienation of his property, or the receipt of his debts from such as are privy to his bankruptcy; for they are no longer his property, or his debts, but those of the future assignees.

If an execution be sued out, but not served and executed on the bankrupt's effects till after the act of bankruptcy, it is void as against the assignees. But the king is not bound by this fictitious relation, nor is within the statutes of bankrupts; for if, after the act of bankruptcy committed and before the assignment of his effects, an extent issuer for the debt of the crown, the goods are bound thereby.

As these acts of bankruptcy may sometimes be secret to all but a few, it is provided by statute (Bankrupts, 1745), that no money paid by a bankrupt to a bona fide or real creditor, in a course of trade, even after an act of bankruptcy done, shall be liable to be refunded. Nor, by statute (Bankrupts, 1603), shall any debtor of a bankrupt, that pays him his debt, without knowing of his bankruptcy, be liable to account for it again. The intention of this relative power being only to reach fraudulent transactions, and not to distress the fair trader.

The assignees may pursue any legal method of recovering this property so vested in them, by their own authority; but cannot commence a suit in equity, nor compound any debts owing to the bankrupt, nor refer any matters to arbitration, without the consent of the creditors, or the major part of them in value, at a meeting to be held in pursuance of notice in the *Gazette*.

⚖ DISTRIBUTION OF ASSETS — When they have got in all the effects they can reasonably hope for, and reduced them to ready money, the assignees must, within twelve months after the commission issued, give one and twenty days notice to the creditors of a meeting for a dividend or distribution; at which time they must produce their accounts, and verify them upon oath, if required. Then the commissions shall direct a dividend to be made, at so much in the pound, to all creditors who have before proved, or shall then prove, their debts. This dividend must be made equally, and in ratable proportion, to all the creditors, according to the quantity of their debts; no regard being had to the quality of them.

Mortgages, for which the creditor has a real security in his own hands, are entirely safe; for the commission of bankrupt reaches only the equity of redemption. So are also personal debts, where the creditor has a chattel in his hands, as a pledge or pawn for the payment, or has taken the debtor's lands or goods in execution. Upon the equity of the statute (Distress; Execution: Landlord and Tenant, 1709, which directs that, upon all executions of goods being on any premises demised to a tenant, one year's rent and no more shall, if due, be paid to the landlord), it hath also been held, that under a commission of bankrupt, which is in the nature of a statute execution, the landlord shall be allowed his arrears of rent to the same amount, in preference to other creditors, even though he hath neglected to distrain, while the goods remained on the premises: which he is otherwise entitled to do for his entire rent, be the quantum what it may.

But, otherwise, judgments and recognizances (both which are debts of record, and therefore at other times have a priority) and also bonds and obligations by deed or special instrument (which are called debts by specialty, and are usually the next in order), these are all put on a level with debts by mere simple contract, and all paid pari passu (in an equal degree). Nay, so far is this matter carried, that, by the express provision of the statutes, debts not due at the time of the dividend made, as bonds or notes of hand payable at a future day certain, shall be proved and paid equally with the rest, allowing a discount or drawback in proportion. Insurances, and obligations upon bottomry, bona fide made by the bankrupt, though forfeited after the commission is awarded, shall be looked upon in the same light as debts contracted before any act of bankruptcy.

Within eighteen months after the commission issued, a second and final dividend shall be made, unless all the effects were exhausted by the first. If any surplus remains, after paying every creditor his full debt, it shall be restored to the bankrupt. This is a case which sometimes happens to men in trade, who involuntarily, or at least unwarily, commit acts of bankruptcy, by absconding and the like, while their effects are more than sufficient to pay their creditors. If any suspicious or malevolent creditor will take the advantage of such acts, and sue out a commission, the bankrupt has no remedy, but must quietly submit to the effects of his own imprudence; except that, upon satisfaction made to all the creditors, the commission may be superseded. This case may also happen, when a knave is desirous of defrauding his creditors, and is compelled by a commission to do them that justice which otherwise he wanted to evade.

Therefore, though the usual rule is, that all interest on debts carrying interest shall cease from the time of issuing the commission, yet, in case of a surplus left after payment of every debt, such interest shall again revive, and be chargeable on the bankrupt, or his representatives.

TITLE BY TESTAMENT, AND ADMINISTRATION

☙☙ WILLS AND ADMINISTRATION — There yet remain to be examined, two other methods of acquiring personal estates, viz., by testament and administration. These I propose to consider in one and the same view; they being in their nature so connected and blended together, as makes it impossible to treat of them distinctly, without manifest tautology and repetition.

In the pursuit, then, of this joint subject, I shall, first, inquire into the original and antiquity of testaments and administrations; shall, secondly, show who is capable of making a last will and testament; shall, thirdly, consider the nature of a testament and its incidents: shall, fourthly, show what an executor and administrator are, and how they are to be appointed; and lastly, shall select some few of the general heads of the office and duty of executors and administrators.

☙☙ ORIGIN AND HISTORY OF WILLS AND ADMINISTRATIONS — First, as to the original of testaments and administrations. We have more than once observed, that when property came to be vested in individuals by the right of occupancy, it became necessary for the peace of society, that this occupancy should be continued, not only in the present possessor, but in those persons to whom he should think proper to transfer it; which introduced the doctrine and practice of alienations, gifts, and contracts. But these precautions would be very short and imperfect, if they were confined to the life only of the occupier; for then upon his death all his goods would again become common, and create an infinite variety of strife and confusion.

The law of very many societies has therefore given to the proprietor a right of continuing his property after his death, in such persons as he shall name; and, in defect of such appointment or nomination, or where no nomination is permitted, the law of every society has directed the goods to be vested in certain particular individuals, exclusive of all other persons. The former method of acquiring personal property, according to the will of the deceased, not expressed, indeed, but presumed by the law, we call in England an administration; being the same which the civil lawyers terms a succession ab intestato (from an interstate), and which answers to the descent or inheritance of real estates.

⚖️   ANTIQUITY OF WILLS — Testaments are of very high antiquity. We find them in use among the ancient Hebrews; though I hardly think the example usually given, of Abraham's complaining that, unless he had some children of his body, his steward Eliezer of Damascus would be his heir, is quite conclusive to show that he had made him so by will. Indeed a learned writer has adduced this very passage to prove, that in the patriarchal age, on failure of children or kindred, the servants born under their master's roof succeeded to the inheritance as heirs at law. But (to omit what Eusebius and others have related of Noah's testament, made in writing and witnessed under his seal, whereby he disposed of the whole world), I apprehend that a much more authentic instance of the early use of testaments may be found in the sacred writings, wherein Jacob bequeaths to his son Joseph a portion of his inheritance double that of his brethren: which will we find carried into execution many hundred years afterwards, when the posterity of Joseph were divided into two distinct tribes, those of Ephraim and Manasseh, and had two several inheritances assigned them; whereas the descendants of each of the other patriarchs formed only one single tribe, and had only one lot of inheritance.

Salon was the first legislator that introduced wills into Athens; but in many other parts of Greece they were totally discountenanced. In Rome they were unknown, till the laws of the twelve tables were compiled, which first gave the right of bequeathing; and, among the northern nations, particularly among the Germans, testaments were not received into sue.

This variety may serve to evince, that the right of making wills, and disposing of property after death, is merely a creature of the civil state; which has permitted it in some countries, and denied it in others: and, even where it is permitted by law, it is subjected to different formalities and restrictions in almost every nation under Heaven.

⚖️   TESTAMENTARY POWER IN ENGLAND — With us in England this power of bequeathing is coeval with the first rudiments of the law: for we have no traces or memorials of any time when it did not exist. Mention is made of intestacy, in the old law before the Conquest, as being merely accidental; and the distribution of the intestate's estate, after payment of the lord's heriot, is then directed to go according to the established law. "If anyone through negligence or sudden death die intestate, let not the lord take any part of his effects, except what is due to him of right as a heriot. But let his possessions be distributed among his wife, children, and next of kin, to everyone according to their right."

But we are not to imagine that the power of bequeathing extended originally to all a man's personal estate. On the contrary, Glanville will inform us, that by the common law, as it stood in the reign of Henry II, a man's goods were to be divided into three equal parts; of which one went to his heirs or lineal descendants, another to his wife, and the third was at his own disposal: or, if he died without a wife, he might then dispose of one moiety, and the other went to his children; and so e converso, if he had no children, the wife was entitled to one moiety, and he might bequeath the other: but, if he died without either wife or issue, the whole was at his own disposal. The shares of the wife and children were called their reasonable parts; and the writ de rationabili parte bonorum (of the reasonable part, or share, of the goods) was given to recover it.

⚖ DEVELOPMENT OF THE LAW OF WILLS — This continued to be the law of the land at the time of magna carta, which provides, that the king's debts shall first of all be levied, and then the residue of the goods shall go to the executor to perform the will of the deceased: and, if nothing be owing to the crown "let them resign all the chattels to the will of the deceased; reserving to his wife and children their reasonable shares."

In the reign of King Edward III, this right of the wife and children was still held to be the universal or common law; though frequently pleaded as the local custom of Berks, Devon, and other counties: and Sir Henry Finch lays it down expressly, in the reign of Charles I, to be the general law of the land. But this law is at present altered by imperceptible degrees, and the deceased may now by will bequeath the whole of his goods and chattels; though we cannot trace out when first this alteration began. Indeed, Sir Edward Coke is of opinion, that this never was the general law, but only obtained in particular places by special custom: and to establish that doctrine, he relies on a passage in Bracton, which in truth, when compared with the context, makes directly against his opinion.

Bracton lays down the doctrine of the reasonable part to be the common law; but mentions that as a particular exception, which Sir Edward Coke has hastily cited for the general rule. Glanville, magna carta, Fleta, the Year-Books, Fitzherbert, and Finch, do all agree with Bracton, that this right to the pars rationabilis (reasonable part, or share) was by the common law: which also continues to this day to be the general law of our sister kingdom of Scotland.

Whatever may have been the custom of later years in many parts of the kingdom, or however it was introduced in derogation of the old common law, the ancient method continued in use in the province of York, the principality of Wales, and in the city of London, till very modern times: when, in order to favor the power of bequeathing, and to reduce the whole kingdom to the same standard, three statutes have been provided.

⚖ INTESTATE ESTATES — In case a person made no disposition of such of his goods as were testable, whether that were only part or the whole of them he was, and is, said to die intestate; and in such cases it is said that by the old law the king was entitled to seize upon his goods, as the parens patriae (parent of the country), and general trustee of the kingdom. This prerogative the king continued to exercise for some time by his own ministers of justice: and probably in the county court, where matters of all kinds were determined: and it was granted as a franchise to many lords of manors, and others, who have to this day a prescriptive right to grant administration to their intestate tenants and suitors, in their own courts-baron and other courts, or to have their wills there proved, in case they made any disposition.

Afterwards the crown, in favor of the church, invested the prelates with this branch of the prerogative; which was done, saith Perkins, because it was intended by the law, that spiritual men are of better conscience than laymen, and that they had more knowledge what things would conduce to the benefit of the soul of the deceased. The goods, therefore, of intestates were given to the ordinary by the crown; and he might seize them, and keep them without wasting, and also might give, alien, or sell them at his will, and dispose of the money in pious usus (to pious uses): and, if he did otherwise, he broke the confidence which the law reposed in him. So that properly the whole interest and power, which were granted to the ordinary, were only those of being the king's almoner within his diocese; in trust to distribute the intestate's goods in charity to the poor, or in such superstitious uses as the mistaken zeal of the times had denominated pious. As he had thus the disposition of intestate's effects, the probate of wills of course followed: for it was thought just and natural that the will of the deceased should be proved to the satisfaction of the prelate, whose right of distributing his chattels for the good of his soul was effectually superseded thereby.

☙☙ ORIGIN AND HISTORY OF ADMINISTRATIONS — The goods of the intestate being thus vested in the ordinary upon the most solemn and conscientious trust, the reverend prelates were therefore not accountable to any, but to God and themselves, for their conduct. But even in Fleta's time it was complained "that the ordinaries, who take possession of goods of this kind in the name of the church, make no distribution of them or at least no due distribution."

To what a length of iniquity this abuse was carried, most evidently appears from a gloss of Pope Innocent IV, written about the year 1250; wherein lays it down for established canon law, that "in Britain a third part of the goods left by an intestate is to be distributed for the benefit of the church and the poor." Thus the popish clergy took to themselves (under the name of the church and poor) the whole residue of the deceased's estate, after the parties rationabiles (reasonable portions), or two-thirds, of the wife and children were deducted; without paying even his lawful debts, or other charges thereon. For which reason it was enacted by statute that the ordinary shall be bound to pay the debts of the intestate so far as his goods will extend, in the same manner that executors were bound in case the deceased had left a will: a use more truly pious, than any requiem, or mass for his soul.

This was the first check given to that exorbitant power, which the law had entrusted with ordinaries. But though they were now made liable to the creditors of the intestate for their just and lawful demands, yet the residuum, after payment of debts, remained still in their hands, to be applied to whatever purposes the conscience of the ordinary should approve. The flagrant abuses of which power occasioned the legislature again to interpose, in order to prevent the ordinaries from keeping any longer the administration in their own hands, or those of their immediate dependents: Therefore the statute (Administration of Estates, 1357), provides, that, in case of intestacy, the ordinary shall depute the nearest and most lawful friends of the deceased to administer his goods; which administrators are put upon the same footing, with regard to suits and to accounting, as executors appointed by will. This is the original of administrators, as they at present stand; who are only the officers of the ordinary, appointed by him in pursuance of this state, which singles out the next and most lawful friend of the intestate; who is interpreted to be the next of blood that is under no legal disabilities.

The statute (Administration of Estates, 1529), enlarges a little more the power of the ecclesiastical judge; and permits him to grant administration either to the widow, or the next of kin, or to both of them, at his own discretion; and, where two or more persons are in the same degree of kindred, gives the ordinary his election to accept whichever he pleases.

Upon this footing stands the general law of administrations at this day. I shall, in the further progress of this chapter, mention a few more particulars, with regard to who may, and who may not, be administrator; and what he is bound to do when he has taken this charge upon him: what has been hitherto remarked only serving to show the original and gradual progress of testaments and administrations: in what manner the latter was first of all vested in the bishops by the royal indulgence; and how it was afterwards, by authority of parliament, taken from them in effect, by obliging them to commit all their power to particular persons nominated expressly by the law.

⚖️ CAPACITY TO MAKE A WILL — I proceed now, secondly, to inquire who may, or may not make a testament, or what persons are absolutely obliged by law to die intestate. This law is entirely prohibitory; for, regularly, every person hath full power and liberty to make a will, that is not under special prohibition by law or custom: which prohibitions are principally upon three accounts; for want of sufficient discretion; for want of sufficient liberty and free will; and on account of their criminal conduct.

⚖️ INFANTS AND NON COMPOTES MENTIS — In the first species are to be reckoned infants, under the age of fourteen if males, and twelve if females; which is the rule of the civil law. Though some of our common lawyers have held that an infant of any age (even four years old) might make a testament, and others have denied that under eighteen he is capable, yet as the ecclesiastical court is the judge of every testator's capacity, this case must be governed by the rules of the ecclesiastical law. So that no objection can be admitted to the will of an infant of fourteen, merely for want of age: but, if the testator was not sufficient discretion, whether at the age of fourteen or four and twenty, that will overthrow his testament.

Madmen, or otherwise non compotes (not in their right senses), idiots or natural fools, persons grown childish by reason of old age or distemper, such as have their senses besotted with drunkenness,—all these are incapable, by reason of mental disability, to make any will so long as such disability lasts. To this class also may be referred such persons as are born dead, blind, and dumb; who, as they have always wanted the common inlets of understanding, are incapable of having animum testandi (testamentary discretion), and their testaments are therefore void.

⚖️ PERSONS UNDER DURESS — Such persons, as are intestable for want of liberty or freedom of will, are by the civil law of various kinds; as prisoners, captives, and the like. But the law of England does not make such persons absolutely intestable; but only leaves it to the discretion of the court to judge, upon the consideration of their particular circumstances of duress, whether or no such persons could be supposed to have free testamentary discretion.

⚖️ MARRIED WOMEN — With regard to feme coverts, our laws differ still more materially from the civil. Among the Romans there was no distinction; a married woman was as capable of bequeathing as a feme sole. But with us a married woman is not only utterly incapable of devising lands, being excepted out of the statute of wills (1542), but also she is incapable of making a testament of chattels, without the license of her husband. For all her personal chattels are absolutely his own; and he may dispose of her chattels real, or shall have them to himself if he survives her: it would be therefore extremely inconsistent, to give her a power of defeating that provision of the law, by bequeathing those chattels to another.

Yet by her husband's license she may make a testament; and the husbands, upon marriage, frequently covenants with her friends to allow her that license: but such license is more properly his assent; for, unless it be given to the particular will in question, it will not be a complete testament, even though the husband beforehand hath given her permission to make a will. Yet it shall be sufficient to repel the husband from his general right of administering his wife's effects; and administration will be granted to her appointee, with such testamentary paper annexed. So that in reality the woman makes no will at all, but only something like a will: operating in that nature of an appointment, the execution of which the husband by his bond, agreement, or covenant, is bound to allow. A distinction similar to which we meet with in the civil law. For, though a son who was in the power of a parent could not by any means make a formal and legal testament, even though his father permitted, yet he might, with the like permission of his father, make what was called a donation mortis causa (a donation depending on the event of the death of the donor).

🐝🐝 QUEEN CONSORT — The queen consort is an exception to this general rule, for she may dispose of her chattels by will, without the consent of her lord: and any feme covert may make her will of goods; which are in her possession in auter droit (in the right of another), as executrix or administratrix; for these can never be the property of the husband: and, if she has any pin-money or separate maintenance, it is said she may dispose of her savings thereout by testament, without the control of her husband. But, if a feme sole makes her will, and afterwards marries, such subsequent marriage is esteemed a revocation in law, and entirely vacates the will.

🐝🐝 TRAITORS AND FELONS — Persons incapable of making testaments, on account of their criminal conduct, are in the first place all traitors and felons, from the time of conviction; for then their goods and chattels are no longer at their own disposal, but forfeited to the king. Neither can a felo de se (suicide) make a will of goods and chattels for they are forfeited by the act and manner of his death; but he may make a devise of his lands, for they are not subjected to any forfeiture.

Outlaws also, though it be but for debt, are incapable of making a will, so long as the outlawry subsists, for their goods and chattels are forfeited during that time. As for persons guilty of other crimes, short of felony, who are by the civil law precluded from making testaments (as usurers, libelers, and others of a worse stamp), by the common law their testaments may be good. In general the rule is, and has been so at least ever since Glanville's time, that the last will of everyone be free.

🐝🐝 NATURE AND INCIDENTS OF WILLS — Let us next, thirdly, consider what this last will and testament is, which almost everyone is thus at liberty to make; or, what are the nature and incidents of a testament. Testaments both Justinian and Sir Edward Coke agree to be so called, because they are testatio mentis (a testifying of the mind): an etymon, which seems to savor too much of the conceit; it being plainly a substantive derived from the verb testari (to testify), in like manner as juramentum (an oath), incrementum (an increase), and others, from other verbs.

The definition of the old Roman lawyers is much better than their etymology; "the legal declaration of a man's intentions, which he wills to be performed after his death." It is called sententia to denote the circumspection and prudence with which it is supposed to be made: it is voluntatis nostrae sententia, because its efficacy depends on its declaring the testator's intention, whence in England it is emphatically styled his will: it is justa sententia; that is, drawn, attested, and published with all due solemnities and forms of law because a testament is of no force till after the death of the testator.

⚭ KINDS OF WILLS — These testaments are divided into two sorts: written, and verbal or nuncupative; of which the former is committed to writing, the latter depends merely upon oral evidence, being declared by the testator in extremis (in his last moments) before a sufficient number of witnesses, and afterwards reduced to writing. A codicil, codicillus, a little book or writing is a supplement to a will; or an addition made by the testator, and annexed to, and to be taken as part of, a testament: being for its explanation, or alteration, or to make some addition to, or else some subtraction from the former dispositions of the testator. This may also be either written or nuncupative.

⚭ NUNCUPATIVE WILLS — But, as nuncupative wills and codicils (which were formerly more in use than at present, when the art of writing is become more universal), are liable to great impositions and may occasion many perjuries, the statute of frauds, (1677), enacts: 1. That no written will shall be revoked or altered by a subsequent nuncupative one, except the same be in the lifetime of the testator reduced to writing, and read over to him, and approved; and unless the same be proved to have been so done by the oaths of three witnesses at the least; who, by statute (Wills, 1705), must be such as are admissible upon trials at common law. 2. That no nuncupative will shall in anywise be good, where the estate bequeathed exceeds 30 pounds; unless proved by three such witnesses, present at the making thereof (the Roman law requiring seven) and unless they or some of them were specially required to bear witness thereto by the testator himself; and unless it was made in his last sickness, in his own habitation or dwellinghouse, or where he had been previously resident ten days at the least, except he be surprised with sickness on a journey, or from home, and dies without returning to his dwelling. 3. That no nuncupative will shall be proved by the witness after six months from the making, unless it were put in writing within six days. Nor shall it be proved till fourteen days after the death of the testator, nor till process hath first issued to call in the widow, or next of kin, to contest it if they think proper.

Thus hath the legislature provided against any frauds in setting up nuncupative wills, by so numerous a train of requisites, that the thing itself is fallen into disuse; and hardly even heard of, but in the only instance where favor ought to be shown to it, when the testator is surprised by sudden and violent sickness. The testamentary words must be spoken with an intent to bequeath, not any loose idle discourse in his illness; for he must require the bystanders to bear witness of such his intention: the will must be made at home, or among his family or friends, unless by unavoidable accident; to prevent impositions from strangers: it must be in his last sickness; for, if he recovers, he may alter his dispositions, and has time to make a written will: it must not be proved at too long a distance from the testator's death, lest the words should escape the memory of the witnesses; nor yet too hastily and without notice, lest the family of the testator should be put to inconvenience, or surprised.

WRITTEN WILLS — As to written wills, they need not any witness of their publication. I speak not here of devises of lands, which are quite of a different nature; being conveyances by statute, unknown to the feudal or common law, and not under the same jurisdiction as personal testaments. But a testament of chattels, written in the testator's own hand, though it has neither his name nor seal to it, nor witnesses present at its publication is good; provided sufficient proof can be had that it is his handwriting. Though written in another man's hand, and never signed by the testator, yet if proved to be according to his instructions and approved by him, it hath been held a good testament of the personal estate. Yet it is the safer and more prudent way, and leaves less in the breast of the ecclesiastical judge, if it be signed or sealed by the testator, and published in the presence of witnesses: which last was always required in the time of Bracton; or, rather, he in this respect has implicitly copied the rule of the civil law.

WILLS INOPERATIVE BEFORE DEATH — No testament is of any effect till after the death of the testator. "For every testament is established by death, and the will of the testator is revocable until his death." Therefore, if there be many testaments, the last overthrows all the former: but the republication of a former will revokes one of a later date, and establishes the first again.

WILLS HOW AVOIDED — Hence it follows, that testaments may be avoided three ways: 1. If made by a person laboring under any of the incapacities before mentioned: 2. By making another testament of a later date: and, 3. By cancelling or revoking it. For, though I make a last will and testament irrevocable in the strongest words, yet I am at liberty to revoke it: because my own act or words, cannot alter the disposition of law, so as to make that irrevocable which is in its own nature revocable.

This, saith Lord Bacon, would be for a man to deprive himself of that, which of all other things is most incident to human condition; and that is, alteration or repentance. It hath also been held, that, without an express revocation, if a man, who hath made his will, afterwards marries and hath a child, this is a presumptive or implied revocation of his former will, which he made in his state of celibacy.

The Romans were also wont to set aside testaments as being in-officiosa (deficient in natural duty) if they disinherited or totally passed by (without assigning a true and sufficient reason) any of the children of the testator. But if the child had any legacy, though ever so small, it was proof that the testator has not lost his memory or his reason, which otherwise the law presumed; but was then supposed to have acted thus for some substantial cause: and in such case no querela inofficiosi testamenti (complaint of an undutiful will) was allowed. Hence probably has arisen that groundless vulgar error, of the necessity of leaving the heir a shilling or some other express legacy, in order to disinherit him effectually: whereas the law of England makes no such constrained suppositions of forgetfulness or insanity; and therefore, though the heir or next of kin be totally omitted, it admits no querela inofficiosi, to set aside such a testament.

🙰 EXECUTORS AND ADMINISTRATORS — We are next to consider, fourthly, what is an executor, and what is an administrator; and how they are both to be appointed.

🙰 EXECUTORS — An executor is he to whom another man commits by will the execution of that his last will and testament. All persons are capable of being executors, that are capable of making wills, and many others besides; as feme coverts, and infants: nay, even infants unborn, may be made executors. But no infant can act as such till the age of seventeen years; till which time administration must be granted to some other, durante minore aetate (during minority). In like manner as it may be granted durante absentia (during absence), or pendente lite (pending a suit); when the executor is out of the realm, or when a suit is commenced in the ecclesiastical court touching the validity of the will.

This appointment of an executor is essential to the making of a will: and it may be performed either by express words, or such as strongly imply the same. But if the testator makes his will, without naming any executors, or if he names incapable persons, or if the executors named refuse to act; in any of these cases, the ordinary must grant administration cum testamento annexo (with the will annexed) to some other person; and then the duty of the administrator, as also when he is constituted only durante minore aetate, etc., of another, is very little different from that of an executor.

This was law so early as the reign of Henry II, when Glanvill informs us, that "those should be executors of a will whom the testator shall have chosen, and to whom he himself shall have committed the trust; but if the testator shall not have named any, the relations of the deceased may take this duty upon themselves."

⚖ ADMINISTRATORS — But if the deceased died wholly intestate, without making either will or executors, then general letters of administration must be granted by the ordinary to such administrator as the statutes direct. In consequence of which we may observe;   1. That the ordinary is compellable to grant administration of the goods and chattels of the wife, to the husband or his representatives: and of the husband's effects, to the widow, or next of kin; but he may grant it to either, or both, at his discretion.   2. That, among the kindred, those are to be preferred that are the nearest in degree to the intestate; but, of persons in equal degree, the ordinary may take which he pleases.   3. That this nearness of propinquity of degree shall be reckoned according to the computation of the civilians; and not of the canonists, which the law of England adopts in the descent of real estates: because in the civil computation the intestate himself is the terminus, a quo (the limit from which) several degrees are numbered; and not the common ancestor, according to the rule of the canonists.

Therefore in the first place the children, or (on failure of children), the parents of the deceased, are entitled to the administration: both which are indeed in the first degree; but with us the children are allowed the preference. Then follow brothers, grandfathers, uncles or nephews (and the females of each class respectively), and lastly cousins.   4. The half blood is admitted to the administration as well as the whole: for they are the kindred of the intestate, and only excluded from inheritances of land upon feudal reasons. Therefore the brother of the half blood shall exclude the uncle of the whole blood; and the ordinary may grant administration to the sister of the half, or the brother of the whole blood, at his own discretion.   5. If none of the kindred will take out administration, a creditor may, by custom do it.   6. If the executor refuses, or dies intestate, the administration may be granted to the residuary legatee, in exclusion of the next of kin.

Lastly, the ordinary may, in defect of all these, commit administration (as he might have done before the statute Edward III) to such discreet person as he approves of: or may grant him letters ad colligendum bona defuncti (for collecting the goods of the deceased), which neither makes him executor nor administrator; his only business being to keep the goods in his safe custody, and to do other acts for the benefit of such as are entitled to the property of the deceased.

If a bastard, who has no kindred, being nullius filius, or anyone else that has no kindred, dies intestate and without wife or child, it hath formerly been held that the ordinary might seize his goods, and dispose of them in pios usus (to pious uses). But the usual course now is for someone to procure letters patent, or other authority from the king; and then the ordinary of course grants administration to such appointee of the crown.

⚖ RESPECTIVE INTERESTS OF EXECUTORS AND ADMINISTRATORS — The interest, vested in the executor by the will of the deceased, may be continued and kept alive by the will, of the same executor; so that the executor of A's executor is to all intents and purposes the executor and representative of A himself; but the executor of A's administrator, or the administrator of A's executor, is not the representative of A. For the power of an executor is founded upon the special confidence and actual appointment of the deceased; and such executor is therefore allowed to transmit that power to another, in whom he has equal confidence; but the administrator of A is merely the officer of the ordinary, prescribed to him by act of parliament, in whom the deceased has reposed no trust at all; and therefore, on the death of that officer, it results back to the ordinary to appoint another. With regard to the administrator of A's executor, he has clearly no privity or relation to A; being only commissioned to administer the effects of the intestate executor, and not of the original testator.

Wherefore in both these cases, and whenever the course of representation from executor to executor is interrupted by any one administration, it is necessary for the ordinary to commit administration afresh, of the goods of the deceased not administered by the former executor or administrator. This administrator, de conis non (of the goods not administered), is the only legal representative of the deceased in matters of personal property. But he may, as well as an original administrator, have only a limited or special administration committed to his care, viz., of certain specific effects, such as a term of years and the like; the rest being committed to others.

⚖️ OFFICE AND DUTIES OF EXECUTORS AND ADMINISTRATORS — Having thus shown what is, and who may be, an executor or administrator, I proceed now, fifthly and lastly, to inquire into some few of the principal points of their office and duty. These, in general, are very much the same in both executors and administrators; excepting, first, that the executor is bound to perform a will, which an administrator is not, unless where a testament is annexed to his administration, and then he differs still less from an executor: and, secondly, that an executor may do many acts before he proves the will, but an administrator may do nothing till letters of administration are issued; for the former derives his power from the will and not from the probate, the latter owes his entirely to the appointment of the ordinary.

⚖️ EXECUTOR DE SON TORT — If a stranger takes upon him to act as executor, without any just authority (as by intermeddling with the goods of the deceased, and many other transactions) he is called in law an executor of his own wrong, de son tort, and is liable to all the trouble of an executorship, without any of the profits or advantages but merely doing acts of necessity or humanity, as locking up the goods, or buying the corpse of the deceased, will not amount to such an intermeddling, as will charge a man as executor of his own wrong. Such a one cannot bring an action himself in right of the deceased, but actions may be brought against him. In all actions by creditors, against such an officious intruder, he shall be named an executor, generally; for the most obvious conclusion, which strangers can form from his conduct, is that he hath a will of the deceased, wherein he is named executor, but hath not yet taken probate thereof. He is chargeable with the debts of the deceased, so far as assets come to his hands; and, as against creditors in general, shall be allowed all payments made to any other creditor in the same or a superior degree, himself only excepted. Though, as against the rightful executor or administrator, he cannot plead such payment, yet it shall be allowed him in mitigation of damages; unless perhaps upon a deficiency of assets, whereby the rightful executor may be prevented from satisfying his own debt. But let us now see what are the power and duty of a rightful executor or administrator.

⚖️ BURIAL OF DECEASED — He must bury the deceased in a manner suitable to the estate which he leaves behind him. Necessary funeral expenses are allowed previous to other debts and charges; but if the executor or administrator be extravagant, it is a species of devastation or waste of the substance of the deceased, and shall only be prejudicial to himself, and not to the creditors or legatees of the deceased.

☙ PROBATE OF WILL — The executor, or the administrator must prove the will of the deceased: which is done either in common form, which is only upon his own oath before the ordinary, or his surrogate; or per testes (by witnesses), in more solemn form of law, in case the validity of the will be disputed.

When the will is so proved, the original must be deposited in the registry of the ordinary; and a copy thereof in parchment is made out under the seal of the ordinary, and delivered to the executor or administrator, together with the certificate of its having been proved before him: all which together is usually styled the probate.

In defect of any will, the person entitled to be administrator must also at this period take out letters of administration under the seal of the ordinary; whereby an executorial power to collect and administer, that is, dispose of the goods of the deceased, is vested in him: and he must by statute (Statute of Distribution, 1670), enter into a bond with sureties, faithfully to execute his trust. If all the goods of the deceased lie within the same jurisdiction, a probate before the ordinary, or an administration granted by him, are the only proper ones: but if the deceased had bona notabilia (goods of sufficient value to be accounted for); or chattels to the value of a hundred shillings, in two distinct dioceses or jurisdictions, then the will must be proved, or administration taken out, before the metropolitan of the province, by way of special prerogative; whence the court where the validity of such wills is tried, and the office where they are registered, are called the prerogative court, and the prerogative office.

☙ INVENTORY —.The executor or administrator is to make an inventory of all the goods and chattels, whether in possession or action, of the deceased; which he is to deliver in to the ordinary upon oath, if thereunto lawfully required.

☙ COLLECTING ASSETS — He is to collect all the goods and chattels so inventoried; and to that end he has very large powers and interests conferred on him by law; being the representative of the deceased, and having the same property in his goods as the principal had when living, and the same remedies to recover them.

If there be two or more executors, a sale or release by one of them shall be good against all the rest; but in case of administrators it is otherwise. Whatever is so recovered, that is of a salable nature and may be converted into ready money, is called assets in the hands of the executor or administrator; that is sufficient or enough (from the French assez) to make him chargeable to a creditor or legatee, so far as such goods and chattels extend.

Whatever assets so come to his hands he may convert into ready money, to answer the demands that may be made upon him: which is the next thing to be considered; for,

PAYING DEBTS — The executor or administrator must pay the debts of the deceased. In payment of debts he must observe the rules of priority; otherwise, on deficiency of assets, if he pays those of a lower degree first, he must answer those of a higher out of his own estate.

First, he may pay all funeral charges, and the expense of proving the will, and the like. Secondly, debts due to the king on record or specialty. Thirdly, such debts as are by particular statutes to be preferred to all others; as money due upon poor rates, for letters to the post office, and some others. Fourthly, debts of record; as judgments, statutes, and recognizances. Fifthly, debts due on special contracts; as for rent (for which the lessor has often a better remedy in his own hands, by distraining), or upon bonds, covenants, and the like, under seal. Lastly, debts on simple contracts, viz., upon notes unsealed, and verbal promises. Among these simple contracts, servants' wages are by some with reason preferred to any other: and so stood the ancient law, according to Bracton and Fleta, who reckon, among the first debts to be paid "the services of attendants and the wages of servants." Among debts of equal degree, the executor or administrator is allowed to pay himself first; by retaining in his hands so much as his debt amounts to.

But an executor of his own wrong is not allowed to retain: for that would tend to encourage creditors to strive who should first take possession of the goods of the deceased; and would besides be taking advantage of their own wrong, which is contrary to the rule of law. If a creditor constitutes his debtor his executor, this is a release or discharge of the debt, whether the executor acts or no; provided there be assets sufficient to pay the testator's debts: for, though this discharge of the debt shall take place of all legacies, yet it were unfair to defraud the testator's creditors of their just debts by a release which is absolutely voluntary. Also, if no suit is commenced against him, the executor may pay any one creditor in equal degree his whole debt, though he has nothing left for the rest: for, without a suit commenced, the executor has no legal notice of the debt.

⚖ LEGACIES — When the debts are all discharged, the legacies claim the next regard; which are to be paid by the executor so far as his assets will extend; but he may not give himself the preference herein, as in the case of debts.

A legacy is a bequest, or gift, of goods and chattels by testament; and the person to whom it was given is styled the legatee: which every person is capable of being, unless particularly disabled by the common law or statutes, as traitors, papists, and some others. This bequest transfers an inchoate property to the legatee: but the legacy is not perfect without the assent of the executor: for if I have a general or pecuniary legacy of 100 pounds, or a specific one of a piece of plate, I cannot in either case take it without the consent of the executor. For in him all the chattels are vested; and it is his business first of all to see whether there is a sufficient fund left to pay the debts of the testator: the rule of equity being, that a man must be just, before he is permitted to be generous; or, as Bracton expresses the sense of our ancient law, "from the effects of the deceased are to be answered, first, the demands of necessity; afterwards, what expediency requires; and lastly, the requisitions of bequest."

In case of a deficiency of assets, all the general legacies must abate proportionably, in order to pay the debts; but a specific legacy (of a piece of plate, a horse, or the like) is not to abate at all, or allow anything by way of abatement, unless there be not sufficient without it. Upon the same principle, if the legatees have been paid their legacies, they are afterwards bound to refund a ratable part, in case debts come in, more than sufficient to exhaust the residuum after the legacies paid. This law is as old as Bracton and Fleta, who tell us, "if there should be more due, or more legacies bequeathed, than the chattels of the deceased are sufficient to satisfy, let an equal abatement be made on all the legacies, the privilege of the king being excepted."

If the legatee dies before the testator, the legacy is a lost or lapsed legacy, and shall sink into the residuum. If a contingent legacy be left to anyone; as when he attains, or if he attains, the age of twenty-one; and he dies before that time; it is a lapsed legacy. But a legacy to one to be paid when he attains the age of twenty-one years, is a vested legacy; an interest which commences in praesenti (in the present) although it be solvendum in futuro (to be paid at a future period): and, if the legatee dies before that age, his representatives shall receive it out of the testator's personal estate, at the same time that it would have become payable, in case the legatee had lived.

This distinction is borrowed from the civil law; and its adoption in our courts is not so much owing to its intrinsic equity, as to its having been before adopted by the ecclesiastical courts. For, since the chancery has a concurrent jurisdiction with them, in regard to the recovery of legacies, it was reasonable that there should be a conformity in their determinations; and that the subject should have the same measure of justice in whatever court he sued.

But if such legacies be charged upon a real estate, in both cases they should lapse for the benefit of the heir: for, with regard to devises affecting lands, the ecclesiastical court hath no concurrent jurisdiction. In case of a vested legacy, due immediately and charged on land or money in the funds, which yield an immediate profit, interest shall be payable thereon from the testator's death; but if charged only on the personal estate, which cannot be immediately got in, it shall carry interest only from the end of the year after the death of the testator.

⚖ GIFTS CAUSA MORTIS — Besides these formal legacies, contained in a man's will and testament, there is also permitted another death-bed disposition of property; which is called a donation causa mortis. That is, when a person in his last sickness, apprehending his dissolution near, delivers or causes to be delivered to another the possession of any personal goods (under which have been included bonds, and bills drawn by the deceased upon his banker), to keep in case of his decease. This gift, if the donor dies, needs not the assent of his executor: yet it shall not prevail against creditors; and is accompanied with this implied trust, that, if the donor lives, the property thereof shall revert to himself, being only given in contemplation of death, or mortis causa. This method of donation might have subsisted in a state of nature, being always accompanied with delivery of actual possession; and so far differs from a testamentary disposition: but seems to have been handed to us from the civil lawyers, who themselves borrowed it from the Greeks.

⚖ THE SURPLUS OR RESIDUE — When all the debts and particular legacies are discharged, the surplus or residuum must be paid to the residuary legatee, if any be appointed by the will; and if there be none, it was long a settled notion that it developed to the executor's own use, by virtue of his executorship. But whatever ground there might have been formerly for this opinion, it seems now to be understood with this restriction; that, although where the executor has no legacy at all the residuum shall in general be his own, yet wherever there is sufficient on the face of a will (by means of a competent legacy or otherwise), they imply that the testator intended his executor should not have the residue, the undevised surplus of the estate shall go to the next of kin, the executor then standing upon exactly the same footing as an administrator: concerning whom indeed there formerly was much debate, whether or no he could not be compelled to make any distribution of the intestate's estate. For, though (after the administration was taken in effect from the ordinary, and transferred to the relations of the deceased) the spiritual court endeavored to compel a distribution, and took bonds of the administrator for that purpose, they were prohibited by the temporal courts, and the bonds declared void at law. The right of the husband not only to administer, but also to enjoy exclusively, the effects of his deceased wife, depends still on this doctrine of the common law: the statute (Frauds, 1677), declaring only, that the statute of distributions does not extend to this case.

⚖ STATUTE OF DISTRIBUTIONS — But now these controversies are quite at an end; for by statute (Statute of Distribution, 1670), it is enacted, that the surplusage of intestates' estates, except of femes covert, shall (after the expiration of one full year from the death of the intestate) be distributed in the following manner. One-third shall go to the widow of the intestate, and the residue in equal proportions to his children, or if dead, to their representatives; that is, their lineal descendants: if there are no children or legal representative subsisting, then a moiety shall go to the widow, and a moiety to the next of kindred in equal degree and their representatives: if no widow, the whole shall go to the children: if neither widow nor children, the whole shall be distributed among the next of kin in equal degree, and their representatives: but no representatives are admitted among collaterals, further than the children of the intestate's brothers and sisters. The next of kindred, here referred to, are to be investigated by the same rules of consanguinity, as those who are entitled to letters of administration; of whom we have sufficiently spoken. Therefore by this statute the mother, as well as the father, succeeded to all the personal effects of their children, who died intestate and without wife or issue: in exclusion of the other sons and daughters, the brothers and sisters of the deceased. The law still remains with respect to the father; but by statute (Administration of Estates, 1685), if the father be dead, and any of the children die intestate without wife or issue, in the lifetime of the mother, she and each of the remaining children, or their representatives, shall divide his effects in equal portions.

⚖️   ANALOGIES OF THE STATUTE — It is obvious to observe how near a resemblance this Statute of Distributions bears to our ancient English law (concerning the reasonable share of the goods), spoken of at the beginning of this chapter; and which Sir Edward Coke himself, though he doubted the generality of its restraint on the power of devising by will, held to be universally binding (in point of conscience at least) upon the administrator or executor, in the case of either a total or partial intestacy.

It also bears some resemblance to the Roman law of succession ab intestate (from an intestate): which, and because the act was also penned by an eminent civilian, has occasioned a notion that the parliament of England copies it from the Roman praetor: though indeed it is little more than a restoration, with some refinements and regulations, of our old constitutional law; which prevailed as an established right and custom from the time of King Canute downwards, many centuries before Justinian's laws were known or heard of in the western parts of Europe.

So likewise there is another part of the Statute of Distributions, where directions are given that no child of the intestate (except his heir at law), on whom he settled in his lifetime any estate in lands, or pecuniary portion, equal to the distributive shares of the other children, shall have any part of the surplusage with their brothers and sisters; but if the estates so given them, by way of advancement, are not quite equivalent to the other shares, the children so advanced shall now have so much as will make them equal.

This just and equitable provision hath been also said to be derived from the collatio bondrum (commingling of property for the purpose of equal division) of the imperial law: which it certainly resembles in some points, though it differs widely in others.

⚖️   REPRESENTATION BY THE STATUTE — Before I quit this subject, I must, however, acknowledge, that the doctrine and limits of representation, laid down in the Statute of Distributions, seem to have been principally borrowed from the civil law: whereby it will sometimes happen, that personal estates are divided per capita (share and share alike), and sometimes per stirpes (by representation); whereas the common law knows no other rule of succession but that her stirpes only.

They are divided per capita, to every man an equal share, when all the claimants claim in their own rights, as in equal degree of kindred, and not jure repraesentationis (by right of representation), in the right of another person. As if the next of kin be the intestate's three brothers, A, B, and C; here his effects are divided into three equal portions, and distributed per capita, one to each: but if one of these brothers, A, had been dead leaving three children, and another, B, leaving two; then the distribution must have been per stirpes; viz., one-third to A's three children, another third to B's two children; and the remaining third to C the surviving brother: yet if C had been also dead, without issue, then A's and B's five children, being all in equal degree to the intestate, would take in their own rights per capita; viz., each of them one-fifth part.

Index

CAPRICORN TITLES

201. *Hauser*, DIET DOES IT. $1.35.
202. *Moscati*, ANCIENT SEMITIC CIVILIZATIONS. $1.65.
203. CHIN P'ING MEI. $2.45.
204. *Brockelman*, HISTORY OF ISLAMIC PEOPLES. $2.45.
205. *Salter*, CONDITIONED REFLEX THERAPY. $1.85.
206. *Lissner*, LIVING PAST. $1.95.
207. *Davis*, CORPORATIONS. $2.45.
208. *Rodman*, CONVERSATIONS WITH ARTISTS. $1.45.
209. *Falls*, GREAT WAR. $1.95.
210. MEMOIRS OF A RENAISSANCE POPE. $1.95.
211. *Schachner*, FOUNDING FATHERS. $2.45.
212. *Viereck*, UNADJUSTED MAN. $1.85.
213. *Cournos*, TREASURY OF CLASSIC RUSSIAN LITERATURE. $2.45.
215. *Guerdan*, BYZANTIUM. $1.45.
216. *Mandeville*, FABLE OF THE BEES. $1.65.
217. *Bradford*, OF PLYMOUTH PLANTATION. $1.65.
218. *Taylor*, COURSE OF GERMAN HISTORY. $1.45.
219. *Frankfurter*, LAW & POLITICS. $1.75.
220. *Shelby Little*, GEORGE WASHINGTON. $1.95.
221. *Peterson*, ANCIENT MEXICO, $1.65.
223. *Isaacs*, IMAGES OF ASIA. $1.85.
224. *Krafft Ebing*, ABERRATIONS OF SEXUAL LIFE. $1.95.
226. *Grekov*, SOVIET CHESS. $1.65.
227. *Ernst-Loth*, REPORT ON THE AMERICAN COMMUNIST. $1.45.
228. *Adler*, THE PROBLEM CHILD. $1.85.
231. *Fine*, FIFTY CHESS LESSONS. $1.45.
233. *Barraclough*, ORIGINS OF MODERN GERMANY. $2.45.
235. *Skeat*, ETYMOLOGICAL DICTIONARY. $2.45.
236. *Hauser*, GAYLORD HAUSER COOK BOOK. $1.65.
237. *Fulop Miller*, THE JESUITS. $2.45.
238. *Shenton*, RECONSTRUCTION. $1.75.
239. *Blitzer*, COMMONWEALTH OF ENGLAND. $1.65.
240. *Wright*, GREAT AMERICAN GENTLEMAN. $1.65.
241. *Braeman*, ROAD TO INDEPENDENCE. $1.65.
242. *Bridgebaugh*, CITIES IN THE WILDERNESS. $2.65.
243. *Bridenbaugh*, CITIES IN REVOLT. $2.65.
244. *de Riencourt*, COMING CAESARS. $1.95.
246. *Weinberg*, THE MUCKRAKERS. $2.45.
247. *Hays*, FROM APE TO ANGEL. $2.65.
248. *James*, ANCIENT GODS. $2.25.